FORT ST. GEORGE

Archaeological Investigation of the 1607-1608 Popham Colony on the Kennebec River in Maine

Jeffrey Phipps Brain

**With the collaboration of
Peter Morrison and Pamela Crane**

**Occasional Publications in Maine Archaeology
Number 12
2007**

**The Maine State Museum, The Maine Historic Preservation Commission,
and The Maine Archaeological Society
Augusta**

Occasional Publications in Maine Archaeology
Series Editor: Arthur Spiess

ISBN 978-0-935447-19-4

Fort St. George Excavations

1994
Sponsored by Peabody Essex Museum
Funded by a grant from the Committee for Research and Exploration
of the National Geographic Society

1997-2005
Sponsored by the Maine State Museum
Funded by the Friends of the Maine State Museum
supplemented by private contributions and National Park Service grants
awarded by the Maine Historic Preservation Commission

Cover art: Conjectural reconstruction of Fort St. George in early October 1607
based on the Hunt map and archaeological evidence
(Sam Manning 2006)

see p. p 10-11
438

THIS VOLUME

IS DEDICATED TO

JANE, BUD, JOHN AND DEEDEE

THANK YOU, MY FRIENDS

Frontispiece. Raleigh Gilbert, now Sir Raleigh, some few years after the adventure on the Sagadahoc. The portrait was painted by Cornelius Jansen (usually referred to as "the younger" in order to distinguish him from the contemporary theologian) who was active in England from 1618 to 1643. (Courtesy of Geoffrey Gilbert, direct descendant of Sir Raleigh)

CONTENTS

FIGURES

Frontispiece. Raleigh Gilbert.
1. Detail from Boasio1588 map.
2. Land grants to the London and Plymouth Companies of Virginia, 1606.
3. Famous families in southwest England connected by marriage.
4. Detail from Velasco 1611 map.
5. Fort St. George as drawn by John Hunt, October 8, 1607.
6. The Popham Colony was a cornerstone in the foundation of English America.
7. Location of Fort St. George at the mouth of the Kennebec River.
8. Champlain 1605 map of the Quinibequy (Kennebec) River.
9. Detail from Pasquine 1688 map.
10. Detail from John North 1751 map.
11. Detail from USGS 1868 map.
12. Thayer 1891 map of "Point Popham."
13. Fort Baldwin 6 inch rifled gun overlooking the mouth of the Kennebec River.
14. Detail from U. S. Army Corps of Engineers 1917 map of Fort Baldwin Military Reservation.
15. Temporary buildings at Fort Baldwin in 1918.
16. Detail from Fort Baldwin State Park 1981 map.
17. Approximate locations of excavations at the Popham site by Wendell S. Hadlock in 1962 and 1964.
18. Plan and photo of Hadlock's 1962 excavations.
19. U. S. Army Corps of Engineers 1865 contour map of Sabino Head and same with John Hunt 1607 map of Fort St. George superimposed on it.
20. Topographic map of Popham site showing the predicted line of the fort trace.
21. Plan of excavations at the Popham site in 1994.
22. Stratification in excavation unit P100.
23. Stratification in excavation unit P104.
24. Plan of Fort Baldwin-era utility trench in excavation units P104-P106 and P108.
25. Stratification in excavation unit P110.
26. Stratification in excavation unit P113.
27. Stratification in excavation units P119-P120 and P122.
28. Stratification in excavation units P170-P183.
29. Seventeenth-century artifacts from trench 2.
30. Large posthole and post mold in excavation units P181-P182.
31. Plan of excavation units P184-P190.
32. John Hunt 1607 map of Fort St. George superimposed on modern topographic map of the Popham site.
33. The storehouse as drawn by John Hunt.
34. Plan of excavations on state park land in 1997-2005.
35. Storehouse excavations 1994, 1997-1999, 2004-2005.
36. Plan of excavation units P163 and P400.
37. Plan of excavation units P166 and P410.
38. Plan of postholes and post molds found in excavation units P423, P424, P430 and P431.
39. Stratification in excavation units P444 and P452.
40. Base of post from excavation units P465, P466 and P472.

TABLES

PREFACE

This project had its genesis in a raffle. A friend had won a weekend at a cottage on Bailey's Island, Maine in June 1990. He invited myself, my wife, and two other couples to share his good fortune. On a bright sunny day, we packed a picnic lunch and went touring. I insisted on visiting all of the historic sites along that stretch of the coastline, and one of these was the Civil War-period Fort Popham at the mouth of the Kennebec River. We ate lunch there and enjoyed watching the harbor seals splashing about in Atkins Bay. Inside the fort was a small exhibit, since removed, that gave a brief history of the area, as well as the fort. On one side was a board which proclaimed that the 1607 Popham Colony had been planted nearby. I remember being quite bemused by this claim, and finally decided that local chauvinism had gotten the better of historical fact. Everyone knew that 1607 belonged to Jamestown! Upon leaving the fort, we detoured through the nearby Ft. Baldwin State Park, but there was nothing to see there except some twentieth-century concrete bunkers that soon lost our interest, and we went on our way.

The following year, I had relocated to the Peabody Museum of Salem where I was happily involved in co-curating an exhibit entitled "We Claim These Shores: Native Americans and the European Settlement of Massachusetts Bay" (Brain and Grimes 1992). While doing the background research for the exhibit, I read everything I could find about the European exploration and colonization of New England. To my surprise, I came across repeated references to the 1607 Popham Colony. Intrigued, I delved further and discovered that it was indeed a historical fact, but that no one knew exactly where it had been established. There were many theories, and most of these pointed to a specific place, but the location had never been confirmed. Interestingly, the favored place was part of that otherwise so uninspiring Ft. Baldwin State Park. It obviously was a job for archaeology.

In fact, archaeological excavations had been carried out at the park in 1962 and 1964 under the supervision of Wendell S. Hadlock, Director of the Farnsworth Art Museum in Rockland, Maine. His results were inconclusive, as described below. During the intervening thirty years, however, the practice of historical archaeology had undergone many changes, both in the sophistication of its methodology and in the improved knowledge of material culture. In short, we had a better idea of what to look for and how to find it. With cautious confidence, therefore, I concluded that a new archaeological investigation was in order. I contacted the appropriate state agencies and colleagues in 1991, and preparations were well advanced when personal complications intervened in 1992. It was not until the summer of 1993 that the project could be brought back on track. Funding and personnel were in place by the spring of 1994 when preliminary surveys and mapping were completed.

The first excavations were carried out between June 27 and August 13, 1994. The expedition was sponsored by the newly reconstituted Peabody Essex Museum; authorized by the Maine Bureau of Parks and Recreation, Maine Historic Preservation Commission, and Maine State Museum; and funded by a grant from the Committee for Research and Exploration of the National Geographic Society. The core crew under my direction consisted of Lorinda Goodwin, Andrew Veech, Peter Morrison, and John and Sharon Belmont. Additional assistance was rendered by James Goodwin, Orloff Miller, Ruth Benander, and Pamela Crane. Altogether, they comprised a most professional and personable group, and to work with them was a privilege and a pleasure.

The results of the initial session were minimally encouraging. As described in the following pages we did find features and artifacts that we could reasonably relate to Fort St. George and therefore felt confident that we had established its location. However, it must be admitted that our confidence was based as much on the intuition of the experience as solid evidence. In fact, only one feature was thoroughly convincing, and one feature, of course, does not a fort make. After a period of reflection on how to make that one feature lead us to the larger entity, we returned to the field in 1997. This time the excavations were sponsored by the Maine State Museum and funded through their field school program. During a nine-day period in September and October we found many more features that matched the first one found in 1994 and together constituted part of the storehouse at the fort. We now had absolute proof that we were at the right location, which was sufficient impetus to begin an annual program of investigation with continuing support from the Maine State Museum supplemented by National Park Service grants awarded by the Maine Historic Preservation Commission, as well as private contributions.

In 1998 and 1999 we exposed the entire footprint and much of the floor area of the storehouse. In 1999 we located the nearby house of Admiral Raleigh Gilbert and in 2000 completely explored the remains of that structure. The professional crew during these years, all veterans of 1994, were Lorinda Goodwin, Peter Morrison, and Pam Crane; Tim Dinsmore replaced Lorinda in 2001 when we began to investigate other areas of the site. These supremely gifted career archaeologists supervised the field school students and were assisted by a cadre of trained local volunteers. The latter included John Bradford, Mary Concannon, Judy Dunsford, Nicia Gruener, Orman Hines, Peter Hutchinson, Christa and Fritz Mueller, Jay Robbins, Suzanne Stone, Bud Warren, Peter Woodruff and Cheryl Yeaton. Historical archaeologists Scott Cooper and Erica Stepler-Cavin also generously donated their talents in 2003. When necessary, large amounts of dirt were moved gratis with mechanical equipment operated by Curtis Doughty with incredible finesse.

The field school students who participated after 1994 were a hard working bunch and most were so committed that they returned for multiple sessions. There are too many to list here, but all are acknowledged in the annual reports (Brain 1997-2005). Of particular interest is the fact that at least three are Popham descendants.

During the course of the project, I gratefully acknowledge the encouragement and assistance of my Maine colleagues. Especially helpful have been Alaric Faulkner, Emerson Baker, Leon Cranmer, Bruce Bourque, Gerald Bigelow, and the late Robert Bradley, all of whom welcomed an outlander into their midst with most hospitable collegiality. Arthur Spiess was instrumental in establishing first contacts with the historical archaeology community in the state, even though as a prehistoric purist he considers those "pesky Europeans" to be unwanted interlopers on the archaeological scene. My thanks to all.

Encouragement was also forthcoming from the directors of the Maine state agencies who had to approve the excavation permit: Earle G. Shettleworth, Jr. of the Maine Historic Preservation Commission, Joseph R. Phillips of the Maine State Museum, and Thomas Morrison and David Soucy of the Maine Bureau of Parks and Lands. I especially appreciate the enthusiastic support of Robert Bradley, former Assistant Director of the Historic Preservation Commission, and Denis Thoet, Executive Director of the Friends of the Maine State Museum and administrator of the Field School Program. Denis was succeeded by Michael Hamer in his position as Director of Development. Sheila McDonald, first as Historic Site Specialist of Parks and Lands, and later Assistant Director of the Maine State Museum, also championed the project and guided the paperwork through the Augusta bureaucracy. The park rangers who administered Forts Popham and Baldwin were also a major asset at the site. Under the leadership of Park Managers Ben Kreiton and Brian Murray they provided logistical support, patrolled the grounds during the off-hours, and were a source of local contacts and information. Ben Kreiton even came to our rescue once during a confrontation with a gun-toting fellow who considered his treasure hunting more important than our research!

That research was greatly assisted by a very important non-archaeological line of investigation that was contributed by Peter A. Sablock of Salem State College. In 2004 and 2005, Professor Sablock ran ground-penetrating radar surveys on selected areas of the site. This noninvasive procedure provided considerable information on subsurface features and spared us a considerable amount of effort. The results of his surveys are discussed in the appropriate section and the complete report is reproduced in Appendix C.

Laboratory processing of the artifacts was initially undertaken by dedicated members of the crew and students while still in the field. Upon return to the museum, further processing, cataloguing and analysis of the 1994 collection was accomplished with the volunteer assistance of the following students: Kevin Cahill,

Aaron Goldberg, and Allison Morgan. After 1997, the lab was supervised by John Bradford, who was assisted in later years by Nicia Gruener and Judy Dunsford. Judy also contributed her considerable expertise in computer graphics for creating field maps and report illustrations. Radiographic examination of metal artifacts was performed by Martha Watts and Sherry Lewis using equipment and film provided by Dr. Stephen Sand. Conservation of the metal was most capably accomplished by Molly Carlson who also offered very useful insights into the identifications of some of the cleaned artifacts.

During the analytic and writing stages, many expertises were drawn upon. Bob Bradley of the Maine Historic Preservation Commission and Ric Faulkner, University of Maine at Orono, were constant sources of information on the historical archaeology of Maine. Ivor Noël Hume, William Kelso, and Bly Straub of the Jamestown Rediscovery Project identified artifacts of the 1607 dateline, and also shared data from the excavations at our sister colony; I would especially like to thank Noël for his early and continuing encouragement. Steven Pendery, chief archaeologist with the North Atlantic Region of the National Park Service, generously offered his considerable knowledge of English and American earthenwares. Giovanna Vitelli, honorary research associate with the Institute of Archaeology, Oxford, guided us through the mysterious world of seventeenth-century glass. Arthur Spiess of the Maine Historic Preservation Commission, Bruce Bourque of the Maine State Museum, and Brian Robinson of the University of Maine at Farmington were the principal advisors for the aboriginal artifacts.

Peter Morrison and Pamela Crane participated in all ten years of fieldwork and assisted in the reanalysis of the entire collection of seventeenth-century artifacts. Their collaboration has been crucial to the success of the Popham project and is appropriately recognized on the title page. Peter also provided the artifact distribution maps and an appendix for this volume.

Publication of the volume was funded by the combined resources of the Maine State Museum, Maine Historic Preservation Commission, Maine Archaeological Society, and private contributions. Such broad support is most gratifying and made possible a superior production. Final editing and design benefitted from the sensitive suggestions of Art Spiess, series editor of the *Occasional Publications in Maine Archaeology*. It is most fitting that Art, who played such an important role in getting the project started, should also participate in the final act of publication.

Finally, there are four people of Phippsburg-Popham Beach whose contributions to the project were so fundamental that it is doubtful that we could have achieved such success without them. Earle "Bud" Warren, Chairman of Maine's First Ship, cheerfully took on the position of project coordinator, essentially providing the infrastructure for the field school. His sense of humor, efficiency, and caring stewardship created just the right atmosphere and such a smooth-running operation that I was able to concentrate on matters archaeological. We all especially appreciated his talent for arriving on site with popsicles or hot coffee and cocoa, depending upon the weather. I am spoiled and never want to take the field again without Bud. The second indispensable soul is Jane Stevens, our greatest local supporter and owner of part of the site. Jane stuck with us throughout the lean days of discouraging results and never wavered in her encouragement. She embodies the patience and perseverance so vital to the success of any archaeological investigation. She also provided some of the amenities that civilize the field experience, and even served her time in the trenches. And then there are John and DeeDee Bradford. John not only became an expert field excavator and laboratory supervisor, but also a partner in research and advisor on all matters pertaining to Maine. John and DeeDee hosted me at their West point home during the 1998-2005 seasons and a finer refuge from the fray cannot be imagined. To all these good friends I dedicate this volume.

A note on presentation: generally throughout the text the first person plural will be used in recognition that during the course of the project the strategies, tactics and interpretations were often guided by group discussions among the professional team and the long-term volunteers. Of course, none of these fine folk is responsible for the way his or her advice was translated onto the following pages, but it is hoped that in the main they find sufficient concordance with the results to justify their participation.

JPB
Salem, Massachusetts
2007

INTRODUCTION

This volume focuses on the excavations that located and then investigated the remains of Fort St. George, the principal settlement of the 1607-1608 Popham Colony at the mouth of the Kennebec River in Maine. The colony was the first official attempt to establish an English claim to present-day New England. But when it occurred, this venture was just the latest event in a long-standing interest in the area by the English and other Europeans dating back at least to 1497. And although the colony failed and was abandoned after only a year, it was an important building block in the developing campaign of English colonization of these shores. Its credentials are quite impeccable: sister colony to Jamestown (the first permanent English colony in America) and essential precursor to the Pilgrims (the first successful colony in New England), it was a cornerstone in the foundation of English America. It is only in context, then, that the historical significance of the colony may be fully understood.

HISTORICAL BACKGROUND

The Popham Colony did not just happen. The colonists were the beneficiaries of nearly a century of exploration and experience by various European nationalities in the New World. Although it is doubtful that John Cabot ventured farther south than Newfoundland in his voyages of discovery, and it is unclear where the Corte Real brothers made their landfalls, the northern coasts including Maine may have been probed by unknown mariners early in the sixteenth century. The first explorer of record definitely to have sailed along the Maine coast and describe its landforms and natives was Giovanni da Verrazzano. Sailing under the flag of France in 1524, he reconnoitered the entire Atlantic Coast from the Carolinas to the Canadian Maritimes. In May, after a friendly visit with the Native Americans living around Narragansett Bay which he named "Refugio" Verrazzano and his French crew rounded Cape Cod and sailed north to Maine. From the sea, the coast was described as being fair, open, and bare, with high mountains visible in the distance. A rocky cliff on the shore is of special note because it was the only place where the natives would "truck" (i.e., trade) with the explorers – by means of baskets lowered from the top of the cliff to the sailors approaching in small boats from below. Samuel Eliot Morison believed they may have been in Casco Bay (1971, pp. 308-309), and the only two locations matching such a description are to be found at the mouth of the Kennebec River: on Seguin Island or at Bald Head. Morison felt the latter was more likely, which is of particular interest to us since Bald Head is part of the same peninsula as Sabino Head, the site of Fort St. George and the Popham Colony. Thus, Verrazzano's descriptions of what he called the "Land of Bad People" could be relevant.

The Bad People greeted Verrazzano's landing parties with war cries and arrows before fleeing into the woods. They would confront Verrazzano's men only from their cliff-top vantage point, and even then for the sole purpose of bartering for knives and fishhooks. All they desired of these men from the sea were metal tools. Verrazzano, for his part, considered "The people all different from the others [i.e., those already encountered to the south], and as much as those passed were of cultivated manners, these were full of uncouthness and evil manners, so barbarous that we were never able, with howsoever many signs we made them, to have any intercourse with them.... They had no regard for courtesy, and when they had nothing more to exchange, at their departing the men made at us all the signs of contempt and disdain which any brute creature could make, such as exhibiting their bare behinds and laughing immoderately" (Morison ibid.; Cumming, Skelton, and Quinn 1971, p. 84). In light of the disasters to come, one can only sympathize with such a display of angst.

Verrazzano was followed within a year by Estévan Gomez, a Portuguese in the pay of Spain. He sailed past the Kennebec, which he named the *Rio de buena madre,* but did not explore it. Soon after these voyages, the myth of Norumbega began to take form and circulate widely in Europe, given credence by the reports of unidentified mariners and the tall tales of that continental trekker, David Ingram. A native region originally centered on the Penobscot was transformed into a fabled city which under Ingram's elaborations came to rival the Seven Cities of Cibola and Marco Polo's golden cities of Cathay in the covetous imaginations of sixteenth-century European explorers.

Norumbega was the direct inspiration when official voyages of exploration along the Maine coast were resumed in 1579-1580. This time, it was the English who ventured forth, finally exercising their rights of discovery based on the voyages of John Cabot. These new explorations were undertaken at the behest of Sir Humphrey Gilbert, half brother of Sir Walter Ralegh. The brothers had been commissioned by Queen Elizabeth to colonize English claims in the New World: Sir Walter the southern coasts which were named Virginia in her honor, and Sir Humphrey the land of Norumbega which included all of the continent from the Hudson River north to the Canadian Maritimes (Figure 1). Although the reconnaissances of the Penobscot failed to find the City of Norumbega, Sir Humphrey still intended to plant his colony there. His attempt in 1583 was thwarted by shipwreck, and got no farther than Newfoundland; he himself was lost at sea and the venture failed before it was fairly started. It was, however, the first step in a continuing effort that was to become a family tradition. His son, Raleigh Gilbert, was to make it to Norumbega – or northern Virginia as it was then renamed – 24 years later, after the hiatus enforced by war with Spain. But first there were others.

At the beginning of the seventeenth century, the English returned to northern waters with special attention initially focused on relocating the hospitable Refugio described by Verrazzano, and setting up there a small trading post. Bartholomew Gosnold was the first in 1602. In the ship *Concord*, he explored the coasts and islands of southern New England, or "North part of Virginia" as he was the first to call it (Brereton 1602). It is odd that he should adopt this nomenclature since he apparently sailed without the knowledge or official permission of Sir Walter Ralegh who now held the patent for all of Virginia. The *Concord* returned with a hold full of sassafrass, a highly desired medicinal at the time[1] which should have enriched Ralegh, but it was sold before he knew about it.

Gosnold did plant a temporary settlement on Cuttyhunk Island (Brain 2003c), but it only lasted a few weeks and was not an official attempt at colonization. It was of no more consequence than the fleeting visitations already described above. The momentum was building, however. Even if sassafrass was losing its value, Brereton's *Relation* of the voyage – a nifty bit of propaganda – spurred interest in this northern region.

The very next year, Martin Pring sailed in command of two small ships for "sundry of the chiefest merchants of Bristol." The participation of promoters from Bristol emphasizes the growing role of that important western English port in overseas ventures. Although a new undertaking, previous experience was not ignored. Some of Gosnold's men accompanied Pring, and this time the expedition set forth with Ralegh's blessing. The objectives were the same as Gosnold's: to explore the commercial prospects of northern Virginia and to establish a summer trading camp. Both Gosnold and Pring had made first landfall on the southern Maine coast, which Gosnold called the "North Land," but they did not stick around when neither sassafrass (which is rare north of Massachusetts) nor Native Americans (who may have continued the standoffish behavior experienced by Verrazzano) were found. They headed farther south to search for Refugio.

By 1604, the sassafrass market was glutted and it had been found by Gosnold and Pring, and confirmed by the contemporary French explorer Samuel de Champlain, that fur trading was unrewarding in sassafrass

---

[1] Sassafrass was "a plant of souereigne vertue for the French Poxe [the English term for syphilis" and other assorted ills, according to the medical wisdom of the times (Quinn and Quinn 1983, pp. 224-225).

Figure 1. Detail from Boazio 1588 map. At this time, the English divided the east coast of North America north of Spanish Florida and south of French Canada into Virginia and Norumbega. The latter would be renamed northern Virginia, consolidating the English claim, by the beginning of the seventeenth century, and then in 1614 would be called New England by John Smith, forever establishing the English claim. (Jay I. Kislak collection, Library of Congress)

country. Thus it was that when the English next sailed forth in 1605, it was with other objectives in mind. There actually were two driving forces, fishing and colonization, that would considerably broaden English interests if they were given impetus. The right to establish a permanent presence, rather than simply profiting from uncoordinated trading voyages, was a unilaterally English interpretation of the Treaty of London with Spain in 1604.

The 1605 expedition was led by George Waymouth, whose father had subscribed to the voyages of Sir Humphrey Gilbert, thus forging another connection in the closely related community of Elizabethan-Jacobean adventurers. Waymouth was an experienced navigator who shared the dream of a Northwest Passage and had already failed in one attempt to find it in 1602. In addition to this doomed project, he was also bitten by the colonization bug. He wrote a thoughtful treatise on the subject that included detailed plans for fortified towns which he presented to King James in 1604. This effort apparently won him the attention of Sir Thomas Arundell and the Earl of Southampton, prominent English Catholics who wished to find a suitable place to plant a colony of their religious brethren. It is probable that they had Refugio in mind.

The second initiative was sponsored by Plymouth merchants and other Devonians who were anxious to explore the prospects for establishing seasonal or permanent camps to exploit the excellent fishing grounds in the waters off North Land described by Gosnold and Pring. These two commissions, colonizing on the one hand and fishing on the other, would have been difficult to fulfill in a single voyage if the geographic objectives were as widely separated as indicated. They become complementary ventures, however, if combined in a single region. Although James Rosier's *True Relation* of the voyage suggests that Waymouth had intended to sail more southerly waters (Quinn and Quinn 1983, pp. 257-261), it is probably no coincidence that this Devonshire man concentrated his efforts precisely where his Plymouth backers had expressed their interests. It was to be a fateful turn of events. Waymouth confined his entire exploration of

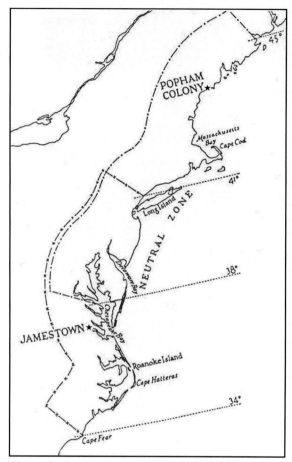

Figure 2. Land grants to the London and Plymouth Companies of Virginia, 1606.

about a month to Monhegan and the Georges Islands and the St. George River. He confirmed the bountiful fishing to be found offshore and touted the river as a suitable colonial site. He also captured five Native American men from Pemaquid at the mouth of the St. George River. These men – Nahanada, apparently sagamore of the Pemaquid village, Amooret, Skidwarres, Manida, and Assacomoit – were to be taken back to England where, learning English, they could give detailed reports of their country and then serve as interpreters in future expeditions.

When Waymouth returned to England in the middle of July 1605, he found that his Catholic backers had turned to other projects. A new colonizing syndicate soon formed, this time composed of West Country men, but Waymouth was not invited to lead further ventures. Nevertheless, his influence was enormous. James Rosier's *True Relation* of the brief voyage had an immediate impact and focused intense interest on the central Maine coast. Furthermore, Waymouth's Native captives had their desired effect as the stories they had to tell about their "Country of Mawooshen" fell on ready English ears. Two of those ears belonged to Sir Ferdinando Gorges, who at the time was the captain of Plymouth Fort. In this official capacity he took charge of three of the Native Americans – Skidwarres, Manida, and Assacomoit – whom he pumped for more information. Sir Ferdinando was impressed, and from that moment until his death forty years later he was a major figure in promoting the English colonization of northern Virginia, or New England when it acquired that name.

Sir Ferdinando enlisted the interest and participation of Sir John Popham, Lord Chief Justice of England, in what was to be the first systematic attempt to colonize northern Virginia. Sir John was motivated by a desire to find a foreign refuge for superfluous members of society: ex-soldiers, vagabonds, perhaps even criminals. Thus, the intervention of Gorges and Popham signalled a major shift in the objectives and scale of English ventures in northern Virginia. The new adventure was even more significant in that it was part of a larger enterprise, the economic exploitation of all Virginia, and was coordinated with a similar expedition to southern Virginia that was to become the successful Jamestown Colony. A joint stock company, the Virginia Company, was formed by an alliance of merchant and gentlemen stockholders, and a royal charter for the venture was sought from James I. The charter, signed and sealed on the tenth of April 1606, was an innovation in English overseas expansion for it endowed the entire endeavor with official sanction. It thus became a geopolitical, as well as economic, venture.

The Virginia Company was divided by the royal charter into two ventures, named the London Company and the Plymouth Company. The London Company was granted that part of Virginia lying between 34° and 41° N, while the Plymouth Company was assigned the more northerly latitudes of 38° to 45° N. Each company was to plant its initial colony within the nonoverlapping portions of the respective grants. The degrees of overlap between 38° and 41° were to be claimed by the first colony that was strong enough to do so. The London Company Colony, also known as the Southern Colony or the First Colony – and ultimately to history as the Jamestown Colony – was to become the first permanent English settlement in North America. This distinction has obscured the fact, fame, and fate of the Northern, or Second, Colony which is more popularly called the Popham Colony (Figure 2).

The Popham Colony was named after Sir John Popham, the principal investor in the venture, and his kinsman George Popham,[2] who was the first president of the colony (Table 1). Although Sir John was the most important financial backer of the Plymouth Company, many other west country interests, including adventurers from Bristol and Exeter, were also enticed to risk their capital. Nevertheless, the actual colonizing attempt was primarily a family affair (Figure 3).

In addition to George Popham, there was his nephew Edward Popham (Sir John's great nephew). Sir John's son, Sir Francis, was treasurer of the company and thus responsible for supplying the colony. Second in command of the colony, titled admiral, was Raleigh Gilbert, despite the fact that he was half nephew of Sir Walter Ralegh[3] who had been sentenced to death

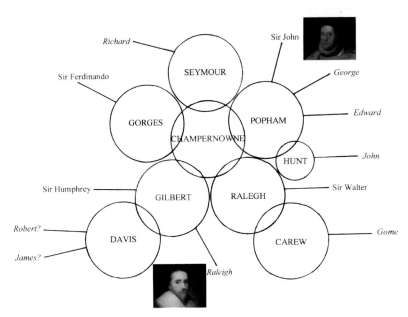

Figure 3. Famous families in southwest England connected by marriage. Members who were Popham colonists are indicated in italics. (Also see Table 1.)

by the Lord Chief Justice. Raleigh's brother, Sir John, was president of the Plymouth Company and a member of the colony's governing council back in England. The Gilberts were related to the Gorges family through their grandmother, Catharine Champernowne. Sir Ferdinando Gorges, a major backer of the colony who assumed the role of prime mover after the death of Sir John in 1607, was therefore a cousin of the Gilberts. Richard Seymour, chaplain, was a cousin to both the Gilberts and Sir Ferdinando, and was also related to the Pophams via the Champernowne connection. Gome Carew, designated searcher (for mines), was related by marriage to the Gilberts and Raleghs; so close was the relationship that Sir Walter Ralegh had a brother and a nephew named Carew. Captains Robert and James Davies probably belonged to the same Devonshire family as John Davis, the great navigator who also may have been related to the Gilberts by marriage (which perhaps was the inspiration for naming his eldest son Gilbert).

Whether such a comfortable coterie sacrificed competence is a question we shall revisit after examining the archaeological evidence. For now, we may venture the opinion that despite the obvious nepotism it is clear that an effort was made to select wisely from the available family-related pool of candidates. The Plymouth Company organizers were well acquainted with the literature of exploration and were attentive to the advice contained therein. For example, Richard Hakluyt and John Brereton (1602) had recommended that the personnel be carefully chosen: it was "to be wished that some ancient captains of mild disposition and judgment be sent" with men skilled in the arts of fortification, mineral prospecting, drug extraction, fishing, salt making, husbandry, and gardening. Thus it is no coincidence that the Popham company included soldiers, searchers (for mines), fishermen, and farmers, as well as carpenters, shipwrights, a cooper and a blacksmith. Moreover, George Popham, the first president of the colony, was described by Gorges as "an honest man, but ould, and of an vnwildy body, and timerously fearfull to offende, or contest with others that will or do oppose

---

[2] George Popham has been variously described as a brother, cousin, or nephew of Sir John (Thayer 1892, pp. 243-244, 250-253; Burrage 1906, p.397, 1914, p. 65; Banks 1929, p. 315; Andrews 1967, p. 745; Viereck 1967, p. 105; Popham 1976, p. 51; Quinn and Quinn 1983, pp. 78, 446fn1, 446fn2). Conclusive evidence that he was a nephew (son of Sir John's brother Edward) was recently discovered in a Popham family genealogy (Popham 1752).

[3] We follow Sir Walter's preferred spelling, although Raleigh Gilbert did not.

Table 1. Personnel of the Popham Colony.

GENTLEMEN OF QUALITY
    Council Members:
    Capt. George Popham, President[1]
    Capt. Raleigh Gilbert, Admiral[2]
    Capt. Edward Harlow, Master of Ordnance
    Capt. Robert Davies, Sergeant-Major, Captain of *Mary and John*[3]
    Capt. Ellis Best, Marshall
    Capt. James Davies, Captain of the Fort
    Capt. John Elliott, Captain of *Gift of God*[4]
    Mr. Robert Seaman, Secretary
    Mr. Gome Carew, Chief Searcher (for mines)
Other Gentlemen:
    John Havercome, Master of *Gift of God*[4]
    Richard Seymour, Chaplain
    Edward Popham[5]
NOTABLES
    Master Turner, Physician[3]
    John Hunt, Draftsman[3?]
    Christopher Fortescue, Ship Master

OTHER PERSONS
    Master Patterson, Killed by Indians?
    Master Digby, Shipwright
    Peter Grisling, Master's Mate of *Gift of God*[4]
    John Diamond, Quartermaster of *Gift of God*[4]
    Timothy Savage, Quartermaster of *Gift of God*[4]
    Lancelot Booker, Cooper of *Gift of God*[4]
    John Fletcher, Sailor of *Gift of God*[4]

COMMONALTY, LANDSMEN, PLANTERS
    Approximately 100 persons who included:
    Soldiers -- like Jamestown, soldiers recently discharged from one army or another probably formed the largest group.
    Craftsmen -- in addition to the shipwrights and cooper listed above, the Hunt map shows a smith, and all the structures certainly indicate carpenters; Carew as chief searcher may have been an alchemist.
    Farmers -- "The garden place" on Hunt map.
    Traders -- probably not a separate category, but activities overseen by Gilbert?
    Riffraff? -- the last vacancies may have been filled as Aubrey says "out of all the gaols of England"; in fact, Sir John Popham himself was instrumental in securing legislation requiring "banishment beyond the seas" as a penalty for vagrancy. As Thayer (1892, p. 210) so elegantly puts it: "We get a blurred but not wholly misleading view of the colonists, as at least in part a low class of men, of light weight in character by former practices, or by reaction from former pressure of severe administration of law, inclined to be lawless and emulous of base and wicked deeds." Our researches, however, suggest a more favorable characterization of the general run of colonist.

---

1. Nephew of Sir John Popham. Age 50. Some suggest he was considerably older, perhaps a septuagenarian (see Thayer 1892, p. 251; Popham 1976) but this has been disproven . Experienced soldier and privateer.
2. Youngest son of Sir Humphrey Gilbert and half nephew of Sir Walter Ralegh. Age 25. Qualifications other than blood--that is, descent from such famous Elizabethan sea-dogs/explorers/colonists as Gilbert and Ralegh, and other family relationships noted below--unknown.
3. Returned to England on the *Mary and John*, October 8 or 9, 1607.
4. Returned to England on the *Gift of God*, December 16, 1607 with 50 men and boys.
5. Nephew of George Popham, great nephew of Sir John.

him, but otherwayes a discreete, carefull man" (Quinn and Quinn 1983, p. 450). The very embodiment of Brereton's "ancient captain," he was chosen for his qualities of experience, judgment, and honesty, and despite the fact that he was "well stricken in years...and had long been an infirme man" (ibid., p. 345).[4] On the other hand, Raleigh Gilbert, second in command of the colony with the title of admiral, was a youth of 25. He was described as "desirous of supremasy, and rule, a loose life, prompte to sensuality, little zeale in Religion, humerouse, head-stronge, and of small iudgment and experiense, other wayes valiant inough" (ibid., p. 450). These are just the sort of characteristics one might expect in a stereotypical adventurer, a man who could effectively lead a body of armed men in a wilderness, but perhaps was not patient enough for the prosaic politics of founding a colony and managing its business affairs.

Sir Ferdinando Gorges, George Popham, and Gilbert's father and step-uncle were all experienced in foreign enterprises, especially the attempts to plant Protestant colonies in Ireland. The Irish plantations were the English prelude to New World colonization, and this proving ground would have provided invaluable preparation for men adventuring into uncharted, potentially hostile lands. The family connections between these protagonists also furnished a structure for organizing the endeavor, and concentrated the capital, political savvy and trust required for its success. In short, the Plymouth Company leaders and colonists were probably as prepared and qualified as any of their contemporaries to undertake the venture to northern Virginia. But all of these people, especially Sir John and Sir Ferdinando, also viewed the New World from a medieval perspective: they shared with Sir Walter Ralegh and Sir Humphrey Gilbert the conception of American settlement as an undertaking by aristocrats who would transfer all the rights, privileges, and trappings of feudalism to their vast new domains. This flawed dream contained the seeds of failure when the first enterprises fell on bleak shores.

At Sir John's urging, the Plymouth Company was the first to venture forth. In August 1606, Captain Henry Challons sailed in the *Richard* with 29 Englishmen and two Abenaki natives.[5] He never reached his destination, however. Contrary to orders, he sailed the southern route via the Canaries and Caribbean and was captured off Florida on November 10 by the Spaniards. A second ship commanded by Thomas Hanham, Sir John Popham's grandson,[6] and the experienced shipmaster Martin Pring, who had previously explored these waters in 1603, left England in October and sailed the direct northern route.

The plan was for the two ships to meet at Pemaquid, explore, select a suitable site for the colony, and set up an advance post that would greet the main body of colonists the following year. Failing to rendezvous with Challons, Hanham and Pring abandoned any thought of settlement and limited their mandate to exploration and site selection. In this they seem to have been more diligent than Waymouth had been, for they obviously explored a longer stretch of coast and islands. They were disappointed in the prospects offered by the St. George River, but sailing west they found the Sagadahoc – perhaps guided by one of Waymouth's Pemaquid natives, Nahanada, whom they had brought back with them – which seemed to offer much better opportunities for a colony. This was the recommendation they carried back to England, arriving just in time to redirect the main expedition under George Popham and Raleigh Gilbert.[7]

---

[4] Although it has been argued that he was a septuagenarian (Thayer 1892, p. 251), which would seem an impossibly ancient age to go adventuring, he was still too old for such business at his actual age of about 50.

[5] Manida and Assacomoit who had been captured from Pemaquid by George Waymouth in 1605. After a year in England learning the English language and customs, they were being brought back to serve as translators and guides.

[6] Also identified as Thomas Hanham the elder, Sir John's son-in-law (Thayer 1892, p. 245), but the younger seems more likely for such a voyage of exploration (Burrage 1914, pp. 58-59; Quinn and Quinn 1983, pp. 76, 342). In any case, Sir John's prediliction for keeping the entire proceeding in the family is manifested once again.

[7] But how different the beginning of English America might have been if Challons and Hanham had rendezvoused as planned in the autumn of 1606 and established their colony. There is no reason to expect that the St. George River would have provided a more welcoming venue than the Sagadahoc, but it must be acknowledged that when 20 years later permanent English colonization began to take hold along the southern Maine Coast Pemaquid was one of the earliest settlements to flourish.

Table 2. Chronology of the Popham Colony, 1607-1608 (o.s.).

May 31, 1607	*Gift of God* and *Mary and John* set sail from Plymouth
June 1	Pass the Lizard
June 10	Sir John Popham died
June 25-July 1	At and near the Azores; ships separated
July 30	*Mary and John* made landfall (Nova Scotia)
August 7	*Gift of God* joined *Mary and John* off Pemaquid
August 12	Both ships sailed for Sagadahoc
August 13	*Gift of God* arrived at Sagadahoc
August 16	*Mary and John* arrived at Sagadahoc
August 17-18	River Sagadahoc explored
August 18 PM	First landing at colony site
August 19	Sermon and formal taking of possession
August 20	"All our companyes landed & thear began to fortefye"
August 20-September	Most, if not all, labored on fort and buildings
August 31	Storehouse started by this date
September 7	Began to unload *Mary and John* (storehouse partly done)
September 26	Storehouse finished?
October 8 or 9*	*Mary and John* sailed for England
December 1	*Mary and John* arrived at Plymouth
December 16	*Gift of God* set sail with 50 men/boys
February 5	President George Popham died at Fort St. George
February 6 or 7	*Gift of God* arrived at Plymouth
By March 20	Two resupply ships sailed for Sagadahoc
May ?	Supply ships arrived (with news of Sir John Popham's death)
May-June ?	Supply ships returned to England
July 9	Death of Sir John Gilbert
After July 9	*Mary and John* sailed for Sagadahoc
By early September	*Mary and John* arrived at Sagadahoc (with news of Sir John Gilbert's death)
September or October	Colony abandoned; all set sail in the *Mary and John* and the *Virginia of Sagadahoc*
November ?	All returned to England

---

* The 8th according to the Hunt map, but at least one other witness indicated the 9th (Quinn and Quinn 1983, p. 460).

Two ships, the *Mary and John* and *Gift of God*, left Plymouth on May 31, 1607 (Table 2). On board, were more than 100 colonists (see Table 1), about the same number that had been sent out by the London Company a few months before to found the Jamestown Colony. The *Gift of God*, described as a "flyboat," had been provided by the Pophams and accordingly was commanded by George Popham. The *Mary and John* was a "good ship" of approximately 200 tons and had been chartered for the voyage by the Plymouth Company.[8] She carried the admiral, Raleigh Gilbert. Although the ships sailed out together, they parted company off the Azores on June 29 when the *Mary and John* was briefly waylaid by two Dutch ships. Skillful navigation and their pilots' obvious familiarity with those northern waters and landmarks brought them together again near Pemaquid on August 7. Anchoring offshore, they landed delegations to establish contact

---

[8] Like the Jamestown fleet, originally three ships had been planned, but apparently the third ship was deemed unnecessary since the combined tonnage of the two ships was greater than the displacement of all three Jamestown ships. The *Mary and John* alone, at 200 tons (Quinn and Quinn 1983, pp. 335, 458), more than equaled the *Susan Constant* (120 tons), *Godspeed* (40 tons), and *Discovery* (20 tons). English flyboats were small, shallow draft, easily maneuvered ships that were ideal for coastal exploration. They ranged in size from 20 to 150 tons (Morison 1971, p. 126). We do not know the tonnage of the *Gift of God*, only that it was smaller and more maneuverable than the *Mary and John*. *Gift of God* was a popular name for ships: an 80 tonner homeported in Barnstaple is recorded in 1591 and 1598 (Andrews 1964, pp. 256, 270) and another namesake listed at 130 tons arrived at Jamestown in 1622 (Noël Hume 1994, p. 381). It is not known whether either of these ships carried George Popham in 1607.

with the Pemaquid Indians and their sagamore, Nahanada. Despite (because of?) their earlier relations with Nahanada, the Englishmen were received with initial hostility, then cautious hospitality mixed with no little suspicion of their motives. A native of Pemaquid, Skidwarres, another of Waymouth's captives, had been brought back on the *Mary and John* to serve the colony as intermediary. Once back home, however, Skidwarres abandoned his carefully groomed role and refused to go along when the ships sailed for the Sagadahoc on the twelfth of August. Thus the colony was bereft of its native guide and translator.

Weathering a storm along the way, first the more maneuverable *Gift of God,* and then on August 16 the *Mary and John,* entered the Sagadahoc River (Figure 4). The first order of business for the colonists was to explore their new home and select a site suitable for fortification. Manning the boats from both ships with about half their company, Popham and Gilbert sailed up the river 14 leagues on August 17. They returned on the 18th, impressed by the "gallant ryver," and chose Sabino Head on the west bank near the mouth for their colony. On the 19th, the chaplain delivered a sermon, their "pattent" was read, the officers invested, and the plan of the fort laid out. Construction was started on August 20 when "all our companyes Landed & thear began to fortefye our presedent Capt popham Sett the fryst spytt of ground unto ytt and after hem all the rest followed & Labored hard in the trenches about ytt," and in the following days "all hands Labored hard about the fort Som in the trentch Som for fagetts & our ship carpenters about the buildinge of a small penis [pinnace] or shallop" (Thayer 1892, p. 67). The fort was named St. George.

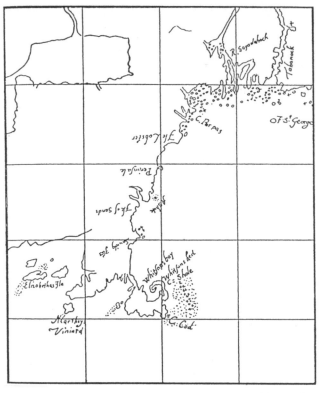

Figure 4. Detail from Velasco 1611 map. This section depicts the coast of northern Virginia (later New England) as it was known to the early seventeenth-century English explorers and Popham colonists. The Sagadahoc (Kennebec) River is in the upper right. The St. George offshore refers to an island, not the fort of the Popham Colony. North at top. (Original in the Archivo General de Simancas.)

The above quotations are taken from the only surviving journal which was written by Robert Davies[9] (see Appendix A1). Unfortunately, there is little additional information about the physical aspect of Fort St. George, merely references to its ongoing construction with emphasis on the storehouse. The ship captains impatiently awaited the completion of the storehouse so that they could unload their vessels and return to England while the sailing was still fair. We do learn from these brief descriptions, however, that the fortifications were composed of a ditch, the dirt from which would have been thrown up into a rampart that was reinforced with fagots (fascines). The journal stops after the October 6 entry, presumably because Davies returned with the *Mary and John* when she sailed for England two or three days later.

However, we also have the drawing of Fort St. George which was dated October 8 and also was sent back on the *Mary and John* (Figure 5). It is an extremely important document since it is the only detailed plan we have of an initial English settlement anywhere in the western hemisphere. The draftsman was one John Hunt, who may have been the brother-in-law of Edward Popham, George's nephew, and thus another

---

[9] Although there has been some confusion about the identity of the author, Strachey clearly names him as Robert Davies (Quinn and Quinn 1983, p. 401n3).

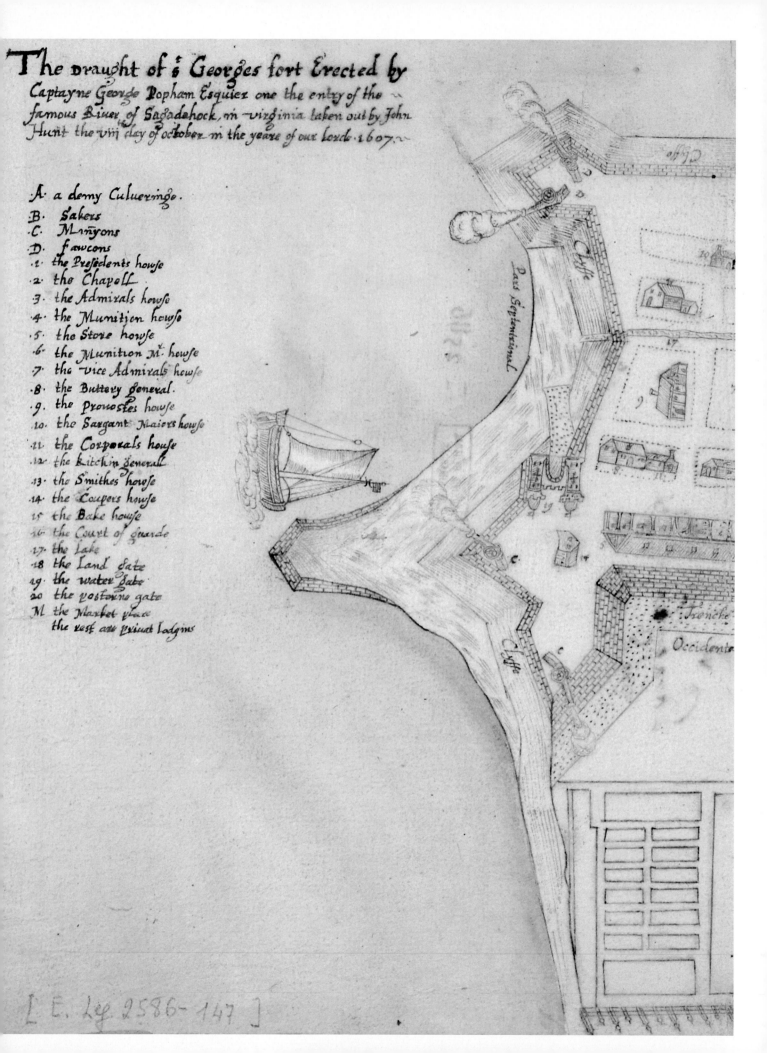

The Draught of ý Georges fort Erected by

Captayne George Popham Esquier one the entry of the
famous Riuer of Sagadahock, in virginia taken out by John
Hunt the viii day of october in the yeare of our lord 1607

- A. a demy Culueringe.
- B. Sakers
- C. Minyons
- D. fawcons
- 1. the Presidents house
- 2. the Chapell
- 3. the Admirals house
- 4. the Munition house
- 5. the Store house
- 6. the Munition Mr house
- 7. the vice Admirals house
- 8. the Buttery generall
- 9. the Prouostes house
- 10. the Sargant Maiors house
- 11. the Corporals house
- 12. the kitchin generall
- 13. the Smithes house
- 14. the Coupers house
- 15. the Bake house
- 16. the Court of guarde
- 17. the Lake
- 18. the Land gate
- 19. the water gate
- 20. the posterne gate
- M the Market place
  the rest are priuat Lodgins

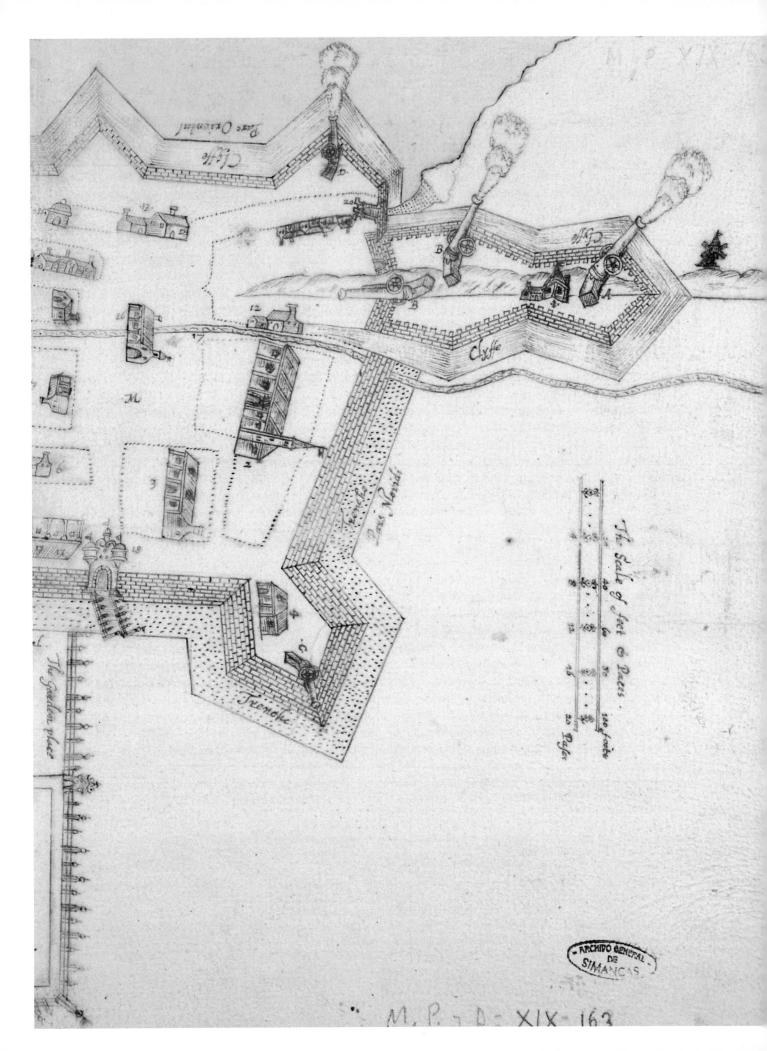

Pars Orientbul

Clyffe

Clyffe

Clyffe

The Scale of feet & Paces.

The Garden place

Figure 5 (pages 10 and 11). Fort St. George as drawn by John Hunt on October 8, 1607. Reproduced at full scale, but borders have been omitted (see Figure A2). This map was acquired by the Spanish ambassador to England who sent it to his sovereign, Philip III, in 1608. Fortunately, it was then deposited in the Spanish archives at Simancas where it was preserved until it was rediscovered nearly three centuries later. (Ministerio de Cultura de España, Archivo General de Simancas, MPD, 19, 163)

family connection.[10] Hunt drew a completely finished fort with nine cannons, battlemented gates (emblazoned with flags and pennants), and at least 25 structures within the compound (Figure 5). This seems unrealistic considering the drawing was made only seven weeks after construction began. It will also be noted that the pinnace built by the colonists, to be christened the *Virginia*, was also finished: afloat and fully rigged. It has always been suspected that Hunt's rendering was more a depiction of aspirations than reality at the time it was drawn. William Strachey says as much in his summary account of the colony when he notes that "After Capt. Davies' [of the *Mary and John*] departure they fully finished the fort, trencht and fortefied yt with twelve pieces of ordinaunce, and built fifty howses, therein, besides a church and a storehowse" (Thayer 1892, p. 84). That is, *after* the map was drawn Fort St. George was *fully* finished. Nevertheless, Strachey does seem to confirm Hunt's magnitude of the establishment and even adds three more guns and doubles the number of structures. Fifty houses seems impossible, as well as unnecessary. There was not enough time to build that many, nor space for them within the fort compound; and after mid December, when half the colonists returned to England, there would have been more houses than people. Most scholars assume the "fifty" is a misprint, but if construction units (bays, rooms, additions, etc.) are counted rather than individual structures the number can be reconciled with the Hunt map (Quinn and Quinn 1983, p. 441; see the *Oxford English Dictionary* for this contemporary meaning of "house"). The archaeology seems to support Hunt's rendering, exclusive of some of the obvious elaborations, although we cannot assume that all of the structures shown were actually constructed (see Appendix A2).

We can be certain that the storehouse was built: it was the structure most mentioned in the accounts, and of course it was the most necessary. The ships could not leave until it was serviceable, so it is probable that it was nearly, if not fully, finished when Hunt drew his map. It may have been the only major structure that had been completed by that time. According to Hunt's rendering, it would appear to have comprised eight bays, perhaps two rooms deep. We will find that archaeology confirms the construction of the storehouse, but corrects Hunt's record somewhat.

The only other structure we can be sufficiently confident about is Capt. Raleigh Gilbert's house (no. 3, "the Admirals house," on the Hunt map). It is mentioned repeatedly in legal depositions taken after the failure of the colony (Banks 1929). The deponents referred to a meeting of the ruling council that occurred in Gilbert's house just before the *Gift of God* sailed in mid December. So as winter set in we can be certain of only two major structures. Presumably, the president's house had been built, as well as some of the other facilities, but the documents are silent on the matter. Just why the council was meeting in Gilbert's house, rather than President Popham's house, is not explained either, but it suggests that interior space was a problem.[11]

---

[10] Edward's sister, Katherine, married a John Hunt (Popham 1976, p. 27). That this was the same John Hunt who was at Fort St. George and drew the map becomes a very real probability when it is also realized that Edward was married to Dorothy Bartlett, daughter of a Richard Bartlett (ibid., p. 29). Although the latter could have been a relatively common name, it seems too much of a coincidence that he could have been other than the famous military engineer and cartographer whose style was closely followed by John Hunt (Brain 1998).

[11] Or else, perhaps, a power shift was taking place within the colony, lending credence to Sir Ferdinando Gorges' dark mutterings about "childish factions" that were reported to him by those returning on the *Mary and John*. He put the blame on "ignorant timerous, and ambitiouse persons" (Quinn and Quinn 1983, p. 449) which is suspicously reminiscent of his description of Raleigh Gilbert if the reference is to temerity, and also George Popham if he really meant timerity. In fact, Raleigh outranked George in social standing which would not have been overlooked even in such changed circumstances. It may indeed be no coincidence that Gilbert had a bigger house – in fact, the largest heated structure in the fort – than the president, although the latter occupied the most prestigious spot within the citadel.

If space was at a premium, then the problem was about to be alleviated. The reason for the council meeting was to arrange for the departure of the *Gift of God* with half of the colonists. We do not know who was selected to go, or how they were selected. Probably including the ship's company, they are simply described as 50 men and boys. It is clear that even more of a problem than inadequate facilities was the lack of supplies. They were running out of food, and in order to last out the winter they sent half their number back – and those poor wretches were not even given enough sustenance to last the voyage according to the depositions.

Nevertheless, George Popham put on the best face he could in dispatches he sent back with them to England. The only document to survive is an extraordinary letter written in Latin that he sent to his sovereign, James I (see Appendix A3). Popham describes as products of the country such tropical spices as nutmeg, mace and cinnamon, even though he was already experiencing the frozen depths of a Maine winter, and claims that the Northwest Passage had at last been found for he was assured by the natives that what he interpreted as the Southern (Pacific) Ocean was only a seven-day journey from Fort St. George! These distortions of fact may reveal a rather naive and short-sighted appraisal of his countrymen's credulity – certainly Sir Ferdinando Gorges back in Plymouth did not believe them – but differ only in the magnitude of outrageous detail from the flood of overly favorable treatises that were promulgated by contemporary explorers and colonists.

After the *Gift of God* sailed, 45 colonists were left to winter over. The only ones who can be identified with certainty are George Popham and Raleigh Gilbert. Popham died on February 5, which left Gilbert in charge. In truth, Gilbert may already have assumed much of the leadership. He was the one who went exploring up and down the Maine coast during the fall months, who met with various chiefs, and who was primarily responsible for developing the fur trade.

There is a dearth of information about the colony from this point until the following fall when it was abandoned. We know that it was resupplied twice, which demonstrates the resolve of Gorges and Sir Francis Popham to keep the venture going after Sir John's death the previous year. The first ships to arrive in the spring of 1608 "found all things in good forwardness, and many kinds of furs obteyned from the Indians by way of trade; good store of sarsaparilla gathered, and the new pynnace all finished" (Thayer 1892, p. 85). But when the *Mary and John* arrived with the second resupply in the early fall, it also brought news of the death of Sir John Gilbert, Raleigh's brother. Raleigh was Sir John's heir, and the lure of title and lands back in England apparently was more appealing than the prospect of another Maine winter, so he decided to return home and claim his inheritance. The rest of the colonists, bereft of their leaders, gave up the venture and went with him. Thus the fort was abandoned, Gorges says "dismantled," and the entire company embarked on the *Mary and John* and the newly built pinnace, *Virginia*,[12] and set sail for home. "And this was the end of that northerne colony upon the river Sachadehoc" (ibid., p. 86).

The unexpected return of the colonists was the death warrant of the Plymouth Company, as well as a "wonderful discouragement" (Quinn and Quinn 1983, p. 338) to further ventures in northern Virginia for the next dozen years. The colonists excused their withdrawal by blaming it on the climate. The Sagadahoc, they said, was "a cold, barren, mountainous, rocky desert" and "an intolerably cold and sterile region, not inhabitable by our English nation" (Thayer 1892, pp. 213-214). As succinctly stated by Gorges: "Our hopes were frozen to death" (ibid.).

The failure probably owed more to the disappointingly sparse terrestrial resources. No mines of exploitable minerals had been discovered, and the fur trade was not as productive as had been hoped, in part because of deteriorating relationships with the native tribes. The searching and the trading were in the hands of Raleigh Gilbert who may not have been the best choice for the job, as already suggested above, because diplomacy and patience with the Native Americans were required. In fact, it is clear from the English

---

[12] One of the few accomplishments of the Popham venture was the construction of the *Virginia*, the pinnace that was sturdy enough to carry some of the colonists home in 1608 and see subsequent transatlantic service. Thus was born at this very place the North American ship building industry for which the Kennebec was to become so justly renowned.

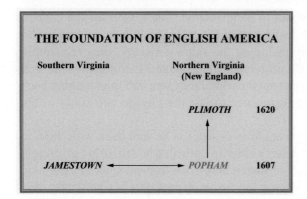

Figure 6. The Popham Colony was a cornerstone in the foundation of English America.

documents that relations with the Native Americans were strained initially and continued to deteriorate during the following year. After Popham's death, whatever brake he might have had on Gilbert's temperament was released. Father Biard, visiting the Kennebec in 1611, recorded Native American complaints that the English were not only inhospitable, but also beat them and set dogs on them (Thwaites 1896, p. 223). The natives, themselves, preserved even more dire tales that probably exaggerated the conflicts with the retelling (Williamson 1832, pp. 200-201), but attest to the troublesome depths to which relationships had declined. Not forged between these peoples was the peace of Massassoit.

But the greatest problem was certainly the loss of leadership and lack of motivation among that disparate band, for when more resolute leaders and colonists were put upon these shores they succeeded.[13] Sir Ferdinando Gorges and other prime movers of the Virginia Company had learned lessons that would serve them well in future ventures. The Popham Colony, then, was an important experience in the ongoing campaign of English colonization (Figure 6). The lessons learned were easily understood, if not as easily put into practice. The right combination of strong leadership and a people committed to enduring regardless of hardships was not to be found for a dozen years. But that lonely little outpost on the Sagadahoc, bravely named Fort St. George, had begun a new era.[14]

HISTORY OF THE SITE

The site of Fort St. George, which we shall know by the name of "Popham" in recognition of the nomenclature that historically has been most associated with it, is found on the west bank at the mouth of the Kennebec River on the tip of a north-facing headland named Sabino Point or Sabino Head (Figure 7). The coordinates are Latitude 43° 45' 11" N, Longitude 69° 47' 20" W. It is within the modern community of Popham Beach in the Town of Phippsburg, Sagadahoc County, Maine. Today, the core of the site is a small part of Fort Baldwin State Park, but portions of Fort St. George also lap over onto contiguous parcels of private land to the east, west, and south (see Figure 16). The number for the historic occupations at the Popham site in the Maine state designation system is ME 348-001; the number for the prehistoric components is Maine Archaeological Survey 15.139.

Located strategically at the mouth of an important river, the Popham site and vicinity are unusual for that rocky and barren coast in having sandy beaches and arable land. Given the geographic and natural assets, it should, indeed, be expected that the Popham site has a long history of human occupation, during the course of which a variety of cultural activities are manifest. A brief review of the prehistoric and historic occupations (Table 3) will provide the context for the archaeological data to be presented in the following pages.

[13] In this regard, it is often forgotten how close Jamestown came to failure. The colonists had actually given up in 1610 and were sailing down the James River when they were met by the new incoming governor, Thomas West, Lord De La Warr, who turned them around and forced them to resettle, instituting a strict regimen that saved the colony.

[14] Those who require more detailed historical background than can be offered in this treatise would do well to consult the following sources: for the broad perspective of Elizabethan and Stuart expansion and colonization, the works of A. L. Rowse and Peter Mancall; for a detailed treatment of the New England ventures, the many excellent studies by David B. Quinn (especially Quinn and Quinn 1983), and the volume by Emerson Baker, et al.; and for practically everything there is to know about the Popham Colony, the classic treatment by Henry O. Thayer (1892).

Table 3. Historic occupations of the Popham Site.

DATE	PERIOD	CULTURAL AFFILIATION	DIAGNOSTIC ARTIFACTS
2000			
	POPHAM BEACH	American Park	Recreation/Picnic
	FORT BALDWIN	American Shore Defense	Military
1900			
	PHIPPSBURG	American Residential	Agricultural/Maritime
1800			
		Hiatus	
1700			
	KENNEBEC	Native American	Colonial/Aboriginal
1600	FORT ST. GEORGE	English Colonial	Military/Trade
		Abenaki	Prehistoric

The prehistoric use of the site probably began during the Middle Archaic period, and continued through the Late Archaic and Woodland (Ceramic) periods. It is assumed that there were breaks in this continuum when the site was abandoned for some time. Even when in use it was probably occupied primarily on a seasonal basis by groups that migrated between the coast and inland regions. During the summer, bands of closely related families established camps and erected temporary shelters. When in residence, the natives were perfectly situated to exploit a rich diversity of estuarine and terrestrial resources. Fish and shellfish must have been the primary foodstuffs extracted: Samuel de Champlain noted a fishing village when he visited in July 1605, and the site is covered with shell middens, especially on the western and southeastern sides. These middens form the first observable human modification of the natural landforms.

Champlain and his men were the first known Europeans to definitely see, if not set

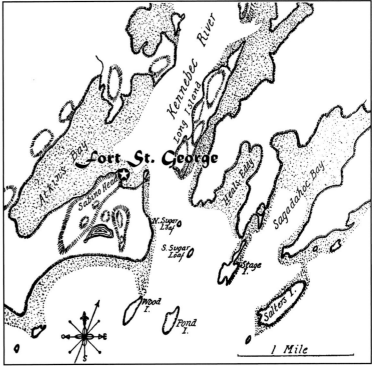

Figure 7. Location of Fort St. George at the mouth of the Kennebec River.

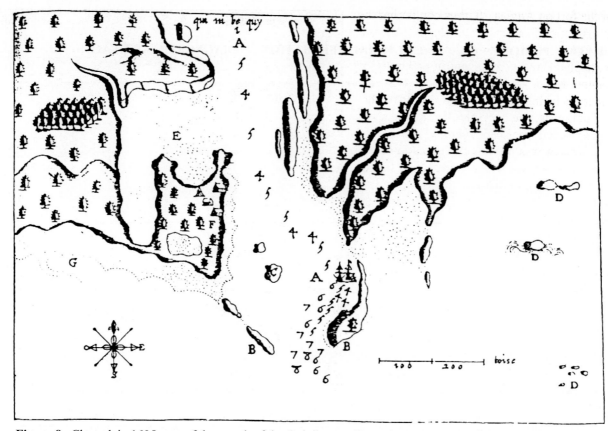

Figure 8. Champlain 1605 map of the mouth of the Quinibequy (Kennebec) River. The accuracy of the map may be appreciated by comparing it with the modern chart in Figure 7. Sabino Head is just below the "E" on this map. The native fishing village is indicated by the conical and rectangular wigwams on the right side of the peninsula ("F"). (Collection of the author)

foot on, the site. We know this as a fact because Champlain was a master cartographer and he drew a marvelously detailed map (Figure 8). Not only are the major topographical features at the mouth of the "Quinibequy" rendered with relative accuracy, but even the contours of Sabino Head are immediately recognizable. This attention to detail attests to Champlain's interest in the strategic value of the location and its suitability for possible colonization.

The same interest was, of course, shared by the Popham colonists two years later when they selected the tip of Sabino Head for the location of Fort St. George. On August 18, 1607, they "ad Choies of a place for our plantation wh^ch ys at the very mouth or entry of the Ryver of Sagadehocke [Kennebec] on the West Syd of the Ryver beinge almoste an Illand of a good bygness" (Thayer 1892, p. 66). The choice of location for the fort was dictated in instructions issued by the Virginia Company.[15] Although the instructions to the Popham Colony have not survived, a parallel set to the Jamestown colonists specifies that "you shall Do your best Endeavor to find a Safe port in the Entrance of Some navigable River making Choise of Such as one runneth furthest into the Land" (Spectre and Larkin 1992, p. 14). These instructions apparently were influenced by Richard Hakluyt who 25 years earlier in his *Divers Voyages* advised that colonies should "plant upon an island in the mouth of some notable river or the point of the land entering the river, if no island be" (Quinn 1974b, p. 274). Sabino Head fit these instructions admirably, and it was the perfect place to hide an exposed outpost that could be defended from waterborne attack. The colonists landed and began construction

---

[15] It is possible that Hanham and Pring influenced this decision. When they selected the Sagadahoc as a preferable venue for a colony the previous year they may also have noted the suitability of Sabino Head for fortification.

of the fort on August 20, thus continuing the human modification of the land. The odd configuration of the fort is explained by the particular shore contour and topography of Sabino Head. Thus the site found a new function in the hands of European soldiers and colonists, and so it served until the fall of 1608 when it was abandoned.

That it was not a perfect location for a fort, however, was noted by the Jesuit, Father Biard, and a party of Frenchmen who visited in 1611 (Thwaites 1896, p. 35). At first, they recognized the virtues of the choice, but then the shortcomings became apparent. Most serious of these was that the fort was confined to the tip of the point and was commanded by the higher ground that comprised the rest of Sabino Head. The fort was indefensible from land attack. It could also be cut off from water communication by a counter fort on the nearby Hunnewell Point. It is no wonder, then, that when the next generation of forts was built in the vicinity they were placed on Hunnewell Point, for although it was more exposed it was at the same time more easily defended from both land and water attack. But lest it be perceived that the military sense of the colonists was faulty, it must be noted that the Sabino site selected for Fort St. George perfectly fulfilled their immediate requirements: viz., an easily fortified location that was accessible to the sea and home, but was hidden from direct observation by French ships reconnoitering along the coast; and should the French happen to find them, then the earthen ramparts and canons would provide a doughty defense against any naval assault.

There were other visits by Englishmen later in the century, and it is clear from their comments that the site remained an abandoned ruin. For example, about 1625 Samuel Maverick found only "Rootes and Garden hearbs and some old walles" (Thayer 1892, p. 129), and in 1660 Henry Gardiner reported that just "Ruins and fruit Trees remain to this day" (ibid., p. 101). The site seems to have been avoided by the early European settlers. According to local legends, however, the vic-

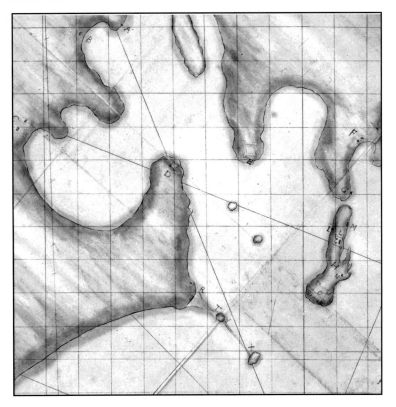

Figure 9. Detail from Pasquine 1688 map, *Carte de l'entrée de la rivière de Quinibequi et de ses environs et plan de l'isle et fort de Sakdeak* [Sagadahoc]. French familiarity with the Kennebec in the late seventeenth century is attested by this map and the notations locating several habitations (A, B, C, F, G), including one occupied by a Frenchman who had lived on this river for 28 years. Many fortifications are also indicated, especially Fort de Sagadahoc on Stage Island (H). Although the map shows some improvement from the map of Champlain in knowledge of the landforms and islands at the mouth of the river, it incorrectly depicts those details of most interest to us: specifically, Sabino Head and Hunnewell Point are merged into one feature, and the reach of Atkins Bay is considerably foreshortened. Clearly, the cartographer had not sailed upstream and so was denied the perspective that enabled Champlain to be more accurate in these regards. The cartographic confusion is especially frustrating because at the tip of the combined Sabino-Hunnewell peninsula is indicated an English fort (D) that the notation says was destroyed by the Kennebec Indians nine years before. This would place the destruction about the time of King Philip's War. The existence of such a facility is not otherwise recorded, but it is entirely possible that some sort of fortification had been established at this strategic location. However, although the map confuses the situation, it is more likely that by this time such a fort would have been placed on Hunnewell Point where it could exercise better control of the river, as were all later fortifications during King George's War, the Revolutionary War, the War of 1812, and the Civil War. In short, this map tells us nothing about Fort St. George. (Bibliothèque Nationale de France, GE SH18E PF135 DIV3 P6)

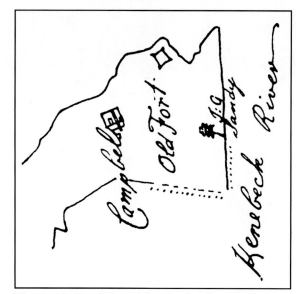

Figure 10. Detail from John North 1751 map showing settlements around the mouth of the Kennebec River. The map confirms the location of Fort St. George at the tip of Sabino Head, and the regularity of outline even suggests that ruins might still be visible. In any case, the closest indications of contemporary settlements or house sites are on the other side of the headland. (Collections of Maine Historical Society, R10.)

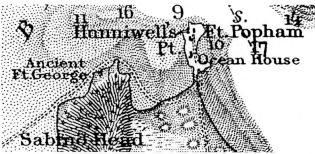

Figure 11. Detail from USGS 1868 map. "Ancient Fort George" is still associated with the tip of Sabino Head, and the nearest development has been the construction of Fort Popham and the resort hotel Ocean House on "Hunniwell's" Point.

inity was used as a gathering place for Native American was bands during King Phillip's War (Lane 1966, p. 3), and fortifications may have been constructed on the nearby Hunnewell Point by this time (Figure 9). It certianly is to be expected that the abandoned Fort St. George was visited by native salvagers looking for scraps of metal, and that the site was briefly reoccupied at these times is indicated by the presence of aboriginal pottery and artifacts that in many locations are found in a thin layer overlying the remains of Fort St. George. The few later seventeenth-century European artifacts that have been found at the site may be reasonably assigned to these native activities.

Not only is there no evidence of a Euroamerican presence at the site for the remainder of the seventeenth century, but it is also apparent that settlers continued to avoid that particular place during most, if not all, of the eighteenth century as well. The only eighteenth-century maps we have found that are detailed enough to indicate settlement patterning and land use at Sabino Head show an absence of development at the location of Fort St. George, and in fact identify the location only with the fort (Figure 10). The site clearly was unutilized, except possibly for some farming, for nearly two centuries. We shall see that the artifact inventory from the archaeological excavations confirms this hiatus.

The land had not been ignored, however. A 250-acre tract including Sabino Head had been acquired from a local sagamore soon after 1630 by an English settler, John Parker. The land apparently was sold by Parker's widow to the Clarke and Lake Company after 1654 (Isaacson 1965, p. 42), as part of that company's land acquisition program. Clarke and Lake centered its operations farther upriver on the northern end of Arrowsic Island (Baker 1985, p. 10), however, and the Sabino tract must have been deemed surplus for it was sold to Ambrose Hunnewell on June 25, 1662 (Isaacson, ibid.). The Hunnewell family retained the land long enough to leave its name attached to Hunnewell Point where the Civil War Fort Popham was built (Fig. 11).

In the 1730s, the land was bought by Job Lewis, and then passed to James McCobb. When McCobb died in 1788, this property, which included all of what is now Sabino Head, Popham Beach and Small Point, was still referred to as "Honeywell Farm, containing 250 acres" (ibid.). The land then seems to have been subdivided among McCobb's heirs, and his stepson, Mark Langdon Hill, received a portion that included the tip of Sabino Head which was renamed temporarily "Hill's Point" (ibid., p. 43). Sometime between 1788 and 1831, Hill built a "large dwelling" on his point which is probably the early nineteenth-century feature encountered in the 1994 excavations (see discussion under excavation unit P110). During the later nineteenth century, other families moved onto the point, most notably the Olivers and Perkins, and a map drawn in 1891 (Figure 12) shows several houses on and near the site of Fort St. George, although Hill's "large dwelling" had been removed. Three of the houses are still standing.

Beginning in 1905, a major development occurred. The U. S. Army acquired most of Sabino Head, including a large part of the site of Fort St. George, in order to build a modern fort of their own. Named Fort Baldwin, in honor of a Revolutionary War hero, it consisted of three batteries mounting five rifled guns (Dunnack 1924, pp. 139-141). Each battery was a large reinforced concrete bunker situated on the upper part of the headland. The guns had a clear field of fire that could command the entire mouth of the Kennebec and its approaches (Figure 13). This was but an elaboration of the military arts and technology that had already been recognized on a smaller scale by the Popham colonists who had placed their largest caliber guns on the highest point of the headland contained within their fort compound.

Although the batteries, themselves, did not directly impact the site of Fort St. George, ancillary constructions were more damaging. First, a railway was built from the site of the batteries, down the hill to the point, and out onto a pier into Atkins Bay where ships off-loaded their cargoes of cement and steel for the construction of the batteries. This railway ran right across the fort site, and the tip of the point was substantially reinforced where the pier was anchored to the land. Then, all the support facilities for Fort Baldwin – barracks, mess hall, storehouse, hospital, administration building, and so forth – were built on the western part of the site of Fort St. George (Figures 14,15). We hoped that these buildings were temporary structures without foundations or cellars, and so they proved to be (except for one nineteenth-century house, the "Nath'l Perkins" house on the 1891 Thayer map, that had been retained and was converted to army use). Nevertheless, we did encounter in the excavations various features that dated to Fort Baldwin, such as utility trenches, postholes, and other intrusions.

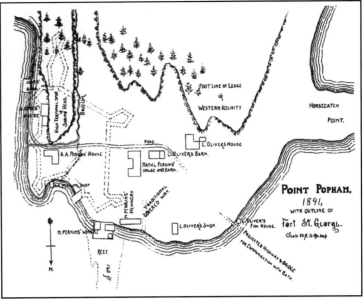

Figure 12. Thayer 1891 map of "Point Popham" with outline of Fort St. George superimposed according to Thayer (1892). Fortunately, the "projected highway and bridge" to Bath was never constructed. Note that the north arrow points down.

Figure 13. Fort Baldwin 6 inch rifled gun overlooking the mouth of the Kennebec River. This was the largest caliber mounted at the fort and although it was not much larger than the 4.5 inch demi-culverin brought by the Popham colonists for the same purpose, its range and firepower were superior. (From Dunnack 1924, p. 138)

However, far greater damage – at least for the archaeology of Fort St. George – occurred after Fort Baldwin was deactivated in 1924 and the temporary buildings were removed. In that year, the military reservation was sold to the State of Maine. The state apparently leased the arable land on the point, where the

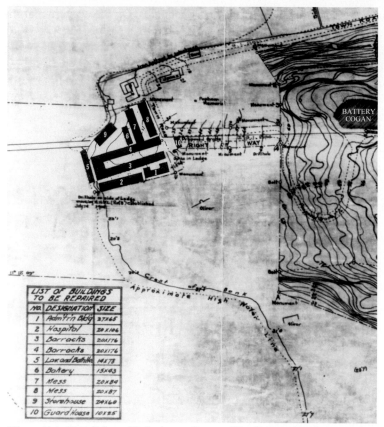

LIST OF BUILDINGS TO BE REPAIRED		
NO.	DESIGNATION	SIZE
1	Adm'trn Bldg	27x65
2	Hospital	30x106
3	Barracks	20x176
4	Barracks	20x176
5	Lav and Bath Ho	14x73
6	Bakery	15x43
7	Mess	20x84
8	Mess	20x87
9	Storehouse	24x60
10	Guard House	10x25

Figure 14. Detail from U. S. Army Corps of Engineers 1917 map of Fort Baldwin Military Reservation. Battery Cogan was the first of three batteries placed on the top of Sabino Head; the support buildings are shown at the tip of the headland overlying part of the site of Fort St. George. Note that north is to the left. (National Archives, RG77 fortifications file)

Figure 15. Temporary buildings at Fort Baldwin in 1918. The building with the shed entrance right of center was a barracks (#4 in Figure 14) and was situated on the site of Admiral Raleigh Gilbert's house. Curiously, these buildings were similar in form and probably even construction to the storehouse built by the colonists. The Nathaniel Perkins house in the background was converted for use as the administration office of the fort. (Photo by Ernest W. Oliver)

army's facilities had been, to a local truck farmer in the 1930s and 1940s. This simple plowing operation destroyed and mixed the historical strata from Fort St. George to Fort Baldwin over much of the state-owned portion of the site.

Fort Baldwin was reactivated during World War II, but with the exception of a gatehouse on the road at the bottom of the hill all new construction was confined to the area of the batteries on top of the headland. After the war, the land reverted to the state and since then it has been conserved as a state park under the management of the Bureau of Parks and Lands. The small part that concerns us, the flat area at the tip of Sabino Head where the support facilities of Fort Baldwin had been placed, has suffered only minor modification during this period (Figure 16). The nineteenth-century Perkins house that had survived Fort Baldwin was torn down and the cellar hole was filled in. More fill was brought in to construct a parking lot on the north side of the road. A flagpole was erected, a post-and-rail fence installed along the shore, and a few postholes have been dug for signs that have come and gone over the years. Otherwise the impact of the park has been minimal, and the surface has been stabilized with grass and plantings that are consistent with the new usage of this historic land for leisure-time activities.

This part of the park is surrounded by private land on all sides, except for the northern shore front and a right-of-way on the south that leads to the battery area on the summit of the headland. The strip of shorefront along the eastern side of the site occupied by Fort St. George is divided into two properties, occupied by two nineteenth-century houses: on the northeast the Perkins-Freeman house, and on the southeast the Jones-Stevens house, as they are identified on the 1891 Thayer map (Figure 12) and by the modern occupants. On the western margin of the park, outside of Fort St. George proper, but including the proposed garden area depicted on the Hunt map (see Figure 5), is land that may have been farmed in the eighteenth century and along the shore of which were structures related to fishing activities in the nineteenth century. To the southwest, the later nineteenth-century Oliver-Abraham house was built at the base of Sabino Head. The fact that all of these properties have been residential at least since the nineteenth century and were never owned by the federal or state governments gives us hope that they were not subjected to the various depredations of Fort Baldwin or the between-the-wars truck farming. Some indication of the potential was found in small tests on these lands that are among the excavations described in the next section.

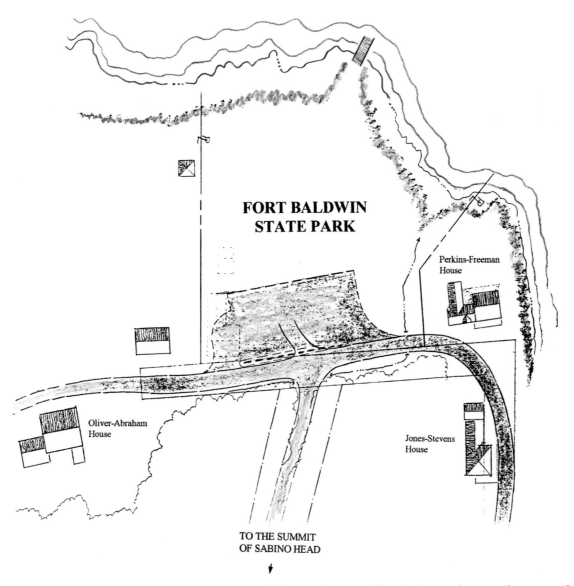

Figure 16. Detail from Fort Baldwin State Park 1981 map. The core of Fort St. George is presently preserved within the boundaries of the state park, but important elements overlap onto private lands contiguous to the east, south, and west. North at top. (Maine Bureau of Parks and Lands).

EXCAVATIONS

The site of Fort St. George has been excavated professionally by three different investigators. The first was Wendell S. Hadlock of the Farnsworth Art Museum in Rockland who dug many trenches across the site in 1962 and 1964. The second was Dr. Robert L. Bradley of the Maine Historic Preservation Commission who tested a small area in 1981. The third investigation began in 1994 under the direction of the author. All of these excavations had as the principal objective the location and verification of the remains of Fort St. George. After the first exploratory investigation in 1994, the present project continued in 1997 with intensive excavations of various structures within the fort. Following a brief discussion of prior efforts, our 1994 and 1997-2002 excavations will be described.

PREVIOUS EXCAVATIONS: LOOKING FOR FORT ST. GEORGE

The 1962 excavations were opened up by Hadlock on May 1, 1962, and continued until July 1. Hadlock[1] explored four separate areas of the site (Figure 17). A series of small excavations were placed in the center of the state park and on the south edge near the base of the granite outcrop. These efforts apparently were unrewarded as there is no record of the results nor artifacts so attributed in the Hadlock collection. The third area was on private land west of the park where a 110-foot-long trench was dug parallel to the bank of the shore. This trench cut into an extensive prehistoric shell midden, as well as pockets of nineteenth-century trash.

The fourth area explored by Hadlock was back on the park land, near the northern shore of the point. This was the principal area of his investigation and he excavated a large grid of narrow trenches. A plan of these excavations exists (Figure 18), but it was not initially possible for us to place it in relationship to existing landmarks. We encountered segments of these trenches in our excavations, however, so that eventually we were able to reconstruct the entire grid and position it precisely. We found that the trenches were approximately 15-18 inches in width, and averaged the same in depth (Lane 1962). Such limited exposure failed to provide sufficient perspective for Hadlock's crew to confirm the location of Fort St. George, and indeed we discovered many instances where their trenches cut right through fort features without being recognized. But they made many useful observations which could be integrated with our findings and thus significantly aid interpretations.

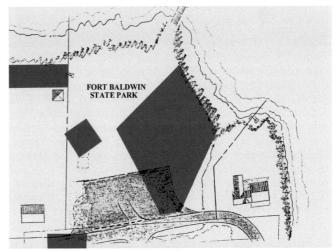

Figure 17. Approximate locations of excavations at the Popham site by Wendell S. Hadlock in 1962 and 1964 are indicated by shaded areas. North at the top.

---

[1] Throughout we shall use "Hadlock" and the third person singular in reference to these excavations, although Hadlock was rarely present. The working crew actually consisted of David Oxton, foreman, and Gardner Lane, recorder, with occasional additional assistants.

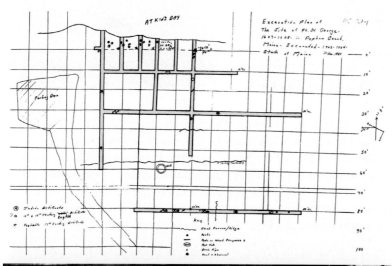

Figure 18. Plan and photo of Hadlock's 1962 excavations in the northeastern corner of the park (see Figure 17). As shown in the plan, the trenches (highlighted here with a gray tone) were placed parallel and perpendicular to the shoreline on a grid oriented approximately 60° east of north. We found sections of these trenches in our excavations which enabled us to correlate his grid with ours (see Figure B1) and determine that his "zero point" (datum) was at or near N11 E39 in relation to our datum (see Figure 21). In 1964, Hadlock returned to dig out the bank along the shore where seventeenth-century artifacts seemed to be most numerous, as indicated by the many symbols below the "Atkins Bay" legend. The photo was taken after trenches O-V had been excavated, but before the 10', 30' and 80' trenches had been started. Fort Popham is in the upper right corner.

Although they were unable to identify features, Hadlock's crew did find an assortment of artifacts in this area that within the knowledge of the day appeared to include some dating to the seventeenth century. Hadlock returned to the site for a brief period in August - September 1964 to "mine" (as he put it) more of these artifacts from the most productive area along the bank of the shore (Figure 18). His first uncertain conclusion was that while there had been a seventeenth-century occupation on the site, Fort St. George had not been identified and might not even have been at this location (W. Hadlock 1962, Simpson 1963). Reconsideration of the artifactual evidence, however, gave him greater confidence and he later decided that the fort probably had been there but had been entirely destroyed (Isaacson 1964, Fournier 1965, Lane 1966).

The 1981 investigation by Bob Bradley was equally inconclusive (Bradley 1981). On May 20, a small square 18 inches on a side was excavated 26 inches into subsoil in order to test the ground where the new parking lot was to be constructed. The first 22 inches of soil were found to be badly disturbed and no features were observed. All of the artifacts, whether prehistoric or historic, were found mixed together throughout this topsoil, and of 42 items only 3 – two handwrought nails and a white glass bead (variety WIA5 in the classification of Brain 1979, p. 108) – possibly dated to the seventeenth century. Bradley correctly observed, however, that they were not sufficiently diagnostic out of context and concluded that "no features or artifacts were identified which can be assigned to the Popham Colony."

These unsuccessful attempts to verify the presence of remains attributable to Fort St. George left the question open, and it was considered that even if the fort had been at Popham all evidence of it had been destroyed by human agency – farming, quarrying bedrock for Fort Popham, constructing Fort Baldwin – and/or erosion (Wahll 1980; Bradley 1981; Quinn and Quinn 1983, pp. 431, 515-519). The matter was so much up in the air that the professional community of historians and archaeologists cautiously referred to the "alleged" site of Fort St. George.

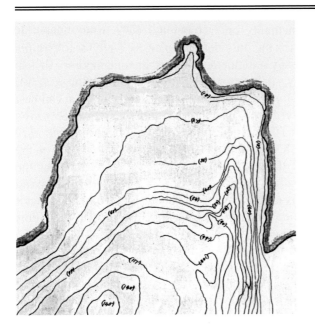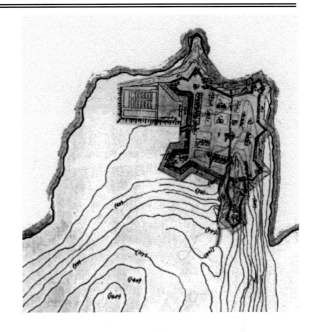

Figure 19. U. S. Army Corps of Engineers 1865 contour map of Sabino Head, and same with John Hunt 1607 map of Fort St. George superimposed on it. North at the top. (National Archives RG 77, DR 9, SH 24)

1994 EXCAVATIONS: FINDING FORT ST. GEORGE

The location of Fort St. George has never really been a matter of serious doubt. Although the issue was obscured by the influential works of Sullivan (1795) and Williamson (1832) who suggested various alternative sites because the original had been forgotten, the discovery of the John Hunt map (see Figure 5) in the Archivo General de Simancas more than a century ago put the matter beyond doubt (Hill 1891; Thayer 1892, pp. 167-187). This map was drawn by Hunt on or before October 8, 1607, and sent back to England on the first returning ship, the *Mary and John*. A copy quickly fell into the hands of the Spanish ambassador, Pedro de Zuñiga, who sent it to his overlord Philip III in 1608. There the map reposed in obscurity for the next 280 years and so there can be no question about its authenticity. On internal evidence, too, the map is clearly genuine: the odd configuration and other details reveal that Hunt obviously drew the map on the ground, accurately depicting a fortification and layout that conformed to unique topographic features. This is clearly illustrated when the Hunt plan is oriented and scaled to the site location on the promontory known since the seventeenth century as Sabino Head. It precisely matches the natural outline and contours drawn on a U. S. Army Engineers map before any modern changes could have occurred (Figure 19). Note especially the coincidence of natural and man-made features along the shoreline, in the flat garden area, and on the high-relief citadel. Even the stream course depicted by Hunt follows the natural contours of the topographic map. Thus the exact location was as certain as could ever be determined through the analysis of historical cartography and topography.

On the other hand, there is an aspect of the Hunt map that has troubled all who have considered it. The plan was drawn less than two months after the colonists had landed, and yet we see depicted a finely finished fortification with castellated and bannered gateways surrounding a large number of buildings – including storehouse, chapel, guard house, kitchen, bakery, buttery, magazine, blacksmith, residences – that would have done credit to a flourishing colony after some years of effort. Most commentators have assumed that Hunt indulged in a bit of artistic license, and that he was indicating the plans and aspirations of the colonists rather

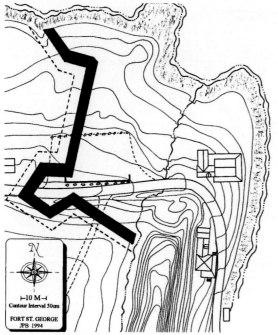

Figure 20. Topographic map of Popham site showing the predicted line of the fort trace.

than actuality on October 8, 1607. In any case, his record is the only detailed plan we have for a Virginia Company settlement, or any other contemporary British colony, so that as stated by Noël Hume in *The Virginia Adventure*: "In the continuing search for what can best be described as the *character* of the Virginia Company's James Towne [and, of course, any other contemporary English site], no archaeological site ranks higher on the list of things needing to be completed than does the excavation of Sabino Point" (1994, p. 116). Having already reached the same conclusion, we decided that it was time for a new archaeological investigation of Fort St. George to see what might have been overlooked in the earlier excavations.

Again, the principal objective of the 1994 excavations was to confirm the site as the location of Fort St. George, and in the process we hoped to identify specific features, and to determine the potential for future intensive archaeological exploration. Our expectations were high because, unlike the site of James Fort, the initial settlement of Jamestown that had been intensively occupied for the century following its founding, Fort St. George had been abandoned after a year. The history of the site recounted above indicates that the ground remained essentially unoccupied for the next two centuries, and that nineteenth-century disturbance was probably very localized. The most serious problem was expected to be the construction and garrisoning of Fort Baldwin, but even that was not anticipated to be completely destructive and we even cherished hopes that it might have been protective in some instances. In fact, we were to discover that the most serious impact on the land and the archaeology had been wrought by simple farming practices that may date as far back as the Hunnewell farm, but certainly scoured the land as recently as 50 years ago. In our ignorance, however, the prospects looked good and we were determined to see what remained.

As a guide to the excavations, we drew a detailed topographic map of the site (Figure 20) based upon an instrument survey carried out during the still very cold months of April and May. On it was superimposed the fort trace as drawn by John Hunt in his 1607 plan and reproduced at exactly the same scale. We thought ourselves especially fortunate that Hunt had included a scale of feet and paces on his map (see Figure 5), but we did not know whether it was accurate or a red herring.

The initial strategy of the excavations was to approach the predicted location of the fort by digging one or more trenches from beyond the pale on the west side in an easterly direction until features of the fortifications were encountered. Although we did not expect to find much evidence of the earthen rampart that enclosed the landward side of the fort, we did anticipate that the fortification ditch from which the earth had been taken would be an archaeologically visible scar in the ground. Once the outline and orientation of the fortification had been established, we then intended to test the accuracy of the Hunt map by triangulating in on specific structures and other features within the walls.

Fifty-one excavation units totaling 61.5m^2 were opened up in 1994 and dug to depths varying from 25 cm to 160 cm. These units were assigned numbers between 100 and 302 which were prefixed by the letter P (for Popham) to avoid any confusion with numbers assigned to the excavations in 1962 and 1964 (see Appendix B2). Some of these units were grouped along the initial exploratory trenches, others were strategically placed within the predicted fort compound (Figure 21).

Trench 1

The first west-to-east trench was laid out on the north side of the site and was roughly parallel to the bank line. It was intended to sample the area outside of the fort, to bisect the fortification line, and to discover interior features. This trench was 1 m wide and 46 m in length, and was divided into 2 m segments which thus formed convenient 1 x 2 m units of excavation. These units were numbered P100 to P122. Ultimately, 11½ of these units were excavated within the trench line (Figure 21), the remainder being skipped because it was concluded that they would contain redundant information or were too badly disturbed.

P100

The first excavation unit, P100, was at the extreme western end of trench 1 on private property belonging to Dr. George Abraham. We were confident that it would be outside the fort area, and so it proved. The natural stratification was as typical of the pre-1607 condition of the site as we were to find at any location (Figure 22). Under approximately 10 cm of sod, we dug through 40-50 cm of yellow and brown sandy soils, and then 35-40 cm of glacial till composed of unstratified and stratified deposits of sand, gravel and cobbles, the larger sizes increasing with depth. Finally, at about 100 cm beneath the surface, a compact white beach sand was encountered. Test holes revealed that the sand continued unchanged for at least another 50 cm. No distinct cultural horizons were identified at any level, and the only cultural features isolated were postholes dating to the nineteenth or twentieth centuries.

The cultural materials from this excavation unit were exclusively prehistoric and modern. Aside from one plain Indian potsherd, the sod layer contained only late nineteenth- and twentieth-century artifacts. Native artifacts and numerous shell fragments became more common in the sandy soils, but because of intrusions modern materials were found all the way down to the glacial deposits in this excavation unit.

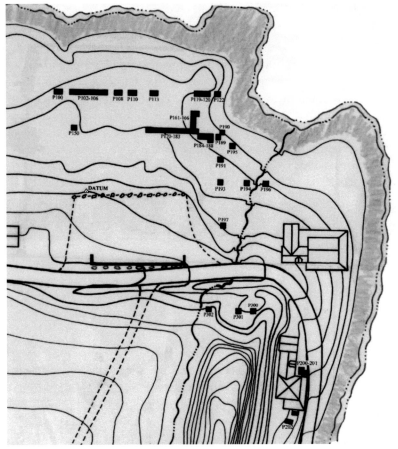

Figure 21. Plan of excavations at the Popham site in 1994, north to top. Datum is an arbitrarily established point near the northwestern corner of the parking lot which was later determined by GPS to be at Latitude 43° 45' 11.3660" N, Longitude 69° 47' 19.9801" W (NAD83); all horizontal and vertical measurements for all of our excavations are in reference to this point.

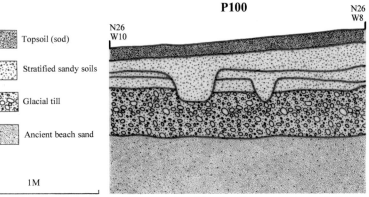

Figure 22. Stratification in excavation unit P100, north profile.

P102

Excavation unit P101 lay athwart the property line between Mr. Abraham's land and the state park, and so it was skipped in order to avoid questions of artifact ownership. Thus the trench was continued with P102. The stratification of this unit was similar to that found in P100, except that there was even more disturbance, including a trashpit and drainpipe line. Cultural materials were abundant and again consisted of prehistoric and recent artifacts. Although cultural surfaces and features still could not be isolated, and disturbance contaminated much of the unit, general horizons were apparent. The sod contained only twentieth-century artifacts, while only aboriginal artifacts were found on the surface of the glacial drift. A mixture of these materials was included in the intervening sandy soils, as were nineteenth-century items.

P103

The excavation of P103 confirmed the same basic soil stratification and cultural stratigraphy that were found in P100 and P102. The only significant difference is that this unit was not as badly disturbed as P102, but still there was no evidence of seventeenth-century features. It also became apparent that the upper half of the sandy layer beneath the sod was more homogeneous than the lower half above the glacial deposits, indicating that the upper soils had been mechanically mixed to an average depth of approximately 25 cm below the surface. We later identified this phenomenon as the result of truck farming in the 1930s and 1940s, and since it is a consistent feature across the state-owned portion of the site it shall be referred to formally as the "agricultural zone."

P104-P106

According to our predictions, we expected to encounter evidence of the fort trace about where these units were located next in line to the east of P103. We did, indeed, uncover an encouraging disconformity in the natural stratification in the eastern half of P104: a roughly vertical cut that extended down into the glacial deposits and was filled with layers of fine silty sand (Figure 23). Unfortunately, the top of this intrusion was truncated by the agricultural zone and the eastern side was obliterated by a Fort Baldwin-era utility trench that ran through units P105-P106 (Figure 24). Thus, the original height and width of the feature could not be established. If it was the remains of the ditch around Fort St. George, however, it certainly would have been a rather modest attempt at fortification, bearing little resemblance to John Hunt's elaborate plan.[2] No other features were found to support the identification, and the absence of seventeenth-century artifacts throughout these units precluded confirmation. In fact, the only artifacts found in the feature were prehistoric and modern. Nearby the feature, a prehistoric copper bead was found on top of the glacial deposits in an undisturbed portion of P105, and an Orient Fishtail point came from the same level.

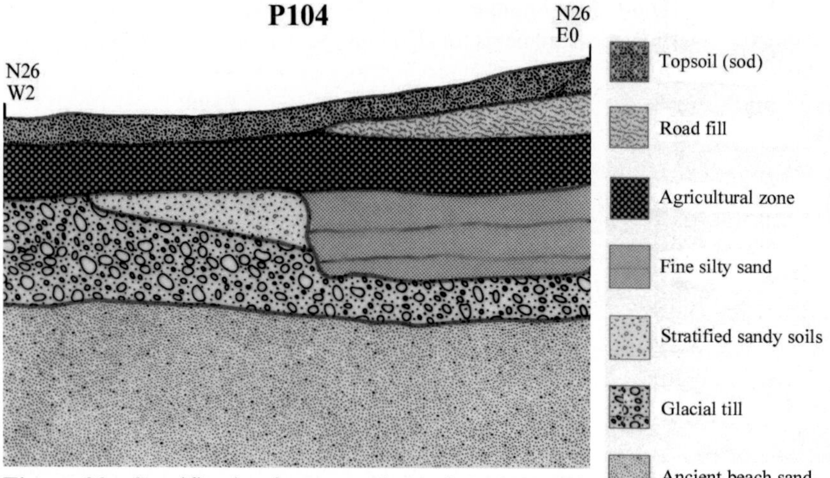

P104

N26 E0

N26 W2

Topsoil (sod)

Road fill

Agricultural zone

Fine silty sand

Stratified sandy soils

Glacial till

Ancient beach sand

Figure 23. Stratification in excavation unit P104, north profile

---

[2] The recent excavations at Jamestown do offer support for the possibility that these initial fortifications were not up to European standards. What has been interpreted as the first palisade of James Fort is a very flimsy affair indeed (Kelso 1996).

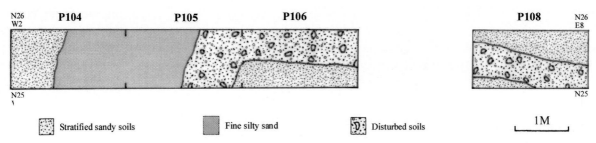

Figure 24. Plan of Fort Baldwin-era utility trench in excavation units P104-P106 and P108, depth below surface approximately 50cm.

P108

Excavation unit P108 was placed on what had been predicted to be the interior side of the earthen rampart of Fort St. George. It was hoped that it would reveal evidence of the rampart and/or features within the fort. Fort features were indeed encountered, but they related to Baldwin, not St. George. The most prominent of these was a large utility trench 40-65 cm wide and 120 cm deep that ran through the center of the unit and was the same destructive feature that was found in units P105-P106 (Figure 24). This trench extensively disturbed the natural stratification, cutting down through the sandy soils into the glacial till. It was truncated by the agricultural zone which lay just beneath the sod. The purpose of the trench was not identified, for whatever had been laid in it had subsequently been removed, and it was filled with Fort Baldwin-era trash and architectural debris. Outside the trench, the sandy soils contained some nineteenth-century artifacts, while the agricultural zone had artifacts from the recent, Fort Baldwin, nineteenth-century, and prehistoric periods. The latter, which included six copper beads, presumably had been churned up by the utility trench.

P110

The placement of P110 was also determined by the continuing search for the Fort St. George fortifications. To this point, we had no convincing evidence of a seventeenth-century occupation, neither features nor even artifacts. Once again, our hopes were to be frustrated. Although we knew we would be clear of the Fort Baldwin utility trench, which was trending off to the south of our trench line, we encountered yet other disturbances.

Initially, we were encouraged by finding among the usual assortment of nineteenth- and

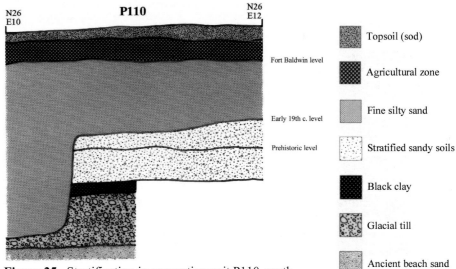

Figure 25. Stratification in excavation unit P110, north profile.

twentieth-century artifacts in the sod and agricultural zone a pipestem that appeared to date to the seventeenth century. However, we then encountered an *in situ* paving of bricks in the southeastern portion of the unit. This paving was 25 cm beneath the surface and represented an intact level from Fort Baldwin (Figure 25). Beneath it was 50 cm of grayish brown sandy silt fill that contained a fine collection of early to

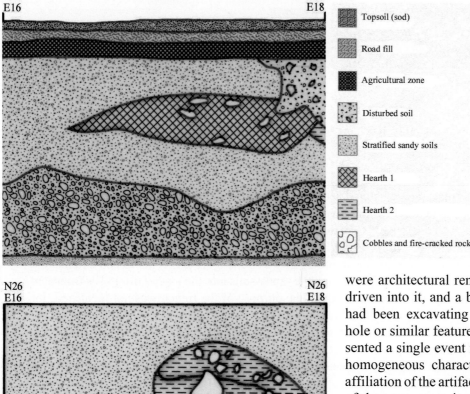

Figure 26. Stratification in excavation unit P113, north profile, and floor plan at approximately 100 cm beneath the surface showing hearth 2.

mid nineteenth-century domestic artifacts. An early nineteenth-century occupation surface was revealed in the eastern two-thirds of the unit at a depth of approximately 100cm, and 15 cm below it was an aboriginal zone that overlay the glacial till. In the western third of the unit, the overlying fill intruded another 75 cm down into the glacial deposits and at the bottom were architectural remains: a beam with cut nails driven into it, and a brick. It would seem that we had been excavating a nineteenth-century cellar hole or similar feature. That the fill episode represented a single event is indicated by the relatively homogeneous character of the soil and cultural affiliation of the artifacts, and by the fact that pieces of the same ceramic vessels were found scattered throughout the fill from the bottom to the top.

In summary, this excavation unit revealed evidence of an aboriginal occupation on the old glacial deposits, which was overlain by an early nineteenth-century house site. This was covered over by fill containing early to mid nineteenth-century refuse that in turn was capped by the Fort Baldwin installation. Above that was the agricultural zone, and finally the sod of the state park. This was a very clear and informative sequence of cultural stratigraphy, but one unfortunately lacking an early seventeenth-century component. The only encouragement was a single artifact – the pipe stem – which was, however, out of useful context since it was found in the sod layer.

P113

Excavation unit P113 continued the search for the now elusive Fort St. George. Once again, we were to be disappointed in our primary objective, but we did isolate some of the best prehistoric contexts that we found during the course of the excavations.

The now familiar stratification was revealed once again: sod, agricultural zone, a thick layer of sandy soils, glacial till, and beach sand (Figure 26). The base of the sod was highly compacted and represented fill that had been brought in to form a road and parking lot for the state park in the recent era after World War II (and still visible in photographs of the 1962 excavations; see also Figure 18). The agricultural zone was unusually thin at this location, presumably having been altered by the road construction, but it was sufficiently destructive to have obliterated all historic surfaces. The underlying sandy soils contained exclusively prehistoric artifacts, except for an intrusion in the northeastern corner of the unit that is probably attributable to Fort Baldwin. Two other features, however, were purely aboriginal. They were partially superimposed hearth areas that contained pottery, lithics, fire-cracked rock, burned bone, and shell. The fact that both hearths contained cord marked pottery suggests closely sequent occupations probably dating to Ceramic Periods 4 or 5 (Petersen and Sanger 1991).

P119 - P120, P122

By this point, we had tested at intervals along trench 1 for a distance of 28 m without finding any evidence of Fort St. George and, frankly, were becoming rather discouraged. Therefore, we skipped to the eastern end of the trench on the northern point of the shoreline where John Hunt placed the water gate on his map, suggesting an area of exceptional

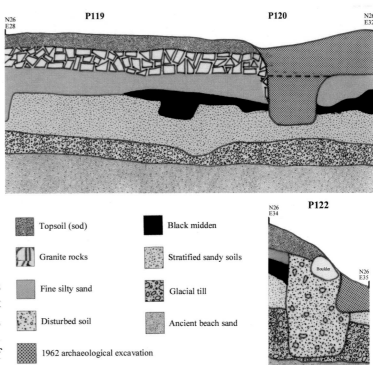

Figure 27. Stratification in excavation units P119-P120 and P122, north profiles.

activity. The credibility of the Hunt map was now at stake. We knew, however, that the task was going to be complicated by transformations of this point that occurred during the construction of Fort Baldwin. A railway trestle had been built from the point out into Atkins Bay where ships could offload their cargoes of cement, steel, coal, and lumber. Where the trestle met the land the bank had to be reinforced and raised. Thus we expected to encounter a considerable amount of disturbance and overburden. The trade-off, we hoped, would be that surfaces and features attributable to Fort St. George survived intact and had been protected from the plow by the trestle footings. We excavated 2½ units here, the eastern half of P122 being over the edge of the bank (Figure 27).

Beneath the sod layer was a zone of granite rocks approximately 25 cm thick. All of the rocks had been quarried from the same source and brought in as fill and riprap for the base of the trestle. When the granite had been removed, an old sod line was revealed. It was the surface of an undifferentiated layer of dark brown silt that was up to 30 cm in thickness. At the base of this silt in most of the units was a layer of black midden. Below that were approximately 40 cm of the familiar sandy soils, then 20 cm of the glacial till, and finally the white beach sand at a depth of 130 cm beneath the present surface. Disrupting this stratification in P120 and P122 was evidence of the 1962-1964 archaeological excavations, as well as an earlier Fort Baldwin-era intrusion.

Despite the complex stratification, the cultural stratigraphy was relatively straight forward. A very strong (and pure when the intrusions are discounted) prehistoric record is preserved in the sandy soils and reaches a climax in the black midden. The dark brown silt and upper layers are increasingly contaminated by nineteenth- and twentieth-century materials. Also scattered throughout these contexts, however, we finally found a few seventeenth-century artifacts: North Devon earthenware, handwrought nails, and English flint. Although these items were out of context, or at least not associated with any definable Fort St. George features, we were grateful for the encouragement. We were nonplussed by the lack of features, but we determined to try again with trench 2.

Trench 2

Trench 2 was located parallel to, but 10 m south of, trench 1 (see Figure 21). It, too, was designed to explore from west to east across the site until seventeenth-century features were encountered. Also 1 m wide, this trench was 41 m in length. Unlike trench 1, however, it was divided into 1 m segments for greater flexibility. Ultimately, twenty-eight 1 x 1 m units were excavated along this trench line and contiguous to it. These units were assigned numbers P150 to P190.

P150

Excavation unit P150 anchored the west end of trench 2 and was positioned to intercept the feature encountered in P104 (see Figures 23-24). If that feature continued south along the same axis observed in P104, its interpretation as the fort ditch would be enhanced.

The fort ditch was not confirmed. Directly beneath the sod was approximately 20 cm of soil with a high concentration of shell. Presumably, we had struck the edge of the prehistoric midden that was found on the private property to the west during the 1962 excavations. But, aside from a few stone flakes, the artifacts from this layer dated to the nineteenth and twentieth centuries. Underlying the shell midden were the usual sandy soils, and then at approximately 50 cm below the surface the glacial deposits were revealed. No cultural materials were present in these lower levels.

P170-183

Discouraged by our initial effort in trench 2, we skipped 20 m and then opened up fourteen units in line. This exposure was designed to cover the gaps left in the excavation of the parallel trench 1 (see Figure 21).

Under the sod in units P170-P175 was a layer of compacted gravelly fill up to 40 cm thick that was brought in to make the road and parking lot described above in the discussion of unit P113. This layer contained only nineteenth- and twentieth-century artifacts. It lay upon the old plowed surface which averaged about 15 cm in thickness. The cultural content of the agricultural zone in these units was a mixture of Fort Baldwin-era and prehistoric materials. Below that lay 40-50 cm of sandy soils which were sparsely sprinkled with stone flakes and charcoal, indicating some prehistoric activity during formation (as was the case elsewhere on the site). A large disturbance in the southeastern and perhaps western part of unit P170 contained a fine silty sand fill similar to that found in the P104-P105 feature, but the alignment was considered to be somewhat off for the fort ditch (see further discussion on p. 97) and again there was no artifactual confirmation. The glacial till was 10-30 cm thick, and at about 100 cm beneath the surface the white beach sand was exposed.

This stratification was modified in units P176-P183. First of all, the road fill petered out, and secondly, there was a considerable amount of subsurface disturbance (Figure 28).

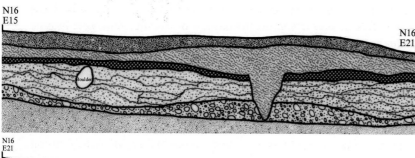

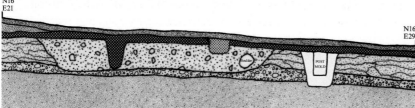

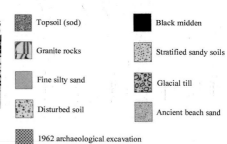

Figure 28. Stratification in excavation units P170-P175 (upper) and P176-P183 (lower), north profiles.

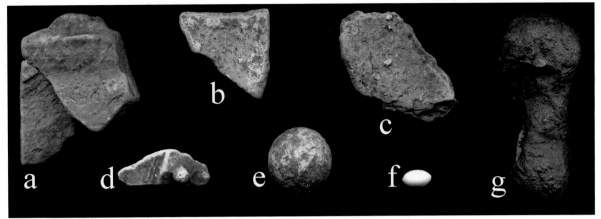

Figure 29. Seventeenth-century artifacts from trench 2: a-c, North Devon and West of England potsherds (P188A, P189A, P189C); d, lead sprue (P183A1) e, .75 caliber lead musket ball (P176D); f, glass bead (P182B2-4); g, iron spike (P182B3-4). The bead and spike were found in the posthole. (1:1)

Although some of the disturbances were clearly recent intrusions, including in P180 one of the 1962 excavation trenches, others were caused by more ancient activities. In units P177- P180, we bisected a very large feature in which all of the soils below the agricultural zone were completely intermixed. At first, it seemed to be the perfect candidate for the fort ditch we had been seeking. The problem with that theory was that the excavation had been refilled with the same soils that had been removed before either the soils or the exposed surfaces had been

Figure 30. Large posthole and post mold in excavation units P181- P182, looking west. Note chock stone. Diameter of posthole ca. 70cm.

weathered for any appreciable amount of time. On the other hand, no agency alternative to the colonists is credible: it certainly was not a natural or prehistoric feature, nor was it made during the nineteenth or twentieth century although it contained some recent intrusions. Furthermore, whereas we found no artifacts in the feature itself (except for the contamination in the recent pits), it is noteworthy that the artifact-bearing agricultural zone above included for the first time in trench 2 seventeenth-century items, in addition to prehistoric and modern. There was a large .75 caliber musket ball near the edge of the feature in P176, and then a persistent and ever increasing representation of North Devon earthenware, as well as pipestems, handwrought nails, and other items, in units P177-P183 (Figure 29). Although these artifacts were not diagnostically early seventeenth century, they certainly could have occurred then (and in fact will be found to be typical elements in the Fort St. George assemblage). We have never resolved the significance of the large pit feature, but subsequent work has revealed that it was contained entirely within the storehouse and so may have been an additional subterranean, perhaps temporary, storage area.

The first feature that we could definitely identify with the storehouse was encountered in units P181-P182. The feature was a very large posthole containing a single post mold (Figure 30). The lower part of the posthole that remained undisturbed below the agricultural zone was 70 cm in diameter and 65 cm in depth. The post mold revealed that the post had been hewn to a roughly square cross section. The upper portion of the mold contained charcoal and earth that had been fired *in situ*, indicating that the post and structure to which it had belonged must have burned. In the bottom of the post mold some of the wood of the post was preserved and has been identified as a hard pine, probably pitch pine (*Pinus rigida*), which is common in the area (Hoadley 1998). The only artifacts found within the posthole again were consistent with the early seventeenth century: North Devon earthenware, a glass trade bead (IIA1 in the classification of Brain 1979, p. 101), and fragments of handwrought nails and a spike (Figure 29f, g). The size and location of the feature encouraged the interpretation that the post had been a supporting member of the storehouse which is the largest structure shown on the Hunt map (Figure 5). We finally felt confident that we had found a genuine Fort St. George feature.

P161-166

Excited by the prospect of defining the dimensions, construction, and perhaps even content of the storehouse, we extended the excavations with a series of units to the north of P182 (see Figure 21). We hoped that the structure had been oriented to the cardinal directions and that we would uncover at least one more posthole on a line north from the one found in units P181-P182. Unfortunately, the storehouse had a different orientation from our grid and we did not notice any more features attributable to it in these units, and we ran out of time before we could explore further. The proximity of the storehouse or another important Fort St. George component, however, was confirmed by the relative abundance of seventeenth-century artifacts.

The now familiar stratification was revealed once again: sod, agricultural zone, sandy soils, and glacial till (at which the excavations were halted). The upper two layers contained a mixture of artifacts from prehistoric to modern, with the majority relating to Fort Baldwin. At the interface between the agricultural zone and the sandy soils, the artifacts were generally confined to aboriginal and seventeenth-century colonial items when modern intrusions were disregarded. The sandy soils were prehistoric and several native occupations were indicated by what appeared to be three hearths that were encountered in units P163, P165, and P166 (however, see p. 39 for reinterpretation of one of these features). These hearths contained only undiagnostic materials, such as charcoal, burned earth, fire-cracked rock, and unutilized stone flakes. Thus, although we cannot be specific about the temporal and cultural affiliations, the Native American settlement of this part of the site is corroborated.

P184-P190

Units P184-P187 and P189 formed a continuation of trench 2, but were offset 1 m to the south in order to bypass a stand of trees (see Figure 21). P188 was removed from this series and attached to the south side of P187 because it was obvious from a surface depression that its place in line had been extensively disturbed by one of the 1962 archaeological trenches. (We were soon to find that it was not the only one.) Unit P190 anchored the eastern end of trench 2 in line.

The basic stratification of these units was the same as already described above except that there was no sod because we had entered a wooded area. Thus, beneath a thin layer of leaf mold we were directly into the agricultural zone. The excavations were generally halted at the top of the sandy layer unless features were observed. After the features were removed, shovel tests confirmed the stratification down into the glacial till.

The topsoil (humus and agricultural zone) ranged in thickness from 25 cm in P184 to 45 cm in P190 which was at the edge of the bank. This layer contained the usual assortment of prehistoric to modern artifacts, but early seventeenth-century items were more abundant than had yet been found elsewhere on site. Beneath the topsoil in units P184, P185, and the western part of P186 we encountered a layer of mixed soils approximately 30 cm thick: humus, coarse yellow sand, glacial till, and fine white beach sand were randomly intermingled (Figure 31). This was clearly spoil from an excavation somewhere nearby, but our excavations did not intersect the parent feature and there were no artifacts in the layer to aid our interpretation. That the redeposited soils might have been caused by activities at Fort St. George is suggested by two features on the eastern edge of the disturbance in P186. A large rectangular block of gneiss had clearly been roughly dressed and placed in position by human agency. The purpose of the block was not ascertained, but that it was

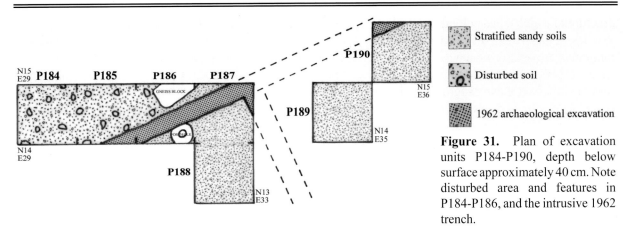

Figure 31. Plan of excavation units P184-P190, depth below surface approximately 40 cm. Note disturbed area and features in P184-P186, and the intrusive 1962 trench.

structural might be indicated by the direct association of at least one handwrought nail. The second feature was a posthole, another structural element. The only artifact in the posthole was a native potsherd, but the fact that the hole was 80 cm deep makes it more likely that it was of colonial origin than aboriginal.

Our interpretations were hampered by the recent intrusion of a 1962 archaeological trench. This trench cut across units P185, P186 and P187, where it intersected another perpendicular trench, and continued on to P190 (Figure 31). Although the trench caused interpretive problems in these units, the documentation of a length of it, and also part of a cross trench, enabled us to correlate the principal 1962 excavation plan with our grid.[3] This correlation was to enhance our interpretive capability overall because it was then possible to integrate some of the earlier findings, especially artifact distributions, with ours.

Strategic Excavations

Now that we had some indication of the probable location of Fort St. George, it was necessary to gain an idea of its overall dimensions and surviving features. Thus, small 1 x 1 m units were widely scattered over all accessible landforms that might contain elements of the fort. These units were assigned numbers between P191 and P302; P191 and P193-P197 were still on state land, while three units each in the P200 and P300 series were placed on two separate parcels of private property (see Figure 21).

P191

This unit was excavated in order to confirm the 1962 excavation plan by relocating one of the outer trenches. It was also an opportunity to investigate an extensive area of burned soil that was reported for that trench. Both missions were accomplished.

Topsoil was 40 cm thick and within it was a recent intrusion that was interpreted as evidence of the 1962 trench. The cultural content of the topsoil was predominantly nineteenth to twentieth century, although there was a modest representation of seventeenth-century earthenware and nails. Beneath the topsoil was a layer of orange clay, the color indicating that it had indeed been subjected to fire or intense heat *in situ*. A small pit feature on the western side of the unit contained charcoal and ash, further supporting a burning event. No artifacts were associated with either the orange clay or the pit feature, so we could not be certain of their origin.

---

[3] According to the 1962 site map, the excavations were oriented 67½° east of north (see Figure 18), apparently so that the trenches would be parallel and perpendicular to the bank line at that location. We found the overall orientation of the grid to be closer to 60°, but the individual trenches often deviated from this standard (see Appendix B1).

P193-P197

These units were scattered farther to the south and east in order to test precincts within the inner fort compound, especially what we expected to be high activity areas along the banks of the shore and stream (see Figure 21). Since we now knew the approximate position of the 1962 excavation trenches, we could place our units to avoid those disturbances.

Unit P193 was 5 m south of P191. It was dug to explore the extent of the burned layer found in P191. If it continued in this direction we hoped to find features or other evidence that would allow us to determine the cause and cultural origin of the conflagration. The recent humus and agricultural zone contained the usual mix of prehistoric to modern artifacts, but there was a strong representation of early seventeenth-century items which was very encouraging. Evidence of burning was encountered at a depth of about 25 cm. The burned earth and charcoal was concentrated in the eastern half of the unit in what was initially interpreted as a prehistoric hearth, because the only cultural materials found within it were aboriginal lithics and potsherds dating to Ceramic Period 3, ca. 1650-1350 B.P. (Petersen and Sanger 1991). The overall context, however, was obviously churned and also contained nineteenth-century artifacts. Clearly missing were any features or artifacts that could be linked to Fort St. George.

Unit P194 was placed 6 m due east of P193 on the west bank of the modern drainage ditch that approximately follows the course of the stream that originally flowed across the site. The topsoil here was an exclusively Fort Baldwin-era dump. The sandy soil appeared at approximately 30 cm, and at the interface was the usual mix of prehistoric through nineteenth-century artifacts. The seventeenth century was represented by a single sherd of Bellarmine stoneware, and possibly some unclassified earthenware and bottle glass fragments.

P195 was perched on the edge of the bank along the shore between the stream and trench 2. It was also squeezed in between two of the 1962 trenches and the strip along the shore frontage that had been mined for artifacts in 1964. Many seventeenth-century items had been recovered here in those earlier excavations, and we were hoping that some proper Fort St. George contexts had been preserved. We found only the usual stratification of mixed topsoil overlying a layer of sandy soils, and the same mix of prehistoric to modern materials in the agricultural zone. We did confirm once again that the top of the sandy soil contained only aboriginal and seventeenth-century colonial artifacts, but the contemporary Fort St. George surface had been destroyed by the plow and no intrusive features were revealed.

P196 was also positioned near the shore, but on the east bank of the stream 4 m due east of P194. We had high hopes for this area because it did not appear that this side of the stream had been plowed, but unfortunately our investigation was confined to a narrow strip of state-owned land. As was the case in P194, we also found in P196 that this location was a favored dumping ground for modern occupants of the site. The first 20 cm was full of recent twentieth-century domestic refuse, presumably from the Perkins-Freeman house situated some 10 m to the southeast. Below that was 50 cm of midden, most of which was probably attributable to Fort Baldwin. Only then did we come upon an old surface that sloped precipitously down to the beach. This was the top of the sandy layer, and once again seventeenth-century artifacts were present. But despite the protection of the overburden, and the absence of plowing on this side of the stream, there were no features attributable to Fort St. George – probably because in the seventeenth century, too, it was sloping ground that was unused, as well as being subject to erosion.

P197 was 10 m south of P193 and P194 on the west side of the stream. This was the southeastern corner of the park and as far as we could go on state-owned land in this direction. The actual placement was simply selected at random. The first 20 cm was topsoil that had a nice sample of nineteenth-century housewares, in addition to the usual Fort Baldwin presence. These became increasingly mixed with seventeenth-century and prehistoric artifacts until we were entirely in the sandy soils at 30 cm when all cultural materials vanished. Once again, the plow had clearly destroyed all historical surfaces and there were no intrusive features, although there was an abundance of what appeared to be burned earth, charcoal and ashes. Furthermore, the early seventeenth-century artifacts confirmed that we were still within the compound of the fort.

We needed to investigate farther to the east and south to establish the bounds of the fort, but we had run out of state land in those directions. We could not investigate the northeastern corner of the site because the landowner refused to even discuss the possibility. The refusal was most unfortunate since this part of the site appears to have escaped the truck farming that occurred on the state-owned land, so there is the possibility that intact seventeenth-century surfaces may have survived. If this land ever becomes available it should be investigated at the first opportunity. But we still had two other pieces of private property to the south to test.

P200-P202

The southeastern corner of the site is owned by Miss Jane Stevens who lives in a duplex frame house nestled at the base of the granite outcrop (see Figure 16). Jane is the enthusiastic historian of Popham Beach and our foremost champion. Unlike her neighbor to the north, she insisted that we dig up her front lawn. Actually, her lawn is very small and had known areas of disturbance, but we were able to squeeze in two small excavation units by her front door. These were numbered P200 and P201. A third unit, P202, was placed on the south side of the house (see Figure 21).

Unit P200 was 1.5 x 0.75 m and P201 was 1.5 x 1 m. These units were contiguous and revealed essentially the same stratification so they can be discussed as a single excavation. The sod capped 25 cm of recent fill that Jane had brought in for her lawn. It contained nineteenth- and twentieth-century artifacts. Below the fill was the humus line of the old surface which protected a prehistoric shell midden up to 30 cm thick. The midden had accumulated on natural sandy soils overlying a reddish brown clay. Small pits of unknown function intruded from the shell midden down into the culturally sterile subsoils, and a builder's trench for Jane's house cut through the midden and underlying soils in the western part of unit P201. The shell midden was deposited throughout the Ceramic Period until about the time the Popham colonists arrived. That the latter moved right in is attested by a fine representation of North Devon earthenware, handwrought nails, and possibly other early seventeenth-century artifacts that were found concentrated in the upper centimeters of the midden. A row of "privat lodgins" appears on the John Hunt map at approximately this location (see Figure 5).

P202 was originally laid out as a 1 x 1 m square, but when a drain pipe was found to run through the northern half it was reduced to a 1 x .5 m unit. Beneath the sod was 25 cm of badly disturbed sandy loam which contained nineteenth- and twentieth-century artifacts, and then sandy soils and reddish brown clay similar to the culturally sterile subsoils found in P200-P201. There was no evidence of a shell midden here, but a projectile point and other possible stone artifacts were found at the interface between the sandy deposits and the topsoil.

P300-P302

Units P300, P301, and P302 were three 1 x 1 m excavations that were placed at the foot of the granite outcrop on its western side just south of the town road (see Figure 21). This was on land that at the time belonged to Dr. George Abraham (on whose property elsewhere we had commenced operations with unit P100). Because of the uneven and sloping terrain, there were minor differences in stratification and soil composition between these units, but a basic description suffices for all.

Since at least the time of Fort Baldwin, this location has been wooded and it may well have been that way for centuries. We first dug through a thick (10-25 cm) mat of leaf mold and other forest detritus. When that was removed we encountered various silty deposits, with pockets of sand and clay, that were probably eroded from the higher elevations of Sabino Head. Solid granite ledge halted excavation at 50-60 cm. An ashy, charcoal-flecked layer up to 30 cm thick was found in a pocket of the ledge in unit P300. This excited our imagination because the John Hunt map shows the "kitchin generall" to have been situated near the foot of the granite outcrop on this side (see Figure 5). Unfortunately, there were no artifacts associated with this layer, although there was a fair representation of early seventeenth-century North Devon earthenware, pipestems, and handwrought nails in the silts above it, as well as in the humus layer of units P301 and P302.

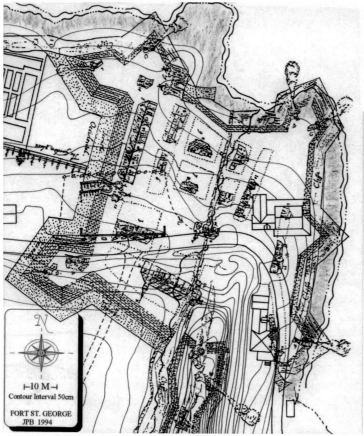

Figure 32. John Hunt 1607 map of Fort St. George superimposed on modern topographic map of the Popham site. The Hunt map has been rotated approximately 20 degrees east of magnetic north as determined in 1994. Note that the eastern wall of the fort has been swung out slightly in order to improve the alignment with the topography on that side; otherwise the fit is remarkably precise. The cartographic and topographic correlation is supported by evidence from the 1962 and 1994 archaeological excavations, and in turn provides a predictive guide for investigation of constructions within the fort.

There also was a great quantity of very poor quality brick or daub in these layers, but since there was the usual nineteenth- and twentieth-century contamination, as well, the cultural affiliation of this architectural debris remains in doubt. Nevertheless, the artifactual evidence extended Fort St. George to the granite outcrop, the presumed citadel area shown on the John Hunt map.

Summary of 1994 Excavations

Fort St. George was certainly an ephemeral presence at the Popham site, but enough features were found to corroborate the historical documentation and the John Hunt map. Conclusive evidence was provided by the artifacts that identify an English colonial venture consistent with the 1607-1608 dateline. The excavations also revealed that this presence was a brief interlude that was intermediate to much longer sequences of features and artifacts attributable to both prehistoric and post-colonial periods. Nevertheless, we felt confident that we had finally confirmed the site of Fort St. George and that significant remains were retrievable. The problem we now faced was designing the most efficient approach to the investigation of these remains.

1997-2005 EXCAVATIONS: EXPLORING FORT ST. GEORGE

The objectives of the 1994 excavations had been, first, to establish the presence and exact location of Fort St. George on the Popham site and, second, to assess the potential for further archaeological investigation. At the conclusion of the excavations, we felt that we had found the fort, but were uncertain about the archaeological parameters and potential. In the preliminary reports, I concluded that "Fort St. George was significantly smaller than was indicated by the scale on John Hunt's map" (Brain 1994, p. 11; Brain 1995, p. 82). The conclusion was influenced by the meager, albeit sufficient, evidence that confirmed the former presence of the fort. However, during reanalysis of the data in the winter of 1996-1997, while preparing a volume describing all 8000 years of archaeology at the site (Brain n.d.), I became increasingly uncomfortable with this conclusion, finally writing instead that "Fort St. George was depicted with incredible accuracy by John Hunt." In fact, I had now come to believe that John Hunt drew his plan exactly to scale. I was forced to this reinterpretation when the earlier impressions from the field were discarded and a fresh

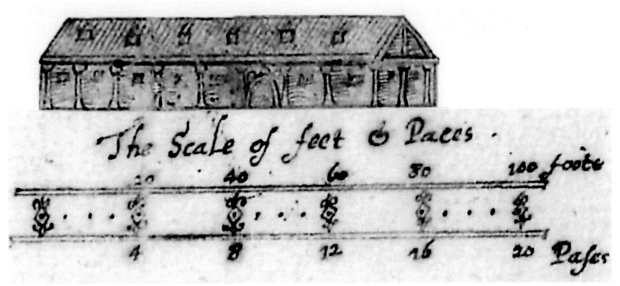

Figure 33. The storehouse as drawn by John Hunt and reproduced at the same scale as the "The Scale of feet & Paces" included on the map. An average interval of approximately nine feet between the wall posts would seem to be indicated.

perspective of the archaeological data, the topographic map of the site, and the Hunt map revealed what appeared to be a precise correlation.

The particular correlations that excited my attention were the one-to-one matching of the Hunt plan to the site outline and contours – as had been hypothesized before the 1994 excavations seemed to suggest otherwise – and the realization that the archaeological data did not contradict the possibility, in fact could as reasonably be interpreted as supportive. The crucial clue was the realization that the best fit of the topography and Hunt plan oriented the long axis of the fort approximately 20° east of modern magnetic north (Figure 32). It is entirely possible that because of changes in declination this direction coincides with magnetic north in 1607.

The most significant feature attributed to Fort St. George in the 1994 excavations was the large posthole containing the mold of a hewn timber in excavation units P181-P182 (see Figures 28, 30). The size and approximate position of this feature had led us to the conclusion that it represented the remains of a support post of the largest and most important building within the fort: the storehouse. This theory still seemed valid and so it was logical to draw a line oriented 20° east of north through this feature and suppose that it delineated a wall of the storehouse, hypothetically the east which is drawn so carefully by Hunt. In fact, the elevation drawn by Hunt is so detailed that every support post of the wall is clearly shown. There are nine in all and when compared with the scale Hunt placed on his map it appeared that the interval between the posts (center to center) was approximately nine feet (Figure 33).

In the last days of the 1994 excavations we had tried to find companions to the P181-P182 posthole. In the absence of any other clue, we simply ran a series of excavations (P161-P166) on magnetic north from P182 and found nothing that seemed to resemble another posthole. However, in reanalysis when the new line was followed nine feet to the northeast the edge of a feature was found to have been encountered in P163. At the time, this feature was interpreted as a prehistoric hearth, several of which had already been found in the immediate area. Now it looked suspiciously like another posthole. Of course, we still needed confirmation, but it was sufficient encouragement to plan an excavation program in which we might expect to find additional postholes at approximately 9' intervals along this line of 20° east of north. Coincidentally, it was at this point (February 1997) that the Maine State Museum offered its field school.

Thus began a series of annual excavations that examined various features within the fort. From this point on, our investigations were restricted to the state-owned portion of the site, which appeared to include most

Figure 34. Plan of excavations on state park land in 1997-2005. Portions of 1994 excavations also included for reference purposes. The standard excavation unit was a 1 x 1 m square, although topographic or archaeological concerns occasionally required deviation from this standard. North at the top.

of the western fortification wall, the storehouse, admiral's house, and the smaller structures clustered around the central square or "market place." The first objective was to confirm the storehouse, the most important building within the fort and the one for which we thought we already had archaeological evidence. As it was defined, attention moved on to other structures within the fort compound. First, the admiral's house in 1999, in 2000 the fortification trace, and then in 2001 the vice admiral's house and other smaller structures. Finally, we returned to the storehouse in 2004-2005. The excavation plan during these years is in Figure 34.

We knew that the storehouse, admiral's house and fortifications had been constructed because they are specifically mentioned in other documents besides the John Hunt map. Other structures, such as those identified by Hunt as the vice admiral's house, the munition master's house, the provost's house, and the buttery with attached corporal's house are not independently documented, so the first question before us was whether they had actually been built. This was, then, to be a crucial test of the Hunt map. A separate building for the storage of butts (casks) of spiritous liquors protected by a corporal's guard would be a logical facility within the fort. So, too, would homes for such important military personages as the officer in charge of ordnance and munitions, the provost, and a vice admiral. The conundrum we are presented with, however, is that no such offices nor personages are described in the colony's charter, manifest, or other documents. Thus our quest doubled in importance: it was not just a check on Hunt, but also an inquiry into the structure and functioning of the colony. The change in objectives is reflected in a new presentation format in which the descriptions of the excavations will be anchored to the structures and other features shown on the Hunt map.[4]

Storehouse

The 1997 excavations focused on the storehouse and were designed to test the new theories of its orientation and pattern of construction (Figure 35). These excavations were successful as five more posts of the east wall of the storehouse were revealed. Once it had been established, attention was then expanded during the last days of field work in an effort to find the west wall. In 1998 another post of the east wall, a large segment of the west wall, the north end, and a section of the interior of the storehouse were exposed. More of the interior and the south end were excavated in 1999. The objectives of the 1998 and 1999 seasons were to complete the footprint of the storehouse so that we had its exact dimensions, to gather as much information about the construction as we could so that the structure could be compared with contemporary architecture and the details illustrated in the Hunt map, and to expose whatever activities may have been performed by the colonists within the storehouse. We returned in 2004 and 2005 to pursue these objectives further.

East Wall

The excavations recommenced in 1997 with unit P400 which was placed contiguously to the east of P163 where the suspicious feature had been found in 1994 (Figure 36). The two units were overlapped 10 cm to ensure than none of the

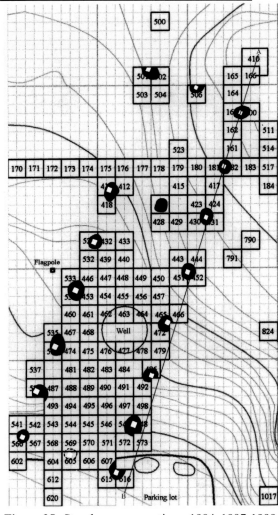

Figure 35. Storehouse excavations, 1994, 1997-1999, 2004-2005. The postholes and molds that were actually exposed are shown. The thin diagonal line A-B was the predicted line for the east wall of the storehouse when excavations recommenced in 1997.

Figure 36. Plan of excavation units P163 and P400 showing position of large posthole and post mold. Depth below surface approximately 50 cm, and depth below datum -260 cm.

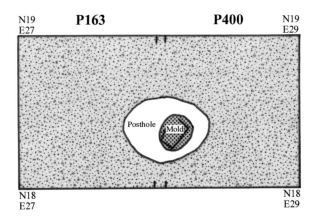

---

[4] Those who prefer a chronological account of the excavations are referred to the annual reports (Brain 1997-2005), complete sets of which are available at the following repositories: Maine State Library, Phillips Library at Peabody Essex Museum, Tozzer Library at Harvard University, and the Totman and Popham Beach Libraries in Phippsburg..

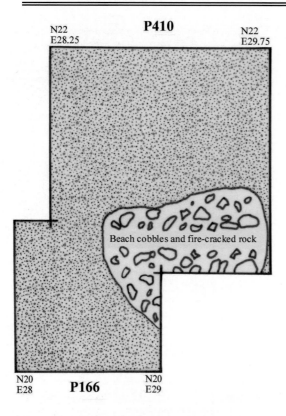

Figure 37. Plan of excavation units P166 and P410. No artifacts were found in the feature, but fire-cracked rock and charcoal indicated that it had been an aboriginal hearth.

feature would be overlooked. The standard procedure followed here and elsewhere, except as noted, was based on our 1994 experience of the natural and cultural stratification. The sod (level A) was cut and placed aside, and then the disturbed plow zone was removed as level B until subsoil was encountered. The surface of the subsoil (level C) was then inspected for disturbances. In this case, a large feature (C1) was found as anticipated and it was soon apparent that it was indeed another posthole similar in size and configuration to the one encountered in P181-P182 in 1994. This oval posthole, comprising the parts found in P163 and P400, was 45-60 cm in diameter and 65 cm in depth beneath the plow zone. The bottom was defined by a large flat rock embedded in the white beach sand at -305 cm below datum. Within the hole was a post mold that exhibited a roughly rectangular cross section approximately 20-25 cm on a side. Pieces of the heartwood of the post were encased in the mold near the bottom. The base of the post was found at -287 cm below datum. Chock stones had been placed beside the post and shims underneath it. The shimming suggests a leveling operation indicating that the post may have been one of a pair in prefabricated post-and-beam construction, thus raising our hopes that the storehouse had been constructed in regular bays as drawn by John Hunt.

The artifactual content of the posthole included a wrought nail, a white glass bead (IIA1), charcoal and daub fragments, and unidentified seeds. There were also aboriginal stone flakes.

Thus we had our first encouragement that we were on the right track in confirming the precise configuration of the storehouse. We needed to make a slight revision of our predicted orientation and measurements, however: comparing the two post holes we now had, the orientation seemed to be slightly east of 20° and the interval between the posts closer to 9.5' than 9'. We continued to test north and south at intervals along this line.

In 1994, we had encountered in the northeastern corner of excavation unit P166 part of a feature that again was interpreted at the time as an aboriginal hearth. Since this feature was approximately 9' northeast of the P400 posthole we now wondered if it could instead be another posthole. We therefore set up unit P410 to explore this possibility. P410 was enlarged from the standard 1 x 1 m dimensions to 1.5 x 1.5 m to ensure that the entire feature, whatever it was, would be revealed. This unit also intentionally overlapped the northeastern corner of P166 so that its data could be directly integrated into the new findings (Figure 37).

The feature was rediscovered in the southeastern corner of P410 and was completely revealed. It was confirmed to have been a prehistoric aboriginal hearth. There were no artifacts within it other than fire-cracked rock and charcoal. Only undisturbed subsoil was found in the rest of the unit. It therefore could be concluded that the northeast corner of the storehouse had been found in P400, a conclusion that seemed quite reasonable considering the proximity of the shore line and the position of the structure on the Hunt map (the credibility of which was being reinforced at every turn). We could now direct all our attentions to following the line of the wall southwards.

The next interval to the south along the line where a predicted post was expected was between units P424 and P431 of the new excavation grid. As a control, however, two units (P415 and P417) were opened up first in areas where no features were anticipated. Both units exhibited the usual stratification of sod, disturbed plowzone, and undisturbed subsoil. The latter was the glacial till which we now understood to be more accurately described as a winnowed till: sandy soil containing pebbles and cobbles that increased in number and size with depth until it was mostly cobbles. Beneath the cobble layer was a white beach sand. The only feature found intruded into the subsoil in either unit was a small Fort Baldwin-era disturbance in the east-central part of P417.

The next units excavated were P429 and P431. The only feature found in P429 was a small pit that was bisected by the west wall. The artifacts within it were aboriginal stone flakes, three fragments of wrought nails, and three sherds of red earthenware, at least two of which were North Devon. Although there was no clue as to what caused the disturbance, the artifactual content attributes it to Fort St. George. In P431 we were rewarded with what appeared to be one quarter of a posthole in the northwest corner: right on schedule, if slightly farther west than originally predicted. We then opened up units P423, P424 and P430 in order to isolate the entire feature.

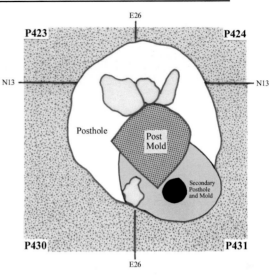

Figure 38. Plan of postholes and post molds found in excavation units P423, P424, P430 and P431. Note the rocks used for chocking the post.

When first encountered beneath the disturbed zone, the roughly circular posthole had a maximum diameter of 75 cm (Figure 38). It extended for another 25 cm before bottoming out in the white beach sand at a depth of -260 cm below datum. The post mold within the hole revealed that the timber had been hewn to a square cross section approximately 35 cm to a side. The post had been chocked with cobbles, but no shim stones were found beneath the flat base. A large piece of heartwood survived from the bottom of the post.

As the posthole was being excavated, a large piece of wood was found lying on the south side of the post mold. At first, this was thought to be an extra chock, but further excavation revealed the remains of a secondary post that had been placed next to the first timber. That is, at a time subsequent to the planting of the first post, a second post was inserted. This was accomplished by making a new posthole in the southern portion of the original posthole which was dug out to a depth of -273 cm below datum and then refilled. The new fill was distinctly different, being much more loamy than the original fill. The post, too, was of a different order: round in cross section and only 12 cm in diameter. None of the wood was preserved, indicating that it was a different, less hardy species than that used for the other posts. The bottom of the post was tapered, although still flat. There were no chock stones – presumably the post was secured in place by being attached in some manner to the primary post – but the base sat on shim stones 8 cm in thickness. The addition appears to be an original alteration rather than a repair and in fact may be interpreted as the jamb for the door which was drawn by Hunt as being in this bay.

The artifacts from the P423-P424-P430-P431 posthole consisted of aboriginal pottery and stone flakes, and European items comfortably attributed to the early seventeenth century (sherds of North Devon ceramics, a wrought iron nail, and an iron object that might be the handle of a knife). Daub and charcoal were also present. No artifacts were found in the small posthole for the secondary post, suggesting that it may have been dug and refilled quickly.

According to the original prediction, the next posthole in line to the south was to be found in the middle of excavation unit P444. No such feature was found, however, and we were just about ready to close down the unit in disappointment when a disturbance was observed in the southwestern corner. We had just nicked a large feature which exhibited the characteristic soil content, color and texture found in the other postholes. By this time, too, we had refined the original model, angling the line slightly farther to the west and increasing the interval between the posts to 9.5'. According to these revisions, the disturbance was in precisely the right place for the next posthole.

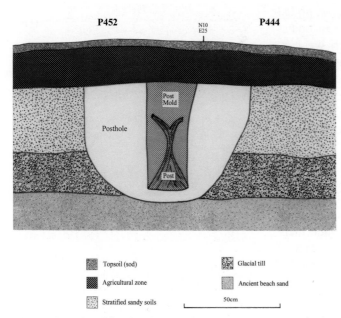

Figure 39. Stratification in excavation units P444 and P452, west profiles. Note remains of post heartwood in the bottom of the mold: the arcing "arms" are decay-resistant knots which are characteristic of native pitch pine.

Figure 40. Base of post from excavation units P465, 466, and P472.

We opened up the contiguous unit to the south, P452, and confirmed the presence of the posthole which we bisected all the way to the white beach sand (Figure 39). We then excavated the southeastern quadrant of unit P443 and northeastern quadrant of P451 to complete the exposure of the feature. This posthole was approximately 80 cm in diameter when it was first encountered beneath the plowzone, and intruded 60 cm into subsoil. The bottom was -251 cm below datum. The post mold indicated the former presence of a square hewn timber that measured about 20 cm to a side. The bottom of the post was 6 cm above the bottom of the posthole. No shims were observed, but chock stones, some quite large, had been placed around the post. A large piece of heartwood from the base of the post was still preserved in place. No artifacts were found in the posthole, except for a few aboriginal stone flakes. Some pieces of charcoal were also present.

The next posthole was found in units P465, P466 and P472 which were placed on the north side of a steep rise in ground elevation (see Figure 35). The distinctive hump was assumed to be an alteration in the topography that occurred during the Fort Baldwin occupation, or perhaps was associated in some fashion with a nearby nineteenth-century well. Much to our surprise, however, we were to discover that both here and in the following set of excavations described below the general lay of the land was of some greater antiquity. The surface levels exhibited the usual disturbance and preponderance of Fort Baldwin-era artifacts, but these overlay earlier cultural levels that protected an original 1607-1608 ground surface (see below).

The initial prediction had expected a posthole in the north-central part of excavation unit P466, but the revision relocated it to the southwestern corner of the unit. We were not disappointed: even before we had defined the posthole, spikes of preserved heartwood of the post were encountered in the angle of the corner. In order to excavate the feature, it was necessary to open up contiguous units P465 and P472; P473 could not be excavated because of a nearby tree, so one quarter of the posthole was not investigated although the remains of the post were entirely removed (Figure 40). The posthole was ca. 70 cm in diameter and 66 cm deep (-241 cm below datum). The post mold and well preserved base of the post were 25 cm square. The wood of the post was identified as pitch pine (Hoadley 1998). There were chock stones around the post, but no shims beneath it even though the base was 31 cm above the bottom of the hole. Artifacts within the posthole were restricted to aboriginal items: a stone biface and chert flakes, as well as charcoal.

To our delighted astonishment, a new layer of soil was encountered in unit P472 at ca. -175 cm below datum that appeared to be an *in situ* living surface that was littered with aboriginal and European artifacts, as well as

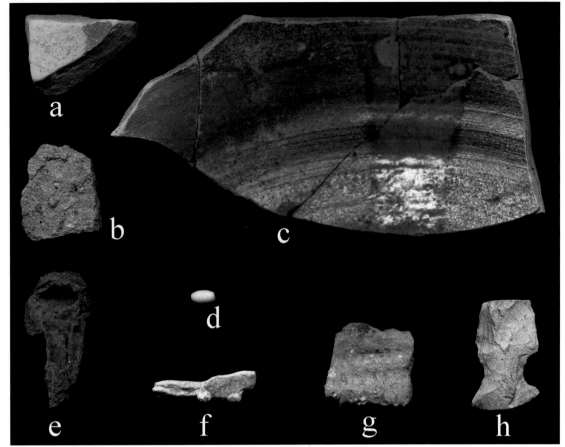

Figure 41. Sample of artifacts found *in situ* on the floor of the storehouse in excavation units P472, P478 and P486 (see Figure 42): a-b, West of England potsherds (P472C, P486C); c, portion of a fine North Devon pitcher or jug (P486C); d, white glass bead (P486C); e, cast of wrought iron nail associated with charred sill (P478C); f, lead sprue (P486C); g, aboriginal pottery (P472C); h, unclassified side-notched point (P472C). (1:1)

a considerable amount of charcoal and burned earth. Fortuitously, the overburden at this location had preserved the floor of the storehouse interior. Lying on this floor were charred boards and thatch, which attest to destruction by fire that preserved these structural elements, and an assemblage of period artifacts that included both English and aboriginal items (Figure 41). This exciting discovery encouraged us to excavate the intervening units in our continuing quest for the next posthole in line.

The revised line and interval placed the next posthole in excavation unit P486 (Figure 42). Units P478 and P479 were also opened up in order to expose more of the floor encountered in P472. Just beneath the sod in these units were many large blocks of gneiss. We were to discover that these were part of the nearby nineteenth-century masonry wellhead that had been leveled when the park was landscaped in 1981. Beneath the blocks were layers dating to Fort Baldwin and the nineteenth century into which several disturbances intruded, including a trench across unit P479 that had been dug for a water pipe that ran from the well to the nearby Perkins-Freeman house. The floor of the storehouse was bisected by this trench, but otherwise was undisturbed. More charred boards and thatch and numerous artifacts were found *in situ*. At least one of the boards was pierced by wrought nails, but at this stage of the investigations it was not possible to determine whether it and the other pieces represented flooring or some part of the superstructure.

Unit P486 was excavated to the floor level (-165 cm below datum), at which point the posthole and post mold were confirmed. The hole was about 80 cm in diameter and the mold indicated a post conforming to

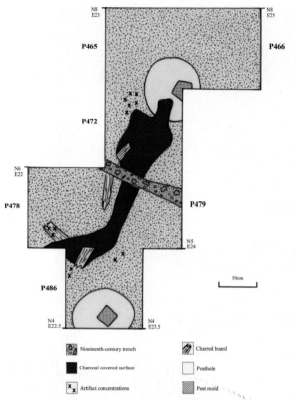

Figure 42. Plan of excavation units P465, P466, P472, P478, P479 and P486 showing positions of postholes and posts, as well as concentrations of artifacts, burned boards, thatch and charcoal on the floor of the storehouse. The floor is ca. -165 cm below datum and ranges from 42 cm below the surface in P472 to 65 cm deep in P486.

Figure 43. Alignment of posts of east wall of storehouse, looking northeast from P486 in foreground.

the standard 20-25 cm square. On the floor north and west of the P486 posthole were many artifacts: ceramics, sprue, a white glass bead (IIA1), wrought nails and unidentified iron fragments, as well as aboriginal pottery, chert flakes, and the proximal end of a point (see Figure 41). Because we were running out of time, excavation was halted at this point.

By the conclusion of the 1997 excavations, then, we had found six posts of a wall of the storehouse. These posts were in perfect alignment (Figure 43), attesting to the skillful construction of a timber-framed building. That this wall was the east side of the storehouse was confirmed during the final days of the 1997 excavations when we triangulated in a post of the west wall, as described below.

When excavations continued in 1998, units P547, P548, P572 and P573 were opened up because the next post in line going south along the east wall of the storehouse was predicted to be near the intersection of these units. Since they were on the north edge of the parking lot, we encountered up to 60 cm of unconsolidated sand and gravel fill that had been brought in to level off this side of the lot. After this overburden was removed unit P573 was discontinued. The other three units were taken down into a dark brown soil that represented a buried A-horizon. This old sod layer contained a mix of artifacts from prehistoric to modern eras, but as it blended into the underlying B-horizon, a former agricultural zone approximately 40 cm thick, the artifacts became sparser and predominantly nineteenth century. By the bottom of the layer the artifacts were nonexistent. At -150 cm from datum (approximately 110 cm below the local surface), a band of black staining oriented NNE-SSW appeared in all three units. When isolated this band was found to consist of charcoal and was clearly a burned timber about 25 cm wide and 3 cm thick. It was covered and sur-rounded by fragments of carbonized thatch and what may have been wattling and unfired daub. Associated artifacts included six wrought nails, as well as aboriginal stone flakes and pottery. In unit P548 the timber was interrupted by a dark gray feature that was 30 cm in diameter. This was the mold of the post we had been seeking, and it was now obvious that the horizontal timbers were sills (Figure 44). Seven centimeters north of the post mold a wrought nail had been toenailed into the sill on a slant from north to south. It appeared to be too far away from the mold to be involved in the joining of the sill and post, and too close for attaching a stud, so we are uncertain about its architectural purpose. The sills were removed and we found that originally they had been joined to the post 5 cm above the natural red-dish-yellow sandy subsoil. The post had been set into a hole that was up to 1 m wide. After the features had been drawn and photographed we left them *in situ* for future investigation.

In 2004, we returned to open up units P497 and P498 so that we could follow out the wall as it went north from P547 and P548. We were hoping to refine some of the constructional details. A mass of charcoaled wattling and burned earth from the wall was uncovered (Figure 45), but when it was removed we found no trace of the sill which apparently had disintegrated completely. There was a line of four wrought nails along where the sill would have been, but we were unable to dis-cern how they might have been employed in joining the structure.

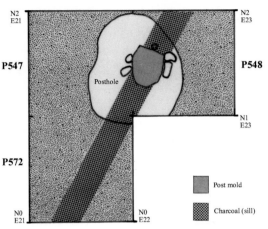

Figure 44. Plan of posthole, post mold and sills in excavation units P547, P548 and P572.

Figure 45. Detail of interwoven wattle from east wall of storehouse in excavation unit P498.

We completed the east wall line in 2005 with the excavation of unit P492. This time, beneath the layer of burned wattle we were able to trace the charcoal stain left by the sill, thus confirming the integrity of the construction. Apparently, charcoal leaching down into subsoil from the overlying burned wattle had obscured the remains of the sill in unit P498.

The excavation of the east wall of the storehouse had revealed an earthfast, timber-framed structure that had interrupted sills, wattle-and-daub walls and a thatched roof. It had not yet been established whether the building had been constructed in bays and whether the normal or reverse method of construction had been used.

West Wall

During the last days of the 1997 excavations, an attempt was made to establish the width of the storehouse. Hunt's drawing of the gable end seemed to indicate that the structure was two bays wide and that the interval between posts was somewhat less than that along the sides. Therefore, we estimated an interval of 8' for a total width of 16'. Assuming that the line of postholes we had confirmed represented the east wall

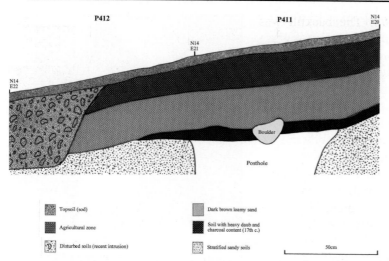

Topsoil (sod)

Agricultural zone

Disturbed soils (recent intrusion)

Dark brown loamy sand

Soil with heavy daub and charcoal content (17th c.)

Stratified sandy soils

50cm

Figure 46. Stratification in excavation units P411 and P412, south profiles. Note the layer of dark brown loamy sand overlying the posthole that contained a large amount of daub and charcoal.

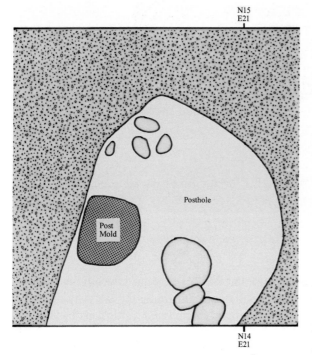

Figure 47. Plan of posthole and post mold found in excavation unit P411.

of the storehouse, and hypothesizing that the regularity of the placement of those posts indicated that they were paired with similarly placed posts along the other side, we turned a 90° angle to the west from two of the posts along the east wall line and measured off 16'. The first location we explored was P433, and although we found North Devon ceramics and a white glass bead (IIA1) in the disturbed plow-zone we were unrewarded with any features relating to Fort St. George. We then focused on P411 and P412. This time we tried two intervals: 16' brought us to P412, but if 9.5' was the standard for width as well as length of each bay then two times 9.5' is 19' which fell in the next unit, P411.

As was the case in P433 no obvious features were found in P412, although a mottling of the soil was observed along the western wall of the unit (see below). A wrought iron nail and other encouraging objects were found in the plowzone. P411, however, provided the answer we were looking for. At a depth of approximately 40 cm below the surface a layer of dark soil was encountered that contained a high proportion of charcoal, low- fired daub, and what appeared to be unfired daub (Figure 46). Artifacts associated with this layer included North Devon ceramics, as well as stone flakes and a large piece of bone. When we took up this layer we found directly beneath it at a level of -190 cm below datum the western wall post and hole that we were seeking. The posthole was an irregular oval measuring 70 cm by more than 80 cm (Figure 47). The eastern edge of it extended a short distance into unit P412 and was the mottling noted above. The post mold indicated a rectangular timber measuring 20 cm by 24 cm. This post was the mate to the one found in P431 from which our measurements were made. The post was about 40 cm south of the 90° line drawn west from the P431 post, but that certainly would have been within the tolerances for them still to be considered a pair in timber-framed construction. Perhaps there was a slight curve in the connecting beam. Such a condition might also explain the unusually elongated shape of the posthole and the off-center position of the post in the hole.

The entire feature was excavated only another 10 cm, sufficient to clarify the details of the plan, then plastic was laid in and the unit was temporarily refilled. We had run out of time, but we had our confirmation of the west wall and it seemed likely that the storehouse had been constructed with paired posts set according to a uniform standard of regular intervals or bays.

We continued the excavation in 1998. The backfill was removed from P411, exposing again the posthole and mold, and we opened P418 in order to get at the southern part of the posthole and provide adequate working room for the excavation of the entire feature. As was the case in P411, and unlike the areas to the north where they had been destroyed, some very distinct strata were revealed in P418. Beneath the sod was the usual dark brown sandy loam which was the former agricultural zone containing a mix of artifacts dating from the prehistoric to modern eras. At approximately 20 cm below the surface was a layer of cobbles and coarse sand up to 10 cm thick that at first was thought to be a man-made pavement but when found at other locations presented a less organized appearance. Associated with it were early to mid nineteenth-century domestic artifacts, such as annular pearlware, redware, glass, and pipe fragments. The cobbles formed an abrupt boundary separating the plow zone above from an underlying layer of dark brown loam that also was about 10 cm thick and appears to represent the hiatus between the Fort St. George occupation and the early nineteenth century. The artifacts in this layer included aboriginal pottery and flakes, North Devon ceramics and glass beads, charcoal and daub which apparently had migrated up from earlier levels. At a depth of 40 cm beneath the surface and -175 cm below datum we encountered a very dark brown soil that contained much charcoal, ash and daub, as well as North Devon and Iberian ceramics, glass beads, and wrought nails. This was the floor level of the storehouse. Running diagonally across it from NE to SW was a charcoal streak that probably represented the remains of a sill (Figure 48). Beneath the floor was the usual sandy subsoil into which the posthole, now fully revealed, had been intruded. The posthole was the same irregular oval that had been observed in 1997, the full measurements of which were now determined to be 70 cm by 95 cm. The post mold indicated a hewn timber with a rectangular cross section measuring 20 cm by 25 cm. The feature was completely excavated and the post was found to have been chocked with many large stones (including a crystal of beryl). A large part of the base of the post was preserved and the bottom was recorded at a depth of -267 cm below datum; the bottom of the hole was at -278 cm. There were no shims beneath the post. The wood of the post again was identified as pitch pine (Hoadley 1998).

The next three posts in line to the south were predicted in the northeast corner of unit P531, the northeast corner of P534, and the southeast corner of P535. In addition to these units we also opened P532, P533 and P536 in order to investigate the intervening spaces for the possibility of sills. The stratification in all these units was similar and revealed a more clearly defined and complex cultural stratigraphy as we now entered the better protected part of the site (Figure 49). The top 10 cm was sod, the artifacts from which are typical of those left behind by park visitors: bottle glass, tab tops from aluminum cans, cigarette filters, sheets of foil and plastic, and plastic spoons and forks. Beneath the sod was the usual 20 cm layer of dark brown sandy loam. This soil is the well mixed agricultural zone from the truck farming in the 1930s and 1940s which contains artifacts from the prehistoric to modern eras, the largest proportion being from the Fort Baldwin occupation. At a depth of

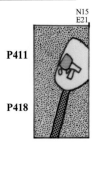

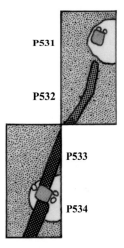

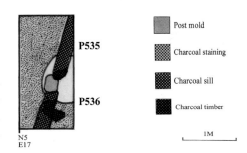

Figure 48. Plan of postholes, post molds and sills found in excavation units P411, P418 and P531-P536, delineating the west wall of the storehouse.

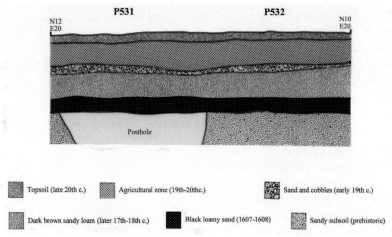

Topsoil (late 20th c.)   Agricultural zone (19th-20thc.)   Sand and cobbles (early 19th c.)

Dark brown sandy loam (later 17th-18th c.)   Black loamy sand (1607-1608)   Sandy subsoil (prehistoric)

Figure 49. Stratification in excavation units P531 and P532, east profiles. Note that there has been about 50 cm of soil accumulation since the Fort St. George occupation.

25-30 cm below the surface we again encountered the layer of yellowish brown sandy soil in which were many cobbles. This layer was 5-7 cm thick and clearly related to the one found in P418, although it did not now appear that the cobbles were set in any purposeful arrangement. We were finally to conclude that this soil was ejecta (back dirt) from the nearby well when it was dug out in the early nineteenth century. Artifacts were sparse, but again they dated to the first half of the nineteenth century and earlier. This is an important stratigraphic boundary for under it is another 20 cm layer of dark brown sandy loam which is a buried A-horizon predating the nineteenth century. It is essentially featureless, except where it has been disturbed by later occupations, and probably represents slow natural soil accretion. There is no definitive evidence that it was ever subjected to the plow. This soil is contaminated by only a few (presumably intrusive) nineteenth-century artifacts and contains mostly aboriginal materials, as well as a few early seventeenth-century items and daub. Considering the preponderance of native artifacts, it is probable that the bottom of this layer represents a seventeenth-century Abenaki reoccupation of the site after Fort St. George had been abandoned. Underlying this layer is a black loamy sand that is approximately 10 cm thick. It contains few aboriginal materials, but much charcoal and daub, as well as early seventeenth-century artifacts. This is the 1607-1608 Fort St. George level: the living surface and post-destruction building debris. Within it are the structural remains of the storehouse. These lie upon a reddish sandy soil, the pre-1607 A-horizon, which blends into a coarse sandy yellowish brown subsoil – the winnowed till – by a depth of 70 cm.

The structural remains we found in these units are most informative. We did, indeed, confirm three more postholes and molds (see Figure 48). We now had five posts of the west wall and could see that they, too, were set at regular intervals of approximately 9.5'.[5] We also could now verify that the foundations of the wall sections between the posts were interrupted sills. In units P411 and P418 the evidence for sills was little more than a streak in the soil, black staining from charcoal that had disappeared. In the better preserved area to the south, however, the sills began to take form, first as linear flakes of charcoal and then larger and larger fragments until by P535 and P536 the actual charred timbers were discovered *in situ*. Their dimensions are comparable to those in P547 and P548 that measured 25 cm wide and at least 3 cm thick. Insofar as could be determined by rocks sitting under and next to the sills they must have been joined to the posts about 5 cm above the contemporary ground surface. The method of joining was not determined, but in the absence of nails mortise and tenon is presumed. Lying on the sills was daub and a considerable amount of charcoal debris, including large pieces of wood that probably were remains of the wall posts or studs, but could have been joists, rafters, or other elements. Many of these timbers disappeared into the eastern walls of the excavations and were explored further in contiguous excavations within the interior of the storehouse described below.

We now had a good piece of the west wall and confidently skipped the next post in line to what we expected would be the penultimate post on that side. We were so certain of the location that we excavated only a single 1 x 1 m unit to uncover it.

---

[5] The posts in P501, P411 and P534 were removed in 1998 and 1999, the others left *in situ*.

The stratification in unit P566 was quite familiar and compared closely to that already established elsewhere on the site. Beneath the sod was a thick layer of coarse sand and gravel that had been brought in to level off the parking lot in the early 1980s. This is the same unconsolidated fill that was found in Units P547, P548, P572, and P573 discussed above. Here it was up to 40 cm thick and overlay a buried soil horizon that contained a high proportion of Fort Baldwin period artifacts and constructional debris. This layer was a dark brown sandy loam that averaged about 30 cm in thickness. It could be distinguished from an even darker, almost black, layer of sandy loam that also averaged 30 cm in thickness. Except where there were Fort Baldwin intrusions, the artifacts in this layer were

Figure 50. Charred timbers and wattle from the west wall of the storehouse in excavation units P541 and P542, looking south. A section of Hadlock's trench 80 cut right through these remains and while the charcoal was noted its significance was not recognized.

nineteenth-century. This is the first time that a stratigraphic break between these two components could be differentiated: elsewhere on site the two layers have been mixed into one layer by plowing although differences in artifactual distributions (Fort Baldwin predominating near the top, nineteenth-century near the bottom) were often recognized. The lense of well ejecta encountered in units north of the well was not present here, so the next underlying stratum was a dark brown sandy loam that represents the hiatus in site occupation during the later seventeenth and eighteenth centuries. It is thicker here, however, averaging about 35 cm. This layer was bisected by a later intrusion, but where it was undisturbed the artifacts were restricted to aboriginal materials and some unidentified earthenware that could date to Fort St. George. Fortunately, the disturbance just missed the objective of this excavation: at -140 cm below datum a layer of charcoal was revealed in the northeast corner and beneath it a spike of wood protruded up from the subsoil. The charcoal was part of a sill, the wooden spike the remnant of the eighth post. Once confirmed, the post was left *in situ.*

Artifacts associated with these remains and the general Fort St. George level were quite numerous, but still limited in variety. There were the nails, of course, which presumably had been used primarily for structural purposes. Contents of the storehouse were indicated by North Devon and Iberian ceramics and glass beads. The beads were relatively abundant in this area, dozens being found along and just inside the wall. All but two are the typical plain white drawn beads (IIA1) that have occurred elsewhere on the site; the two exceptions represent a plain blue variety (IIA7). A .75 caliber musket ball was found on the sill on the north side of the P534 post mold.

We returned to the west wall in 2004 when we explored units P541 and P542. These units are just north of the P566 posthole and we hoped to learn more about how the wall was constructed. The overlying stratification was similar to that found in contiguous units and when the Fort St. George level was revealed at ca. -145 cm below datum we found a great mass of charred debris remaining from the destruction of the storehouse (Figure 50). Bands of interwoven pieces of charcoal obviously had been wattle, but there was little evidence of daub in association. When the wattle was removed we expected to see a reasonably solid sill, but all we discovered was a black stain containing a few fragments of charcoal which was about 12-15 cm wide. That this shadow represented all that remained of the sill is apparent from its orientation and dimensions. The disparity between the preservation of the sill and the wattle above it might have been due to differential carbonization of the components or the durable qualities of the different species utilized.

We continued the exposure of the west wall in 2005 with the excavation of units P537-P538. We expected to find a wall post in P538 and indeed were rewarded with a fine mold and hole beneath a burned

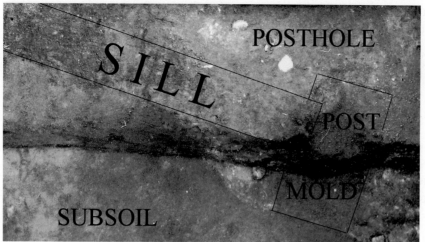

Figure 51. Burned sill, post mold and posthole in excavation unit P538. The remains of the sill can be seen lying across the posthole and extending into the mold, proving that the sill and post were joined with mortise and tenon. Note that the floor level is stepped down between the "Post" and "Mold" which provides a vertical profile of the mold. When extracted, the post was found to be a squared timber of pitch pine that measured 30 cm on a side (see Figure D1). The butt of the post sat directly on the bottom of the posthole at a depth of -223 cm below datum.

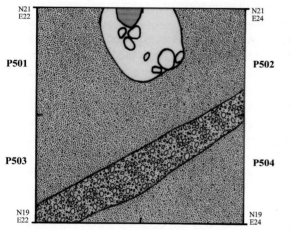

Figure 52. Posthole and post mold in excavation units P501 and P502; also note Hadlock trench running through units P502, P503, and P504.

sill and layer of wattle. Over the years, we had found evidence that the interrupted sills had been mortised into the wall posts and now we were presented with un-equivocal proof (Figure 51).

North Wall

The north gable end of the storehouse was established in 1998. Triangulating from the west wall post (P411) and the northeast corner post (P400) that had been had been discovered in 1997, we pre-dicted that the northwest corner post would be found in unit P501.[6] The intermediate ridgepole post depicted by John Hunt was ex-pected in unit P506.

Because the predicted location of the northwest corner post was in the southeastern corner of unit P501, units P502, P503 and P504 also were opened in order to ensure that we could excavate the entire posthole feature (see Figure 35). Once the sod had been removed we encountered a dark brown sandy loam, the agricul-tural zone, that was approximately 25 cm thick. It contained mostly modern and late nineteenth-century artifacts. At a depth below surface of 30-35 cm a mottled gray soil appeared. This layer was only about 5 cm thick and the cultural content was restricted to aboriginal and early seventeenth-century artifacts. Beneath that was the reddish sandy subsoil. Several features that intruded into this subsoil were poorly defined but were potential candidates for the posthole. It was neces-sary to go deeper before these were sorted out. One linear feature, however, was more obvious and easily interpreted. This was a trench that was found running through units P502, P503 and P504 on a NE-SW line (Figure 52). This trench was 30-40 cm wide and had been dug to a maximum depth of approximately 50 cm. It contained a mixture of soils and artifacts, including modern cigarette butts. The location, dimensions, orientation and contents of this feature readily identified it as a section of trench 5 dug by Wendell Hadlock's crew in 1962 (see Figure 18 and Appendix B1).

---

[6] In 2003, we excavated unit P500, 9.5' north of P501, and proved that the storehouse did not extend that far, confirming what we had already learned in the excavation of P410 in 1997.

Fortunately, Hadlock's trench just missed the northwest corner posthole. This feature was finally defined at a depth of 70 cm below the surface. The post turned out to be 50 cm farther north in P501 than predicted, and the posthole overlapped into P502. The posthole was found to be an oval measuring 60 cm by 70 cm, and the post mold revealed a squared timber measuring about 25 cm to a side. The bottom of the post was set -288 cm below datum; only a few fragments of wood from the post remained in this less well preserved part of the site. Chock stones had been placed around the post, but no shims beneath it. An aboriginal potsherd, a stone flake, and calcined bone fragments were associated with it. The bottom of the posthole was found at a depth of -297 cm below datum and intruded into the grayish white beach sand that underlies the reddish yellow winnowed till across the site.

We were so certain now that we could home in on individual posts that

Figure 53. Posthole and post mold in excavation unit P506, looking north. The posthole is the darker semicircular feature on the north side of the floor, and within it is the slightly pedestaled mold.

when we went after the gable end ridgepole post we set up only a single 1 x 1 m excavation unit: P506. The sod was removed and a brownish gray soil was found that was equivalent to the dark brown and mottled gray sandy loams that had been found in excavation units P501-P504. The strata had been mixed by the plow and contained a variety of artifacts, from prehistoric to modern. At a depth of 25 cm beneath the surface the reddish yellow sandy subsoil (winnowed till) was encountered, and within centimeters the outlines of the posthole and mold were defined (Figure 53). The posthole had a diameter of 75 cm, and the mold measured 25 cm by 30 cm. Both measurements are similar to the standard already discovered for the wall posts. This post had also been set as deep as the wall posts, a piece of the heartwood the size and shape of a cigar being found at -301 cm below datum. The posthole bottomed out at -306 cm and so it is probable that in this instance the post sat directly on the bottom of the hole.

We thus confirmed the north gable end of the storehouse as drawn by John Hunt. The most interesting finding was that the ridgepole post was as substantial an element as the wall posts, i.e., it was as large a timber in cross section and had been set as deeply into the ground. It was, however, identified as spruce (Hoadley 1998) which is not as strong or durable as the pitch pine used for the wall posts (Dwelley 1980, p. 14).

South Wall

One of the objectives of the 1999 season was to complete the outline of the storehouse so that we had the exact form and dimensions. The final piece of the footprint that we needed was the south wall. In 1998 we had found the seventh post from the north end in the east wall and the eighth post in the west wall, so we expected to uncover a trapezoidal section bounded by the penultimate east wall post, the southeast and southwest corner posts, and the gable end post.

In order to confirm the length of the building and provide secure reference points for the other posts, we began the excavations at the predicted locations of the southwest and southeast corner posts in unit P617 and at the intersection of units P630-P631, P638-P639. Much to our surprise, we found no evidence of a post,

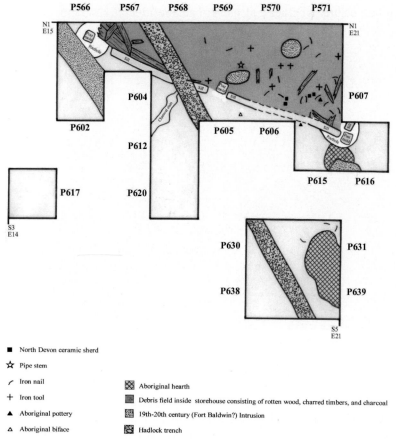

P566   P567   P568   P569   P570   P571

N1
E15

N1
E21

P604

P602

P612

P617   P620

S3
E14

P605   P606

P607

P615   P616

P630   P631

P638   P639

S5
E21

■ North Devon ceramic sherd
☆ Pipe stem
ⱱ Iron nail
+ Iron tool
▲ Aboriginal pottery
△ Aboriginal biface

▨ Aboriginal hearth
▦ Debris field inside storehouse consisting of rotten wood, charred timbers, and charcoal
▦ 19th-20th century (Fort Baldwin?) Intrusion
▨ Hadlock trench

Figure 54. Plan of excavations in the south end of the storehouse. The south wall is defined by the interrupted sills that connect the corner and gable end posts. The earthen floor inside the building had been leveled off at approximately -150 cm below datum and was covered with charred debris and artifacts. Note that a section of Hadlock's trench 80 ran right through the southwestern corner of the storehouse, but they interpreted the remains as dating from the Fort Baldwin occupation.

posthole, or any structural remains relating to the storehouse at either location. Meanwhile we also had opened units P602, P612, and P620 in what we anticipated would be the interior of the storehouse, but these too were completely uninformative regarding the storehouse although a smattering of appropriate artifacts were found. By now we were receiving a very clear message: to wit, the storehouse simply did not extend that far.

In short, we discovered that the storehouse was seven bays long, not eight bays as drawn by John Hunt. The post we had found in P566 in 1998 was the southwest corner post of the structure and the southeast corner was now exposed in units P615-P616 (Figure 54). The gable end post was then easily located in P605. Confirmation that these posts represented the south end of the storehouse was provided by the interrupted sills that connected them. Before the sills had been laid, however, we found that the ground under the entire south end of the storehouse had been excavated to a depth of approximately 23 cm beneath the contemporary 1607 ground surface. The cut bank was still visible along the south side of the sills.[7] And here we have a possible solution to our conundrum regarding the discrepancy between Hunt's drawing and the archaeological revelation. We know from our earlier excavations in the northern part of the storehouse that it had been built on a ground surface that sloped down slightly toward the shore. At an average gradient of 5%, the degree of slope was inconsiderable and the floor was essentially level for all practical purposes. Near the south end, however, the ground apparently rose sharply (as it still does today even discounting the added parking lot fill), and therefore in order to maintain an approximate level the extra soil was removed. It is a reasonable conjecture that the effort caused the builders to reconsider their original plan for eight bays and they terminated construction at this stage.

Interior

As the formal dimensions of the storehouse took shape, we began exploring the interior floor spaces in 1998 looking for features and artifacts that would further inform us about constructional matters, as well as contents and activities. Some of the topics we hoped to address included: the structure of the roof; the organization of interior space; the types of *matériel* that were stored and used by the colonists; the kinds of

---

[7] As may be seen in Figure 54, Hadlock's crew dug through the south end of the storehouse in 1962. Although they did not realize what they had encountered, they did note the presence of wood, daub, and charcoal (which they attributed to Fort Baldwin), as well as a seven inch "drop" in subsoil where we defined the cut bank (Lane 1966).

activities that occurred within the storehouse, and especially whether it also ever had a residential function; and finally the determination of when the building was destroyed.

Although we had excavated units inside the storehouse in previous seasons these had not been specifically placed for that purpose and indeed in some instances the relationship was not even realized. In 1994, trench 2 had unknowingly been dug right through the north end of the storehouse and in the 1997 search for wall posts some units were opened within the storehouse but most of these were also in the poorly preserved northern end where the 1607-1608 floor level had been destroyed. But once we had established the precise layout of the building we began examining the better preserved southern half for interior structural, spatial and behavioral details.

Our first efforts were directed to gaining a better understanding of the basic structure of the storehouse and the organization of interior space. In 1998, we excavated four units in a search for ridgepole posts along the median long axis. The presence or absence of a ridgepole would reveal much about the sophistication of construction, presence being presumed to mean more competent carpentry. Although we did not expect to find evidence of the element itself, we could infer its existence if we found the remains of supporting posts. If we found ridgepole posts, the principal questions we then had were whether they were set as regularly as the wall posts, whether there was one for every pair of wall posts, and whether these interior posts were as sturdy and as deeply set as the outside wall posts.

Our point of reference, of course, was the gable end post that had been found in P506. The first units we opened in this search were P421 and P428 which were half way between the third pair of posts south from the north end (see Figure 34). A double unit was necessary to allow for some deviation in the location of the predicted feature. The excavation of P428 also gave us the opportunity to explore further a small pit that had been found in the west profile of unit P429 in 1997. This pit had contained Fort St. George period artifacts and we hoped that its further excavation would inform us about contents or activities within the storehouse. But we were completely disappointed in our expectations. There was no more evidence of the artifact pit or any other feature. Once we were certain we were below any possible Fort St. George level, the unit was dug deeply into subsoil to provide additional working room for the investigations in unit P421.

Although this area had been badly disturbed, all historic occupation levels being removed, we did find the bottom of a large posthole in P421 that intruded into the subsoil. This hole was 70 cm in diameter and bottomed out at -237 cm below datum. All that remained of the post was a circular area of dark mottling near the center of the hole. Below it were flat rocks 15 cm thick that might have been shim stones; the bottom of the post may thus be estimated at -222 cm below datum. The post not being set as deeply as the companion wall posts would seem to indicate that it was not quite of the same order, unlike the gable end post. But it is still reasonable to conclude that it functioned as a ridgepole post and that the ridgepole did not need as much support as the walls.

The lighter load that needed to be carried also seems to be confirmed by the other two units excavated: P523 and P476. The first unit was placed between the second pair of wall posts and P476 between the sixth. At neither location was there any evidence of a post or posthole, and thus it is probable that the support interval was longer than for the walls. Of course, there could have been king posts between the beams and ridgepole at the intervening locations, but in either case it would appear that interior space was minimally obstructed.

We then proceeded to explore that interior space. In 1998 we opened units P476, P477, P483 and P484.[8] This block was contiguous to units P478 and P486 which had been excavated in 1997 when we were defining the east wall and where we first found that the 1607-1608 floor level was preserved in the southern end of the building. Lying *in situ* on the small section of floor that was exposed along the interior side of the wall were artifacts and architectural elements, such as daub, charred timbers and carbonized thatch. Also in 1998

---

[8] All of these units had the standard 1 x 1 m dimensions, except for P484 which was 1 x 1.5 m in order to account for the half-meter deviation of the contiguous unit P486 which had been shifted that amount so that the sixth post and hole of the east wall could be confirmed as economically as possible during the closing days of the 1997 season.

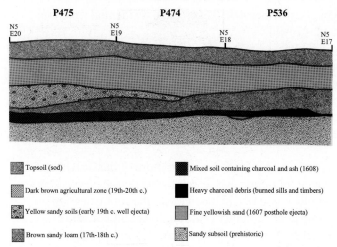

P475   **P474**   **P536**

Topsoil (sod)

Dark brown agricultural zone (19th-20th c.)

Yellow sandy soils (early 19th c. well ejecta)

Brown sandy loam (17th-18th c.)

Mixed soil containing charcoal and ash (1608)

Heavy charcoal debris (burned sills and timbers)

Fine yellowish sand (1607 posthole ejecta)

Sandy subsoil (prehistoric)

Figure 55. Stratification in excavation units P474, P475 and P536, south profiles, within the storehouse.

excavations along the west wall line in units P531-P536 revealed excellent information on wall construction and especially had provided evidence of the use of interrupted sills. Lying on and inside these sills in some places were pieces of wood the grain of which was perpendicular to the sills. Furthermore, numerous nails in and on the sills could not definitely be interpreted as part of wall construction (joining sills and posts or studs) and there was the thought that they might instead have been used for securing floorboards to the sills. In order to look for further evidence of flooring, we opened up units P446, P453, P460 but were not able to take them down to the constructional layer before time ran out in 1998. In 1999, we completed these units and also opened up the contiguous units P461, P467, P468, P474 and P475. This block connected with units P476, P477, P478, P483 and P484 which altogether gave us a complete cross section of the storehouse. Also in 1999, the southernmost end of the storehouse was exposed in units P567-P571 and P605-P607 while we were tracing the south wall (see Figure 54). The remaining interior area between the 1997, 1998 and 1999 excavations was explored in 2004 (units P495-P498, P541-P543, P545-P546) and 2005 (P481-P482, P487-P491, P493-P496, P544-P546).

The stratigraphy at this location followed the well-established sequence, differing only in slight variations in the thicknesses of individual layers and the occurrences of unique features. A representative profile is illustrated in Figure 55. Beneath 15 cm of sod topsoil was the usual layer of dark brown sandy loam approximately 25 cm thick. This layer had been disturbed by the plow, and contained nineteenth- and twentieth-century artifacts. The bulk of the artifacts related to Fort Baldwin were concentrated in the upper part of the layer, while nineteenth-century domestic items were found near the bottom. The early nineteenth century was defined by an underlying layer of yellow sand and cobbles – now identified as the ejecta from the nineteenth-century well – that was up to 20 cm thick in the center of the excavations, but gradually tapered out to a barely distinguishable line to the west and south. Beneath it was a brown sandy loam that contained only a few artifacts, most of which were of aboriginal manufacture. This layer ranged from 5 cm to 20 cm in thickness and represented a two-century hiatus in site occupation following a brief Abenaki resettlement after the destruction of Fort St. George. The 1607-1608 level was 2 cm to 8 cm thick and was defined by evidence of destruction, such as charcoal and ash, as well as early seventeenth-century artifacts. Excavation was generally halted at this level, except where features intruded down into subsoil.

A major disturbance at this location was the early nineteenth-century well that was found in units P462-P464 and P476-P477. This well had been dug down from the surface of the lower brown sandy loam layer. It was stone-lined and the stone casing extended far enough above the ground surface so that it was still visible in 1962 when Hadlock noticed it and had it cleaned out. He discovered that it had been dug down through 6' of subsoils to bedrock. At the bottom he found modern trash and one of the few diagnostic later seventeenth-century artifacts found at the site: a kaolin tobacco pipe of a type essentially identical to examples from the nearby Clarke & Lake trading settlement that was occupied from 1654 to 1676 (Baker 1985, pls. 5e, 7a). When the park was landscaped in 1981, the rough blocks of the casing still above ground were pushed aside and the interior of the well was filled with the same unconsolidated sand and gravel that was used as fill in the parking lot, which thus relates the two events. Although destructive of the archaeology in the immediate vicinity, the well is an important key to the interpretation of the site. First, it provides an anchor for the Hadlock excavation plan (see Figure 18 and Appendix B1), helping us to place it on our site map so that we could more accurately trace his trenches. Even more importantly, when the well originally

ARTIFACTS

- ■ Ceramic sherd
- ☆ Tobacco pipe fragment
- ◻ Glass sherd
- ○ Glass bead
- ✳ Iron caulking tool
- ☾ Iron nail
- ☉ Iron rove
- ✛ Iron artifact
- ● Lead artifact
- △ Shell bead
- ★ English flint
- ✗ Daub

FEATURES

- Ash
- Charred timber
- Burned wattle
- Charcoal stain
- Later 17th c. pit
- Fort Baldwin intrusion
- Mid 20th c. trench
- 1962 Hadlock trench
- 1981 well infilling

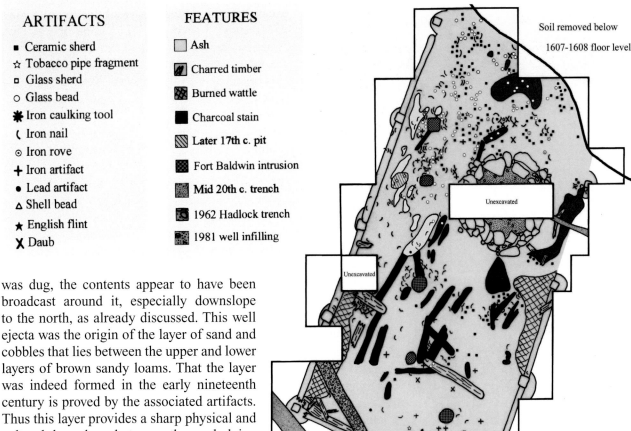

Soil removed below 1607-1608 floor level

Unexcavated

Unexcavated

Figure 56. Distribution of features and artifacts on the floor of the storehouse. The floor of the storehouse sloped from -140 cm in the southwestern corner to -175 cm at the fifth post north along the west wall and from -149 cm in the southeastern corner to -172 cm at the fourth post north along the east wall.

was dug, the contents appear to have been broadcast around it, especially downslope to the north, as already discussed. This well ejecta was the origin of the layer of sand and cobbles that lies between the upper and lower layers of brown sandy loams. That the layer was indeed formed in the early nineteenth century is proved by the associated artifacts. Thus this layer provides a sharp physical and cultural boundary between the underlying natural soil accretion of the later seventeenth and eighteenth centuries and the overlying nineteenth- and twentieth-century soils. It is an important reference point in site occupation.

Although the preservation of structural information on the interior of the storehouse was not as good as had been anticipated, we were able to add some important details concerning its construction and destruction. On the west side of the building, we were able to trace the charcoal and ash stains of timbers sufficiently to answer one of our questions. As is evident in Figure 56, the absence of regularity in the patterning of the stains, especially the lack of consistent orientation with the sills, was strong evidence against their being the remains of floorboards, at least for the ground floor. The random orientation of the many handwrought nails within this debris added to the impression of chaotic destruction and collapse, rather than *in situ* burning. In marked contrast was the more regular patterning of nails along the sills that had been observed in 1998 which may now be interpreted as probable anchors for the wall studs rather than floorboards. If the studs were toenailed to the sills, however, it would suggest a joinery more akin to balloon framing than that expected for the early seventeenth century.

A considerable litter of burned debris was found on the floor of the storehouse south of the well. The remains of many timbers could be observed, but most were badly deteriorated and were visible only as charcoal stains, alignments of wooden knots and patches of organic matter. It was difficult to make sense from this jumble or to identify specific architectural elements, but clearly they represented sections of the superstructure of the collapsed building. The largest structural feature was a fallen timber that lay diagonally

Figure 57. Features and artifacts on the floor of the storehouse in excavation units P545 and P546. The fallen post lies diagonally across the units from top left (southeast) to bottom right (northwest). The knot pairs are clearly evident along the length of the timber. The iron artifact at lower left was a badly deteriorated knife blade. Two decorated glass beads lay directly on the timber.

Table 4. Early seventeenth-century artifacts found inside the storehouse.

CERAMICS
West of England[1]	285
Olive Jar	67
Delft	3
Bellarmine	13

TOBACCO PIPES 61

GLASS
Bottle	16
Wine/ale glass	2
Bead	160
Window	6
Mirror	2

IRON
Nail	1303
Washer	35
Tool	3
Armor	69
Gun part	1

LEAD/PEWTER
Munition[2]	41
Miscellaneous	1

COPPER/BRASS 7
OTHER MATERIALS[3] 4

[1] Including North Devon, Totnes and other West of England types, and unclassified.
[2] Lead pistol and musket balls, sprue, drips and scrap.
[3] Flint, shell.

across the floor (Figure 57). Most of the timber had been reduced to a thin black stain 20-25 cm wide along which were scattered pieces of charcoal and wood. The latter, well preserved, were found in pairs along the length of the timber and were clearly knots. The fact that they had resisted decay while the rest of the timber had almost entirely disintegrated is characteristic of pitch pine: the knots "are so filled with resin that they resist decay long after the stump has rotted away" (Peattie 1950, p. 23). Pitch pine has already been recognized as the wood used for wall posts and this timber had obviously been a major post, but the angle at which it had fallen does not fit well with the wall. It might have been a median post, but we were unable to find a posthole in which it would have been set. It could have rested directly on the ground, but that would not match the median post found in the northern end of the storehouse that had been set in a posthole. If this was indeed an interior median post, then the angle of the knots shows that it had stood in an inverted position – that is, with the base upwards – a common practice at the time (Cook 1982, p. 24; Sobon and Schroeder 1984, p. 27).

The most informative constructional detail was observed in P487 where relatively well preserved overlying timbers were clearly joined with nails, confirming that the large number of nails found within the storehouse were probably used in its construction. Nailing would have enabled the colonists to build the storehouse more rapidly, if not as strongly as with mortise-and-tenon joinery. A corollary is that they were well supplied with building hardware.

Aside from the wrought iron nails used in construction, artifacts were relatively rare in the storehouse (Table 4). There were diagnostic sherds of earthenware, including North Devon, fragments of

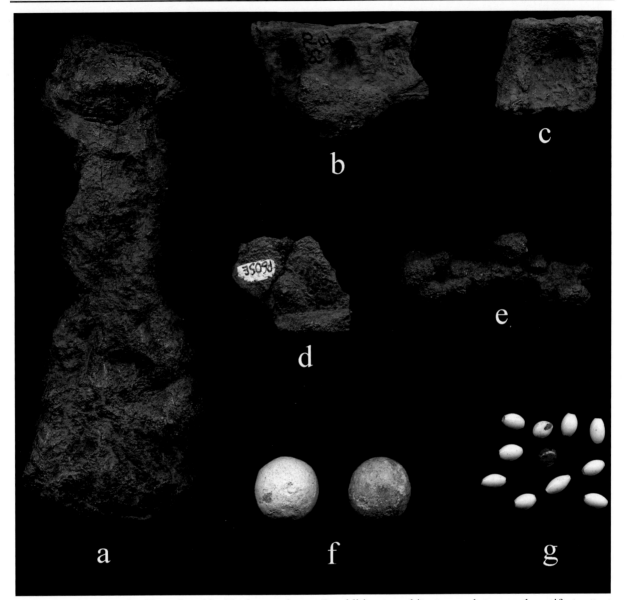

Figure 58. Sample of artifacts found inside the storehouse. In addition to architecture and storage, the artifacts attest to some of the principal activities of the colonists, such as boat building, military duties, and trading with the natives: a, caulking iron (P607D); b, strip of iron washers or roves (P570E); c, large rove (P461D); d, piece of armor, probably tasset lame (P605E); e, snaphaunce safety lever (P484H3); f, lead musket balls (P474E, P534C); g, glass beads exhibiting the ratio of ten white to one blue (P447D, P461D). (1:1)

tobacco pipes, glass beads, and iron items (Figure 58). The latter were concentrated in the southeastern corner and included many pieces of armor which appeared to be tasset lames. A small buckle, riveted straps, and iron washers used in attaching the lames were in association. Lead balls, shot, and sprue, and the safety lever from a snaphaunce lock were found nearby. This concentration of military artifacts suggests that the south end of the storehouse may have served as the armory of the colony.

Glass beads, on the other hand, were mostly confined to the central part of the storehouse along the western wall which suggests that this area may have been used for the storage and/or processing of trade goods. These beads are monochrome: many white and a few blue in imitation of wampum (there was even a wampum bead mixed in with them). Two decorated beads, however, were segregated some distance away.

Figure 59. Isometric reconstruction of the storehouse based on the Hunt drawing and archaeological evidence. Note that the wall posts are earthfast and that the south end of the building stops at the cut slope. (Drawing by Judith Dunsford)

One is dark blue with longitudinal white stripes (variety IIB1 in the classification of Brain 1979, pl. 2), while the other is a compound bead with a light green inner layer and an opaque brick red outer layer (variety IVA2, ibid.). The latter is a distinctive type that is so widely distributed in space and time it has been given a name: "Cornaline d'Aleppo" These are the fanciest beads that have been found at Fort St. George and their separate provenience suggests that they were withheld from the general trade.

Iron roves were also common in the central part of the storehouse. Roves were used in shipbuilding, and together with the caulking iron found in P607 remind us of the foremost success of the colony: that is, the construction of the pinnace *Virginia.*

Overall, the relative scarcity and fragmentary condition of the artifacts support the conclusion that the storehouse had been cleaned out before its destruction.

Summary of the Storehouse

After five seasons of excavations focused on the storehouse, we may offer some confident conclusions and tentative interpretations; we are also still left with a few puzzling questions. We have confirmed that it was a timber-framed, post-in-ground structure that had interrupted sills connected to the posts with mortise-and-tenon joinery. We may presume that the posts were tied together with beams and wall plates which supported the roof trusses, conforming to the common English vernacular box framing (Figure 59). The walls were infilled with wattle-and-daub between the posts, although surprisingly small amounts of fired daub were found in the excavations. The lack of daub might be due to the fact that the fire which destroyed the building was a slow and relatively low temperature burn, a condition that also would explain the abundance of only partially charred wood among the debris that covered the floor of the building. The floor itself was earthen, as there was no evidence of floorboards or joists. And so, too, the lack of flooring seems to deny the presence of an upper story or loft. The composition of the roof was substantiated by charred thatch (and globules of glassy slag that may be silica bubbled from the grasses during burning). All of this is consistent with Hunt's drawing.

Archaeology also provides several surprises concerning the construction. The most startling revelation of all, of course, was that the storehouse was one bay shorter than drawn by Hunt. We had already discovered that it was wider than he had indicated so we should have been forewarned that length could deviate as well. Overall dimensions were finally determined to be about nineteen feet wide and sixty-nine feet long.

Another interesting discovery was the large number of nails used, most apparently for the joining of lesser elements in the superstructure of the building. Although the join might not have been as strong as one made with a mortise and tenon, nailing could have speeded up construction. That this technique must have been considered sufficient is supported by the omission of all but one or possibly two median posts.

As to whether the building was assembled by the normal or reverse method, the evidence is not conclusive. A case has been made in favor of normal construction (Morrison 2002, pp. 63-75) and an updated version that also contains a useful summary of construction details is presented in Appendix E. Despite the compelling argument, however, the method of framing remains a question. Morrison's case for normal construction rests primarily upon the positions of the posts within the postholes, but the actual positions do not seem to be uniformly supportive of the proposition although they could have been altered by the final leveling and alignment procedures. Additional circumstantial evidence for normal framing is that the defining tie-beam-over-wall-plate joinery that is required is most characteristic of English box-frame construction (Harris 1980, pp. 19-20), and a close examination of Hunt's drawing of the storehouse reveals that the tops of the posts are expanded as though they have been fashioned into a jowled or gunstock form typical of such joinery. On the other hand, Hunt may simply have been indicating that the posts had been placed in an inverted position with the base upwards.

The argument for reverse construction, on the other hand, is based on the challenges faced by the builders. The carpenters were commissioned to build a large and sturdy storehouse as quickly as possible so that the ships could be off-loaded. Their choice of the longhouse form may have been dictated by the barn-like structures of their experience. These were commonly cruck-built, but a similar result would be achieved with box-framing utilizing reverse assembly. In this form of construction, post-and-beam bents are assembled first, arranged in bays and then tied together with wall plates. It is a logical way to put together a long, narrow building and has several advantages. First, the post-beam-wall plate joinery is simpler and thus the whole process can be accomplished more quickly. Second, it is easier, and thus quicker, to position and align the bents and insert the interrupted sills between them. Third, it avoids the difficulties of raising and leveling a long side wall on sloping terrain. It also makes it easy to simply omit a bay when the grade becomes so steep that ground must be removed to maintain any sort of level within the structure. Finally, there is an intriguing clue in the Davies journal which records that the storehouse was still under construction on September 22, but that the *Mary and John* had already begun "discharging her vyttuales [victuals]" on September 7, suggesting that usable space was available which would have been possible after the first couple of bents had been put up and covered, whereas in normal construction the entire substructure must be completed before the building can be roofed. Reverse framing, then, makes more sense in meeting the challenges faced by the builders. But, of course, the actual construction need not have adhered to such a rule of logic and may have been determined by other concerns or simply the traditional techniques with which the carpenters were most familiar. Unfortunately, we cannot be certain which circumstances prevailed at Fort St. George.

In regards to usage, we are informed by Hunt and the documents that the building was intended to function as the primary storehouse. It was the largest public building and the center of communal activities. The possibility that it might also have quartered some of the colonists rested solely upon Hunt's depiction of what appear to be dormers in the roof. However, we could not find evidence of a loft, nor – as the absence of chimneys in Hunt's drawing clearly indicates – provision for heating which would rule out any possibility of a residential function.

The type and quantity of artifacts (Table 4) also do not support an interpretation of midden refuse accumulated during an occupation of the building. Rather, the scattering of items is evocative of storage compartmentalization in which we were able to distinguish different activity areas. For example, there was a concentration of military items in the southeastern corner of the building which suggests that it may have served as the armory for the colony. On the other hand, the number of glass beads and iron roves in the center of the storehouse indicates that those items so essential to the primary economic ventures of the colony, fur trading and ship building, were stored close to the door where they were easily accessible.

The fact that the artifacts found within the storehouse were relatively small in number and consisted mainly of randomly scattered small items and broken pieces – that is, things easily lost or discarded – attests to the fact that the bulk of the stored goods obviously had been removed before the storehouse was destroyed. Together with the fact that there is no evidence of rebuilding, we may conclude that the destruction was not an accidental midwinter catastrophe, as reported by Gorges some years later, but rather a planned event that occurred upon abandonment of the colony.

Figure 60. The admiral, Raleigh Gilbert, and his house as drawn by John Hunt.

Admiral's House

Admiral Raleigh Gilbert's house is one of only three structures at Fort St. George for which we have documentation beyond the Hunt map attesting to its construction. The other two are the storehouse and the chapel, which are mentioned in the surviving Robert Davies journal and in Strachey's summary version of that account. Raleigh Gilbert's house, however, is specifically and repeatedly cited in legal depositions taken down back in England in 1608 as the place where officers of the colony met (Banks 1929). That this should have been the venue for official meetings rather than President George Popham's house might seem strange but could be explained by the fact that it was the largest house in the fort - and third largest structure after the storehouse and chapel - as drawn by John Hunt. Why Raleigh Gilbert rated a larger house than the president raises interesting questions, but for present purposes is irrelevant. Its importance here is that it was definitely constructed and therefore provides a test of Mr. Hunt and his accuracy concerning locational and constructional details.

The admiral's house was located approximately 40' (ca.12 m) south of the storehouse, according to Hunt's scale, and was oriented perpendicularly to it (see Figure 5). As drawn by Hunt, the construction appears to be similar: post-in-ground framing, wattle-and-daub walls, and thatched roof (Figure 60). The latter also displays two of those problematic dormers. The structure was composed of four single bays and, again using Hunt's scale, measured about 30' (9 m) in length and 12' (3.5 m) in width. The door was located in the second bay of the north side closest to the western end where the chimney was placed. The fact that this was the largest heated structure in the fort undoubtedly determined its selection as a preferred meeting place. It also gave us hope for significant structural remains in the form of a stone hearth or chimney base.

A location 40' south of the storehouse did not seem to provide us with much opportunity for finding Raleigh Gilbert's house since that would place most of it beneath the town-owned Fort Baldwin Road, a major artery we dared not broach at this stage. But if Hunt was correct, it appeared that we had a chance to uncover at least the northwestern corner of the house in the southeastern corner of the parking lot. Thus, in 1999, while we were already digging up the parking lot to investigate the southern end of the storehouse, we expanded the excavations to include the predicted location of Raleigh Gilbert's house (Figure 61).

The first excavations we opened at this location in 1999 were selected according to our best interpretation of Hunt's information, which placed the northwest corner post of the admiral's house within

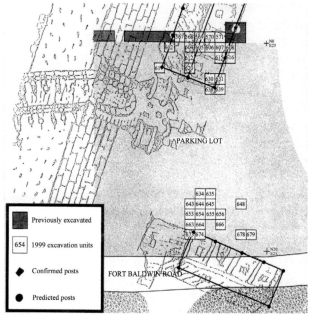

Figure 61. Predicted location of the admiral's house according to the Hunt map, and placement of 1999 excavations. North at top.

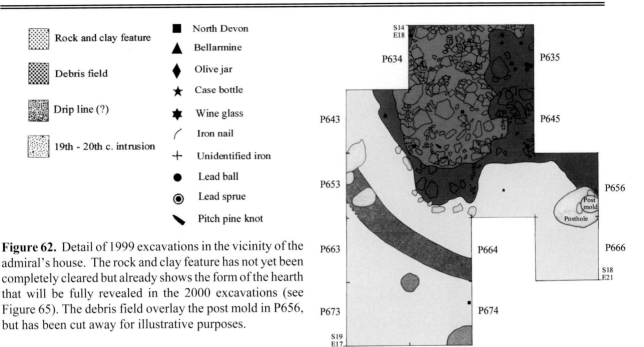

Rock and clay feature

Debris field

Drip line (?)

19th - 20th c. intrusion

■ North Devon

▲ Bellarmine

♦ Olive jar

★ Case bottle

✦ Wine glass

⟨ Iron nail

╀ Unidentified iron

● Lead ball

◉ Lead sprue

➘ Pitch pine knot

Figure 62. Detail of 1999 excavations in the vicinity of the admiral's house. The rock and clay feature has not yet been completely cleared but already shows the form of the hearth that will be fully revealed in the 2000 excavations (see Figure 65). The debris field overlay the post mold in P656, but has been cut away for illustrative purposes.

the square formed by contiguous units P663- P664 and P673-P674. The uppermost levels in these units were composed of very mixed soils among which was a streak of dark, highly organic, and noticeably malodorous material that was immediately attributed to Fort Baldwin by the excavators (although this interpretation perhaps was based more on prejudice than evidence). The artifactual content was equally mixed and included everything from Fort Baldwin to prehistoric. Of greatest interest to us, however, was a fair representation of early seventeenth-century materials. The numbers were not large, but the pieces were bigger, and of more variety and finer quality, than we had been encountering in the vicinity of the storehouse. These included diagnostic sherds of case bottle glass and North Devon ceramics. Already, too, daub and charcoal were appearing, and one piece of daub from P674 was particularly promising since it exhibited the impressions and prolonged exposure to high heat consistent with chinking from a stick chimney. We began to hope that we were indeed in the right neighborhood.

The features we found in these units, however, appeared to offer no encouragement. One of these was a pit that was found precisely at the predicted location of the northwest corner post, but it was clearly non-architectural in origin and, although it contained items of Fort St. George vintage (including a small fragment of white tin glaze, the first evidence of delftware that we had ever found at the site), the most prominent artifact was a piece of Rockingham stoneware. The other feature of note was a dark, slightly curved linear stain that ran across units P663-P664 (Figure 62). It contained highly organic, water-sorted silts and was tentatively interpreted by the excavators as a drip line. No artifacts were found within it, however, and so it could not be related to Fort St. George, much less Raleigh Gilbert's house. Excavations in these units were halted at an average of only 30 cm below the surface (-35 cm from datum).

We needed to expand our exploration and would have looked farther south toward the heart of the predicted location of our objective if the road had not blocked our way (fortuitously as it turned out). Instead, we began opening up contiguous units to the north and east. P654 was the first unit selected because of a possible feature in the northeast corner of P664 that appeared to continue farther north. It was not found in P654, but other intriguing features were uncovered. Stretching across the middle of the unit was a curved band of dark disturbed soil that enclosed a zone of rock and clay along the north wall. The latter clearly was not natural: the clay was out of place geologically, and the rocks were concentrated and arranged in a manner

Figure 63. Some diagnostic artifacts found in the 1999 excavations at Admiral Raleigh Gilbert's House: a-b, North Devon baluster jar (P656B1, P674A); c, Totnes pot (P656B1); d, Delft apothecary jar (P648D); e, Iberian olive jar (P648D); f, Bellarmine jug (P1A3, P643B2); g, light green flask (P648D); h, *cristallo* mirror (P656B); i, jet bead (P648B); j, black glass buttons (P648D); k, blue-green case bottle (P648D); l, window pane (P656E2). (1:1)

that denoted human intervention. It was, in fact, a purposeful construction of rocks, many obviously selected for flatness, that appeared to have been set in the gray clay. Although it was not exactly where we had expected to find it, our immediate thought was that we may have a hearth or chimney base. This thought was reinforced by the fact that many of the rocks appeared to have been subjected to heat.

Hoping for more evidence, we excavated unit P644 and were rewarded with a continuation of the rocks and clay feature. In the north side of the unit many of the flat rocks had been deliberately stacked on top of each other. Embedded in the clay between the rocks were found Bellarmine and North Devon sherds and a pitch pine knot. This was the encouragement we sought, and all contiguous units (P634, P635, P643, P645, P653, P655) were opened up. Most of the feature was thereby exposed (Figure 62) and continued to exhibit the characteristics and artifacts consistent with a man-made structure that dated to the early seventeenth century. But could we say we had found the house of Raleigh Gilbert? For that we needed more definitive architectural and artifactual information. These were forthcoming in units P656/P666, P648, and P678-P679.

P656 had been selected at random, the choice being determined by the desire to explore farther east and the necessity to provide convenient working room between units. It was a lucky choice in terms of encouraging us because we promptly encountered more structural remains that contained an astonishing array of artifacts. The structural evidence was a layer of daub (both fired and unfired), charcoal, and thatch in the northeastern part of the unit. This debris was 20 cm thick in the northwestern corner and following a sloping contour was more than 30 cm thick in the southeastern corner. The debris field continued eastwards at least as far as P648, where it was found throughout the unit, as well as the northwestern corner of P678. In P648 it was more than 40 cm thick, and it was noticed that the proportion of fired daub to unfired clay increased toward the bottom of the layer. The tentative hypothesis at this point was that we had encountered part of a collapsed wall that had been subjected to more intense heat on one side than the other. But as the excavations progressed, we were to determine that the fired daub and unfired clay represented two discrete events.

An effort was made to follow out the debris layer in P666, but surprisingly it did not continue into that unit, nor were there any artifacts below the surface level. It exhibited a totally different stratigraphic situation until at a depth of -50 cm below datum the edge of a feature was revealed that extended into P656 beneath the debris layer. This new feature was a posthole and mold. Charcoal and daub in the mold indicated that the post had burned in place. Because of the immediate association with the debris layer, it was clear that the post was another architectural element of the same structure. Found near the post was a piece of slightly melted glass that seems to be a fragment of a quarrel from a leaded window (Figure 63l). Ghostly images along the two original edges of the quarrel are consistent with the former presence of lead cames, and drips of melted lead on the glass, itself, would seem to confirm such mounting. Apparently, the fire had been hot enough to melt the lead and distort the glass. Other probable pieces of window glass were also recovered. The luxury of glazed windows would add another dimension to the sophistication of the building and the importance of its occupant, and greatly enhance our perception of the colony's preparedness.

So did we have Admiral Raleigh Gilbert's house? At this stage, we did not yet know the form or dimensions, but it was obvious that we had a post-in-ground, wattle-and-daub building with a hearth area (and chimney?) that was in approximately the right place according to Hunt. In fact, the difference between the

Table 5. Early seventeenth-century artifacts found in the admiral's house.

CERAMICS	
West of England[1]	318
Olive Jar	63
Delft	49
Bellarmine	28
TOBACCO PIPES	13
GLASS	
Bottle	473
Wine/ale glass	500
Bead	9
Button	56
Window	27
Mirror	12
IRON	
Nail	769
Washer	3
Tool	1
Armor	10
LEAD/PEWTER	
Munition[2]	62
Miscellaneous	1
COPPER/BRASS	5
OTHER MATERIALS[3]	57

[1] Including North Devon, Totnes and other West of England types, as well as unclassified.
[2] Lead pistol and musket balls, sprue, drips and scrap.
[3] Flint, jet, graphite.

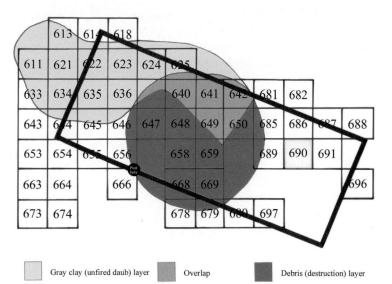

Gray clay (unfired daub) layer   Overlap   Debris (destruction) layer

Figure 64. Plan of 1999-2000 excavations at the admiral's house and predicted footprint for the house in 2000. The placement of the footprint was determined by the hearth area and the posthole that had been encountered in 1999. If the footprint was placed in a reasonably accurate position then additional postholes were expected in the vicinity of units along the outline. Also depicted are the two distinct strata that represent sequent events at this location: a layer of daub and destruction debris that is overlain by a layer of unfired gray clay. The straight edges of the clay layer in units P640, P649 and P650 formed along fallen timbers.

predicted location and the actual location was about 9', or the width of one of the storehouse bays. Since the storehouse was one bay short, the relative positions of the two structures are exactly as drawn by Hunt.

The case for this being the house of Raleigh Gilbert became even stronger when the associated artifacts were analyzed. Not only are they diagnostically early seventeenth-century, but there are qualitative and quantitative differences that set them apart from other locations on the site. The items are generally finer and more varied. The inventory includes sherds of North Devon, Delft and Bellarmine ceramics, fragments of drinking glasses and case bottles, glass buttons, lead munitions, handwrought nails, iron hardware, and pieces of armor (Figure 63, Table 5). Such an assemblage is most appropriate for a leader of the colony. The presence of the finest ceramics that have been found at the site, as well as numerous fragments of liquor bottles and wine glasses indicate that he set a superior table. The many glass buttons, and

also the jet beads, suggest the dress of a gentleman of standing within the community. The armor and lead munitions are evidence of his military role. All together are consistent with the Raleigh Gilbert identification.

Thus the results of these preliminary tests were greatly encouraging and further investigation was clearly in order. When we continued the excavation in 2000 we opened up an area that we expected would contain the entire footprint of the house, except for the southeastern corner which probably lay beneath the town road. The actual placement of the excavations was determined by the position of the hearth and the post mold which we deduced with some confidence to be a major support timber for the south wall of the structure. Around these features we drew a footprint 30' long by 12' wide, the approximate dimensions indicated by John Hunt's scale (Figure 64). Along this outline we predicted where additional wall posts might be found according to the details contained in Hunt's drawing of the house.

The soil stratification at this location revealed the following general profile. At the surface was the recent parking lot fill that was at least 50 cm thick and most of which we removed by machine. Beneath that was a brown silty loam that was clearly mixed and disturbed and contained artifacts from the prehistoric period to the twentieth century. This layer averaged 10-20 cm in thickness and was underlain by Fort St. George layers or at least the 1607 A-horizon of the subsoil. The subsoil was a sandy and cobbly glacial till that was disturbed by numerous Fort St. George intrusions, as well as a few that were identified with Fort Baldwin.

The1607–1608 surface was -35 cm to - 45 cm below datum and was readily identified by a relative abundance of contemporary artifacts. Usually, this surface was stained by charcoal, although even that was hard to find in units on the eastern side. Over most of the area, however, and especially in the central units, there was a layer of debris consisting of daub, charcoal and artifacts (Figure 64). Partially overlapping the debris, but concentrated in the northern units, was another layer of relatively pure gray clay that did not

Figure 65. Hearth area of Admiral Raleigh Gilbert's house: upper left, plan of hearth in excavation units P633-P635, P643-P645 and contiguous units; upper right, close-up of badly heat damaged hearthstones, looking west; lower left, semicircle of coursed stone blocks and cobbles, looking southeast; lower right, reconstruction of semicircular fireplace in earthfast structure based on evidence from the 1630 Allerton house in Kingston, Massachusetts (adapted from Baker 1997, p. 26).

contain as many artifacts. The surface of the clay was often noticed to be scored, creating little ridges and valleys oriented east-west. These were interpreted as fossilized furrows which would be consistent with the obviously mixed agricultural zone lying above. Both the debris and clay were often found associated with the features described below and the different combinations are important to the interpretation of events at Raleigh Gilbert's house.

What was believed to be the hearth area of a residence during the 1999 excavations was confirmed in 2000. Although we had expected the hearth to extend farther to the north, we found that it was confined to P634/P644 and portions of contiguous units. The construction details of this feature are most interesting (Figure 65). First, the subsoil had been dug out to an unknown depth and then a bed of pure clay, the same that was to be used as daubing for the walls, was laid in. Large flagstones of schist set in this clay were the

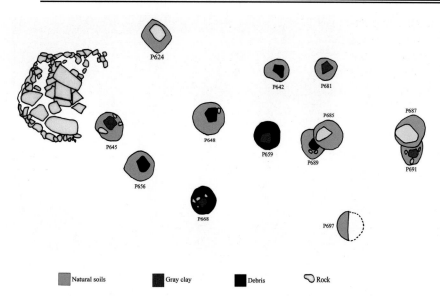

Figure 66. Pattern of postholes and their contents at the admiral's house. A posthole is identified by the unit in which it was mostly contained.

actual hearthstones and their surfaces showed the effects of heat: cracking, delamination, and color change. Around the hearthstones were large boulders. Most of these appeared to have been tumbled out of place and apparently had been disturbed by plowing activities. Originally, they probably formed a fireback. Around all these stones was a semicircle composed of small blocks of schist and cobbles of fieldstone that had been mortared with clay and built to a height of at least several courses. This crude masonry may have provided a foundation for the fireback. The north edge of this construction had been knocked askew, again probably by the plow, but the overall arrangement was still clear. A rounded, or semicircular, hearth area is a logical form in primitive architecture and may have been common in this early period (Fig. 65). The open hearth must have been surmounted by a wattle-and-daub smoke hood and chimney which may have been supported by one of the posts (P645) described below. Many pieces of the chimney daub were found around this end of the house. They differed from wall daub in having a much higher sand content, and the long exposure to heat and smoke had given them a harder firing and more blackened appearance.

The hearth clearly was oriented so that the structure it served was built to the east. In 1999, we had found architectural evidence in that direction consisting of charcoal, daub, and a posthole. In 2000, we set out to locate additional postholes so that we could determine the form, dimensions, and orientation of what we now felt confident was Raleigh Gilbert's house. We also, of course, hoped to learn details about the construction of the house and the activities that occurred within it.

Many new postholes were indeed discovered, but they do not at first glance seem to form a coherent pattern (Figure 66). The problem, however, is greatly alleviated when it is realized that there are differences between them and that the posts they contained were not all contemporary. Most of the postholes contained the mixture of natural soils and rarity of artifacts that typify the first features dug by the colonists, such as the storehouse postholes. Two, however, were filled with the debris (charcoal, daub and artifacts) of a destruction event. Moreover, while five of the post molds were filled with gray clay, four contained debris. Finally, there were four apparent postholes in which we did not find molds. In one case (P697), the excavation revealed only part of the posthole and we did not have time to open up the contiguous unit so the mold could be identified. The other three postholes, however, were entirely exposed and instead of molds we found only large flat rocks. At first, we thought perhaps that these were postholes that were aborted when those impediments were encountered, but the rocks were not really that large and in at least two cases it looked as though the holes had been completely dug and then the rocks were laid in. It now seems likely that these were padstones, or foundation supports for posts (Charles 1981, p. 12.05). They would be an obvious solution when short posts needed extra height, sort of like large shimstones. If they came close to the surface, no mold would be preserved. The presence of both deeply set posts and padstones in the same construction is known from Medieval England (e.g., Dixon 1982, fig. 13.2o).

The inventory of postholes/molds described by content distinguishes four types. There are three postholes with natural fill and clay molds (P645, P681, P691); four postholes with natural fill and molds that contain debris (P642, P648, P656, P689); two post-holes that are filled with debris and have clay molds (P659, P668 [Figure 67]); and three postholes that have natural fill and padstones (P624, P685, P687). There is also the one posthole with natural fill but the mold or support was not ascertained (P697). This discrimination indicates the following sequence of events.

A crude structure was built and inhabited (Figure 68). Sometime during occupation at least the central portion of the building burned as revealed by the heaviest concentration of the debris field and the contents of the post molds in P642, P648, P656 and P689. The posts in each case had burned all the way into the ground and charred pieces of the bases were found at the bottoms of the molds which subsequently were filled with debris. The fire was so hot that it melted glass, copper and brass artifacts.

After an unknown interval, the burned portion of the house was rebuilt. Although we do not know how much time elapsed, the unweathered appearance of the debris suggests that the interval was short. We may imagine that if it occurred during the winter months the rebuilding was hurried, even jury-rigged. The four centrally placed posts that had burned were replaced with new posts (Figure 69). The holes for two of these (P659, P668) were filled with debris confirming the sequence. A fifth post (P687) was apparently set to reinforce a preexisting post, perhaps to stabilize the east end of the structure.

The house was re-occupied, again for an unknown period, and then apparently was abandoned and fell into ruin. That it was not burned upon abandonment is evident in the absence of a second destruction level. Instead, there is the layer of gray clay that was found across the northern side of the house site (see Figure 64). This clay is from the unfired walls or smoke hood/chimney that may have remained standing until the posts deteriorated. Natural weathering washed the clay from the walls and into the hollow postmolds and other depressions in the surface. Most of the artifacts that appeared to be from the clay layer were actually on the old surface and were incorporated in the clay as it flowed around them. Evidence for this hydraulic action, rather than simple deposition from the wall falling over, is clearly stated in the excavators' notes which refer to the clay as being "pooled", "layered", "lensed", and "puddled." These still standing walls might have been what Samuel Maverick (1885) saw

Figure 67. Debris-filled posthole and clay-filled post mold in excavation unit P668. Number 1 is the posthole full of debris, number 2 is the clay mold. Note the chock stones in the hole next to the mold.

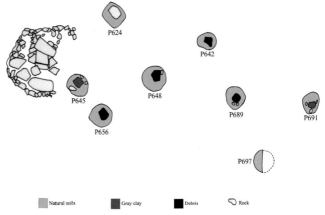

Figure 68. Features relating to the original construction of Admiral Raleigh Gilbert's house. The irregularly set posts could have supported a roof structure, but the walls must have been made of wattle-and-daub, cob, or other impermanent materials.

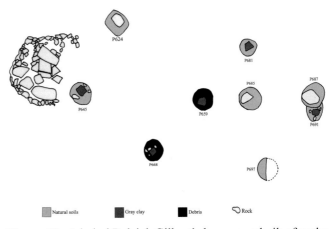

Figure 69. Admiral Raleigh Gilbert's house as rebuilt after the fire. The central posts have been replaced and a reinforcing post added to the east end.

when he visited the site about 1625 and recorded that he found "some old Walles there...which shewed it be the place where they had been." If the walls had been made of cob, which was common in Devonshire (McCann 1995, pp. 3-7), rather than wattle-and-daub, they may well have remained standing for a considerable while (Evans 1974). Cob walls would also be consistent with the irregularity of the posthole pattern and explain the difficulty of defining a precise footprint.

Thus we document the rise and fall of Raleigh Gilbert's house. Many observers, however, have been troubled by the fact that there are not enough posts nor a typical pattern for box-framed, post-and-beam architecture like the storehouse, or even the buttery. Surely, they suppose, Raleigh Gilbert would have lived in no less a construction. But every effort to connect the postholes into regular patterns forming bays has failed, although some ingenious hypotheses have been offered. For example, Morrison (2002, pp. 75-88; updated version presented in Appendix E herein) proposes that rather than the rebuilding of a single structure, there were actually two different houses built on the same site but with slightly different orientations. The regular patterns thus achieved work only if what we uncovered was not the complete footprint of the house(s) and requires that additional features be found outside the area excavated. Except for the southeastern corner still buried beneath the road, however, we would have been most unlucky to have missed at least some indication of these putative features considering the extent of the area we opened up. Morrison also assumes that the clay molds are from posts of the "second" house, although the infilling only describes the final deterioration, not the original setting which could as reasonably have been for the "first" house. Finally, neither orientation of the two houses aligns well with the hearth area. Nevertheless, the Morrison theory is possible and if the opportunity should arise in the future it should be tested by opening up a wider area (an opportunity we were denied when the parking lot was placed off limits after 2000).

Until then we must make do with what we appear to have and that is not the neat box-framed structure exhibited by the storehouse. Instead, we seem to have a much more primitive architecture composed of irregular post placement and perhaps some form of crotchet construction (Charles 1981, 1982; Carson et al. 1988, p. 130) that used unshaped forked posts and scant elements that were nailed together instead of being joined by the sophisticated and more time-consuming mortise and tenon. A seventeenth-century English description of such construction in Ireland fits our archaeological evidence remarkably well:

> They build their cabins by putting two forked sticks of such length as they intend the height of the building, or if they design it longer three or four such forks, into the ground and on them they lay other long sticks which are the ridge timber. Then they raise the wall, which they make of clay and straw tempered with water, and this they call mud; raised to a sufficient height which is perhaps four feet. Then they lay other small sticks with one end on the ridge pole and the other on the wall. These they wattle with small hazels, and then cover them with straw or coarse grass. (Evans 1974: 58)

Similar construction is specifically described for the chapel and houses at Jamestown: "We built a homely thing like a barne, set upon Cratchets, covered with rafts, sedge, and earth; so was also the walls: the best of our houses [were] of the like curiosity; but for the most part farre much worse workmanship" (Smith 1631). And indeed crotchet construction appears to be confirmed in recent excavations at Jamestown (Kelso et al. 2001, pp. 15-17; Kelso 2006, pp. 80-84). That a parallel building program existed at Fort St. George is reasonable and seems to be documented by no less an authority than William Strachey. Privy to firsthand information from Popham, Strachey specifically referred to "ill-built and bleak Cottages": *yet did our men, in their ill-built and bleak Cottages, endure one whole winter there, without any great losse or danger* (1612, p. 35). In other words, despite being ill-built and bleak, their simple dwellings proved adequate to survive the harsh conditions. Cottage, here, is clearly being used in the disparaging sense given in the *Oxford English Dictionary* as "a small temporary erection used for shelter: a cot, hut, shed, etc." What could be more revealing of the housing situation or coincident with the archaeological evidence?

It is easy to imagine that while the few carpenters and other trained craftsmen were put to work on the all-important storehouse, the necessity for housing the colonists and protecting them from the rapidly deteriorating weather forced the hasty erection of crude shelters by the less competent. The admiral may have envisioned something more sophisticated – and the fact that he apparently had brought at least one glazed window along with him suggests that he did – but even he was forced to compromise (actually, he was off exploring for half the time during this period and so he would have been distracted from supervising the construction of his house). Likewise, it has been noted that while the storehouse at the 1604 French settlement on St. Croix was timber-framed, "the other buildings were evidently no more than...huts" (Biggar 1922, pl. LXXI). But it should be noted that

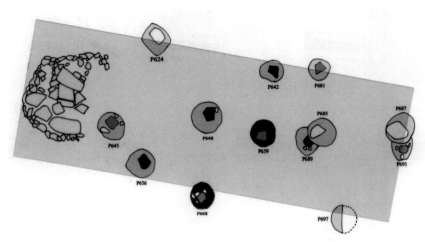

Figure 70. The approximate footprint of Admiral Raleigh Gilbert's house is indicated by the shaded area. The form probably was not as regular as shown here or by John Hunt on his map, but the dimensions, orientation and location are remarkably close to what Hunt drew.

while these "huts" may have been "simple, one-story, unframed, nail-joined structures" (Cotter 1994, p. 17), they can still "fulfil the most basic domestic requirements" (Charles 1981, p. 12.05) and be put together in a fraction of the time required for timber framing. In describing the need for such "transient hovels," Abbott Lowell Cummings (1979a, p. 19) reasonably suggests that "the newly arrived Englishmen may indeed have borrowed from some long-familiar subvernacular building traditions in throwing together the rude structures which were to shelter them for the first winter at least." In fact, this should be our expectation, rather than neat little box-framed houses for which they had neither the time nor resources.

Although the irregularity of construction does not allow us to draw a precise footprint for Raleigh Gilbert's house, the distribution of features define its general dimensions and orientation (Figure 70). Once again, we find that John Hunt was remarkably accurate, although it must be acknowledged that the dimensions of the structure were approximately 33' by 11', instead of 30' by 12', the orientation was 100° east of north rather than the predicted 110°, and the location was a few feet off, but only the most intolerable critic would carp about these minor deviations.

The sample of artifacts recovered from the 1999 excavations at this location was greatly enhanced in 2000 (Figure 71, Table 5). Enhanced, that is, in quantity rather than variety. Although there are a few new types, the same basic categories of artifacts are the same. The lack of variety reflects the parsimonious provisioning of the colony – even a limit to the personal possessions of one of the leaders – and especially the fact that there was only one resupply before Fort St. George was abandoned. The types of artifacts, however, reveal that someone of quality lived in this house. The quantity is partly due to this social distinction, but probably owes even more to the fact that the structure burned while it was being occupied and goods could not be saved from the destruction.

The basic categories of artifacts are divided into ceramics, glass, and various metals. The ceramics are predominantly earthenwares, mostly from North Devon, but also from Totnes and other as yet unidentified West Country sources. There are also delftware from England or Holland, as well as Iberian olive jar and German stoneware.

The North Devon includes both coarse and fine wares. The former are mostly storage containers, such as baluster jars, and large serving vessels, such as bowls. Some of these North Devon jars and vessels are coarsely tempered, but the great majority are not. The finer wares are relatively thin and have a more refined texture, and the glazes are more evenly applied. Most exhibit a family resemblance to the coarser North Devon, and are probably just finer versions meant for the table.

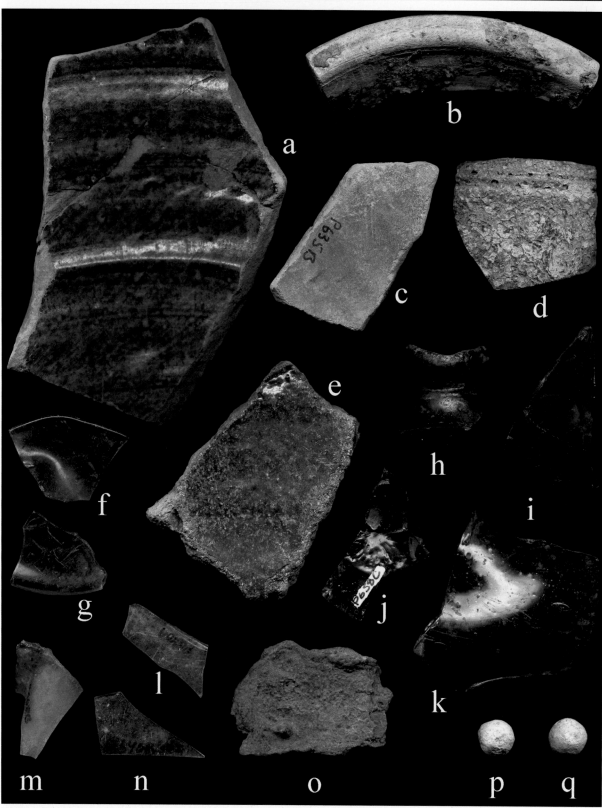

Figure 71. More artifacts from Admiral Raleigh Gilbert's house (see also Figure 63): a-b, North Devon baluster jar (P649DC1, P697D); c-d, West of England (P635B, P642FD3); e, Totnes (P659E1); f, heat-altered wine glass rim (P697D); g, wine glass foot (P627A); h, heat-altered case bottle rim (P642FD3); i, case bottle base (P648E2); j-k, flask bases (P656A, P658C); l-n, window glass (m heat-altered) (P640A, P640B, P668B); o, armor, possibly tasset lame (P635C); p-q, .39 cal. lead balls (P623D). (1:1)

The Totnes pottery was made just down the river Dart from Compton Castle, the Gilbert family seat. Totnes (Allan and Pope 1990) is distinguished from North Devon by a ware that is even coarser and very sandy. It is also distinctive in containing a scatter of black mica inclusions. The color is reddish brown, but the core of thick pieces is gray. The glaze is a thin yellow-green with black mottling. Handles indicate that cooking pots and perhaps pipkins made of this ware were present.

Unclassified sherds fall between these established types, sometimes differing only in minor characteristics of ware or glaze. While many of these are expected to be of West Country origin, some could just as well have been manufactured in other parts of England, or even on the continent.

Distinctive foreign wares from the continent are represented by the examples from Iberia, Holland, and Germany. Fragments of Spanish or Portuguese "olive jars" are common in Raleigh Gilbert's house. Such jars were popular shipping and storage containers throughout Europe and its colonies in the sixteenth to eighteenth centuries. The Middle Style D rim, the only form that we have found at the site, is appropriate for the early seventeenth century. These jars could be, and were, used for a variety of products but were particularly suited for liquids.

The finest earthenware yet found at the site is represented by the delftware, and much that we have found in ten years of excavation was concentrated at Raleigh Gilbert's house. Many sherds of blue-and-white decorated Delft were found around the hearth. These sherds are too small to hazard a guess at vessel forms, but the decorations suggest they may have been from tableware. Monochrome dark blue sherds from the debris field in the center of the house, however, were from an apothecary jar of the typical *albarello* form. While it is still uncertain when the delftware industry truly began in England, it seems probable that at this period most if not all Delft was imported from Holland (Crossley 1990, pp. 260, 264).

Another distinctive foreign ceramic is the stoneware from Germany. The only kind that we have found at Fort St. George is the type commonly called "Bellarmine" or "Bartmann." Vessels of this type are covered with a mottled brown salt glaze on the exterior and may be decorated with molded medallions and face masks. The style of the molded decorations from Fort St. George dates the vessels to the period 1590-1607. Similar examples are known from Jamestown (Kelso 1995, fig. 3). Jugs are the only form and at the time were popular shipping and storage containers for valued liquids, such as wine, ale, or cider. Fragments of at least two jugs have been recovered from Raleigh Gilbert's house.

Glass artifacts from the admiral's house are divided into four groups: bottles, tableware, ornaments, and window glass. Bottles form the largest group, and among the numerous pieces two types have been identified. The first type is the case bottle which is made of blue-green or pale green glass and has square sides, a slightly concave base, rounded shoulders, short neck and a simple everted rim. Case bottles were meant to be packed in boxes and were used for the transport and storage of the best spiritous liquors, such as brandy. Fragments of at least eight case bottles have been found in Raleigh Gilbert's house. The second type is a fully round bottle with a long neck called a flask. These flasks are not to be confused with the well-known, but later, "wine bottles." Typically, they are smaller and made of light green glass. Only recently recognized as being an artifact of this period, these flasks were made in England and were probably used for a variety of liquids.

Tableware is distinguished by the thinness of the metal and a coloration that ranges from a very pale green to almost clear, as well as such formal attributes as foot rings. Because of the thinness of the metal, the glasses broke into many small fragments from at least a half dozen examples. Forms are difficult to reconstruct, but the available evidence and absence of stems, knops or prunts indicate the presence of stemless wine glasses and perhaps ale glasses. The admiral clearly brought along the appropriate glasses for his beverages.

Ornaments include buttons and beads. The buttons are all made of black glass that has been wound around an iron loop that forms the attachment. There are two sizes, small (ca. 8mm in diameter) and large (ca. 12mm). More than fifty of these buttons have been discovered within Raleigh Gilbert's house, leading us to the conclusion that he was dressed as a gentleman should be dressed, even in the wilderness.

Glass beads were not as common in the admiral's house as they had been in the storehouse where the bulk of the trade goods obviously were kept. Nevertheless, it is noteworthy that of the dozen or so beads from this location the rarer (and presumably more valuable) blue beads outnumber the white by a ratio of 2-to-1. In the storehouse, on the other hand, the ratio was more than ten white to one blue. It may be that in the world of barter Raleigh Gilbert, the principal trader, controlled the higher "denomination" of beads. Two pendant beads made of clear faceted glass may also fall into this special class, or they could have been personal possessions of Raleigh Gilbert's.

The presence of window glass at the admiral's house is a sure indication that Raleigh Gilbert came prepared to camp out in style as befitted his status. A piece of glass with traces of the lead cames provides evidence that at least one prefabricated window was included in his baggage. The fact that such an architectural luxury does not seem to fit the archaeological picture of his primitive dwelling (but see Cummings 1979a, fig. 23 for just such an example) emphasizes the discordance between his expectations and the ultimate realities of the situation.

Metal artifacts consisted mostly of wrought iron nails. Hundreds of these have been recovered from the ruins of the admiral's house. The large number and the association with the debris and gray clay layers indicate not only that these were architectural hardware, but that the house had largely been joined with nails again attesting to the more primitive quality of construction. Other iron artifacts include a badly deteriorated dagger blade and pieces of armor.

Items made of lead form the second most important metallic group. Lead balls, sprue, spillage, and scrap were found in front of the fireplace. Clearly, Gilbert was involved in the manufacture of his own ammunition. Of the nineteen balls, fourteen averaged only 10mm (.39 in.) in diameter, a caliber that would be most appropriate for a pistol and further proof that the inhabitant was a leader of the colony.

There are a few unidentified items made of copper or copper alloy. Interestingly, there is no evidence of the copper artifacts that had been made for the Indian trade at Jamestown (Kelso, Luccketti, and Straube 1999, fig. 10). Perhaps that industry was not developed until the colonists had been in place for a few years and learned the natives' preferences.

As noted above, the artifacts were found to be most common around the hearth and in the heaviest concentration of debris in the center of the structure. But there are distinctions between the proveniences of various artifact types. For example, while decorated delftware and lead munitions were clustered around the hearth, the coarse earthenwares and glasswares were more common in the debris field. These differences probably reflect spatial organization of activity and storage areas. On the other hand, the distributions of some artifacts serve to integrate the entire location. Most outstanding in this regard is the distribution of the Bellarmine. Fragments of one of the jugs were found both around the hearth and in the center of the structure, and in a variety of contexts that included a post mold, the 1607-1608 floor level, and the clay layer. Pieces of another jug were recovered from the central debris field and the very eastern end of the location (P688). These interconnections endow the house site with an internal integrity that further supports our architectural reconstruction.

The artifacts and the archaeology also suggest a correction to the historical record. The large number of artifacts in the debris, many of which were altered by fire or heat, attest to the fact that the original structure burned while it was occupied and that a quantity of goods must have been destroyed. A widely cited comment by Sir Ferdinando Gorges (1658) states that "their store-house and most of their provisions burnt the Winter before [i.e., 1607-1608]." Thus we were somewhat puzzled when the excavation of the storehouse revealed that while it had burned, the firing obviously occurred after it had been emptied of all but discarded or lost items, presumably when the fort was abandoned in the fall of 1608. Gorges recorded these recollections fifty years later and his memory may not have served him well (other important inaccuracies in this document have been noted by Quinn and Quinn 1983, pp. 338-347). In fact, a rather different report, probably written by Gorges less than fifteen years after the event, would seem to be more compatible with the archaeological evidence: "in the depth [of winter] thereof, their lodgings and stores were burnt and they thereby were wondrously distressed" (Thayer 1892, p. 92). That is, it was not the storehouse that burned, but stores that were in some of their lodgings. One of these lodgings must have been Raleigh Gilbert's and his distress would have been quite noteworthy.

Buttery and Corporal's House

The buttery was close to the main storehouse, but was separate and closely guarded because of its contents. It was also the nearest building to the water gate in order to minimize the distance that the heavy butts would have to be transported. As drawn by Hunt, the buttery was a simple rectangular building with a doorway that faced the storehouse (Figure 72). Windows high in the gable end and a dormer in the roof suggest that there may have been a loft. Since it was a storage facility there was no chimney. The attached corporal's house, however, was a heated single-story structure.

This location was first investigated by us in 1994 during the course of our preliminary exploration. At that time we encountered a posthole in the southeast corner of unit P186 that we attributed to Fort St. George (Brain 1995, p. 45). The post mold was only 15 cm in diameter, which was smaller than the post that we thought might belong to the storehouse and it was too far removed to be part of that structure. Nor could we connect it to any other feature. A review of the field notes for Hadlock's excavations (Lane 1962), however, revealed that they thought they had found a posthole nearby in their trench 10 between our units P188 and P189 (Figure 73). They believed their posthole probably related to Fort Baldwin, but by now we were skeptical of their identifications and it appeared that both postholes were well within the vicinity of where Hunt placed the buttery and corporal's house. We decided to test this theory in 2001.

Our P186 posthole and Hadlock's putative posthole were about 2 m apart and aligned approximately 110° east of north. If the two posts were part of the same bent then the structure they supported would be oriented precisely with the storehouse as Hunt illustrates. The interval between the posts would seem to be improbably small for a single-bay building, but we were sufficiently intrigued to hypothesize several possible posthole arrangements, depending upon whether the postholes were part of the same bent, belonged to different bents or were irregularly placed within the same structure, or were related to different structures (i.e., one to the buttery, the other to the corporal's house). Starting with the simplest reconstruction that assumed the posts were from the same bent, we predicted additional postholes at 2 m intervals from them along lines 20° and 110° east of north. Excavation units were then selected in 2001 based upon these predictions (Figure 73).

The results of the 2001 excavations were something of a disappointment in regard to features that we could relate to Fort St. George. Of four predicted postholes, three did not materialize, two perhaps because

Figure 72. The buttery and corporal's house as drawn by John Hunt.

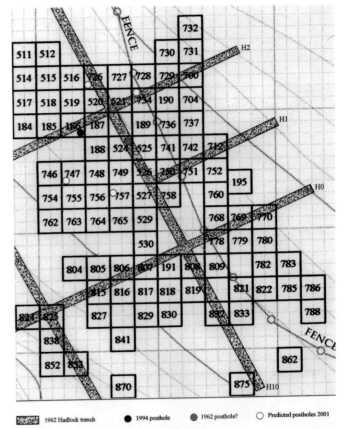

Figure 73. Plan of 1994, 2001, 2003-2005 excavations in the vicinity of the buttery and corporal's house. Hadlock trenches scored the area, but happily missed the postholes and molds that define the footprint of a building.

they had been obliterated by Hadlock trenches, although in other situations we have successfully identified features that they had trenched through. We did find one posthole, however, close to where one had been predicted at the intersection of units P748, P749, P756 and P757. It alone, of course, could not substantiate our hypothetical model but it did contribute to the evidence for earthfast construction in the area, although we were no closer to establishing form or dimensions of the structure much less function. It still seemed to be no coincidence, however, that the two known postholes, P186 and P757, and the possible Hadlock feature were in the vicinity of where Hunt placed the buttery and corporal's house.

Therefore, we returned in 2003 to explore this location further, starting with the two known postholes as the primary reference point. The post molds in these holes were approximately 2.5 m apart and a line drawn through them trended northwest-southeast. The new excavations were laid out at appropriate intervals in these directions with the hope that more postholes would be found along this hypothetical wall line. Additional units were also placed nearby in an effort to rediscover the feature encountered by Hadlock's crew so that it could be identified and hopefully integrated within the plan of whatever structure could be reconstructed at this location.

A large block of units (P511-P512, P514-P519) was excavated in an attempt to find more postholes on the line to the northwest of the known holes. We were also hoping to find other structural evidence: in 1994 a large flat block of gneiss was found just to the north of the posthole in P186 (see Figure 31), and recalling the hearth of such stones in the admiral's house we cherished the hope we were at the edge of a similar feature here. That hope was dashed, however, when no more blocks of stone were found. Nor were there any postholes or any other evidence of building activity in these units. The only cultural features encountered were charcoal-stained lenses in P512 and possibly P515 that may have been the remnants of aboriginal hearths. Native artifacts were relatively common in these units, although pieces of charcoal and calcined bone were not as numerous as would be expected if hearths had been present.

Units P520-P521 and P524-P526 were opened primarily to relocate Hadlock's trenches and especially to find that segment where it was believed a posthole had been encountered (our prediction was that it would be found in unit P524). We found Hadlock's trenches where we expected them to be, running on a diagonal through units P520-P521 and P524-P527. We found no evidence of a posthole, however, nor any other feature they might have interpreted as one. There was a large piece of charcoal in P525 that could have come from a post, and a disconformity where the subsoil appeared to have been dug out in the southwestern corner of P525 and adjacent units that might indicate where a posthole had been thoroughly excavated by Hadlock's crew.

The final three units (P527, P529, P530) were placed to intersect the hypothetical wall line to the southeast. At last we were successful, finding a posthole in P529 that was the same size as the other postholes previously recorded. The post mold was closely aligned with other molds and maintained the same 2.5 m interval.

Although we had not yet defined a structure at this location, we believed that we were in the process of discovering one. The hypothetical wall line had been extended and a vacant space had been revealed between it and the storehouse. Thus, we hypothesized that if more remains of a building were present they were to be found to the east and perhaps south of the latest excavations. Another posthole found in unit P778 in 2001 encouraged this hypothesis, although at that time it was speculated that it and an associated series of post molds might have been associated with the provost's house (Brain 2001, p. 10).

In 2004, we acted upon our hypothesis and the excavations were expanded to the east and south in an effort to find more postholes that would form a coherent whole and provide dimensions for a structure at this location. Since the three known postholes in line were spaced 2.5 m apart, new units were established at approximately that distance both along that line to the south and parallel to it where we hoped to find the eastern wall. The first objective was to confirm the existing wall and because excavations in 2003 had failed to discover evidence of it to the north (which would have been unlikely anyway since it would have brought it too close to the storehouse) we set up units P808 and P819 to the southeast of the posthole that had been found in P529. If the line was valid, it was our expectation that a 2.5 m extension in this direction would lead us to another posthole either in the southwestern corner of P808 or the northwestern corner of P819. We had not seen such a feature in P191 which is contiguous to the west of P808, but that unit had been an isolated test in 1994 and it must be admitted that the lack of perspective and expectation would have hindered our observations. As it was, we had to work hard to find the posthole and mold, but then they appeared precisely as predicted at the interface of units P808 and P819 (Figure 74). Not only was the mold on line at the proper interval, but it also gave us our first indications of form and dimensions of the building since it could represent the southwestern corner: a line drawn at a right angle to the wall at this point goes straight through the P778 post mold found in 2001. The distance between these two posts is about 1.75 m, and since P778 would hypothetically be a gable end post then the overall width of the building could be estimated at approximately 3.5 m.

The accuracy of this dimension was confirmed by two more postholes and molds that were discovered in units P760 and P742 (Figure 75). Together they form a line roughly parallel to the established wall line, but at a distance of 3-3.5 m. A probable post mold was also found in P729, although a posthole could not be distinguished in the very cobbly soil. Nevertheless, this post would be the northeast corner of the building. A feature discovered in unit P521 in 2003 that was tentatively identified as a possible posthole and mold could now be interpreted as the gable end post in the north wall. At this stage, the evidence indicated that we had a structure that was about 25' long and half that in width, but we could not be certain that we had the entire footprint: the southeast corner post had not yet been found and it was possible that the building extended farther east to the edge of the bank. It also was not yet clear whether this structure represented the buttery or the adjoining corporal's house as drawn by Hunt.

These uncertainties were resolved in 2005. First, six units (P700, P704, P712, P731, P732, P752) were placed

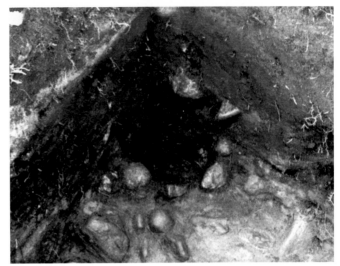

Figure 74. Posthole and post mold in excavation unit P808, southwest corner. The dark area is the mold which is surrounded by chock stones.

Figure 75. Posthole and post mold in excavation unit P742. The mold shows the round post 15 cm in diameter typical of this location, and contains calcined bone giving it the lighter color. The posthole was about 50 cm in diameter and in the fill at the spot marked "X" was a unique glass bottle of probable French origin (see Figure 77n).

to the east of the defined building to ensure that it had not extended any farther eastward. The structure was already very close to the edge of the bank, which did not appear to have eroded very much, and so it seemed unlikely that there was any more of it in this direction, but we had to be sure. A number of features were encountered, but none could be related to the buttery or even to Fort St. George. The most prominent were two Hadlock trenches that were revealed, as expected, in P700 and P712. Despite the lack of good contexts, seventeenth-century artifacts were relatively abundant. Clearly, however, the buttery did not extend any farther to the east and we could be confident that we had defined it on three sides: the west, north and east. We were now free to search for the last main element of the structure.

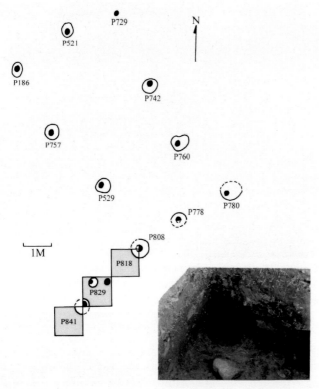

Figure 76. Postholes and post molds that form the outline of the buttery, as well as probable evidence of the corporal's house. Although a small posthole and mold in P829 could not be related, two new posts in that unit align with the south wall of the buttery, providing evidence for the corporal's house. Lower right, the posthole and post mold in the southwest corner of P829 is typical of those found at this location (see Figure 74). The posthole cut down through the burned layer seen on the right in the photo which is a characteristic feature found in the vicinity of the vice admiral's house nearby. As demonstrated here, the burning must have occurred before the buttery was built.

The missing corner of the buttery was predicted to be at approximately the intersection of units P769, P770, P779, and P780. P768 had been partially excavated in 2004, and since it had not been finished it was reopened in order to complete the picture and provide additional working space. In all five units, the usual stratification was encountered which consisted of topsoil, a mixed agricultural zone up to 25 cm in thickness, the reddish brown soil, and finally subsoil at approximately -290 cm below datum. In P768, P769 and P770 the only major feature noticed during excavation was a segment of a Hadlock trench which ran diagonally across all three units. When the south wall of P770 was profiled, however, a feature was observed that began in an ash layer at the top of the reddish brown soil and intruded down into subsoil. This feature overlapped into P769 and was about the size of a posthole typical of the kind we had been finding for the buttery. Units P779 and P780 were then opened up and the posthole was finally exposed at a depth of approximately -273 cm. It was very hard to see and we probably would have missed it here, too, if we had not had the vertical cross section to work from and the expectation that the corner post had to be in the vicinity.

With the footprint of the basic buttery structure now completely defined, we turned to the question of the corporal's house. Hunt shows such a building attached to the south side of the buttery, but it is unclear whether it was placed parallel to the long axis of the buttery or at right angles to it (see Figure 72). Our best interpretation of Hunt's rather odd perspective rendering was that it was perpendicular, but as insurance we took both possibilities into consideration when designing our excavation plan. Units P782, P783, P785, P786 and P788 were placed along the edge of the bank to look for evidence of parallel construction to the southeast of the buttery, while P818, P829, P830, P832, and P841 were positioned to intercept perpendicular construction to the southwest.

The only noteworthy feature in the units excavated to the southeast of the buttery was found in the northeast corner of P782. It resisted our efforts to interpret it as a Fort St. George posthole, but neither did it have all the characteristics of an aboriginal hearth of the sort commonly found along the edge of the bank. Thus it remains an anomaly. Artifacts recovered from the feature and contiguous units were equally ambiguous: they included native pottery, stone flakes and calcined bone, as well as North Devon, Bellarmine, Delft, tobacco pipes, flask glass, lead munitions, nails and daub. Therefore, while a strong colonial presence is certainly verified, a specific structure was not identified in place.

Our excavations to the southwest, however, were more rewarding (Figure 76). A fine Fort St. George posthole was found in the southwestern corner of unit P829, overlapping into the northeast corner of P841. This hole was similar to those defining the buttery, being about 40 cm in diameter and containing the organic mold of a round post 15 cm in diameter. A second probable post mold was found in the northeastern corner

Figure 77. Artifacts from the location of the buttery and corporal's house: a, Totnes base (P742B); b-c, North Devon (P736C, P742C); d, Bellarmine (P728B); e, Bellarmine medallion (P751B); f, Iberian olive jar (P729D); g, lead spill (P729C); h, lead spill showing impression of wood board (P730C); i, lead sprue (P819A), j, .32 cal. lead ball (P730D); k, lead shot (P730C); l, English flint showing use with strike-a-light (P729B); m, typical clay tobacco pipe with small belly bowl and heart-shaped heel (P729E); n, unique glass bottle of probable French origin (P742C). (1:1, except n 1:2)

of P829, although it differed in that it may have been punched into the ground as there was no evidence of a posthole. This mold was filled with water-laid sand indicating that the post had been pulled out. These two posts, together with the southwest corner post of the buttery found in P808 in 2004, form a straight line at right angles to the long axis of the buttery. These posts were set at intervals of about 1.5 m (five feet) which suggests a smaller structure than the buttery. All together, these are tantalizing clues pointing to the corporal's house. Proof, however, requires a second parallel wall and this we could not define before we ran out of time. A desperate attempt was made in the excavation of unit P832, but the only feature found was a segment of Hadlock's trench 10. Thus while the evidence is inconclusive, it is sufficient to reinforce John Hunt's credibility.

That the identification of this location with the buttery and corporal's house might indeed be more than idle speculation is supported by the quantities, kinds and distributions of artifacts which reveal activities characteristic of storage and residence. Our excavations in 1994 had recovered a rich assortment of artifacts attributable to the early seventeenth century in units P184-P190. Hadlock's trenches 2 and 10 had also been very productive in this area. Our 2001 and 2003-2005 excavations contributed hundreds of new items and

Table 6. Early seventeenth-century artifacts found at the location of the buttery and corporal's house.

CERAMICS

West of England[1]	318
Olive Jar	5
Delft	11
Bellarmine	23

TOBACCO PIPES 45

GLASS

Bottle	63
Wine/ale glass	14
Bead	6
Window	9
Mirror	1

IRON

Nail	147
Armor	1

LEAD/PEWTER

Munition[2]	51
Miscellaneous	1

COPPER/BRASS 12

OTHER MATERIALS[3] 4

[1] Including North Devon, Totnes and other West of England types, as well as unclassified.

[2] Lead pistol and musket balls, sprue, drips and scrap.

[3] Flint.

Figure 78. Provost's house as drawn by John Hunt.

confirmed this as a major locus in the occupation of Fort St. George. At least 318 sherds of coarse English earthenwares from the West Country (Figure 77, Table 6) appropriate to the period were recovered. There were relatively few sherds of Bellarmine, and these mostly seemed to be from the jug with the "1599" medallion. The Iberian olive jar is also represented. Glass was rare but pieces of both case bottles and flasks were present, and there was one nearly complete bottle from the P742 posthole. All of these containers would have been appropriate for the storing and dispensing of potables. A residential component is indicated by the relatively numerous pipe fragments, a few glass beads, and a thimble, that ubiquitous symbol of domesticity (Noël Hume 1969a, p. 255). The mandatory military element is represented by the manufacture of lead munitions. Among the latter is a spill that clearly shows the impression of a wood board on one side (Figure 77h), suggesting that perhaps the building had a floor. Other evidence of the structure is provided by dozens of wrought nails and fragments of daub. These artifacts are distributed in a tight cluster, with the highest concentrations being found within the outline of the buttery in units P189, P748, P749, P757. All together, the evidence is compelling in support of an identification à la Hunt.

Provost's House

The structure identified as the provost's house by John Hunt was situated about 45' (13.5m) east of the storehouse according to the scale on the Hunt map (see Figure 5). This distance would place most of the building over and beyond the current bank on the shore of Atkins Bay. Therefore, if Hunt's measurement was accurate, then most of the building must have been lost to erosion. Such a loss would be regrettable for it is depicted on the map as the second largest private residence after Raleigh Gilbert's house. Actually, it is shown as a compound structure consisting of a main house with at least one wing on the east side (Figure 78). Both the house and wing have their own chimneys. It may be that if the principal inhabitant was truly intended to serve as the provost marshal[9] of the colony then the wing was to be the gaol. An architectural feature of note, and of possible archaeological importance, is that Hunt drew in wall posts on the main house. These are not seen on the immediately neighboring structures which could indicate either that they were of inferior construction or that they were simply too small for such artistic detail.

Although most of the structure may have been destroyed, we hoped that we might find evidence of a corner that would at least attest to its existence. Accordingly, four units – P778, P809, P821, P822 – were excavated at the edge of the bank in 2001 (see Figure 73). The 1962 excavations had revealed that the highest concentrations of seventeenth-century artifacts were to be found along the shore (Lane 1962) and in 1964 Wendell Hadlock returned to "mine" this general area (Lane 1966). The depression left from his excavation was still visible to the north of our units which were

---

[9] According to John Smith, Captain Ellis Best was designated marshal of the colony (Quinn and Quinn 1983, p. 353).

Figure 79. Artifacts from the area between the buttery/corporal's house and the vice admiral's house that Hunt identified with the provost's and munition master's houses: a, North Devon (P906B); b, Totnes (P875B); c-f, Delft (P906D1, P889C); g-i, Bellarmine (P917C, P889C); j, wine glass foot (P906D); k, case bottle (P833B); l, flask (P875B); m, clay tobacco pipe (P916B); n, .73 cal. lead ball (P906B); o, .55 cal. lead ball (P917B); p, lead sprue with shot still attached (P906A); q-r, lead sprue (P906D, P917B); s-t, lead spills (P917B, P906D). (1:1)

carefully placed to avoid this activity. The four units excavated at this location in 2001 provided minimal support for the proposition that we were in the vicinity of a structure. A dark organic post mold was bisected at the interface between units P778 and P809. The mold was 10 cm in diameter and it clearly tapered to a point toward the bottom. It appeared to sit in a shallow posthole, but the sharpened point suggests that it may have been set primarily by being driven into the ground (although no stress lines were observed in the surrounding soil). Such a method of setting posts is referred to as puncheon (Carson, et al. 1988, p. 125) and is the most primitive form of earthfast construction.

Further evidence of the puncheon technique might be four more molds that formed a line in P778. These were similar in size to the first post mold but contained a sandy fill indicating that the posts had been pulled before rotting. It was not determined if the posts were tapered, but they definitely were not set in holes. The question in 2001 was whether these molds formed part of the provost's house or some other structure. It was suggested that they might even indicate a fence line which would explain the dotted enclosures Hunt drew around many of the structures, including the provost's house. The puncheon technique and small size of the posts would be consistent with fencing, or perhaps palisades for further protection within the fort (Outlaw 1990, p. 20; Baker 1997, p. 25; Noël Hume and Noël Hume 2001, p. 99, pp. 134-137). In 2004, however, all these features were included within the buttery and/or corporal's house (q.v.). On present evidence we conclude that the provost's house was never built.

Artifacts from these excavations were surprisingly sparse, especially considering the observation by Hadlock's crew that seventeenth-century items were most numerous along the shore (Lane 1962). There were, however, West Country ceramics, fragments of glass, and lead munitions, as well as fine pieces of Bellarmine and tobacco pipes (Figure 79).

Figure 80. Munition master's house as drawn by John Hunt.

Munition Master's House

John Hunt drew a small structure about 20' (6 m) east of the storehouse that he identified as the munition master's house (Figure 80). Although appearing to be hardly more than a shack, its placement on the main square indicates the importance of the occupant and his office. Possibly the officer was Edward Harlow who was designated Master of the Ordnance for the colony according to John Smith (Quinn and Quinn 1983, p. 353; Bradford 2001).

Two of Hadlock's trenches crossed this area in 1962 (see Figure 73) and from them were recovered a moderate number of seventeenth-century artifacts, including West Country ceramics, tobacco pipes, and lead munitions. Of even greater importance, it was reported that a posthole and some rotten wood was encountered in a segment of his trench 0 (Lane 1962). According to our best placement of the Hadlock trenches on the ground, it appeared that the particular segment coincided most closely with our units P815 and P816. These and five contiguous units were opened in 2001 to investigate what Hadlock had found. We also excavated eight more units between P824 and P895 at our best placement of the Munition Master's house on the ground according to John Hunt.

Unfortunately, both efforts failed to find any convincing evidence of seventeenth-century construction. Whatever Hadlock's crew had found in the first location was either destroyed by their trenching or had been misinterpreted. Although several shadowy features were observed, none was a convincing posthole. The rotten wood turned out to be a natural layer of reddish soil. A stack of flat pieces of schist in P817 created a brief flurry of excitement, especially when a typical white glass bead was found under one piece. But then machine-cut nails and a fragment of whiteware in close association revealed that our feature was a nineteenth-century footing. At the second location, the only definite cultural features exposed were more segments of Hadlock's trenches in P825, P838 and P853, a circle of rocks that may have been a nineteenth- or twentieth-century dry well in P870, and a twentieth-century utility trench in P895. Two more units excavated in 2004, P1017 and P1030, also were devoid of any features attributable to Fort St. George, although a posthole containing cut nails was found in P1017.

Fort St. George artifacts from these excavations included a fine assortment of North Devon, Totnes and Bellarmine ceramics, glass, and lead munitions (Figure 79), but none of course could be identified with a certain Fort St. George context. Notably under-represented are architectural remains such as wrought nails and daub which further reinforces the absence of major constructional activity at this location. It is possible that whatever Hunt had envisioned was combined with the nearby structure identified on his map as the vice admiral's house.

Vice Admiral's House

Although none of the colonists is identified as vice admiral of the colony, it has been most reasonably suggested that a logical candidate might be found in the person of Edward Popham because of his high social status (John Bradford, pers. comm., 2001). Edward is not mentioned in the Davies journal, nor in Gorges' letters or memoires, nor in John Smith's list of officers. In fact, the only reference we have to his presence is an offhand mention in George Popham's will (Thayer 1892, p. 250). If indeed he did make it to the Sagadahoc, the silence in the documents indicates his influence was minor despite his social position. But that very silence in the 1608 legal proceedings (Banks 1929) also proves that he did not return home early on either the *Mary and John* or *Gift of God*, for surely if he had been at hand his cousin Sir Francis Popham would have called him as a friendly witness for the family's interests. Thus he must have stayed with the colony the entire year and would have required a residence in Fort St. George.

John Hunt indicates that this structure was located about 50' (15 m) east of the storehouse (see Figure 5). Hunt drew a very modest house, probably consisting only of a single room about 10' square (Figure 81). There is a chimney on the west gable end, and a doorway on the south side faces the market place. Lacking is any indication of wall posts, which could reflect a less intrusive form of construction (that in turn would leave even more ephemeral archaeological remains) or might merely be due to the smaller scale of the building that deterred Hunt from adding such architectural detail.

Figure 81. Vice admiral's house as drawn by John Hunt.

We intensively explored this location in 2001-2004. Our excavations were again guided by our best reconstruction of where the vice admiral's house should be according to Hunt's positioning and scaling (see Figure 32). In our exploration of the storehouse we discovered as we moved south that preservation of Fort St. George features was enhanced due primarily to protective layers of overburden that had been added through natural and human agency. We hoped for a similar situation in this area east of the storehouse, and indeed the excavations at this present location revealed some stratigraphy missing farther north. Whereas in the vicinity of the structures discussed above we generally found a simple sequence of sod, disturbed plowzone, and subsoil into which seventeenth-century features might have intruded, we now encountered some B-horizons and even A-horizons near the top of the subsoil that were contemporary with Fort St. George, although we rarely identified an actual living surface. Offsetting this advantage somewhat were several nineteenth- and twentieth-century intrusions that cut through this part of the site (Figure 82).

The primary effort in 2001 was a north-south series of ten units (P905, P915, P925, P935, P945, P955, P964, P973, P982, P990) that formed a trench which we hoped would intersect some part of the vice admiral's house. Ten more side units (P941, P942, P944, P956, P957, P958, P963, P965, P966, P967) were added in order to follow up on intriguing features and artifact concentrations. The most significant structural features discovered in the 2001 excavations were what appeared to be two postholes in units P915 and P956/P965. No post molds were observed, presumably because the holes were defined only near their respective bottoms below the posts, so we can only consider them probable postholes. One of these did happen to lie precisely on the predicted line of the south wall of the house, but no mates were discovered. The only other possible evidence for a building at this location was an extensive area of burned and heat-altered soils. These layers were found in the western two-thirds of units P905 and P915, and in P925 until they were cut through by a Fort Baldwin

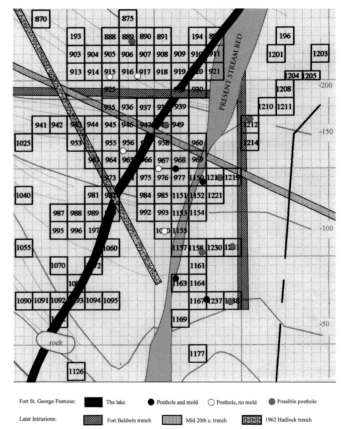

Figure 82. Plan of 2001-2004 excavations in the vicinity of the places identified by John Hunt as the vice admiral's house, lake, market place, and housing for some of the lesser colonists. The area was crossed by several later trenches, but a number of Fort St. George postholes survived although they fail to cluster in discrete patterns resembling a building footprint. The channeled stream, or lake, was clearly defined, however.

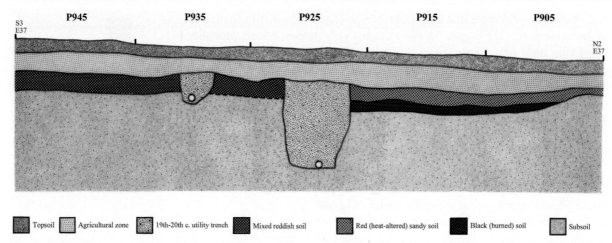

▓ Topsoil	░ Agricultural zone	▒ 19th-20th c. utility trench	▓ Mixed reddish soil	▒ Red (heat-altered) sandy soil	■ Black (burned) soil	□ Subsoil

Figure 83. Stratification in excavation units P905, P915, P925, P935 and P945, west profiles. Of special note are the burned and heat-altered layers in P905-P915. The intrusive trench in P935 carries a water pipe from the nineteenth-century well to the Perkins-Freeman house; the deeper trench in P925 contains a Fort Baldwin pipe.

Table 7. Early seventeenth-century artifacts found in the vicinity of the vice admiral's house (including the lake).

CERAMICS

West of England[1]	136
Olive Jar	15
Delft	66
Bellarmine	135
TOBACCO PIPES	73

GLASS

Bottle	418
Wine/ale glass	146
Bead	4
Button	8
Window	58
Mirror	1

IRON

Nail	143
Washer	2
Armor	15

LEAD/PEWTER

Munition[2]	216
Miscellaneous	2
COPPER/BRASS	11
OTHER MATERIALS[3]	8

[1] Including North Devon, Totnes and other West of England types, as well as unclassified.
[2] Lead pistol and musket balls, sprue, drips and scrap.
[3] Gold, flint, bone.

utility trench (Figure 83). The layers then reappeared as a single mixed stratum of reddish soil that continued south to P945 and west to P942, and may be related to the burned features found in units P193 and P197 in 1994. All together, these features constituted minimal evidence for a structure at this location, and the relative paucity of architectural materials, such as nails and daub, did not improve the case.

A large number of other artifacts, however, were recovered from this location, many in association with the burned layers, and both the quantity and types marked this as an important activity area. The assemblage is very reminiscent of that recovered from Raleigh Gilbert's house in that it is characterized by the presence of what would seem to constitute high class items for 1607 Fort St. George (Table 7). Especially prominent among the latter are the Delft, glass buttons, and wine glass fragments, as well as the relatively large number of sherds from Bellarmine jugs and glass bottles (Figure 84). Overall, the impression was of Admiral Raleigh Gilbert on a slightly smaller scale, or indeed of a *vice* admiral as identified by Hunt. The most significant difference is the far greater amount of lead munitions at this location. The full range of ball sizes (.39-.75 cal.) known from the site is represented, as well as a large quantity of shot, sprue, and scrap or spillage. Just one large puddle of lead from unit P955C weighs 315.1 g, far exceeding the total scrap and spillage otherwise found in all our excavations outside this location. Clearly, this was a major center of munition manufacture. But the large number of other artifacts also confirmed that this was a residential locus and distributions revealed that the highest concentrations were found in units P957 and P958 which happened to fall exactly within the predicted footprint of the vice admiral's house.

At this point, the evidence for a specific building relating to Fort St. George was circumstantial. The probable postholes and evidence of burning certainly indicated that we were in the vicinity of a structure. That it was the vice admiral's house as identified by Hunt was supported by the assemblage of artifacts that attested to the high status presumed

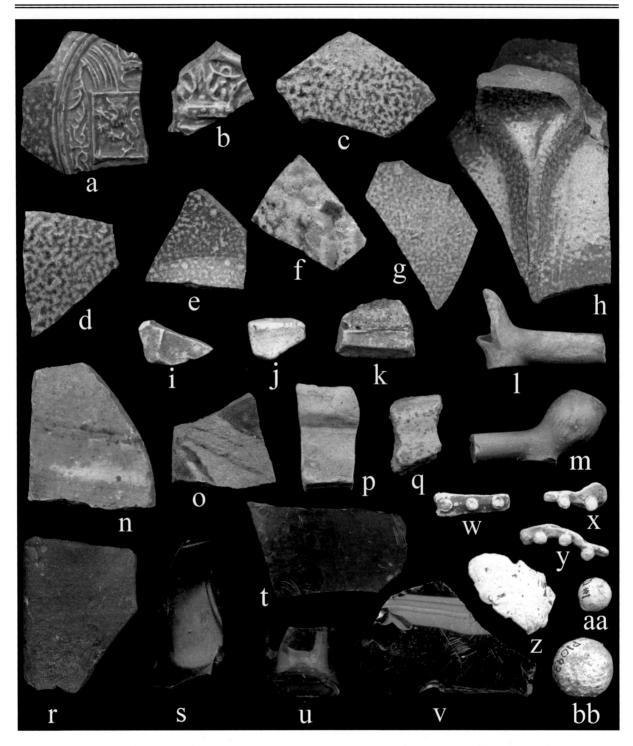

Figure 84. Sample of artifacts found in the vicinity of the vice admiral's house: Bellarmine (P907C, P1203C, P911E1, P1072C, P911D, P890B, P890C, P911E); i-k, Delft; (P909D, P893E); l-m, clay tobacco pipes (P1082C, P893D); n-q, North Devon (P909E, P907C, P1094B, P1082B); r-s, case bottle (P888B, P888A); t, case bottle sherd that has been reused as a scraper (P1092B); u, glass phial (P910D); v, flask (P1082A); w-y, lead sprue (P911E, P890C, P907C); z, lead spill (P907C); aa, .39 cal. lead ball (P907D); bb, .69 cal. lead ball (P1093ED1). (1:1)

for an officer holding such an office. On the other hand, the exceptional abundance of lead balls, shot, sprue and scrap reminded us of the munition master's house which we failed to find at its predicted location. Several questions came to mind: Could Hunt have erred by this order of magnitude in the positioning of these structures on his map; or could circumstances have forced a modification of his master plan whereby only one of the two structures was built, even if it meant putting the two gentlemen under the same roof; or could his rendering have been a complete fabrication and the location was actually occupied by a third party, perhaps Raleigh Gilbert after he was burned out of his first house (thus explaining the similarity, but smaller scale, of the assemblage)? These were all questions that had our attention as we explored further in 2002.

The excavations were expanded with the addition of twenty-five 1 m-square units in 2002. These units were placed primarily to gather more information about any construction at this location. We were particularly interested in establishing the extent of the putative burned area and also hoped to find more postholes from any structure that may have been associated.

The layer of red soil that seemed to indicate an area of burning in 2001 had been found primarily in units P905 and P915. It had also been discovered in test unit P193 that was excavated in 1994. Therefore, four new units (P903, P904, P913 and P914) were placed in the space between these earlier excavations to see if the layer was continuous. Red soils had also been encountered in units P942 and P944 and so P943 was opened to fill in the gap on this western side. Because we knew that a Hadlock trench ran right through P943, unit P953 was added to provide additional information. Finally, the red soil had been found in P197 in 1994, but not in the contiguous P990 in 2001, so unit P989 was excavated in hopes of clarifying the situation on the south edge of the location.

The layer of red soil was found in the eastern parts of units P904 and P914, but it disappeared by the middle of the units and did not extend into P903 or P913 so it was discontinuous with that found in P193. It was found again in the western parts of units P943 and P953, but in P943 it was interrupted by the Hadlock trench which ran diagonally across the unit. The trench continued through the northeast corner of P953, but the red layer had already disappeared by the middle of the unit indicating that it did not continue farther east in either unit. In P989 the red soil was again confined to the western part of the unit, so that although it extended south into P197 it was not found farther east. Thus in all three spots tested, we discovered localized patches of the red soil, but they did not reveal any definite pattern nor could we be certain whether they had been deposited by natural or human agency. We even began to doubt our earlier conclusion that the layer had been heat-altered and indicated the nearby presence of a burned structure. The problem was compounded by the fact that the red soil was noticeably lacking in artifactual content. When this layer was first excavated in units P905 and P915 in 2001, however, it had contained Fort St. George artifacts. Furthermore, it directly overlay an old buried surface (A-horizon) that contained an abundance of charcoal and a few aboriginal artifacts.

The questions concerning the red soil that confronted us, then, were whether it was deposited by natural erosion or by the colonists, and if the latter whether the color was due to heat alteration or added minerals. To address these concerns, we engaged the interest of a pedologist who analyzed a sample of the soil (Wall 2003). Her conclusion was that the red soil was definitely made ground which contained a significant amount of natural iron oxides (49,800 mg/kg). When heated, this natural mineral content could produce the startling red color of the soil (Cornwall 1958, p. 118). The old A-horizon, then, represents the pre-Fort St. George (aboriginal) surface and the red soil was brought in by the colonists at the beginning of their occupation and then subjected to heat. Whether it indicates a structure that was burned at this location remained moot.

This clear stratification is generally obscured elsewhere at this location by mechanical mixing of the two layers, probably during the nineteenth century. The Fort St. George surface was almost entirely destroyed at this time, and only patches of the red soil and underlying aboriginal layer were spared. The resulting mixed layer is characteristic of this location and is consistently described in the field notes as a "reddish" soil which when isolated contains only aboriginal and Fort St. George artifacts. This layer, in turn, was overlain and impacted by Fort Baldwin, the remains of which were thoroughly mixed by the mid-twentieth-century agricultural activity. The resulting plow zone is a dark brown soil that subsumed the upper portions, and sometimes all, of the underlying reddish soil so that the artifactual content reflects the entire sequence from prehistory to the twentieth century. But while we felt more confident about the interpretation of the stratigraphy at this location, Fort St. George had become more elusive.

Therefore, fifteen more units were excavated to explore more fully the central part of the location for structural remains. These units were P936, P937, P949, P960, P968, P969, P974, P975, P976, P977, P984, P985, P992, P993, and P1000. Here we found the stratigraphy described above, although it was often

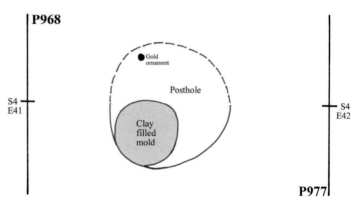

Figure 85. Posthole and post mold in excavation units P968 and P977. A small gold ball was found in the fill of the posthole.

disrupted by nineteenth and twentieth century intrusions. The plowzone contained a rich assortment of artifacts overwhelmingly from the nineteenth and twentieth centuries, but also included a fine assemblage of Fort St. George and aboriginal items (Figure 84). In a number of units (e.g., P936, P937, P960, P968, P984; as also P955, P956, P957, P958, P964, P965, P967, P982 in 2001), some patches of the reddish soil survived intact, preserving the integrity of the earlier materials.

The only specific Fort St. George context discovered in these units was a posthole and mold (Figure 85). Half of this feature was isolated in P977 and consisted of a posthole 38 cm in diameter containing a post mold 20 cm in diameter and filled with gray clay like some of those at Raleigh Gilbert's house. The bottom of the post was at a depth of -194 cm while the bottom of the hole was at -200 cm. No artifacts were found in this part of the posthole but the size of the hole and mold and the clay fill are typical of the smaller Fort St. George structures. The remainder of the posthole in unit P968 to the north was not recognized during excavation, but the area where it would have been was described as disturbed, and within this disturbance was found a small gold ball (Figure 85). This ball was probably a pendant from an ornament and is certainly attributable to Fort St. George.

The origins of two other holes that were revealed in nearby units P976 and P1000 are far more ambiguous. Both features are about the same size as Fort St. George postholes (40 cm and 45 cm respectively), but like the similar "postholes" found in units P915 and P956/P965 in 2001 they do not contain any evidence of post molds. Furthermore, while P976 contained a piece of case bottle glass and some other probable Fort St. George artifacts, there were also brick fragments, coal slag, and a wire nail indicating recent disturbance if not origin. The P1000 hole had some aboriginal flakes and a wire nail. Several apparent post molds, but no postholes, were found in units P903, P904, P913 and P914, but at least two contained wire nails and so all are also presumed to be nineteenth or twentieth century in date. Thus the only certain evidence for a Fort St. George structure in these excavations was reduced to the sole P968/P977 posthole and mold, and as we shall see it actually probably belongs to constructional activities that were centered farther to the east and south (see "private lodgings" below).

Finally, three units (P862, P891, P918) were placed on the northern side in an effort to discover the limits of this location in that direction. In 1994, one test unit (P194) had been excavated here in our random sampling of the site. That unit had been singularly uninformative, or so it seemed at the time. Beneath some 30 cm of plowzone with the usual mixture of prehistoric-to-twentieth-century artifacts, there was the layer of the dark reddish soil in which were aboriginal and Fort St. George artifacts plus some contamination of items from the nineteenth century. Subsoil was encountered at approximately -260 cm below datum. No features attributable to the early seventeenth century were observed. Units P862, P891 and P918 were similarly featureless, but the stratigraphy was more informative. In all units, the dark reddish soil beneath the plowzone was approximately 20 cm thick and contained an almost pure assemblage of Fort St. George artifacts. Under this layer and lying directly on the subsoil in units P891 and part of P918 was a thin

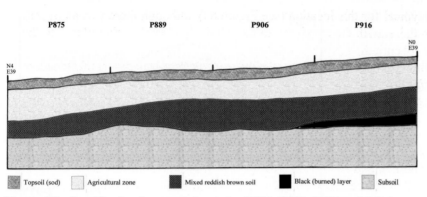

Figure 86. Stratification in excavation units P875, P889, P906 and P916, east profiles. The reddish brown soil typically contains a mix of aboriginal, Fort St. George and nineteenth-century artifacts. The black layer was probably the original ground surface when the fort was established in 1607.

charcoal-laden stratum that had only (prehistoric?) aboriginal artifacts. This stratigraphy matches that found in units P904/P905 and P914/P915 and brings us back full circle.

Thus we had a clear sequence of events at this location: from prehistoric, to the early seventeenth century, to the nineteenth and twentieth centuries. But after two seasons' investigation, we were left with the conclusion that the vice admiral's house was not situated at this precise place as predicted from the Hunt map, although the artifactual evidence of such a personage continued to suggest that he had been in the vicinity.

Dissatisfied with this state of affairs, we returned in 2003 and excavated an additional eighteen and a half 1 m-square units. These were grouped in areas where we hoped to find new structural information or clarify previous observations. Six units (P833, P875, P889, P906, P916, P917) were positioned to define the northern periphery more precisely. Again, it was found that as we progressed north in these units the stratification became simpler and Fort St. George artifacts less common. In unit P833 there were only a few early seventeenth-century artifacts and these were confined to the plowzone. The layer of reddish brown soil between the plowzone and subsoil that we believe to be a disturbed relict of the 1607-1608 occupation did not contain any colonial or aboriginal artifacts. The same stratigraphic situation was present in P875 (Figure 86), although there were a half dozen Fort St. George artifacts from the plowzone. In P889 and P906 there were, respectively, a couple of dozen and more than forty early seventeenth-century items, many of them from the reddish brown layer. Once again, these artifacts included numerous sherds of Bellarmine and Delft, and a large amount of lead balls, shot, sprue and scrap (see Figure 84). The same abundance of artifacts was present in P916 and P917, especially in the reddish brown soil, and there was also the old buried A-horizon between that layer and subsoil. This old surface, as already noted above, would have been the ground level when the colonists arrived in 1607 and it contained much charcoal and calcined bone, as well as fire-cracked rocks, stone flakes and tools. Many of these were associated with what was probably an aboriginal hearth. There was also an unidentified linear feature in P916 and what appeared to be a posthole in P917. The latter was very similar to the postholes found in P915 and P956/P965 in 2001. Like them, no post mold could be discerned, again probably because only the very bottom of the hole was preserved, and it contained no diagnostic artifacts that could identify cultural affiliation.

The four last units (P981, P987, P988, P996) excavated at this location in 2003 were placed on the southwestern periphery in an area where features had been encountered in earlier excavations. Unit P981 was next to P982 where a possible posthole had been encountered in the southwestern corner in 2001. No evidence of this feature was found in P990 that same year, nor in P989 in 2002, however our search for structures required one last effort. Most of P981 was occupied by a large boulder, but it did not impact the southeastern corner where we hoped to find evidence of the posthole. A disturbance was found in the corner that connected with the P982 feature, yet even our most generous interpretations were unable to make it into a posthole.

Units P987, P988 and P996 were placed around P995 where some intriguing features were uncovered in 2002. These features included unusual lensing and a possible post mold. The lensing reappeared and was distinguished primarily by the reddish soil found elsewhere at this location, but no particular significance could be extracted from the stratification. Nor were any other encouraging features observed in these units.

The artifactual assemblage is quite typical for this location (see Figure 84), although there was an overall decrease in quantities which is in keeping with the proximity to the relatively clean "market place" to the south.

In 2004, we made one last effort to find enough postholes to make a coherent structure at this location. The results of the earlier investigations had consisted only of a few isolated postholes and evidence of burning. The most significant feature found was the channeled stream – "lake" – that Hunt shows flowing by the eastern side of the house (see below). In an effort to further define the lake and at the same time hopefully discover more postholes that could be related into some sort of meaningful pattern, nine 1 m-square units were excavated near the shorefront along the northern fringe of this location.

The five units P888, P890, P907, P908 and P909 were positioned to fill gaps in our earlier excavations where we hoped fugitive postholes might yet be discovered. Our hopes were dashed, although we did find more evidence of an intensive fire in the area: part of an original surface burned a bright red and mottled with patches of charcoal was especially evident in P907. Associated with this surface was a fine assortment of Fort St. George artifacts. Especially prominent in this assemblage was the large number of sherds of Bellarmine and Delft, as well as pieces of glass. Again these are ample evidence that a person of some importance was associated with this location. The relative frequency of lead castings continue to raise the question whether that individual was the vice admiral or munition master, but whoever it was we still have not pinned down his residence. Even wrought nails and daub were scarce. The lack of structural evidence is not due to post-Fort St. George disturbance for we are able to trace the nearby stream feature (the lake) through the entire location all the way from the shore to the edge of the town road. Since preservation is not the problem, we must conclude that either there was no such structure at this location or that it was of such an ephemeral nature that it is archaeologically invisible.

The Lake

One of the primary objectives of the 2001-2004 excavations was to find the original course of the little stream that runs through the site. This feature was referred to by Hunt as the "lake," a term which has been interpreted by earlier scholars as a misprint (e.g., Thayer 1892, p. 185), but according to the *Oxford English Dictionary* it would have been a perfectly good word in the early seventeenth century for "a small stream of running water." Since the stream is such a prominent feature on the Hunt map – where it is shown flowing from its source on Sabino Hill, through the fort, and into Atkins Bay – the determination of its exact course would give us another point of reference. Like the fortification ditch, it was expected that the scouring of the stream would have left a visible scar in the earth.

The first question was whether the present stream across the site followed the 1607 course. That prospect seemed unlikely because the stream had been diverted to the east sometime in the nineteenth century (see Figure 12), and when it was redirected back to the north in the twentieth century a dogleg was added to funnel the water through a culvert under Fort Baldwin Road (see Figure 21). Thus it was expected that at least part of the present course must still be east of the original course.

In 2001, we had found what we interpreted as the footings for a nineteenth-century stone foundation in units P957, P958, P965, P966 and P990 (Brain 2001, fig. 11). This feature was encountered again in P974 and P1060 in 2002. Thus when we opened up five new units (P938, P939, P946, P947, P948) just to the north in 2003 we expected that this feature would continue to intrude. We also knew from the previous excavations that a utility trench in which a water pipe had been laid[10] would run through units P946-P948, although we still hoped to find some original contexts that had escaped destruction. In the undisturbed portions of P946-P948 the stratification revealed the usual sequence for this general location of plowzone, reddish brown

---

[10]   We had previously blamed Fort Baldwin for this feature (Brain 2001, p. 15), but it is now clear that the pipe is later and runs from the nineteenth-century well that was dug through the storehouse to the Perkins-Freeman farm house on the northeastern corner of the site (see Figure 82).

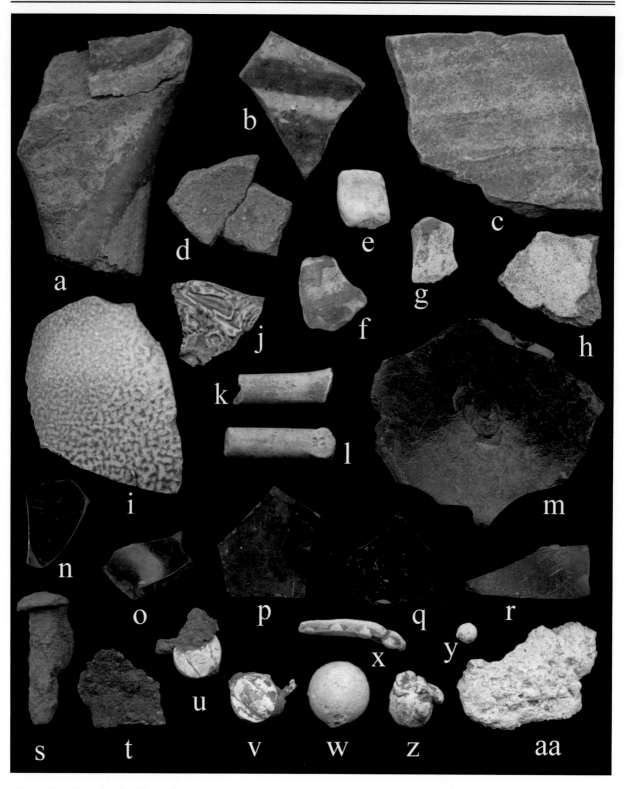

Figure 87. Sample of artifacts from the banks of the lake in the vicinity of the vice admiral's house: a-c, North Devon (P947B, P919C,); d, Totnes (P938C/P948B); e, Delft with glaze missing (P939E); f, Delft with blue glaze (P946B); g, Delft with purple glaze (P948E); h, Iberian olive jar (P939C); i-j, Bellarmine (P930EC1, P939D1); k, pipe stem (P930E); l, pipe stem with incuse mark on heel (P946A); m, glass bottle base with pontil mark (P919B); n, wine glass (P919C); o, flask (P920D); p-r, case bottle (P919C, P948E, P939D); s, iron nail (P929B); t, armor (P920C); u-v, lead seals (P920B, P947B); w-aa, lead munitions (P946B, P938B, P947C, P920E1, P948B). (1:1)

soil and subsoil, and a rich assemblage of artifacts was retrieved (Figure 87). There were no features attributable to Fort St. George in P946 or P947. In P948, we encountered what we thought was the stone foundation exactly where we anticipated it would appear, but as we followed it through P948 and into units P938 and P939 we realized that it was getting rather long for a foundation and that it was beginning to curve a little bit to the east. Furthermore, it was found at the base of the reddish brown soil and intruding into subsoil. In other words, it predated the mechanical mixing that created the reddish brown layer in the nineteenth century. It still could have been earlier nineteenth century, but we now gave pause for thought. And then we arrived at an exciting prospect: could it be evidence of the stream that we had been looking for so long?

When encountered in the past, the feature had been ignored after superficial clearing because of our initial interpretation. Now, with our suspicions aroused, we looked more closely. Upon excavation we found that the feature had been cut into subsoil and then lined with cobbles (Figure 88). In the light of these findings, it is perhaps significant that the *Oxford English Dictionary* also gives as a meaning for lake, "a channel for water." It seems that the stream course had been engineered: that is, the stream had been captured and brought into the fort to provide water. The cobbles would have defined the channel, and

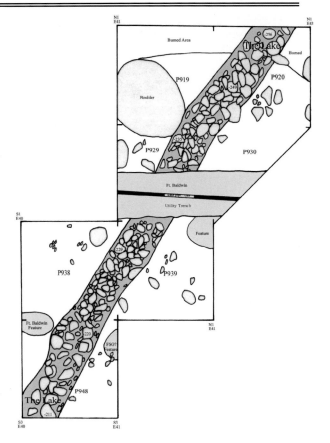

Figure 88. Plan of the lake in excavation units P919, P920, P929, P930, P938, P939 and P948. P930 is only a half unit because the modern stream impinged upon it.

prevented erosion and morass. Although the stream bed was cut by a Fort Baldwin utility trench, we traced it northwards into units P929-P930 and P919-P920. Our reinterpretation was confirmed when the cobbles were removed from the entire exposed length of the channel and only Fort St. George artifacts were found among them (Figure 87).[11]

In 2004, units P893, P910, P911 and P921 were specifically opened up to follow the north end of the lake from where we had left it in P920 to the edge of the shore from whence it would have flowed down the bank into Atkins Bay. The channel was indeed found to continue in units P910, P911 and P893. Again, the channel had clearly been cut and cobbles had been tightly packed in the bottom (Figure 89). A layer of gravelly soil on each side at the top of the channel correlated with a burned Fort St. George layer that had been found in contiguous units immediately to the west in the vicinity of the vice admiral's house.

The south end of the lake was confirmed in units P1072, P1082, P1092, P1093, and P1102 (P1091 and P1094 were also excavated but were outside the course of the stream). The upper portion of the lake on this part of the site had been truncated and contaminated during the nineteenth century, nevertheless heavy rains during the excavations demonstrated the efficacy of this feature as it still collected and channeled water. With this last segment we can now trace the course of the lake from the shore all the way to the town road (Figure 90).

---

[11] With one exception that proves the point: a small piece of a nineteenth-century clay tobacco pipe that was found in P920 but had come from a bowl found in the overlying disturbed soil in P938 and somehow been displaced.

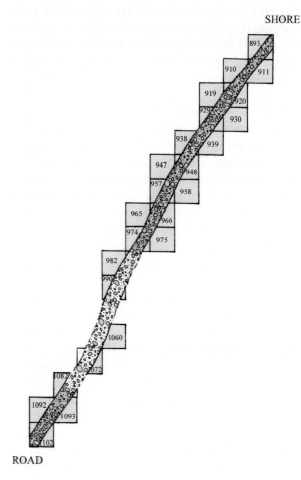

SHORE

ROAD

Figure 89. The lake, looking southwest from excavation unit P893 through unit P911 to unit P910. The channel for this feature has been cut down into subsoil from the Fort St. George layer.

Figure 90. Course of the lake as revealed in the 2001-2004 excavations.

Private Lodgings

East of the lake, directly across from the vice admiral and provost's houses, the Hunt map shows a couple of unidentified structures which must have been intended as "privat lodgins" for some of the less important colonists (Figure 91). Immediately to the south was a building that straddled the stream and is identified as the guardhouse ("court of guarde"), but if Hunt's placement is correct the remains of any such building would be under the present town road. So our expectations focused on the small houses. Our objectives were to establish if there was any evidence of structures at this location, and in the event to identify their function, as well as details of their construction and destruction.

Figure 91. Private lodgings on the east bank of the lake as drawn by John Hunt. The house on the left appears to be one and one-half stories and has a one story wing; the small dwelling on the right may also have a loft. These dwellings are more sophisticated than those built right next door at the sergeant major location or by the postern gate (see Figure 5).

This location is on the very edge of the state land, lying along the boundary with the private property to the east (see Figures 33 and 82). Although the original course of the stream at this location was several meters to the west, it is unlikely at any time in its history to have encroached farther east than its present bed. Therefore, we hoped that this marginal sliver of land between the stream and the boundary line might be relatively well preserved: specifically, that it was minimally impacted by Fort Baldwin and had entirely escaped the later farming of the land. In order to test the situation, fourteen units (P1150- P1155, P1157- P1158, P1161, P1163- P1164, P1167, P1169, P1177) were excavated along the right bank of the stream in 2002.

Of the fourteen units, six unfortunately had Fort Baldwin intrusions and two of these units (P1153, P1155) were so badly disturbed that they were abandoned after the extent of the damage was realized. The mid twentieth-century plowing, however, had apparently not extended this far. Moreover, there was no sod since the state had never planted grass here. Therefore, the basic stratification was quite

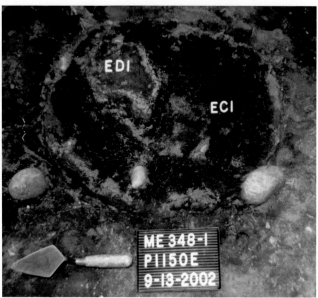

Figure 92. Posthole (EC1) and post mold (ED 1) in excavation unit P1150. Trowel points north.

simple. It consisted of 10-20 cm of dark brown humus which overlay 10-20 cm of the reddish brown soil which rested on subsoil. The humus had the usual mix of artifacts dating from prehistory through the twentieth century. Where it could be isolated, the reddish soil had only aboriginal and Fort St. George artifacts. The total number of early seventeenth-century artifacts, however, was far below the vice admiral's location and thinned out toward the south with only three artifacts attributable to Fort St. George being recovered from P1169 and one from P1177. Although the reddish soil was similar to that described for the vice admiral's location on the west side of the stream, it was mottled with gray clay and had a higher content of charcoal and daub. These indications of the former presence of structures were reinforced by even stronger evidence consisting of at least three good Fort St. George period postholes and molds. A possible fourth mold was found in P1158, but a posthole in P1161/P1164 was finally rejected as probably being a nineteenth-century intrusion.

The three definite Fort St. George features were found in P1150, P1163 and P1167. The P1150 posthole and mold (Figure 92) were very similar to those found on the west side of the stream only about a meter away in units P968/P977 – and here it is important to note that while the present course of the stream separates the P968/P977 and P1150 postholes, both were east of the lake in 1607. The P1150 posthole was slightly larger, being an oval of approximately 40 cm by 50 cm, but the post mold was about 20 cm in diameter and contained the same gray clay fill. The bottom of the mold was at -199 cm below datum and the bottom of the hole was at -204 cm. The clearly defined edge of the posthole showed that it had been dug with a shovel that had a flat blade 25 cm wide. Within the posthole were aboriginal flakes and seven wrought iron nails.

The P1163 posthole was essentially identical in that the hole was 50 cm by 60 cm and again the mold was about 20 cm in diameter and filled with gray clay (Figure 93). It could be determined in this case that the post tapered slightly toward the bottom (to 16 cm). Beneath the post were 8-9 cm of shim stones, so that the bottom of the post was at -169 cm below datum while the hole had been dug down to -178 cm. Within the posthole were aboriginal flakes, a wrought iron nail, and a seed identified as hedge bindweed (Nancy Asch Sidell, pers. comm., 2003).

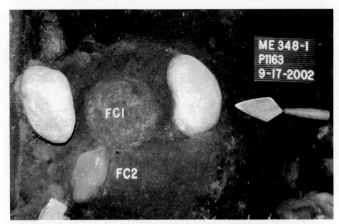

Figure 93. Posthole (FC2) and post mold (FC1) in excavation unit P1163. Note chock stones. Trowel points north.

The P1167 posthole and mold were somewhat different. The hole was larger and more elongated, measuring approximately 60 cm by 85 cm. The mold was filled with the gray clay, but the post had been hewn square and each side measured only 15 cm Furthermore, the post had been set at an angle so that it slanted to the northeast at about 25° off the vertical. The bottom of both the post and hole were at -158 cm below datum. The hole contained more of the hedge bindweed seeds, but no artifacts. Although indisputably a Fort St. George feature, the differences suggested that this post may have served a structural purpose different from the others.

Therefore, when we returned to this location in 2003 one of the first objectives was to complete the excavation of the P1167 posthole in the neighboring unit P1237 into which the mold of the squared timber disappeared. The rest of the posthole was defined in P1237 and another post mold appeared that was typical in being round in cross section and having a diameter of 22 cm. Furthermore, this post had been planted vertically: It was clearly the principal post, while the angled square timber may have been a brace.

Another promising posthole was discovered in P1238, but it was compromised when an iron T-joint for a water pipe and pieces of asphalt shingle were found in association. This unit was truncated on the eastern side by a large Fort Baldwin trench and those artifacts, if not the entire feature, may have been deposited at that time.

Units P1230 and P1231 also were opened in 2003 in order to clarify some streaks of clay and a possible post mold that had been observed in P1158 in 2002. More fired and unfired clay were found in P1230, but no definitive features were revealed. A possible posthole and clay-filled post mold were found in P1231; the posthole contained a wrought iron nail, stone flakes, charcoal, and numerous chock stones. Further exploration to the east was halted by the same Fort Baldwin trench that ran north-south through P1238.

Units P1218, P1219 and P1221 were next to P1150 in which the Fort St. George posthole had been revealed in 2002. Unfortunately, both P1218 and P1219 had been invaded by various intrusions. Foremost among these were the utility trench containing the water pipe running between the well and Perkins-Freeman house and the Fort Baldwin north-south trench already revealed in P1231 and P1238. The water pipe cut through the Fort Baldwin trench in P1219 thus establishing that the water pipe was laid later in the twentieth century. Several other features, including at least one posthole, also appeared to be modern. The absence of Fort St. George features was matched by a lack of contemporary artifacts. P1221 was less disturbed, having only a small hole in the southeastern corner that contained a Coca Cola bottle. No seventeenth-century structural remains were observed, but artifacts were more plentiful than in contiguous units (Figure 94).

Following the artifact trail, we decided to expand the excavations northwards towards the shore. Unit P196, which had been excavated on the nearby edge of the bank in 1994, had yielded a fair number of Fort St. George artifacts associated with an old ground surface beneath a layer of modern trash. Since the stratification seemed relatively well preserved, we placed five units between P196 and P1218-P1219 in 2003.

In P1208 and P1211 we found 25-30 cm of topsoil,[12] beneath which was a layer of dark brown loamy sand that was distinctly different from the usual reddish brown soil. This layer was 10-20 cm thick and con-

---

[12]   Among the modern trash of which was someone's collection of nonnative warm-water shells (conchs, cockles and olives). They are a most appropriate accompaniment to the concrete flamingo lawn ornament found in P196 in 1994.

Table 8. Early seventeenth-century artifacts found in the vicinity of the private lodgings east of the lake.

Figure 94. Sample of artifacts from the 2003 excavations at the location of the private lodgings: a-b, North Devon, both from the same burned baluster jar (P1212C, P1211B); c, Totnes (P1208C); d, Bellarmine mask (P1231B); e-f, pipe stems (P1230C, P1219B); g, pipe bowl (P1208C); h, case bottle (P1221A); i-j, flask (P1219C, P1231C); k, glass button with iron attachment loop (P1221A); l-m, lead scrap (P1210B, P1211C). (1:1)

CERAMICS

West of England[1]	16
Delft	1
Bellarmine	9

TOBACCO PIPES 12

GLASS

Bottle	42
Wine/ale glass	13
Window	4
Mirror	2

IRON

Nail	37

LEAD/PEWTER

Munition[2]	14

COPPER/BRASS 4

OTHER MATERIALS [3] 2

[1] Including North Devon, Totnes and other West of England types, as well as unclassified.
[2] Lead pistol and musket balls, sprue, drips and scrap.
[3] Flint.

tained a large and relatively pure assemblage of seventeenth-century items, both European and aboriginal (Table 8). Many of the Fort St. George artifacts showed evidence of burning, while the aboriginal did not. Unit P1210 did not have the same quantity of artifacts as the neighboring units, but a linear feature was associated with the Fort George layer. It ran across the unit from the southwest corner to the northeast corner. Although there was some speculation that it could be a sill, there was no conclusive evidence. The stratification in units P1212 and P1214 was similar to that already encountered, but there were very few seventeenth-century artifacts, European or aboriginal. The western parts of both units were disturbed by the same north-south Fort Baldwin trench that had been encountered in P1219, P1231 and P1238. The only other features were two postholes in P1212, only one of which might have related to Fort St. George.

Four more units were excavated at this location in 2004 in one last effort to find structural remains that we could associate with the artifact assemblage found in P1208 and neighboring units. P1201 and P1203 were standard 1 m-square units, but P1204 and P1205 measured only 1 m by .5 m in order to preserve a large bush that we wished to leave in place for erosion control purposes. Again we recovered a good assortment of Fort St. George artifacts beneath a thick layer of trash from the nearby nineteenth-century house, but structural remains still eluded us. All we found were trenches relating to Fort Baldwin, although daub and wrought iron nails indicated the proximity of seventeenth-century construction presumably situated on the contiguous private property.

In summary, we were somewhat disappointed in our search for more structural remains at this location. Of course, we were hampered by the restricted area available for investigation, and the extensive twentieth-century disturbance within that area. Nevertheless, we discovered a number of definite and possible postholes attributable to Fort St. George, especially if all those east of the 1607 lake are included (see Figure 82). The sizes of the holes and molds are similar to those found at the admiral's house and the buttery/corporal's house and would have been appropriate for the modest housing shown on the Hunt map. The apparently scattered pattern, however, has stubbornly resisted all attempts to reconstruct specific building footprints. It may be that these structures are indicated by only a couple of principal posts that supported the roofs in the manner of the Irish dwellings cited in the discussion of the admiral's house (see p. 70). Thus one dwelling might have centered on the P968/P977 and P1150 posts and the other on the P1163 and P1167/P1237 posts, the rest of the constructions being composed of less sturdy elements. It may be noted that both sets of posts are in parallel alignment and are perpendicular to the lake, but are too far apart to belong to the same structure. Whatever might have been the case, the clay fill in the post molds reveals that the structures did not burn, but rather deteriorated in place so that the clay daubing from the walls was washed into the molds of the decomposed posts as was also observed at the admiral's house. The presence of daub, charcoal, and heat-altered artifacts, however, suggests that other structures outside the area of the excavations might have burned.

Market Place

The so-called "market place" was the central square or common around which were positioned some of the most important buildings – viz., the chapel, Raleigh Gilbert's house, guardhouse, and vice admiral's house. The location itself would have been free of construction as shown on Hunt's plan. Therefore, excavations placed here in 2002 were intended to reveal whether there was any evidence of structures or other activities. For this reason we adopted an extensive testing program whereby a random sample of eight units (P995, P1040, P1055, P1060, P1070, P1090, P1095, P1126) were excavated over the entire area (see Figure 82).

The usual twentieth-century agricultural zone was found under the sod in all units, except P1090 and P1126 where it was overlain by road and parking lot fill. Beneath it in P1095 and P1126 was only subsoil. In the remaining five units we found at least some evidence of the reddish soil that is so characteristic of the vice admiral's location, although it became more attenuated toward the south until it had disappeared by P1095 and P1126. Under the reddish soil was also the same charcoal-bearing layer that probably represents an old ground surface. In fulfillment of our prediction based on the Hunt map, we found no evidence of construction or any other activity in these units. There was a marked drop-off in frequency of Fort St. George items as we progressed south until only four are recorded for unit P1090, one for P1095, and none for P1126.[13]

---

[13] An artifactual anomaly that gives us pause is the recovery of iron oxide concretions in units P995, P1055, P1070 and P1090 that apparently were associated with the old buried surface. Many could be natural in origin, but more than a few definitely contain pieces of metal which are so badly deteriorated that the original artifacts cannot be identified. No other historic items are present, however, and since the context is otherwise defined only by aboriginal artifacts the possibility of a pre-colonial contact situation might be entertained.

It would seem that this location was indeed a "vacant" place that was devoid of structures or any other invasive activity. The few artifacts present are logically interpreted as creep from the vice admiral's location contiguous to the north. This negative evidence is consistent with the notion of a central square or "market place."

Fortification Rampart and Ditch

One of the principal objectives of the 1994 excavations had been to find the fortification ditch that the colonists excavated. Therefore, our two major trenches were placed where we hoped to intersect it on the west side of the fort. We expected such a major disturbance to be relatively easy to find and identify, and once the fort trace was established we planned to use the Hunt map as a guide to locate the structures he showed within the compound. But although we found some features that we tried hard to interpret as some part of the ditch, we remained unconvinced that we had found it.

Following up on those less than satisfactory results, we tried again in 1997 with the opening of units P401- P407 in that segment of trench 2 that was not investigated in 1994. According to our latest scaling and positioning of the Hunt map we figured that we had just missed the ditch when we skipped that portion of the trench. Unfortunately, when those units were opened up we found a considerable amount of disturbance attributable to Fort Baldwin. Because the abbreviated field season forced us to concentrate our efforts on the storehouse we did not pursue the matter further.

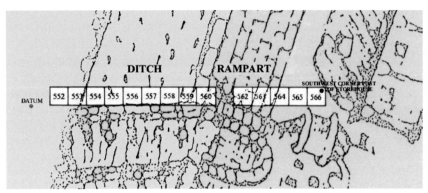

Figure 95. Plan of the trench excavated in 1998 (P558-P566) and 2000 (P552-P557) in the search for the fortification ditch. The relevant portion of the Hunt plan is superimposed at the same scale. Hunt indicates the rampart by the masonry-like pattern and the ditch by the wider stippled area to its left. A post of the storehouse, confirmed as the southwest corner post in 1999, was found in the northeastern corner of unit P566. North at top.

Thus despite several tries we had been frustrated in all efforts to establish the fort trace. Part of the problem had been that those earlier attempts had been placed in the northern part of the site which had been badly disturbed. As we proceeded south in the storehouse excavations, however, we were finding much better preservation and so prospects for all features were considered to be much improved. Furthermore, now that we had a precise fix on the storehouse we could reverse our strategy and use it as the key for predicting the exact line of the fortifications, assuming the accuracy of the Hunt map. Although we did not expect to find much evidence of the earthen rampart, we did hope to find the ditch from which the earth had been removed.

Therefore, in 1998 a 1 m wide trench was excavated on the north edge of the parking lot in what appeared to be the best preserved part of the site that was available to us. This trench was laid out between N0-1 and E7-16 relative to the nearby datum, and was taken out in 1 m units (P558-P566), one of which (P561) was not excavated (Figure 95). The east end of the trench was anchored at the predicted location of the eighth post of the west wall of the storehouse in unit P566. Hunt portrays the storehouse as being right alongside the rampart, the interval between them being only about 5'-6'. If Hunt had it right, therefore, we should look for the inside edge of the rampart in unit P564. We had little expectation that much evidence of the rampart would remain, however, and so our primary hopes rested on finding the scarp of the ditch on the exterior side of the rampart. According to Hunt's measurements, this should appear in unit P559.

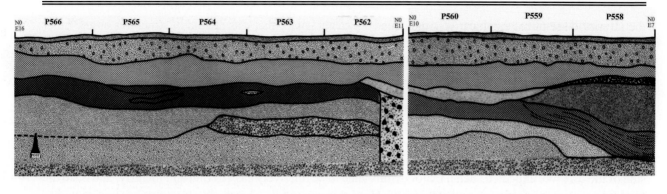

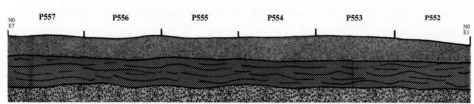

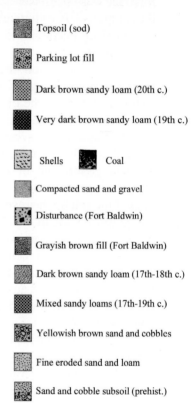

Figure 96. Stratification in excavation units P558-566 excavated in 1998 and P552-P557 excavated in 2000, south profiles. Included for reference purposes, the storehouse post in unit P566 is actually 70 cm north of the wall. The probable base of the rampart is seen in units P562-P564, but is interrupted by a massive Fort Baldwin intrusion in P562. The scarp of the fortification ditch is evident in P559 and P558 where the subsoil has been dug out. The ditch was filled first with a fine particulate matter that could have been washed down from the rampart while the fort was in use and over this a thick layer composed of many lenses of different soils accumulated during the following centuries. Finally, when Fort Baldwin was established the remaining depression was filled.

The stratification of our trench was quite complicated due primarily to depositional events occurring during the past century. These may be condensed for present purposes, and the salient cultural and natural strata that were observed are depicted in Figure 96. What is particularly striking is that there are significant differences from one end of the trench to the other: a story is being told that was consistent with our expectations, although the evidence at hand was just short of proof. The analysis will start at the east end and move west.

In units P566 and P565 the stratigraphic sequence was the same as that described for the southern part of the storehouse area. Beneath the sod was a thick layer of unconsolidated sand and gravel that had been brought in to level off the parking lot in 1982. This overlay a buried soil horizon that capped a dark brown layer which included the agricultural zone of the mid-twentieth century and the Fort Baldwin occupation earlier in the century. Below that was an even darker stratum containing nineteenth-century artifacts. A brown sandy loam up to 35 cm thick was then encountered which had accumulated during the eighteenth and later seventeenth centuries when the site was essentially unutilized. A thin layer of charcoal and occasional artifacts, as well as the appearance of the storehouse post in P566 identified the 1607 ground surface at about -145 cm below datum.

In the middle of the trench the stratigraphy in the uppermost layers was much the same. First, there was the parking lot fill, then the twentieth-century layers, on top of a nineteenth-century level, under which was the post-Fort St. George accumulation. But then there were important new developments. The next stratum encountered was a dark yellowish brown sandy soil that was also very cobbly. This layer was 20 cm thick, and lay directly on subsoil which appeared at about -140 cm below datum, somewhat higher than in P566. In fact, a sharp rise in the subsoil was evident in P564 which coincided precisely with where John Hunt drew the interior edge of the rampart. Whether this was a natural rise or represents redeposited subsoil was not resolved, but the overlying sandy cobbly soil almost certainly is derived from the deeper subsoils that are found just above the white beach sand in other parts of the site. This apparent reverse stratigraphy would seem to indicate a nearby excavation and redeposition of soils. Thus we had a good candidate for a stump of the rampart, but the case could only be made if it could be connected to a contiguous ditch.

The stratigraphic deviations were even more significant and encouraging at the west end of the trench. Under the parking lot fill were several layers attributable to Fort Baldwin. On top was the same layer that was found throughout the trench. Beneath it was a surface

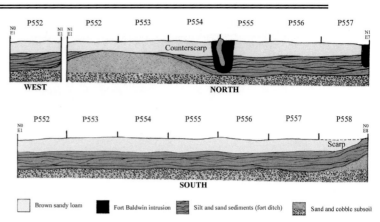

Figure 97. Cross section of fortification ditch in profiles of excavation units P552-P557 excavated in 2000. Unit P558, excavated in 1998, is added to show the scarp of the fortification ditch. The south profile is presented as a mirror image in order to more easily reconstruct the cross section of the ditch from scarp to counterscarp.

composed of hard compacted sand and gravel in units P559- P560 and coal in unit P558. Then there was a large wedge-shaped layer of one-time fill that began in P559 and expanded to more than 50 cm in thickness as it disappeared into the west wall of P558. This was a landscaping event connected with the establishment of Fort Baldwin, for the underlying strata clearly revealed a depression at this location. The underlying strata, in fact, were even more revealing. First, there was a layer of dark brown sandy loam that appeared to be a conflation of the post-Fort St. George and pre-Fort Baldwin accumulations which began to slope downwards in P559 and became ever more striated with lenses of various different soils in P558. The latter were clearly water-sorted depositions eroding into a low point. Below that was another erosional layer that was derived from finer particulates of the sandy subsoil (wash from the rampart?) and was exposed long enough to begin developing an A-horizon as it was being laid down. The fine sandy subsoil, itself, plunged down sharply at this point and disappeared in unit P558. A reasonable interpretation of all this is that we had finally found the edge of the ditch—and precisely where John Hunt drew it. The proof, however, required more excavation.

In 2000, a small team was detached to continue where we had left off in 1998 by extending those excavations farther to the west. Since we had a machine available to remove the parking lot fill above Raleigh Gilbert's house, we also used it to remove about a meter of the overburden at this location. Beneath the sod was the edge of the fill for the parking lot, then the Fort Baldwin and nineteenth-century layers. Prominent in the latter along the south side of the excavation was a brick foundation wall which probably related to the nearby Nathaniel Perkins house. At a depth of -100 cm below datum a level working floor was established and the six excavation units (P552-P557) were laid out. These units were taken down simultaneously as a 1 x 6 m trench.

The uppermost level encountered was the grayish brown sandy loam that contained nineteenth-century artifacts and was probably fill that was brought in when Fort Baldwin was established. This soil was fairly homogeneous and was disturbed in many places by Fort Baldwin-era intrusions. At a depth of approximately -130 cm a dark silty soil appeared in most units. This soil was very organic and had been deposited in thin layers between which were lenses of fine sand. These deposits continued for 30 cm until they were abruptly replaced by cobbly subsoil at about -160 cm.

The silts and sands had obviously been water-laid, and were exactly what we had been looking for. But because they were only about a foot in thickness and could be seen as overlapping horizontal strata across the entire southern profile of the excavations, they were initially interpreted simply as widescale sheet erosion. We had not noticed such a natural phenomenon elsewhere on the site, however, and when we examined the northern profile (Figure 97) we found that the strata sloped up in unit P554 following a contour

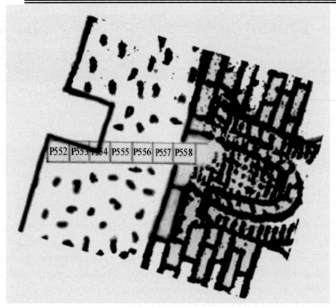

P552 P553 P554 P555 P556 P557 P558

Figure 98. Reconciliation of the profiles of units P552-P558 with the John Hunt map generates the hypothesis that a bridge abutment was left to compensate for the extra width of the fortification ditch. If the 1998 excavations (units P558-P566) really did go through the gateway, as shown here, then it is no wonder we found little evidence of the rampart.

that mirrored the strata previously seen in P558. This must indeed be the counterscarp of the fortification ditch and the alluvial deposits represented the infilling that occurred after the fort had been abandoned.

Although it was obvious that we had finally found the ditch, there were a couple of bothersome questions that needed answering. First, why could we see the counterscarp on the north profile but not on the southern? The answer was found in the fact that while the strata in the southern profile are uncompromisingly flat, as noted, in the western profile of P552 they may be seen to slope upward in a fashion similar to that of the putative counterscarp in P554. A probable explanation is that our excavation trench intersected the fortification ditch at an angle consistent with the proven orientation of the Hunt map. Furthermore, if the location is in the vicinity of where the western ("land") gate and bridge were placed, as shown by Hunt, an abutment may have been left for the bridge in order to span more easily the exceptional width of the ditch (Figure 98).

The second question that bothered us was why the ditch was so shallow. The answer is found in the width: a ditch that was 20' wide did not need to be deep. In these circumstances, the ditch was not the important part of the fortification. It was merely the mine from which the material was extracted for the construction of a substantial rampart. That they did not dig deeper and narrower was probably dictated by the fact that they encountered the nearly impenetrable cobble layer at the bottom of the glacial till, under which was the hard beach sand and then solid rock. They had to go out rather than down. It might also be that the original depth was somewhat greater than is now apparent because the upper portion of the ditch was truncated by later activities.

Figure 99. Ground-penetrating radar survey. The GPR equipment consisted of a GSSI SIR 20 control unit with 200MHz and 400MHz antennae. This equipment was run along transects laid out at 1 m and 2 m intervals. (Photo looking northwest)

In 2004 we were presented with the opportunity to continue our search for the fortification ditch electronically. A ground-penetrating radar (GPR) survey was conducted on the western part of the site on September 17 (Figure 99). This initial survey was followed by two more on October 23 and November 7. The objective of all these surveys was to replicate our findings of 2000 at one or more additional points and

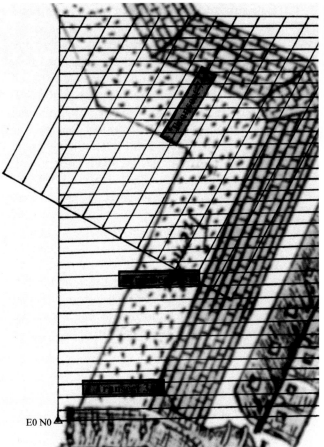

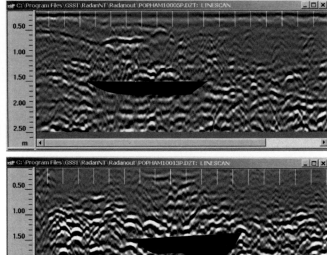

Figure 101. Ground-penetrating radar records of the fortification ditch along the western wall. The black profiles indicate readings along transects 3 (top) and 13 (bottom) of the primary grid that are interpreted as the electronic signatures of the cross sections of the ditch. (Courtesy of Peter Sablock)

Figure 100. Plan of ground-penetrating radar survey of the fortification ditch along the western wall. Two GPR transect grids were employed: the primary grid was oriented east-west and transects were run every meter from N0 to N22, while the secondary grid was angled northeast-southwest and was run at 2 m intervals. Electronic evidence of the ditch was found along most transects: the gray bands indicate where it was recognized along transects 3 and 13 of the primary grid and transect 7 of the secondary grid (see Figures 101-102). As can be seen, these radar signatures correspond closely with the position and width of the ditch as drawn by Hunt.

hopefully delineate the west wall and northwest bastion of the fort. The surveys were conducted by Professor Peter Sablock of Salem State College.

The surveys were run along two grids: the first was coincident with the archaeological grid and consisted of transects running west to east at 1 m intervals from N0E22 to N22E22; the second grid was oriented southwest to northeast along a baseline drawn from N11E15 to N19E0 and was run at 2 m intervals (Figure 100). The results were very encouraging (Appendix C). It seems that the post-Fort St. George ditch fill consisting of naturally water-laid fine silts and sands contrasted sufficiently with the glacial till subsoil composed of poorly sorted sands and gravels to produce a distinctive radar signal. On the primary east-west grid the radar signature shows "a very good correlation with the predicted trace of the ditch both in width and trend as drawn on the Hunt map" (ibid.). Evidence of the ditch was found in all transects from N3 to N13, except for N10 and N11 where another intrusion is evident. These transects show that the ditch is not symmetrical in cross section: a steep scarp is faced by a more gradual counterscarp (Figure 101). "The ditch appears less distinctly" on the southwest-northeast grid "but it appears to have the same characteristic steep scarp and less steep counterscarp" (Figure 102). Interestingly, however, the ditch around the bastion "trends more to the west and south (southerly by as much as four meters) than expected." This may be due to large boulders or bedrock that forced a repositioning of the fortifications. But the data are not as clear here for it is observed that "the further north the transects run the more disturbed the ground becomes, with much more evident post-Popham activity obscuring the ditch signature." It should be noted that these deteriorating conditions

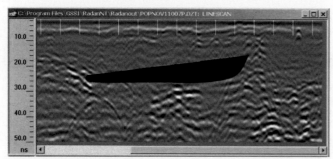

Figure 102. Ground-penetrating radar record of the fortification ditch in the vicinity of the northwest bastion. The GPR reading is along transect 7 of the secondary grid. The ditch appears to be wider here and the north end (to the right in illustration) rests against what is interpreted as a large boulder, perhaps part of the rampart. (Courtesy of Peter Sablock.)

in site integrity from south to north correspond precisely with our archaeological findings.

Sablock returned in 2005 for another day of GPR survey in the southern part of the fort. He ran transects over the parking lot, paved town road, and lower section of the public path up to the Fort Baldwin gun emplacements (Appendix C). He felt confident that he was able to identify more of the ditch relating to the southwest bastion and the south curtain wall about where our correlation of the Hunt and archaeological maps predicted them to be (see Figure 32).

It must be emphasized that the state of electronic remote sensing is not yet sufficient to replace archaeology, for it can not yet achieve the same level of detail nor, of course, retrieve artifacts. It can be an important and very useful complement, however, as demonstrated here. Since we already had identified a segment of our target archaeologically, it was then possible to distinguish its corresponding electronic signature and then replicate it at other locations, thus providing confirmation of the ditch and in the process saving us a considerable amount of labor.

Summary: The Hunt Map and the Construction of Fort St. George

The archaeological revelation of early seventeenth-century structures and other features at the Popham site leads us to conclude that much of Fort St. George was depicted with a high degree of accuracy by John Hunt, allowing for the distortions caused by his isometric renderings. It remains very unlikely that all of the structures on the plan were completed, and the elaborations of a few details reveal a bit of artistic license, but it is also now quite certain that many of the principal constructions were in place when Hunt made his draught. He may have given us a Fort St. George that looks rather more complete and imposing than it really was on that October day when the map left Maine on the *Mary and John* (see cover illustration), but who can blame him for a visionary document that attempted to reconcile actuality with the expectations of the backers in England? For this obviously was a piece of propaganda designed to encourage more support – supplies and colonists – from the company. That this was a conspiracy on the part of the colonists becomes clear two months later on December 16 when George Popham further enhances the picture in his letter to James I (Appendix A3) in which he describes tropical resources and the proximity of the Southern (Pacific) Ocean. Nevertheless, it seems that Hunt's map can be used with confidence not only to guide future excavations at Fort St. George (see Figure 32), but also as an aid to the interpretation of other contemporary English colonies, such as Jamestown. Without the map it is improbable that Fort St. George would ever have been found since the settlement was an ephemeral affair, barely discernible in the archaeological record. Considering that it was an initial outpost on a foreign shore, occupied by a small group of men for little more than a year, and considering subsequent usages of the land in the nineteenth and twentieth centuries, it is remarkable that anything of it survives.

The archaeological excavations were successful, however, for we were able not only to find and define the fort with Hunt's help, but also to recover many details that are not apparent (or even misleading) in Hunt's rendering. Foremost among these are architectural matters that contribute to our knowledge of the building practices of these first English colonists. There is a tendency to think of the initial colonies as little pieces of England transported in their entireties to the New World – like Athena bursting forth full-blown from the brow of Zeus. This expectation may be valid for the fully portable aspects of culture, but the building up of the infrastructure would have required many intermediate steps before achieving results like the neat little settlement depicted by Hunt. Unless they brought prefabricated structures with them, all first comers resorted to compromises, concentrating first on the public buildings before putting up insubstantial dwellings of various levels of sophistication to provide temporary shelter as winter came on. This first housing is always described in contemporary documents with such dismissive terms as "transient hovels," "rude structures," "slight cottages," "poor cabins," and "simple huts." Their actual construction and form would have been determined by many factors, such as the materials and time available, and the skill and experiences of the builders. There may have been master carpenters trained in the English vernacular traditions; gentlemen who recalled the cottages on their country estates; and soldiers who had been exposed to alternative customs on the Continent or in Ireland, and with these templates in mind were accustomed to erecting temporary shelters while on campaign. There were also the Native American traditions and many a colonist was known to have moved into a wigwam or copied many of the features that made it a successful solution to environmental challenges. Those first settlements, then, must have presented a discordant picture of architectural styles, forms and methods of construction. Although we know this to be the general case, nontextual examples have been hard to find. Thus the evidence from Fort St. George is uniquely important.

At Fort St. George, several levels of architectural competence appear to be evident. The only common feature is that all buildings were earthfast and timber framed at least in part. Adhering to their instructions, the colonists started the storehouse on August 21, the day after the first trench was dug for the fortifications. It was still under construction a month later, September 22. The storehouse was the most substantial and sophisticated structure within the fort and for that month must have been the focus of whatever carpentry skills were present. A well-built, box-framed building was required to protect the stores, the very lifeblood of the colony. Only when it was sufficiently finished would attention have been diverted to other necessary public buildings, such as the buttery and chapel, and finally to housing. The buttery may have been a box-framed structure raised in bents or wall sections, but the posts were much smaller than those used in the storehouse and had not been shaped. The chapel, if we may trust Hunt's rendering, may not even have been box-framed, relying instead on a more primitive crotchet construction although the posts may have been regularly spaced. When they could finally turn their attention to the houses, the rapidly deteriorating weather would have encouraged many more compromises in creating enough shelter for all the colonists as quickly as possible. A rather less sophisticated construction is apparent for Raleigh Gilbert's house, but his status was still maintained by the relatively large size of the building and the inclusion of at least one glazed window. For most of the colonists, however, we may imagine simple huts, perhaps only slightly modified wigwams. This primitive architecture is so ephemeral that it is represented only by scattered postholes for the earthfast posts. Although Hunt may have been long at sea by the time these last structures were put up, the great variety of formal and constructional details he depicted on his map may actually be a fairly accurate representation of the architectural mélange that would have been present at Fort St. George as it prepared for the winter of 1607-1608.

There are still many parts of Fort St. George that warrant future excavation. We were able to explore the core of the site on state land, but even there portions of the storehouse, admiral's house, fortifications and other features were left intact so that generations to come can pursue new lines of inquiry. Other important remains are still to be found on contiguous parcels of private land where we were denied permission to investigate. The most interesting of these would be the chapel (where George Popham could have been laid to rest) and the southwestern bastion which might be relatively well preserved (there are interesting topographic disconformities in the general area, but of course they could be the result of more recent activities). Especially important in regard to preservation is the northeastern part of the site. It appears that this corner has never been plowed and therefore would seem to be a promising prospect for recovering those elusive 1607-1608 surfaces.

ARTIFACTS

The collection of artifacts from Fort St. George, a cultural time capsule, identifies the specific years of 1607-1608 and thus provides a unique window into an initial English colony on these shores. It is most humbling, but also eminently satisfying, that the assemblage is essentially identical to that isolated for the earliest post-Indian occupation at Jamestown by John Cotter a half century ago (1958, pp. 12-13) and hypothesized to represent the initial founding of James Fort. The more recent excavations at Jamestown have not improved upon Cotter's insight. The categories listed by Cotter are:

North Devon coarse-tempered, lead-glazed ware
Lead-glazed earthenware (local?)
Delftware
English flint
Dutch gin bottles

White clay tobacco pipes
Locally made brown clay pipes
Building hardware fragments
Wrought-iron nails
Brass spoon

The most notable category missing in this list is military, but arms and munitions are noted in the paragraph following the list (ibid.), and the latter are appended here at the end of the section. Otherwise, we would only omit locally manufactured earthenwares and pipes at Fort St. George, and add some detail to the other categories. We also can define specific types of artifacts within these categories that appear to be diagnostic of a 1607 colonial venture originating in the West of England. Presentation will be under the major headings: Ceramics, Clay Tobacco Pipes, Glass, Metal, Gun Parts and Munitions, and Other.

CERAMICS

The ceramics described here belong to two basic classes: earthenware and stoneware. Earthenware is fired at a low temperature and may be porous. Stoneware is high-fired, well vitrifed, and nonporous.

Earthenware

The seventeenth-century earthenwares from the Popham site commonly exhibit a reddish, oxidized color, although differential firing can also produce a gray core or surface on many examples. Vessels made of these wares were lead glazed. Also present in minor amounts are wares that are not as highly oxidized and tend towards a creamy, buff color. One such ware is coarse and usually unglazed, another is fine textured and tin-glazed.

Red earthenware, or simply "redware," is the common denominator of colonial archaeology. It is ubiquitous on sites from first contact well into the nineteenth century. Unfortunately, because of the simple paste and glaze characteristics, it is often difficult to establish classifications distinguishing chronology, provenance, function, or other useful categories. A large number of the Popham sherds, therefore, are unclassified. Of these, 419 are unglazed and 322 are glazed. Some of these fragments are clearly nineteenth century. These include 43 sherds, all probably from the same vessel, that have a dull opaque green glaze, and another group of 26 sherds with a shiny black glaze. On most of the sherds, however, the glaze is clear or lightly tinged with impurities, typically producing a reddish brown surface color. Many of these might very well be seventeenth-century, but the absence of definitive decorative and formal attributes precludes their assignment at this time.

Six distinctive seventeenth-century types of lead-glazed coarse earthenwares, however, may be distinguished on the basis of paste and glaze characteristics (Table 9). These types are identified as English and are given proper names as closely as they can be placed geographically. The two groups of buff wares are not of English manufacture: one belongs to a large category loosely referred to as "Iberian olive jars," and the other is a distinctive tin-glazed earthenware made in Holland.

Table 9. Measurements of early seventeenth-century English ceramics from Fort St. George.

Type	Color (Munsell)		Texture (Wentworth)	Hardness (Mohs)	Thicknesss (mm)
	Paste	Glaze			
North Devon Variety 1	2.5YR 5/8 Red (ext.) 5 YR 5/1 Gray (int.)	2.5Y3/3;5/6;6/8 Olive 5Y2.5/2 Dark Olive 7.5YR 4/6; 5/8 Strong Brown 10YR 4/6; 5/8 Yellowish Brown	Medium with occasional coarse grains	2.5	4 to 11
North Devon Variety 2	5YR 5/1 Gray	5Y 2.5/1 Black	Medium fine	3.5	3 to 9
North Devon Variety 3	2.5YR 5/8 Red (ext.) 5YR 5/1 Gray (int.)	5Y 5/3 Olive 10 YR 4/6 Dark Yellowish Brown	Very coarse	2.5	4 to 11
Totnes	5YR 4/4 Reddish brown (ext.) 10YR 5/1 Gray (int.)	5Y 3/2 Dark Olive 5Y 6/6 Olive Yellow	Medium with occasional coarse grains	3.5	4 to 10
Unspecified Type A	5YR 4/4 Reddish Brown	5Y 4/3 Olive	Coarse	3.5	5
Unspecified Type B	7.5YR 6/4 Light Brown (ext)	5Y 6/6 Olive Yellow	Medium fine	2.5	5 to 7
Unspecified Type C	2.5 YR 5/8 Red	10YR 5/8 Yellowish Brown	Medium with occasional coarse grains	2.5	3 to 5
Unspecified Type D	5YR 6/6 Reddish Yellow	2.5Y 5/6 Light Olive Brown	Medium	2.5	5 to 10

Note: In the case of mottled glazes, the dominant colors are indicated; see Shepard 1965, pp. 113-121 for a discussion of the Wentworth and Moh scales; thicknesses of sherds are given as ranges.

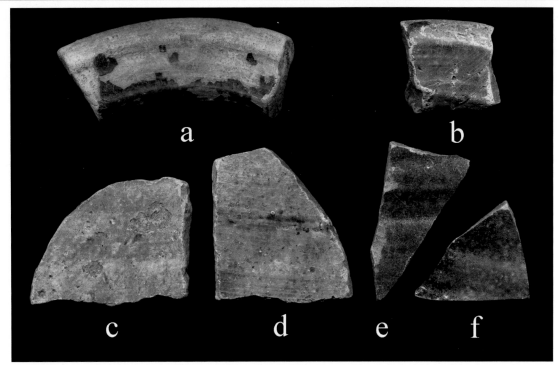

Figure 103. North Devon, variety 1: a-b, rim sherds (P669A, H no provenience); c-f, body sherds showing the range of glaze colors (P742C, P909E, P935D1, P646D). (1:1)

West of England

The most common ceramics found at Fort St. George are coarse earthenwares made in the West of England. The largest number of sherds may be classified within the type North Devon Plain (Watkins 1960). This type is further subdivided here into three varieties which are distinguished by minor differences in ware and glaze. It is important to note that the North Devon is gravel-free, and although there is a variety with coarser tempering it is distinct from the more famous gravel-tempered ware. A second named type was made in the vicinity of Totnes on the River Dart in South Devon. There are also four other unnamed types of earthenwares that are distinct from the North

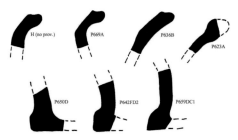

Figure 104. North Devon, variety 1: profiles of rim sherds and bases of baluster jars. (1:2)

Devon and Totnes pottery but that nevertheless display a kinship supporting a general West of England provenance. An additional 48 sherds also share west country characteristics, but do not quite fit into any of the specific types described here. That they are contemporary early seventeenth-century products, however, is evident from their ware and their provenience within Admiral Raleigh Gilbert's house, one of the most secure contexts within the fort.

North Devon, variety 1

Illustrations: Figures 41c, 63a, 71a, 77b-c, 79a, 84n-p, 87b-c, 103, 104.

Sample: 1287 sherds.

Paste: Low-fired, medium to fine textured ware, with fine sand tempering and occasional larger inclusions. Characteristically, the exterior surfaces are oxidized to a pinkish orange color while the interior

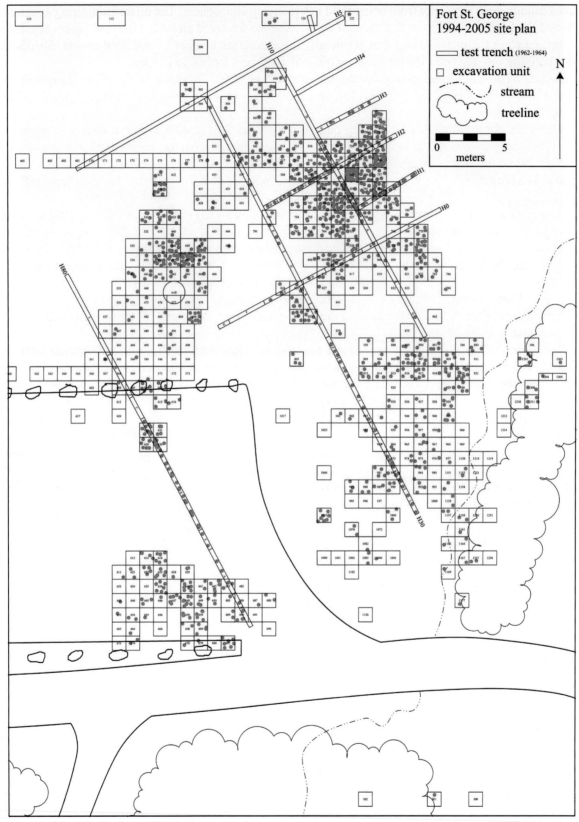

Figure 105. Distribution of North Devon, variety 1.

surfaces usually are a light gray from being fired in a reducing atmosphere. The differential firing apparently weakened the fabric to the extent that most of the sherds also fractured along flat internal planes separating the exteriors from the interiors and thus artificially increasing the number of unglazed sherds. Sherds that exhibit both the interior and exterior surfaces range in thickness from 4 to 11 mm.

Surface treatment: Lead-glazed on the interior surface only. The color of the glaze ranges from a yellowish brown to dark olive (Figure 103). Iron impurities may cause highly variable brown to black mottling.

Additional decoration: None. But poor quality control resulted in differences of ware and glaze that often make it easy to reconstruct subgroupings and even spot pieces from the same vessel. For example, 58 sherds exhibit an olive green glaze with brown speckles (Figure 103e) on a relatively fine paste, while 81 other sherds have a sandier, medium fine paste and a yellow green glaze heavily mottled with brown (Figure 103f).

Forms: The most common form, based on surviving rims and bases (Figures 103a-b, 104),is the tall baluster jar. At least eight individual jars have been identified, but the small size of the fragments and lack of joins do not allow reconstruction of forms or dimensions, except for one baluster rim that has a diameter of 9 cm. Some sherds exhibiting relatively fine and thin ware may be from table pieces, such as bowls or pitchers, but aside from some rim forms no other formal characteristics are known.

Origin: North Devon, probably from the vicinity of Barnstaple or Bideford.

Provenience: Broadly distributed within the compound of Fort St. George, but especially in the buttery and storehouse (Figure 105).

Comments: The baluster jar seems to have been the principal English shipping and storage container for liquids and viscous substances prior to the wide availability of glass containers in the mid-seventeenth century. The finer ware described here is characteristic of Fort St. George. Although Emerson Baker (pers. comm.) urges caution in making such chronological distinctions, it may be that the gravel-free baluster jar is a good marker for the earlier English colonial ventures and that it is replaced by the better known gravel-tempered version later in the century (Watkins 1960, pp. 48-51; Noël Hume 1969a, pp. 133-134, 1982, pp. 195-197; Faulkner and Faulkner 1987, pp. 203-205; Cranmer 1990, pp. 85-86; Deetz 1993, p. 38). Alison Grant (1983, p. 136, no. 10) has observed that the gravel-free jars tend to be smaller than the gravel-tempered examples which suggests that the latter continued in use in the larger size categories after glass containers became popular for smaller measures.

North Devon, variety 2

Illustrations: Figures 63b, 71b, 106, 107, 108, 109a-c.

Sample: 124 sherds.

Paste: Ware that is generally fine textured and relatively thin (3-9 cm). It is tempered with fine sand, and occasionally flat white particles (calcium carbonate?) that may create a laminated appearance. Color ranges from brown to gray that is uniform throughout (i.e., not exhibiting the differential exterior-interior surface colors of variety 1).

Surface treatment: Lead-glazed on the interior surface only. The color of the glaze is a very dark greenish black (Figure 106a-b). Although it is usually thickly applied, on at least one vessel it is thin and streaky in appearance (Figure 106c).

Additional decoration: None.

Forms: The only form recognized is the baluster jar (Figures 107, 108, 109a-c). As determined from surviving rims and bases at least four jars are present in the collection. These have rim diameters of 13 cm and the reconstructed height of one specimen is approximately 25 cm (Figure 108).

Origin: North Devon, but presumably from different potteries than those that produced variety 1.

Provenience: Almost entirely confined to the admiral's house, although a few sherds were found east of the lake near the shore (Figure 110). Two rim sherds, one from each location, join together perhaps indicating that some burned debris from the admiral's house was dumped into the bay.

Comments: This variety formalizes the range of variation within the production of baluster jars from North Devon.

Figure 106. North Devon, variety 2: body sherds from baluster jars showing range of glazes. Bottom left has been burned. (1:1)

Figure 107. North Devon, variety 2: partial baluster jar. (2:3)

Figure 108. North Devon, variety 2: reconstruction of baluster jar. (1:4)

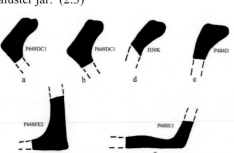

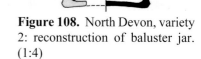

Figure 109. North Devon, varieties 2 and 3: a-c, profiles of rims and base of variety 2 baluster jars; d-e, profiles of rims of variety 3 baluster jars; f, base of variety 3 vessel. (1:2)

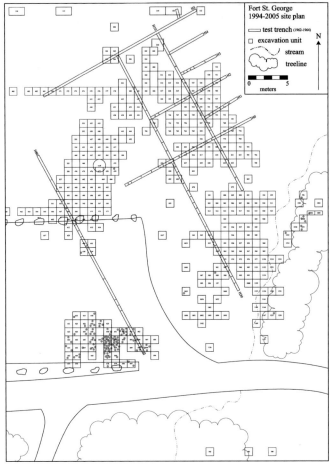

Figure 110. Distribution of North Devon, variety 2. The distribution of this variety is almost entirely restricted to the admiral's house which suggests that the vessels represent a private supply.

North Devon, variety 3

Illustrations: Figures 84q, 87a, 109d-f, 111.

Sample: 56 sherds.

Paste: Ware that is coarse in texture due to heavy tempering with sand and larger chunky particles of calcium carbonate (Figure 111, see especially d). "North Devon Calcareous Temper" wares are known from early seventeenth century sites in Newfoundland (Nixon 1999) and may represent an early ware transitional to gravel-tempered. Whatever the case, their coarseness stands out in comparison to the gravel-free ware more commonly found at Fort St. George. These sherds, however, generally exhibit the highly oxidized exteriors and reduced interiors that is characteristic of variety 1, and thicknesses fall into the same range (4-11 mm).

Surface treatment: Lead glaze interior surfaces and occasionally exterior. Color is generally a greenish yellow to olive brown (Figure 111). Where the glaze is thick or puddled it is dark brown.

Additional decoration: None.

Forms: At least two rims are from baluster jars (Figures 109d-f, 111a) and three pieces of handles indicate some form of pot. Two of the handles are strap handles that are much wider than they are thick. Other rims, bases, and curved body sherds seem to be from simple bowl forms while a large handle fragment may be from a pipkin (Figure 111e).

Origin: North Devon, based on ware and glaze characteristics.

Provenience: Broadly distributed across the site, but with the highest concentration in the admiral's house (Figure 112).

Comments: Although bowl forms are most common, possibly falling within Type no. 3 as illustrated by Grant (1983, pp. 136-137), the rim profiles are most similar to her no. 6 which is a chafing dish. A gravel-tempered chafing dish is known from Jamestown (Watkins 1960, fig. 20), and "chafyng disshes" are among items specifically mentioned as being bought by Sir Ferdinando Gorges for the provision of the Popham Colony (Quinn and Quinn 1983, p. 377). The pipkin and pots are also indicative of food preparation. Overall, the relative rarity of anything approaching gravel-tempered ware underscores the fact that its popularity is later in the century.

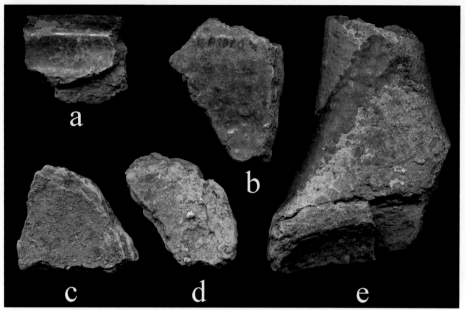

Figure 111. North Devon, variety 3: a, rim (H30K); b-d, body sherds, d especially shows calcareous tempering (P937C, P648D, P189C); e, handle from pot or pipkin (P947B). (1:1)

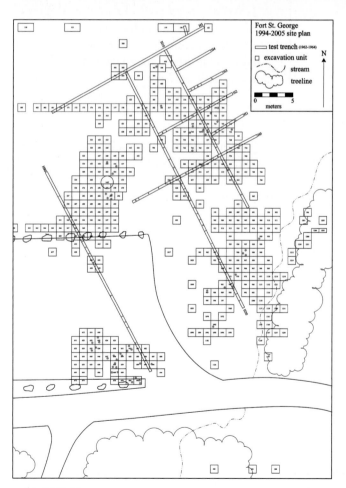

Fort St. George
1994-2005 site plan

test trench (1962-1964)
☐ excavation unit
stream
treeline

0   5
meters

N

Figure 112 (left). Distribution of North Devon, variety 3. This rarest variety of North Devon is broadly distributed, but the highest concentration was found in the admiral's house.

Totnes

Illustrations: Figures 41b, 63c, 71e, 77a, 79b, 87d, 113, 114.

Sample: 82 sherds.

Paste: Medium to coarse sandy ware that characteristically has inclusions of small pieces of black mica. Color is gray to dark gray, although exterior surfaces and sometimes the interiors are commonly oxidized to an orange brown. Thicknesses range from 4 to 10 mm.

Surface treatment: Roughly smoothed with a light to dark olive lead glaze applied to interior surfaces and occasional splatters on exterior (Figure 113).

Additional decoration: None, although horizontal lines may be cut into the exterior while vessel was still on the wheel.

Forms: The only form recognized is a cooking pot with everted rim (Figure 114). At least two large pots are manifested by rim and handle fragments: the two handles are round in cross section and grooved on the outside surface, but are sufficiently different in form to

Figure 113. Totnes: a, rim of pot (P649B, P658B, P659DC1, P685D1); b-c, body sherds (P656B1, P658C); d-e, handles (P625A, P668C); f-h, bases (P742B, P875B, P955B). (1:1)

conclude that they came from two different vessels. Two smaller pots are indicated by a series of relatively thin sherds.

Origin: South Devon, in the vicinity of Totnes which is not far from the Gilbert family seat at Compton Castle.

Provenience: Although found in all the major locations, there is a definite bias in favor of residential locations. Furthermore, there are significant differences between the distributions of the large and small pots.

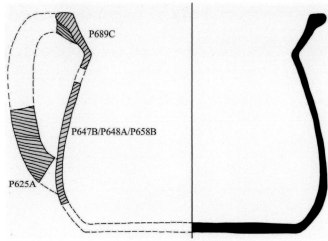

Figure 114. Totnes: reconstruction of pot. (1:3)

Sherds of the former are concentrated in the admiral's house (Figure 115), while most of the sherds from the small pots were found in the vicinity of the vice admiral's house and buttery (Figure 116).

Comments: This type of pottery was not widely distributed even in England and very little has been found in nearby Exeter and Plymouth. In this country, it has only been reported from Jamestown and Newfoundland (Straube 1998, Nixon 1999, Gilbert 2000, Crompton 2000).

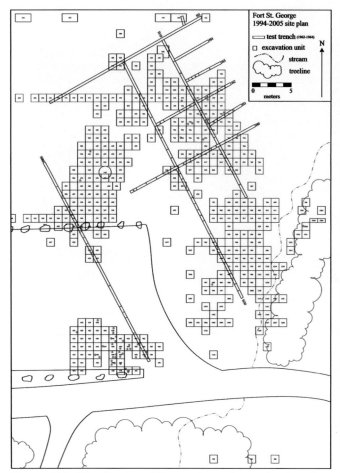

Figure 115. Distribution of Totnes, large form. This form is characteristic of the admiral's house with only a scattering of sherds elsewhere.

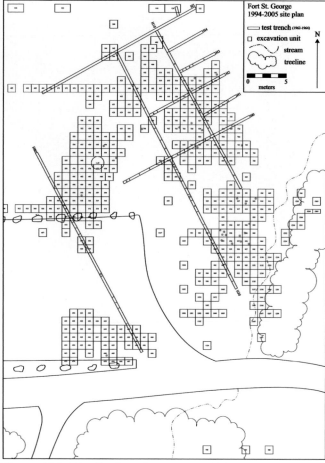

Figure 116. Distribution of Totnes, small form. Sherds of the smaller form were found primarily in the vicinity of the vice admiral's house and buttery.

Figure 117. West of England: a-c, Type A (P804C, P807B, P755C); d, Type B (P642FD3); e-g, Type C (P635B, P460C, P189C); h-k, Type D (P491G1, P490I, H30E, P566E); l, unclassified, Somerset-like (P678B); m, unclassified, similar to Type C but unslipped (P456E). (1:1)

Unspecified West of England, Type A

    Illustrations: Figures 117a-c, 118.

    Sample: 92 sherds.

    Paste: Coarse sand-tempered ware. The basic color is oxidized orange, except for the exterior surface which is reduced gray. This ware is relatively thin, averaging 5 mm in thickness.

    Surface treatment: Interior surfaces only are lead-glazed. The color is a bright, dappled green, although it has deteriorated on many sherds to a pale gray-green (Figure 117a-c).

    Additional decoration: None.

    Forms: Only one sherd exhibits distinctive formal characteristics and that is a rim from a baluster jar (Figures 117a, 118). The jar apparently is similar in size to the standard North Devon jar as the diameter of

Figure 118. West of England, Type A baluster jar rim profile. (1:2)

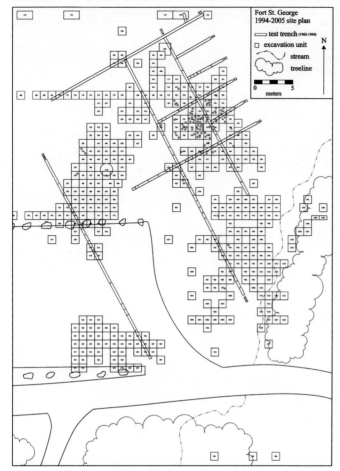

Figure 119. Distribution of West of England, Type A. Almost entirely confined to the buttery, this type must have been used for storage.

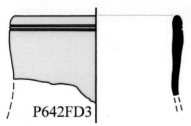

Figure 120. West of England, Type B rim profile. (1:2).

the rim is 13 cm.

Origin: Although at first the characteristics of this ware suggested an Iberian origin, the distinctive baluster form would seem to require the assignment of this type to the West of England, perhaps even North Devon.

Provenience: With only a couple of exceptions, this type is clustered around the buttery (Figure 119).

Comments: The ware and glaze characteristics are very different from anything else in the Popham collection. Since its provenience at the site was almost entirely restricted to a single location it is probable that all of these sherds came from only one vessel.

Unspecified West of England, Type B

Illustrations: Figures 71d, 117d, 120.

Sample: 13 sherds.

Paste: Fine textured ware with very fine sand tempering and occasional pieces of hematite. Color is a pinkish brown, although surfaces may be a pale to dark gray. Thicknesses range from 5 to 7 mm.

Surface treatment: Both interior and exterior surfaces are well smoothed and covered with a thin olive yellow glaze (Figure 117d).

Additional decoration: Incising.

Forms: These sherds are all probably from the same vessel which was a mug or wide-mouthed jug (Figure 120). Two parallel lines are incised around the rim just below the lip and that would suggest that a jug is the more likely form.

Origin: The defining characteristics of this ware are most similar to the published descriptions of Somerset wares most of which were produced at Donyatt (Coleman-Smith and Pearson 1988).

Provenience: All pieces of this vessel were found in the admiral's house (Figure 121).

Comments: The bulk of coarse earthenwares that have been found in the seventeenth-century contexts in Plymouth and Exeter were produced in South Somerset (ibid.). It is widely distributed in the Chesapeake (Kizer 1998), and is "the second most common English coarse earthenware after the North Devon wares" at Ferryland, Newfoundland (Nixon 1999; see also Gilbert 2000). West Somerset was also a major center of pottery production and similar wares were made there (McCarthy and Brooks 1988).

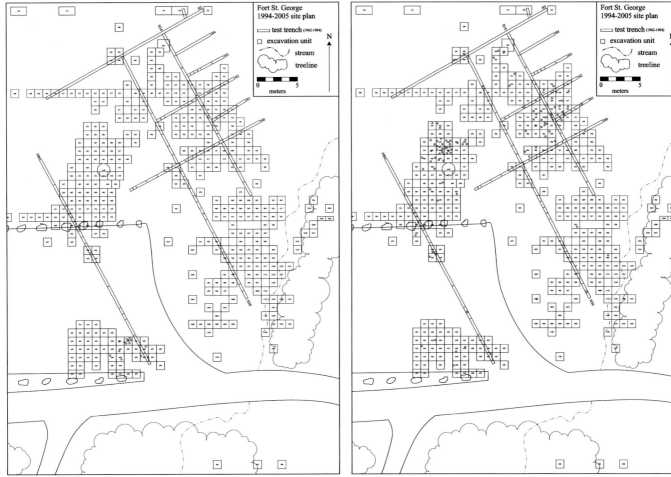

Figure 121. Distribution of West of England, Type B. Confined to the admiral's house, this type was probably used for serving.

Figure 122. Distribution of West of England, Type C. Primarily found in the storehouse and buttery, but the open forms would suggest some other function than storage.

Unspecified West of England, Type C

 Illustrations: Figures 71c, 117e-g.

 Sample: 112 sherds.

 Paste: Medium textured redware tempered with fine sand that occasionally includes larger particles. This ware is uniformly oxidized. Thickness ranges from 3 to 5 mm.

 Surface treatment: These sherds have a white kaolin slip, usually on the interior surface only. A lead glaze was then applied over the slip. The color of the glaze is amber, ranging from a greenish yellow to a yellowish brown, although it is badly deteriorated on most of these sherds (Figure 117e-g).

 Additional decoration: None. West of England slipwares are often incised, but none of these sherds exhibit sgrafitto decoration.

 Forms: None of these sherds is large enough to exhibit specific formal attributes, but the general curvatures and uniform firing of both the exterior and interior surfaces indicate simple open forms such as bowls.

 Origin: The West Country of England attribution is supported by the similarity of the paste and glaze characteristics to North Devon, variety 1.

 Provenience: Although found across the site, this type is concentrated in the storehouse and buttery (Figure 122).

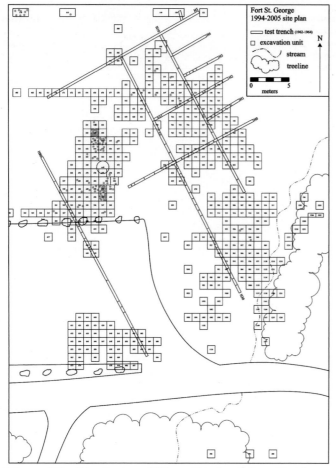

Figure 123. Distribution of West of England, Type D. Almost entirely confined to the storehouse, this type must have been used for a particular kind of storage.

Comments: This pottery would appear to be the same as Watkins' (1960, p. 48) "North Devon Plain Slip-Coated Ware," except that the firing characteristics are more uniform than the standard North Devon product.

Unspecified West of England, Type D
   Illustrations: Figures 41a, 117h-k.
   Sample: 131 sherds.
   Paste: Uniformly oxidized redware with medium texture and no obvious tempering materials; almost brick-like in appearance. Thicknesses range from 5 to 10 mm.
   Surface treatment: Green tinted lead glaze that may contain reddish brown speckles (Figure 117h-k). Glaze is applied to the interior surfaces and occasionally the exterior.
   Additional decoration: None.
   Forms: There are no rims or bases or other formally distinctive sherds. Open vessels such as bowls are presumed.
   Origin: West Country?
   Provenience: This type is particularly common in the storehouse, with a scattering elsewhere (Figure 123).
   Comments: The glaze color and ware of these sherds is very similar to some other sherds typical of the late eighteenth- or early nineteenth-century that also have been found at the site. On the nineteenth-century vessels, however, the green glaze turns clear (so that it appears reddish brown) while these examples

only have green glaze. Furthermore, these sherds have been found in good Fort St. George contexts and clearly must represent an earlier production. Because of the confusion, many sherds undoubtedly were overlooked in earlier sortings

Iberia

The so-called Iberian olive jar was the favored international container for the bulk shipment and storage of a wide range of foodstuffs, liquids and other materials. Made in Spain or Portugal, they are found in every European country and, eventually, European colony. Sherds are easily recognized by their coarse sandy texture, buff to pinkish orange color, and general absence of glaze.

There are 150 olive jar sherds from Fort St. George. These exhibit a medium to coarse sand-tempered ware that is generally a creamy buff or light brownish gray in color, but may be oxidized to a pinkish orange. Sixty-eight sherds are creamy buff with a coarse sandy paste and an average thickness of 9 mm. Most of these (62, including three rims) were found in the admiral's house, but five plus one rim came from the vicinity of the vice admiral's house. Another 79 sherds are pinkish orange in color and tempered with medium to coarse sand (although one rim sherd from the storehouse has very fine sand tempering). Sixty-four of these are from the storehouse. Nine, including one rim, are from the vicinity of the vice admiral's house, while another rim was found in the admiral's house and five sherds came from the buttery location. Many of these appear to

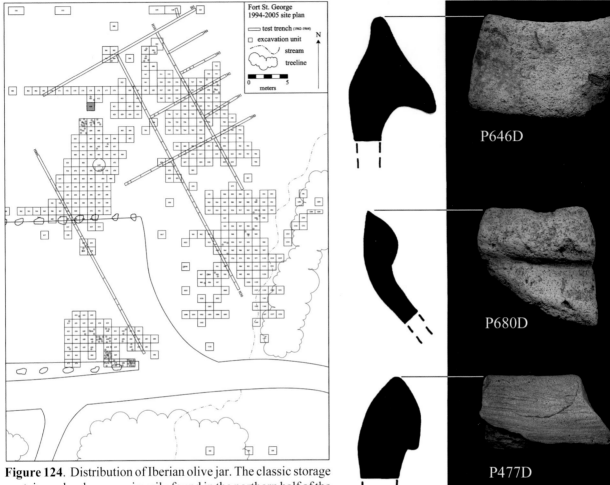

Figure 124. Distribution of Iberian olive jar. The classic storage container, sherds were primarily found in the northern half of the storehouse and the eastern half of the admiral's house, suggesting they had very distinctive contents.

Figure 125. Iberian olive jar rims and profiles. (1:1)

have a whitish slip on the exterior (see Marken 1994, p. 42 for a consideration that such surface finishes were the result of natural erosion or chemical changes during the firing process rather than a purposeful addition). Three more sherds of a light brown color and very coarse sandy paste that average 6 mm in thickness were found in the north end of the storehouse. Differences in ware and rims indicate that at least seven different jars are represented in the collection. Most of these apparently were kept in the northern half of the storehouse and eastern half of the admiral's house (Figure 124).

Although all of the sherds are too small to indicate overall forms, the rims all exhibit the characteristic "donut shape" of a Middle Style D jar (Figure 125) which was common in the early seventeenth century (Deagan 1987, pp. 32-34; Skowronek 1987; James 1988; South et al. 1988, pl. 91). Similar rims have been found at Jamestown where they are identified with Type A olive jars (Kelso, et al. 1999, p. 39; see also Marken 1994, pp. 50-73). Kelso, et al. note that this is the largest standard size of jar and was commonly used for wine (ibid., p. 38).

Holland

A distinctive soft, finely textured, and low-fired ware that is entirely covered with an opaque tin glaze is characteristic of some finer ceramics that were made in Europe in the sixteenth to eighteenth centuries. Collectively, tin-glazed wares made in Holland and England are generically referred to as "delftware" or

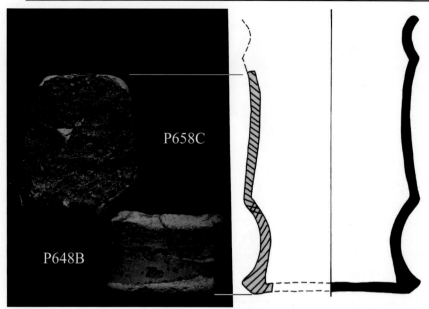

Figure 126. Delft potsherds and reconstructed profile of *albarello* apothecary jar. (1:1)

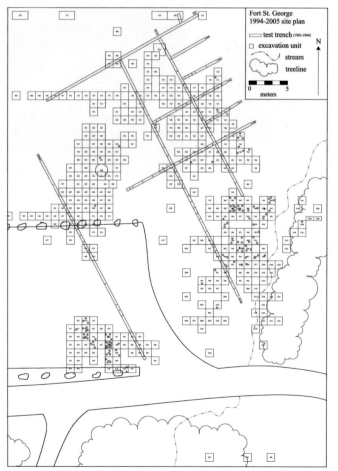

Figure 127. Distribution of delftware. Clearly a prestige item, most of the sherds were found in the admiral's house and vicinity of the vice admiral's house.

"delft" (Noël Hume 1969a, pp. 105-106; Miller and Stone 1970, p. 26). Although delftware production had been introduced into England during the last third of the sixteenth century (Gaimster 1999, p. 220; Stephenson 1999, p. 264), it seems probable that in the early seventeenth century most delft still was imported from Holland (Crossley 1990, pp. 260, 264). The term "Delft" is restricted to ceramics known to have been made in that city. When the word is capitalized in these pages it is to be understood as a requirement of grammatical convention while the meaning always remains generic.

There are 121 delftware sherds and at least five pieces of detached glaze in the collection from Popham. Most of the sherds have lost their tin glaze, presumably due to ground water and frost action that would have caused the soft ware to expand and contract. A partial vessel from the admiral's house still retains its blue painted overglaze, probably because it had been refired in the conflagration that consumed part of the structure (and thus more securely attached the glaze to the ware?). Two other sherds from the admiral's house have a blue design painted on the white ground, but they are too small for decorative motifs to be reconstructed. Two basal sherds, one with a purplish glaze the other with a blue glaze, were found between the vicinity of the vice admiral's house and the buttery. These sherds and the blue glazed vessel from the admiral's house manifest the distinctive *albarello* form of an apothecary jar (Figure 126).

Almost all of the sherds came from the admiral's house or the general vicinity of the vice admiral's house: 49 and 66 respectively (Figure 127). Although there are fewer from the admiral's house they include the biggest and best sherds. Most of those show some evidence of fire, while those from the vice admiral's location do not. The restriction of this finer ceramic to these prime residential loci clearly signifies the importance of the residents.

Stoneware

With the exception of one small gray salt-glazed sherd that may have been made in Raeren, all of the early seventeenth-century stoneware from Fort St. George belongs to a single type that was made in or near Frechen in the Rhineland region of Germany.

Bellarmine

Pot-bellied jugs made of a hard impermeable stoneware were a favored container for the shipping, storage and serving of a variety of liquids before glass bottles became generally available in the mid-seventeenth century. Like the olive jars discussed above, these jugs were widely traded throughout Europe and their presence at a colonial site during this period is quite common.

The ware is hard and finely textured with no visible tempering. Color is a uniform light gray. The surfaces are salt-glazed on the exterior and sometimes interior surfaces. The interior glaze is thin and reveals the surface color through a brownish tinge. The exterior glaze is much thicker and usually mottled with a dark brown iron oxide slip, although it can be a light gray-green color even on the same vessel. The vaporizing of the salt during the glazing creates a characteristic pitted, or "orange peel," appearance. Molded medallions were often added to the body and stylized human face masks applied to the necks (Figure 128).

This type is known as "Tigerware," after the distinctive mottled and streaked appearance of the glaze, as "Frechen," after the district in the Rhineland where most

Figure 128. Modern reproduction of Bellarmine jug, based on sherds from a jug found at Jamestown which is very similar to one from Fort St. George. (1:2)

of it was made, and as "Bartmann," "d'Alva," or "graybeard" when the stylized face masks are applied to the neck area opposite the handle (Noël Hume 1969a, pp. 55-57, 276-279; Brain 1979, pp. 74-75; Wilcoxen 1987, pp. 75-76). We have chosen to retain the "Bellarmine" nomenclature, despite the eponymous discordance, because it is the earliest recorded historical reference (1634) for such vessels in England. Similar ware made in England is called "Fulham," but there is no evidence that it was in production early in the seventeenth century (Crossley 1990, p. 266; Miller 1991, pp. 368-370) and thus there is no reason to suspect that any of the Popham stoneware is not the usual Rhenish product.

There are 213 sherds of Bellarmine jugs in the Popham collection (Figure 129). Portions of sixteen medallions are present, some of which are duplicates (i.e., made from the same molds) that probably came from the same vessel for these jugs often had three identical medallions on the body. Although there are no whole medallions, the duplication often allows reconstruction of much of the design (Figure 129g-j). These exhibit animal, floral and other motifs typical of the early seventeenth century. There are at least seven distinct designs, three of which may be specifically identified as having been made in Frechen (Gaimster 1997, p. 210) and one of these is dated 1599 (Figure 129i). Pieces of at least five masks are also present (Figure 129d-e). A minimum of seven distinct vessels is indicated by the different medallions and masks, as well as multiple crossmends and matches.

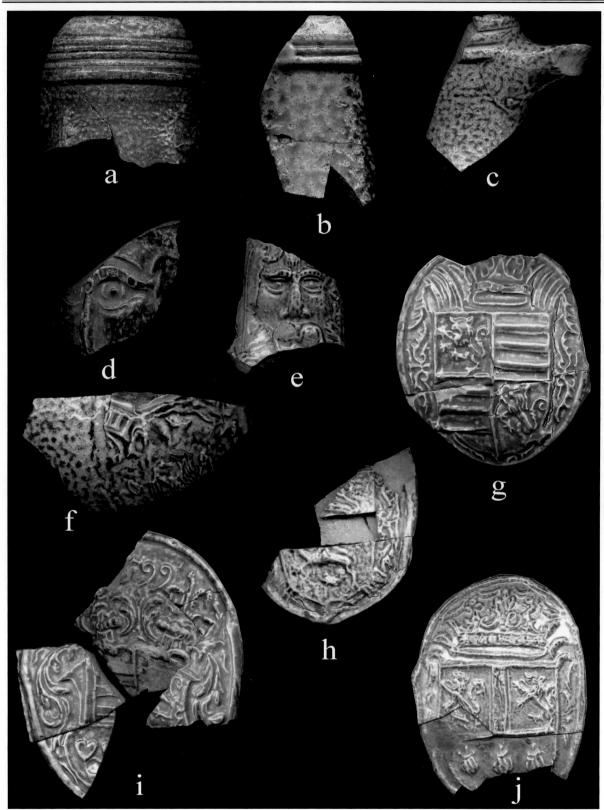

Figure 129. Bellarmine potsherds: a-c, rims (P964B/P992B, P965B/P965D/P984C, P967D); d-e, face masks (P647A, P975C); f, medallion (P862C); g-j, reconstructions of medallions from four different jugs. (1:1)

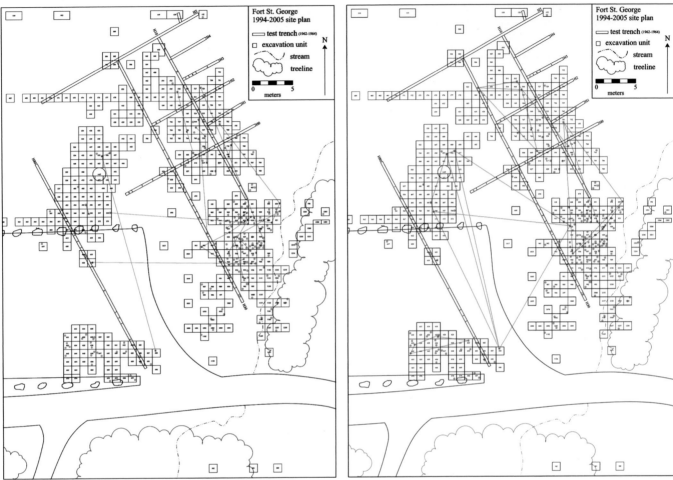

Figure 130. Distribution of Bellarmine. Although scattered broadly across the site, the majority of the Bellarmine sherds were found in the vicinity of the vice admiral's house. Crossmends relate many of these pieces to other locations, however, making this a diagnostic artifact for tying the site together. The fact that more than three quarters of the Bellarmine sherds were found in the vice admiral's and admiral's houses confirms its usual fuction as service ware.

Figure 131. Distributions of fragments of Bellarmine medallions presumed to be from individual Bellarmine jugs. Although some jugs are restricted to a single location, others are found at multiple proveniences.

The majority (63%) of the Bellarmine sherds were found in the vicinity of the vice admiral's house, while 13% were found in the admiral's house, 11% around the buttery, only 6% in the storehouse, and 7% elsewhere (Figure 130). Pieces of the same jugs, and actual joining pieces, were found widely scattered. For example, pieces of one jug were found in the admiral's house, on the floor of the storehouse, and in the vicinity of the vice admiral's house (Figure 131). Others are shared by two locations, such as the vice admiral's house and buttery, while two jugs were restricted to a single provenience.

CLAY TOBACCO PIPES

There are 743 fragments of clay tobacco pipes from the Popham site. Of these, 256 date to the seventeenth century, while the remainder were made in the late eighteenth and nineteenth centuries. All but

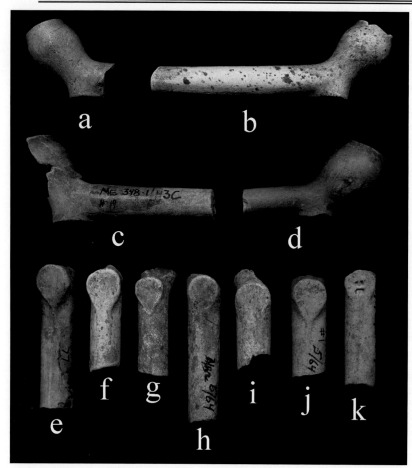

Figure 132. The diagnostic early seventeenth-century type of clay tobacco pipe from Fort St. George: a-d, belly bowls (P529B, P729E, H3C, P893D); e-j, characteristic teardrop-shaped heels (H1A, P911E, H30K, P821B, P1150A, P957A); k, teardrop heel with incuse mark (P946A). (1:1)

three of these were made in Europe of white kaolin clay. The three exceptions are redware pipes that not only post-date Fort St. George, but are the product of an entirely different American industry. These and the later eighteenth- and nineteenth-century pipes are not discussed here.

The seventeenth-century pipes are classified into three types, only one of which is characteristic of the Fort St. George period. The other two types date later in the century and are described below in order to contrast these more familiar styles with the earlier Fort St. George pipes. Eighteen very small fragments of pipe bowls that certainly date to the seventeenth century but are not large enough for formal classification are not included in the following discussion.

The diagnostic Fort St. George type consists of 45 bowl and 170 stem fragments. All of these came from little pipes that are completely undecorated (Figure 132). Bowls are the small "belly" form with constricted rims, the lips of which are plainly rounded or beveled. Heels are flat and exhibit a characteristic teardrop shape. These are all characteristics that identify pipes of the earliest period, ca. 1580-1610 (Oswald 1951, 1955, 1960, 1975, p. 39, nos. 1-3; Noël Hume 1969a, fig. 97; Miller 1991, pp. 639-640). Only one of the heels is stamped with an unidentified incuse impression which may be a maker's mark (Figure 132k).

These pipes are also distinct from the later pipes in manifesting an off-white, pinkish buff, or beige surface coloration. At first, this phenomenon was ascribed to variable soil discoloration, but closer analysis confirmed that it was a consistent characteristic of these early pipes. Indeed, fresh breaks reveal that the clay fired to a creamy, often pinkish, color. The surfaces of these pipes tend to erode easily so that they feel slightly rough in contrast to the hard and smooth, even glossy, finish of the later pipes.

On the other hand, the bore diameters of these pipes are strikingly similar to eighteenth- and nineteenth-century pipes: of the measurable bowls, 2 are 4/64 inches, 10 are 5/64, 8 are 6/64, one is 7/64, and one is 8/64; of the stems, 7 are 4/64, 86 are 5/64, 40 are 6/64, 6 are 7/64, 2 are 8/64 and 29 are unmeasurable. The overall average bore, therefore, is 5.5/64. As has long been recognized, the Harrington-Binford formula is not applicable to this early period of pipe manufacture (Noël Hume 1969a, p. 300).

The length of the stems is unknown, but the mouthpiece tapers to a diameter that is just larger than the bore. Stems from which the mouthpiece has been broken off have been whittled to remove sharp edges.

This type may have been made in London. Although London and the Netherlands seem to have dominated pipe manufacture in the first half of the seventeenth century, there is evidence that Bristol was an important secondary center (Oswald 1960, pp. 42-44). Bristol, in turn, came to dominate the industry later

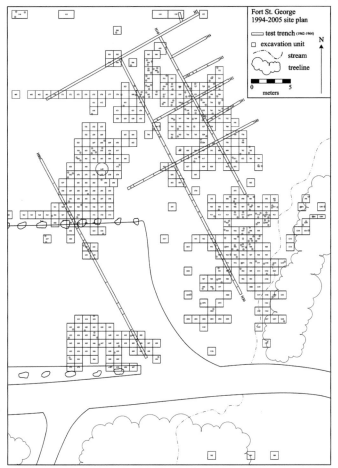

Figure 133. Distribution of the Fort St. George type of clay tobacco pipe. Although broadly scattered across the site, it will be noted that there are relatively few fragments from the admiral's house, suggesting that Raleigh Gilbert may not have indulged in the habit.

in the seventeenth and eighteenth centuries, and perhaps its participation in the early years has not been sufficiently recognized.

Based on the number of distinctive heels in the collection there is a minimum number of 22 pipes, although the more than 200 bowl and stem fragments surely represent many more. These are distributed broadly across the site (Figure 133), but are concentrated around the storehouse (61), buttery/corporal's house (45) and in the vicinity of the vice admiral house (73). It is notable that at the residential locations more than a quarter of the fragments are from bowls, whereas at the storehouse more than 93% are stem pieces.

The later seventeenth-century types of pipes found at the site are easily distinguished from the Fort St. George pipes. They are the only definitively later seventeenth-century artifacts that have been found at the site, and it is probable that they were left by transient populations. One type has a belly bowl, but is much larger than the Fort St. George type, is made of the bright white kaolin clay, and has a stepped round heel (Figure 134a). The only decoration is a single rouletted line below the rim or around the body. This type is similar to no. 4 described by Oswald (1955, p. 245, pl. 1) and probably dates to ca. 1610-1650. Only three reconstructed bowls and four fragments have been found at the Popham site. Two of the bowls have bore diameters of 7/64 and one is 8/64. Six stems with bores of 7/64 and 3 with bores of 8/64 may also be assigned to this type.

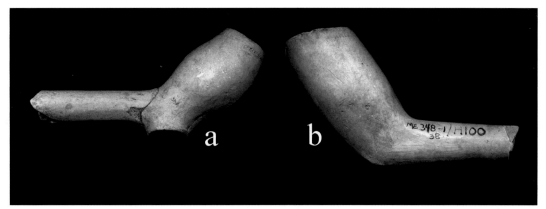

Figure 134. Later seventeenth-century clay tobacco pipes from the Popham site: a, decorated belly bowl type (P460H); b, "export" type (H100). (1:1)

All of the bowls and stems were found in mixed contexts postdating the Fort St. George occupation, although most of one pipe (bowl and four stem pieces) was found in an unusual intrusive pit into the floor of the storehouse. The presence of this type at the site coincides with the native reappearance after the fort was abandoned, and it may be that the pipes were left during the search for salvageable materials.

The second later sixteenth-century type of pipe is often referred to as "export" since it is rarely found in Europe, and because it is similar to some forms of aboriginal pipes and so is believed to have been made specifically for the native trade (Faulkner and Faulkner 1987, pp. 166, 171). These pipes are heelless and the bowls are funnel-shaped, with little or no constriction at the rim (Figure 134b). Unlike eighteenth-century examples where the plane of the rim is parallel to the stem (e.g., Brain 1979, p. 220), the rim plane of the one whole pipe bowl from Popham tilts slightly forward away from the smoker. The only decoration on the bowl is a single rouletted line below the lip. This combination of formal traits dates the type to the third quarter of the seventeenth century. Essentially identical pipes are known from the nearby Clarke and Lake trading settlement that was occupied from 1654 to 1676 (Baker 1985, pls. 5e, 7a). Another pipe from Pemaquid bears the maker's mark "LE" which is believed to stand for Llewellyn Evans who was active in the second half of the seventeenth century (Camp 1975, pp. 57, 60; Oswald 1960, p. 69). A stem fragment from Popham decorated with an intricate rouletted design also dates to this period, if not the same type. Identical examples are known from the Clarke and Lake site and from Pentagoet (Faulkner and Faulkner 1987, fig. 6.8, 1b), and may also have been made by Llewellyn Evans. Our pipes could have been left by warriors who passed through the area during King Philip's War. Only three pipes of this type were found at Popham, all from post-Fort St. George contexts in the vicinity of the storehouse. The best example was found at the bottom of the nineteenth-century well that was cleaned out by Hadlock's crew in 1962. Two more fragments and the decorated stem were found in surface levels nearby.

GLASS

Glass artifacts were relatively rare and expensive at this period. Nevertheless, a variety of items made of glass have been found in Fort St. George contexts. These are discussed in four functional categories: containers, tableware, ornaments and flat glass. A half dozen pieces of melted glass from the admiral's house that have been altered beyond all recognition are not classified here.

Containers

The largest category of glass consists of bottle fragments of various different forms and colors. Although color is considered an unreliable criterion for classifying glass (Jones and Sullivan 1985, p. 12), it is often the only useful attribute in an archaeological collection consisting mostly of small sherds. Also, color does seem to have some significance for establishing chronology, production, and provenance (e.g., Noël Hume 1969a, b; Faulkner and Faulkner 1987, pp. 232-239). For example, the colored container glass from Fort St. George exhibits a range of light green hues that are distinctly different from the dark olive green glass that becomes common later in the seventeenth century. The few examples of the latter that have been found at the site came from post-Fort St. George contexts and are not discussed here. All of the container glass described below is consistent with what is known of early seventeenth-century manufacture. They are classified into four categories on the basis of formal characteristics, presumed function and probable origin (provenance), as well as color.

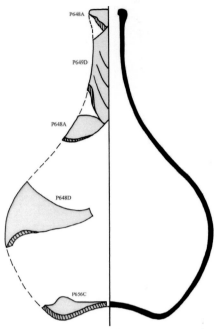

Figure 135. Glass flask reconstruction from fragments found in the admiral's house. (1:3)

Figure 136. Glass flask fragments from the admiral's house. (1:1)

Flasks

There are 213 pieces of light green glass from bottles of a distinctive form known as a flask (Noël Hume 1956, pp. 98-100, Willmott 2002, pp. 79-81). Flasks are round, long-necked bottles with plain rims (Figure 135). These bottles are undecorated, except that the one good neck and two body sherds exhibit what is known as optic-blown wrythen ribbing (Willmott 2002, p. 15 and fig. 98). Bottles of this distinctive form were made in England (ibid., p. 79) and are found in London contexts dating to ca. 1580-1620. They "could have been used to contain all types of liquids" (ibid.). Flasks were made of potash glass and the actual color varies according to the thickness of the glass, being almost clear in the thinnest pieces and quite dark in the thickest (Figure 136). That thickness ranges from 1 mm to 5 mm for body fragments and as much as 10 mm for bases. Bottoms have a slight kick-up and ring-shaped pontil marks. Most of these fragments were found in the admiral's house and in the vicinity of the vice admiral's house (Figure 137). Ninety-four were found in the admiral's house. On the basis of color and formal attributes, especially pontil marks, at least four flasks are represented at that location. Another 95 pieces representing five flasks were found in the vicinity of the vice admiral's house. Because pieces from two vessels overlap both locations, the minimum number of flasks is seven. Of the remaining 24 fragments, 13 were found around the buttery and the rest were scattered about the site. Only one was found in the storehouse. Clearly, flasks were prestige items.

Two bases were not pushed up (Figure 138), indicating that the bodies were entirely globular. In order to function as storage or serving containers they may have been cladded in leather or wicker. Or, they may have been from bottles that had a very different function as urinals (Willmott 2002, p. 103). Such bottles might not seem to be a necessity in the wilderness, but they could have been part of the medical kit of the physician, Master Turner. The illustrated base also was reused by Native Americans who apparently employed it as a scraper as evidenced by a chipped edge. It was found by Hadlock's crew at the bottom of the nineteenth-century well. The other base was found in the vicinity of the vice admiral's house.

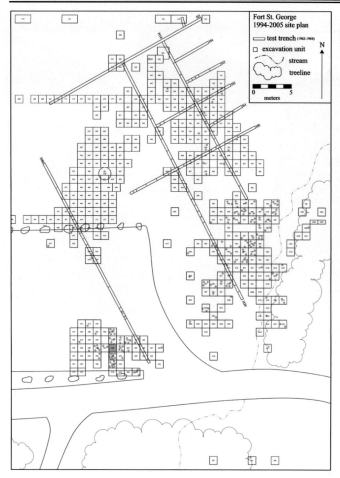

Figure 137. Distribution of glass flasks. Almost entirely restricted to the admiral's house and vicinity of the vice admiral's house, flasks were obviously a prestige item at Fort St. George.

Figure 139. Glass bouteille from the buttery reconstructed by Margaret Burnham (cf. Figure 77n). (1:2, photograph courtesy of Maine State Museum)

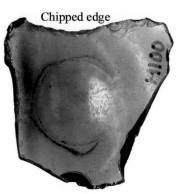

Figure 138. Glass bottle convex base. It has been chipped along one edge and used as a scraper. (1:1)

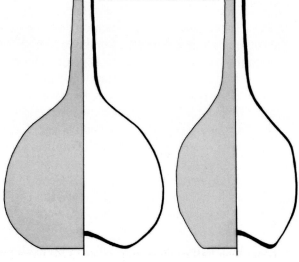

Figure 140. Glass bouteille reconstruction. (1:3)

Bouteille

A nearly complete, but fragmentary, bottle was recovered from one of the buttery postholes (P742). It has a distinctive blue-green color and was flattened so that it has an oval cross section (Figures 139-140). The neck is not ribbed and the rim is unfinished – that is, it was left just as it was when cut off the pontil. Although the glass is about 2 mm thick in the neck and base, the body averages less than 1 mm. It seems likely that such a delicate bottle must have been protected with a wicker covering (Figure 141). In fact, fragments of wicker have been found with pieces of what appear to be very similar bottles at a seventeenth-century site in France (Cabart 1983, p. 252). More of these bottles are known from the 1604-1605 French settlement on St. Croix (Giovanna Vitelli, pers. comm., 2005) and so this type is believed to have been made in France, thus explain-

Figure 141. *Le Dessert de Gaufrettes* by Lubin Baugin. A wicker-covered bottle similar to the bouteille is depicted in this 1630s painting by the Parisian artist. (Musée de Louvre, R.F. 1954.23)

ing the nomenclature used here. What appear to be other examples, however, are known from the Low Countries (Henkes 1994, p. 244) and a 1580s shipwreck off the coast of Croatia (Willmott, pers. comm., 2006), leaving the possibility open for another provenance.

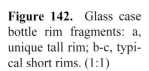

Figure 142. Glass case bottle rim fragments: a, unique tall rim; b-c, typical short rims. (1:1)

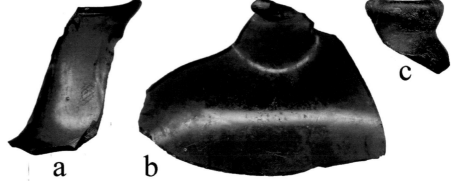

Case Bottles

There are 745 fragments of greenish glass that are from case bottles. These bottles have square bases, flat sides, rounded shoulders, and short everted rims (Figures 142- 143). Thickness of the glass varies from 1.5 mm to 14 mm. Color ranges from light bluish green to light green to yellowish green (Figure 144). The color indicates that the glass was fired in wood-burning furnaces. Since it is believed that the English were turning to coal-burning furnaces at this time (Godfrey 1975, pp. 38-74), these bottles may have been made on the continent. The bluish green color is particularly common in contemporary French products, although other provenances such as Germany and the Netherlands cannot be ruled out.

More than half of these fragments (374) were found in the admiral's house (Figure 145). Many of the sherds are heat altered and so cannot be easily matched. Nevertheless, based on formal characteristics and color a minimum number of five case bottles were found exclusively at that location. Pieces of three more bottles were shared with the vice admiral in the vicinity of whose house 280 fragments were found. Another three bottles from that location could be matched with pieces from the buttery and the storehouse, which had 44 and 13 fragments respectively. Most of the remaining sherds (25) were concentrated east of the lake.

Figure 144. Glass case bottle fragments showing the range of glass color: a-b, blue-green; c, light green; d, yellow-green. (1:1)

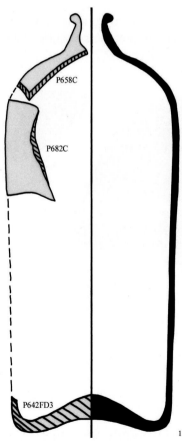

Figure 143. Reconstruction of case bottle. (1:2)

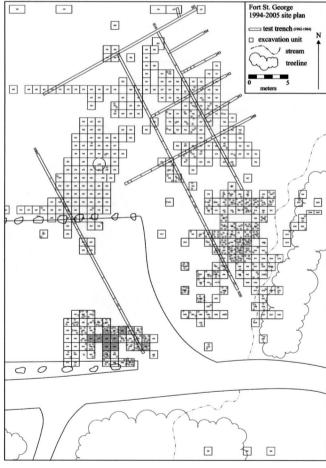

Figure 145. Distribution of glass case bottles. Case bottles were another prestige item found primarily in the admiral's house and the vicinity of the vice admiral's house. Quite a few fragments, however, were also found in the buttery which makes sense considering the primary function of the bottles.

Figure 146. Glass phial fragments. (1:1)

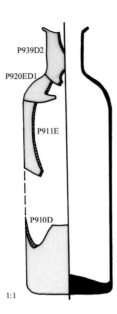

Figure 147. Glass phial reconstruction. (1:1)

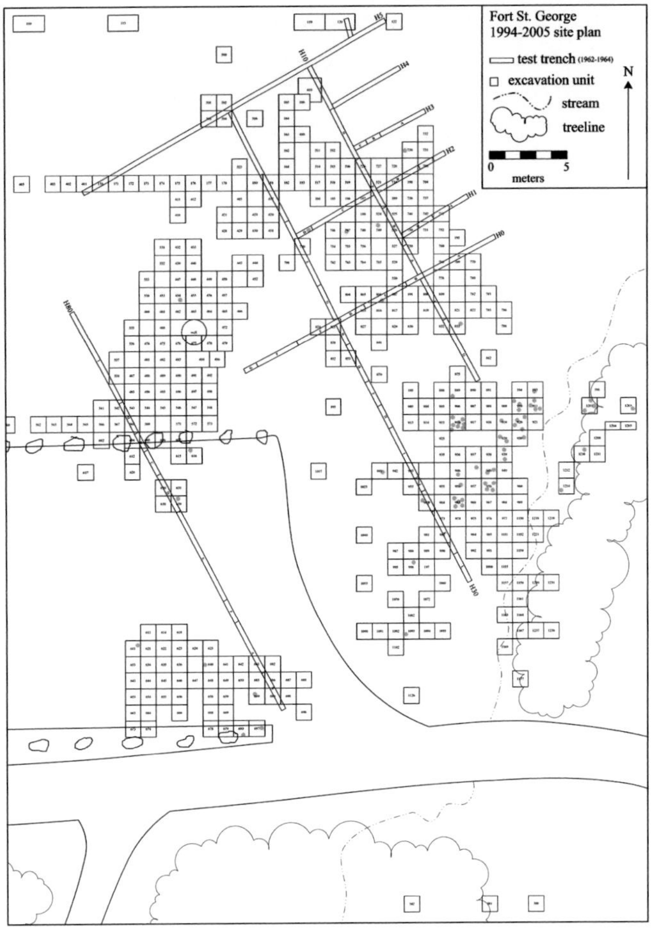

Phials

Sixty-two pieces of clear glass are from small bottles that could be medicine phials. The glass is especially thin, generally 1 mm or less, although bases may be much thicker and exhibit a slight green tinge (Figure 146). A few pieces have formal characteristics that indicate a small cylindrical bottle with a 1 cm neck and everted lip (Figure 147). Another piece is from the shoulder of a bottle that was larger but probably of similar form. The problem is that such phials have not been believed to have existed this early (Cranmer 1990, pp. 91-92; Willmott 2002, pp. 89-90; but see Noël Hume 1969a, p. 72). The majority of these fragments, including the most diagnostic, however, are from good Fort St. George contexts: 43 are from the vicinity of the vice admiral's house and the lake, while five were found in the admiral's house (Figure 148). The preponderance of phials at the vice admiral location, together with the fragment of the possible urinal, suggests the possibility that Master Turner, the physician, may have set up shop there.

Figure 148. Distribution of glass phials. The concentration of phials in the vicinity of the vice admiral's house raises the possibility that the physician, Master Turner, may have set up his practice at this location.

Tableware

There are 677 fragments of glass that are nearly colorless or have only a greenish tinge. Glass with a "clear" metal was superior to the common colored metals, and was reserved for the finer tablewares. Most of these do have a greenish tinge, however, which indicates that they are made of potash-lime glass. They average only 1 mm in thickness, and although the majority are too small to exhibit formal characteristics other than a slight curvature they are probably from drinking glasses. These appear to be wine glasses, rather than

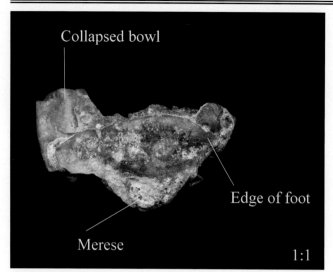

Figure 149. Melted wine glass from the admiral's house. (1:1)

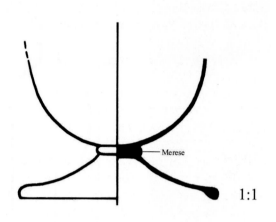

Figure 150. Wine glass reconstruction. (1:1)

tumblers or roemers, but of a stemless type, for there is not a single stem or knop in the collection. Just such a type is confirmed by a large glob of heat-altered glass from the admiral's house (Figures 149-150). Comparable examples of stemless wine glasses were found at Pentagoet where they are referred to as "snifters" (Falukner and Faulkner 1987, fig. 8.13a). At least 51 more rim and foot pieces from Fort St. George represent a minimum number of six glasses.

Four more foot pieces are from another drinking glass, but the reconstructed diameter of the foot ring is 8 cm which seems a little large for a wine glass. Because of the large diameter, one of these pieces that was found in the 1962 excavations was identified by J. Paul Hudson as "a cover for a bowl or sweetmeat dish" (pers. comm. to John Cotter, 1965). Fragments of such "compote" dishes are not unknown in the wilderness of seventeenth-century New England (Faulkner and Faulkner 1987, p. 239, table 8.2). However, an alternative possibility has been offered by Ivor Noël Hume (pers. comm., 1995): He suggests that the "foot" identification is correct, but that it is the base of an ale glass such as are known from Tudor and early Stuart contexts in England (Noël Hume 1962). The foot

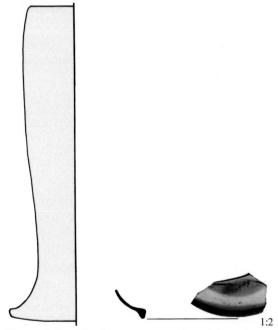

Figure 151. Ale glass reconstruction (from Noel Hume 1962, fig. 3) and fragment of foot found at Fort St. George. (1:2)

rings of these glasses have a range of diameters that comfortably include 8 cm (Figure 151). It must be confessed that we find an ale glass more in keeping with the image of first-colony adventurers than a compote dish.

Five hundred fragments of glass probably from drinking glasses were found in the admiral's house. That the great majority (74%) of these luxury items should be so located attests to the prominence of the inhabitant. Almost all of these fragments were in the central and eastern parts of the structure (Figure 152) which may have been the public space where the leaders of the colony met (see p. 12). Most of the rest of the drinking glass fragments (146) were found in the vicinity of the vice admiral's house. Thirteen more were recovered from the residential area east of the lake, while only 14 were found around the buttery and 2 in the storehouse. Two are unprovenienced.

Ornaments

The glass artifacts from Popham include small ornamental items: beads and buttons (Figure 153). The beads are classified according to the technique of manufacture, i.e., whether they were drawn or wire-wound. There are 166 drawn beads (this includes 29 half beads that are counted as 15 whole beads). Of these, 162 are monochrome: 154 opaque white and seven opaque blue (IIA1 and IIA7 in the classification of Brain 1979, p. 101). The remaining drawn bead is a very small example that is too badly deteriorated to determine color. The white beads average 6.5 mm in length and 4 mm in diameter; the blue beads are round and measure 5 mm in diameter. Three of the beads are decorated: one is dark blue with longitudinal white stripes (variety IIB1, ibid., pp. 103-104), and the other two are of compound construction with a light green inner layer and opaque brick red outer layer (variety IVA2, "Cornaline d'Aleppo," ibid., p. 106). Although these varieties of bead are not sensitive chronologically, they have been found almost exclusively within structures identified with Fort St. George. Most were found in the central of the part of the storehouse: 144 white, 3 blue, and the 3 decorated (Figures 154-155). Of the seven that were found in the admiral's house, four are white and two are blue (the seventh is the deteriorated bead which cannot be classified). Seven white beads were found around the buttery and one in the vicinity of the vice admiral's house.

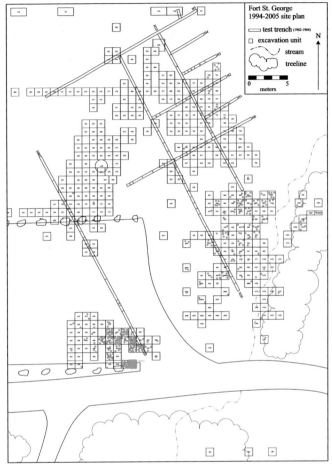

Figure 152. Distribution of wine glass. One of the premier exemplars of prestige, wine glasses cluster in the admiral's house and vicinity of the vice admiral's house. The highest concentration in the southeastern corner of the admiral's house may have been the bar or pantry area.

Figure 153. Glass beads and buttons: a, white drawn beads (IIA1); b, blue drawn beads (IIA7); c, compound green and red drawn beads (IVA2 "Cornaline d'Aleppo"); d, blue and white striped drawn bead (IIB1); e, clear ribbed wire-wound bead (WIIB3 "spiral melon"); f, clear molded pendant bead or button; g, black glass buttons. (1:1)

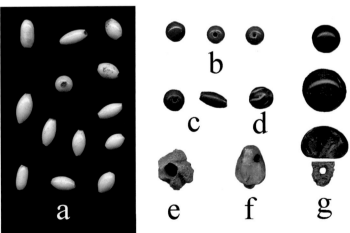

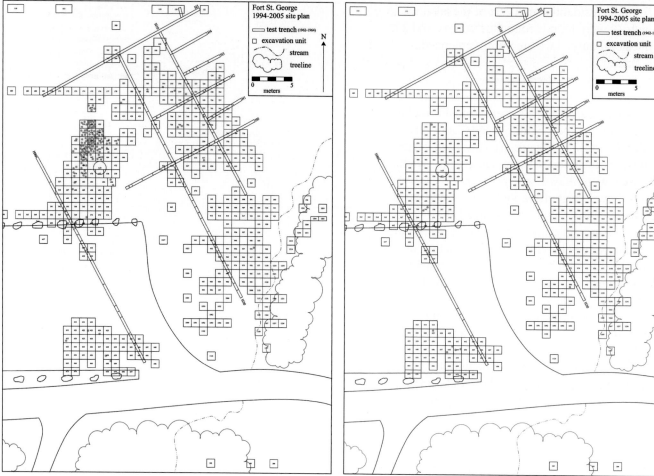

Figure 154. Distribution of white and blue glass beads. These imitation wampum beads were intended for trading with the Indians and were stored in the central part of the storehouse.

Figure 155. Distribution of fancier decorated glass beads. These beads have a distinctly different distribution from the monochrome white and blue beads. They may have been personal possessions of the colonists rather than items specifically intended for the Indian trade.

There are only two wire-wound beads. One is made of clear glass and is molded with longitudinal ribs in the style usually referred to as a "spiral melon" (WIIB3 in ibid. p. 112). This is the earliest known example of this variety, occurrences of which are best known from the eighteenth century. It was found in the vicinity of the vice admiral's house. The other wire-wound bead is opaque white (WIA5 in ibid., p. 108). It may have been found by Bob Bradley in his 1981 test excavation at the site, but this provenience is not secure. Unfortunately, this variety of bead was in use for a long time, and because its context is uncertain the assignment to Fort St. George is tenuous. A similar bead was found at Cushnoc, but not in an undisturbed seventeenth-century context (Cranmer 1990, p. 97).

Four more items could be either beads or buttons. They are made of clear glass (one is slightly milky, probably due to heat alteration) and are pear-shaped (Figure 153f). Three are broken, but clearly have the same measurements as the complete specimen: 8 mm at the widest diameter and 11 mm long. The bodies are decorated with molded longitudinal ribbing and a small knob at the wide end. The narrow end is pierced by a transverse hole. Similar pendant beads made of cut crystal are known from other seventeenth-century contexts (Deagan 1987, pp. 180-181). It has also been suggested that these could just as well have been decorative buttons. Two of these were found in the admiral's house, and two in the vice admiral's.

A large number of definite glass buttons were made by the wire-wound method and are opaque black in color (Figure 153g). A glass filament was wound around an iron wire that was left protruding to serve as the attachment loop. There are 64 of these buttons in the collection and they group into two sizes: 25 small (ca. 8 mm in diameter) and 39 large (ca. 12 mm in diameter). Seven large and one small were found in the vicinity of the vice admiral's house, while all the rest were from the admiral's house (Figure 156). These were mostly concentrated in the debris field in the center of the structure. The restriction of these items to the prime residential areas is to be noted. A glass button is recorded from Jamestown (Cotter 1958, p. 263), and what appears to be an essentially identical example to our buttons was found at an early seventeenth-century site just upriver from Jamestown (Outlaw 1990, p. 150, fig. A3.17, no. 214). These occurrences seem to reflect the peak of black glass buttons which were popular from the late sixteenth century (Egan and Forsyth 1997, p. 222) to the mid seventeenth century (Luckenbach 1995, p. 14).

Flat Glass

There are two categories of flat glass: window and mirror. One hundred and seven pieces of flat glass may be fragments of panes from leaded windows. They are made of potash glass and range in color from green to nearly colorless. One of these has been warped and damaged by heat, but the ghosts of the lead cames in which it was mounted are still visible along the edges and drips of melted lead are apparent on the surface (Figure 157c).

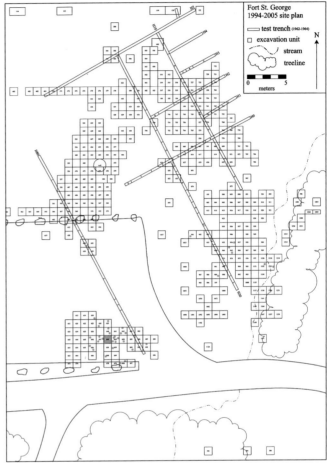

Figure 156. Distribution of black glass buttons. Restricted to the admiral's house and the vicinity of the vice admiral's house, these buttons clearly reflect the dress of a gentleman. That the great majority of large buttons and all but one of the small buttons were found in the admiral's house reveal that Raleigh Gilbert was the best dressed of all, befitting his status and leadership role.

Another completely melted piece is covered with lead oxide. These fragments and 25 more were recovered from the admiral's house (Figure 158). They were mostly pale green in color. Another 58 pieces of generally greener glass were found in the vicinity of the vice admiral's house (Figure 159). Outside of these locations, flat glass is rare: only nine were recovered from around the buttery and six from the storehouse, while the remaining 7 were scattered about the site.

Figure 157. Flat glass from the admiral's house: a-b, fragments of *cristallo* mirror with etched lines and tooled edges; c, diamond-shaped window pane with melted lead drips; d, light green window pane warped by heat. (1:1)

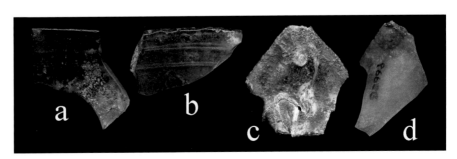

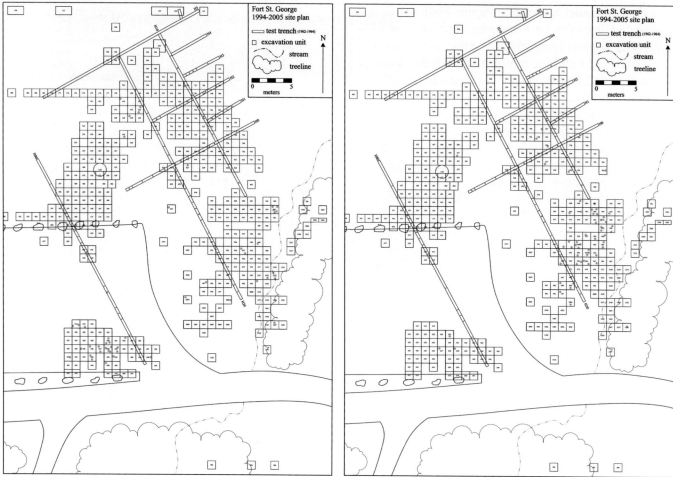

Figure 158. Distribution of pale green flat glass. Believed to be window glass, fragments are concentrated in the admiral's house.

Figure 159. Distribution of green flat glass. The darker green flat glass may also have been for windows, although perhaps it was of lower quality than the paler glass. Fragments were mostly found in the vicinity of the vice admiral's house.

That Raleigh Gilbert, at least, might have brought a glazed window for installation in his abode is a considerable revelation, but certainly not beyond the realm of possibility: A domestic structure built between 1610 and 1620 in Cupids, Newfoundland had glazed windows (Gilbert 2000, p. 16). It must be noted, however, that no lead cames have been found at Fort St. George, although melted lead presumed to be from a came had dripped onto the quarrel from the admiral's house.

Eighteen fragments of glass that are absolutely clear seem to be examples of soda-lime glass or *cristallo*. Many of these pieces have been subjected to heat which has distorted the glass and changed its appearance so that it looks almost like melted sugar. Twelve were found in the admiral's house of which ten were obviously from the same object. Three of these were decorated with parallel etched lines, and our first interpretation was that the admiral had a crystal dish. But when it was realized that the object must originally have been flat and that there was at least one corner piece (Figure 157a) an alternative interpretation was required. Henry Miller at Historic St. Mary's City first suggested a mirror, examples of which he noted were often decorated with etched lines along the edges. Giovanna Vitelli in consultation with Hugh Willmott concurred, and Vitelli pointed out that the surviving edges had been nipped with a grozing iron, a cutting tool used by glaziers. Willmott even supplied a photo of a 1580-1590 rectangular mirror that in his estimation "is a direct parallel to yours" (Figure 160). The final proof came when a red residue on one fragment was submitted to New England ChromaChem Laboratory and found to test positive for the mercury which would have been used in the silvering process (Diderot 1959, pls. 255-256). *Cristallo* was commonly used for mirrors which were made in Venice (Godfrey 1975, p. 8). At Fort St. George, a mirror would certainly have enhanced Raleigh Gilbert's image. All of the pieces were found in the western half of his house (Figure 161) which may have been his personal space. The remaining 6 pieces of *cristallo* were scattered about the site and recovered from disturbed contexts.

Figure 160. Glass *cristallo* mirror from 1580-1590 shipwreck off the coast of Croatia. Note the etched lines and tooled edge. (Courtesy of Hugh Willmott)

METAL

There is a fairly large inventory of metal artifacts from the Popham site that can be securely dated to the early seventeenth century. This is somewhat surprising considering the small scale and parsimonious outfitting of the venture, the brief duration of the colony, the orderly withdrawal giving ample opportunity for the removal of all usable objects, and the presumed scavenging by passing Native American residents of the region who must have mined the site repeatedly for any pieces of metal during the following century.

The artifacts are divided first into material categories as determined by the basic metallic element in the composition: iron, copper, gold, lead. These categories are then subdivided into functional classes and formal types. Finally, a composite category is presented that includes all items that can be identified with firearms and ammunition which together comprise a technological system that is more comprehensively treated as a whole.

Iron

There is a considerable amount of iron/steel from the site. Most of the artifacts date to the nineteenth- and twentieth-century occupations, but there is a significant representation of seventeenth-century hardware, especially handwrought iron nails. The

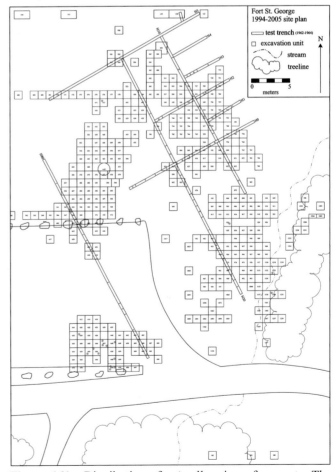

Figure 161. Distribution of *cristallo* mirror fragments. The presence of a mirror in the admiral's house is further evidence of the gentleman who lived there.

Figure 162. Iron handwrought nails: a-b, tacks (P481G, P482H); c-i, architectural nails (Hadlock no provenience, P161C/D, P200C1); j, spike (P182B3-4). (1:1)

exact number of such artifacts, however, is difficult to determine due to the extensive corrosion that has occurred on artifacts of all ages. Hundreds of fragments of badly corroded iron from Fort St. George contexts could not, even after being x-rayed, be placed in an artifactual category with any confidence. Even cleaning by mechanical and electro-chemical processes was not always determinative. The identifications that follow are restricted to relatively well-preserved specimens, and the quantities of each category must be considered the minimum number recovered from the site.

Handwrought Nails

There are at least 2431 whole nails and fragments of nails from the 1962-1964 and 1994-2005 excavations that may be assigned to constructions within Fort St. George. There is no evidence of major architectural activity at the site after the fort was abandoned until houses were built in the early nineteenth century when machine-cut nails were available. The whole nails and heads among the fragments make up about one-third of the total.

All of the handwrought nails have shanks with square cross sections, and large heads with at least three facets. They range in size from small tacks, possibly from furniture or chests, to large spikes (Figure 162). Most clearly were intended for structural purposes, and that they were so used is confirmed by the fact that many were clinched. Some also exhibit firescale from having been subjected to intense heat, most likely because they had been in a building that burned. Sir Ferdinando Gorges recorded that the storehouse and some dwellings caught fire in the winter of 1607/1608 (Quinn and Quinn 1983, p. 337), and even if his memory was faulty on that point (see pp. 61, 74) evidence of fire is apparent at the storehouse, Admiral Raleigh Gilbert's house, and in the vicinity of the vice admiral's house.

The head of a large spike was found in the fill of the P182 posthole identified with the storehouse of Fort St. George (Figure 162j). Most of the shank is missing and the remaining portion is bent (see Figure 29g). It may have been building hardware, but considering the context it must have been damaged and discarded in the early stages of construction. The remaining badly corroded section weighed 42.4 g before cleaning and 34.2 g afterwards.

The distribution of handwrought nails reveals that the largest number have been found in the vicinity of the principal storage buildings and residential areas (Figure 163). At least 1303 were recovered from the storehouse, and another 147 around the buttery. There were 769 in the admiral's house and 143 in the vicinity of the vice admiral's house. The rest were scattered around the site near where Hunt shows the "kitchin generall," "chapell" and "privat lodgins" east of the lake and by the postern gate. These coincide closely with the distributions of daub across the site. It may be that the exceptionally large number of nails– more than half the total count – from the storehouse was due in part simply to their being stored there and so were not all used in its construction. This might explain the high concentration in the central storage area. It would also provide an explanation for the presence of the many small nails that would have been unsuitable for architectural purposes, but might have been from boxes or chests. The nails from the admiral's house, however, were concentrated around the hearth and in the destruction layer of architectural debris, and so they probably were mostly constructional in function.

Tools and Hardware

One of the most exciting finds on the floor of the storehouse was a small caulking iron (Figure 164a). This is the most tangible evidence of the *Virginia* that we could wish for. Although badly corroded, it retains enough of its substance and form to be instantly recognizable. It is 13 cm long and 5 cm wide at the bit; weight after cleaning is 179.2 g.

A large, flat piece of iron or steel was found in the fill of one of the postholes of the storehouse. In its corroded state, it measures 6 cm long, 2.5 cm wide, and approximately 1 cm thick; weight is 33 g. It is rounded on one end

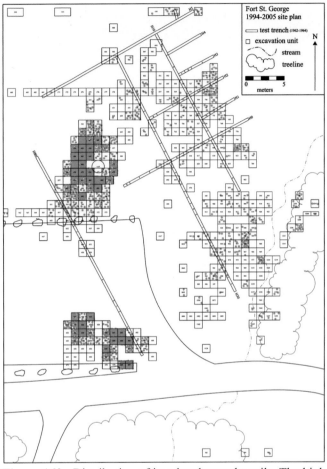

Figure 163. Distribution of iron handwrought nails. The high concentration of nails in the storehouse may have been due as much to storage as to construction, but the large number of nails in the admiral's house suggests that it was more sturdily built than other residences.

and broken on the other, and there are two holes drilled through it. This piece is interpreted as being the handle of a broken knife. Five fragments of what appears to be a dagger blade lay on the floor of Raleigh Gilbert's house. This blade would have been approximately 22 cm long and 3 cm wide; weight of the five fragments is 21 g. Fragments of another knife blade with the remains of a bone handle were found in the storehouse (Figure 165d).

Thirty-five iron washers were found on the floor of the storehouse. These were manufactured in strips that were punched and then scored so that individual rhomboid-shaped washers could be broken off as needed. Both individual specimens and strips were found (Figure 164b-d). There are two sizes: small measuring approximately 18 mm on a side, and large at 25 mm. The small might have been used in fastening pieces of armor together (Outlaw 1990, fig. A3.9, no. 105), but the large were almost certainly used as roves in shipbuilding (Friel 1995, p. 72). These were concentrated in the central and southern part of the storehouse, not far from where the caulking iron was found. Three more roves were recovered from the admiral's house, and two in the vicinity of the vice admiral's house.

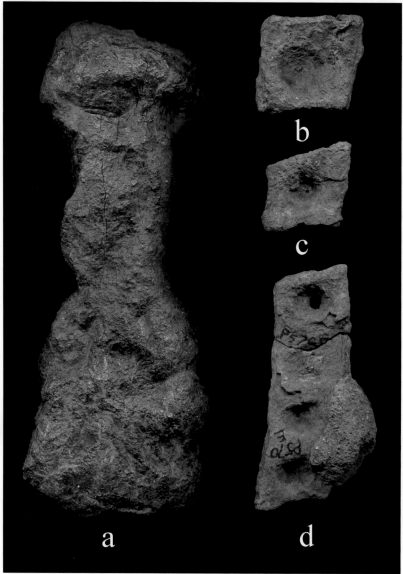

Figure 164. Iron shipbuilding tool and hardware: a, caulking iron (P607D); b, large rove (P461D); c, small rove (P448C); d, strip of small roves (P570E). (1:1)

Armor

At least 95 fragments of iron or steel could be identified as pieces of armor. Most of these were probably tasset lames, that part of an armored suit that was most quickly discarded in New World contexts. These pieces have distinctive rolled edges and some still have rivets in place (Figure 165a). Also present is a helmet cheekpiece (Figure 165c) and a buckle that was probably part of a military harness (Figure 165b). The majority of these (69) were found on the floor of the storehouse, mostly in the southeastern corner. Ten more pieces came from the admiral's house, 15 from the vicinity of the vice admiral's house, and one from the buttery.

Copper

Artifacts of copper or copper alloy datable to the early historic period are especially rare. This is surprising considering the importance of the industry at Jamestown where copper items were manufactured for the native trade (Kelso et al., 2001, pp. 30-31). However, it may be that the copper industry was not seriously developed until after 1609 when Thomas Hariot's advice on the subject was sought by the Virginia Company (Kupperman 1984a, p. 164). There is only one copper trade object that may be assigned with confidence to Fort St. George. This is a tubular bead made of rolled sheet copper (Figure 166a). It is 4 cm long and .5 cm in diameter. The relative crudity suggests that the bead was manufactured on site. Similar examples were found at Jamestown (Kelso et al. ibid., fig. 26).

There are also a few pieces of undatable sheet copper, some of which are engraved with a curvilinear design and probably had an ornamental purpose, but they are too fragmentary to reconstruct original form or function (Figure 166b). A circular cutout of sheet copper was found in Raleigh Gilbert's house that could have been intended as personal ornamentation, or possibly for the native trade (Figure 166c). Also from Raleigh Gilbert's house is an oval ring of sheet copper wrapped around a textile core (Figure 166d). It appears to have been gilded and may have been a decorative clothing item. Fragments of a similar ring were found in the vicinity of the vice admiral's house (Figure 166e).

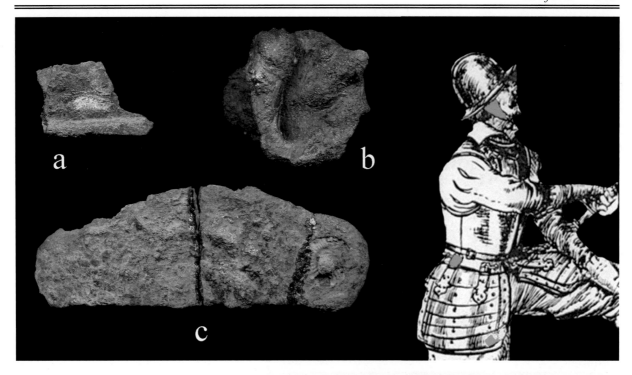

Brass was even rarer at Fort St. George. A fragment of what may have been a small brass button was found on the floor of the storehouse, and two large lumps of melted brass weighing 67.1 g and 100 g (Figure 166f) were recovered from the admiral's house. Otherwise, the only certain early seventeenth-century artifacts are the finial from a brass or latten spoon, which is one of Cotter's specific traits for the early occupation at Jamestown, and a thimble.

Figure 165. Other iron artifacts: a, fragment of tasset lame with rolled edge (P605E); b, buckle (P605E); c, helmet cheekpiece (P571F); d, knife blade (P546H1, photo courtesy of Scott Milliken, Head Tide Archaeological Conservation Laboratory). (1:1)

Seal-top Spoon

Spoons of cast metal were popular in England during the late medieval and post-medieval periods, and a number of types have been defined according to the ornamentation of the finials (Noël Hume 1969a, pp. 180-181). One of the most common was the "seal-top" which ended in a baluster and/ or ball knop that supported a flat disc. Some of these could be quite elaborate with both the baluster and knop, additional annular rings, and molded floral elements (Ruempol and van Dongen 1990, p. 146).

The seal-top from Fort St. George is just that: the stalk and bowl of the spoon are missing (Figure 166g). Enough remains of the finial, however, to establish that it was the simplest form, consisting only of an annular ring, plain ball knop, and flat disc. This variety was most popular in the late sixteenth and early seventeenth centuries. Aside from Jamestown (Cotter 1958, pl. 87; Hudson 1980, pp. 13, 37, no. 1) and the Maine site (Outlaw 1990, fig. A3.7, no. 75) in Virginia, similar examples are known from such other early seventeenth-century sites in New England as Pemaquid (Camp 1975, fig. 36, no. 2), West Ferry (Simmons 1970, ills. 44 middle, 85), and Burr's Hill (Gibson 1980, figs. 56, 127).

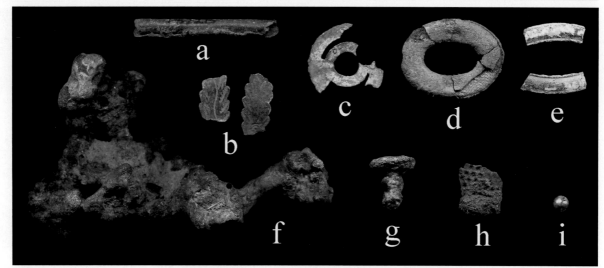

Figure 166. Copper, brass and gold artifacts: a, tubular bead of sheet copper (P572B); b, pieces of engraved sheet copper (P162A); c, sheet copper cutout (P614A); d, oval ring of sheet copper folded over a textile core (P640A); e, pieces of similar ring showing gilding (P929C1); f, large blob of melted brass from admiral's house (P668E); g, finial from brass or latten seal-top spoon (H1-2); h, fragment of brass thimble (P749C); i, gold bead (P968C). (1:1)

Thimble

A portion of a brass thimble was recovered from the buttery/corporal's house. Thimbles are common at later colonial sites where they are an essential element in domestic assemblages (Noël Hume 1969a, p. 255). This example is composed of two sheets of brass: a dimpled outer one which is reinforced by a plain inner lining (Figure 166h). It appears to have a simple edge. These are characteristics of sixteenth- and early seventeenth-century thimbles (ibid., p. 256).

Gold

A small gold ball was found in a Fort St. George posthole (P968C). It is 4 mm in diameter and has a cross-shaped surface blemish where it appears that an attachment fixture has broken off (Figure 166i). Therefore, it is reasonable to suggest that it may have been part of a larger ornament. Just such ornaments appear at the ends of ties or cords in the portrait of Raleigh Gilbert (see Frontispiece).

Lead

Artifacts of lead and lead alloy are an important part of the assemblage from Fort St. George, but oddly are missing from Cotter's definitive list. This must have been an inadvertent oversight because lead munitions, at least, were a basic requirement of all colonizing ventures. These are discussed below under Firearms and Ammunition. In this section are a few items of other significance.

Seal

Two kinds of lead seals are found at the site: one type was used to tag bales of cloth, the other was apparently used for some other purpose. The lead bale seal was found in the 1962 excavations. This type of seal, also called a cloth seal, is composed of two discs, ca. 21 mm in diameter, connected by a narrow strap that is 5 mm wide (Figure 167a). The strap is folded so that the discs are clamped together as they would have been when attached to the cloth. The exterior side of one disc is molded with a central device encircled by an inscription. The device is a stylized madder bag that was used in the seventeenth century as a symbol for the dyeing industry (Egan 1985, fig. 19). The encircling legend is supposed to specify the dyes that were used (ibid.). The letters on this seal are mostly obscured, but they appear to be arranged in three groups of three letters each. The best identifications that a strong light and active imagination can offer are ". . L • V L R • M V P". Somewhere among those letters Geoff Egan (pers. comm. to Robert Bradley, 1981) and Ivor Noël Hume (pers. comm. to Alaric Faulkner, 1988) find an M and W which they interpret as "madder" (red) and "woad" (blue) which together make the color purple.

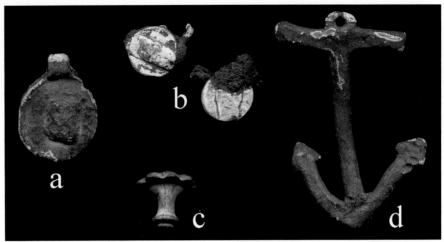

Figure 167. Lead artifacts: a, bale seal (H2A); b, seals for securing wire closures (P920B, P947B); c, pewter finial (H80F); d, anchor pendant (P486B). (1:1)

Although Egan at first seems to have been reluctant to date the seal before 1614 (pers. comm. to Alaric Faulkner, 1981), he apparently has no problem with a Fort St. George provenience in the later letter to Robert Bradley cited above. The acceptance of this dating is shared by Norman Cook of the Guildhall Museum (pers. comm. to Wendell Hadlock, 1963) and Ivor Noël Hume (pers. comm. to Alaric Faulkner, 1988).

Two small lead discs may have been used to seal other items. The discs have a diameter of 14 mm and are 3 mm thick (Figure 167b). They are channeled on one side to receive iron wires; once the latter were in place the channel was filled with molten lead. Corroded iron wires still protrude from the sides of the discs. This general type of seal was "used to label almost every commodity you can think of, from newly minted coins to manure for the fields" (Egan, pers. comm., 2005) and date from the medieval period to modern times (ibid.). Proveniences at Fort St. George were from mixed contexts so that although there were many early seventeenth-century artifacts in association these seals may be of more recent date.

Finial

A mushroom-shaped finial is cast from whitemetal, presumably pewter (Figure 167c). The top is molded into eight lobes or petals. A rivet extends from the top, through the stem, and is broken off at the base. Ivor Noël Hume (ibid.) believes it is probably from the pewter lid of a seventeenth-century German stoneware drinking vessel. It may be no coincidence that it was found in the front yard of Raleigh Gilbert's house.

Anchor Pendant

A crudely cast anchor of lead is 5.8 cm long, 3.6 cm wide at the flukes, and weighs 35 g (Figure 167d). It has a suspension hole at the top of the shank where the ring would be and was clearly intended to be worn on a chain or cord. Wear on the inside of the ring indicates that it was used for an extended period of time. It may have been a charm or amulet and one of the flukes shows a set of dental impressions suggesting that someone may have "bitten the bullet." Although this anchor was found in a post Fort St. George level, a similar example is known from a seventeenth-century context on a nearby island (Peter Woodruff, pers. comm., 1998).

Firearms and Ammunition

Considering the military nature of the site, gun parts and ammunition are important but not overly abundant artifacts at Fort St. George. It is presumed that these items were carefully conserved during the

Figure 168. Safety lever from a snaphaunce gunlock (P484H3). (1:1)

colonial occupation, and that after abandonment the remains were scoured for usable metal. Nevertheless, a gun part, pieces of armor and some lead munitions were found in close proximity in the southeastern portion of the storehouse, suggesting that this corner of the building may have functioned as the armory for the colony.

Gun Part

The gun part that was found on the storehouse floor is of considerable interest because it apparently came from a snaphaunce gunlock (Figure 168). According to an expert on early firearms, it is a safety catch:

> It is the pivoting lever of the external safety of a snaphaunce gunlock of the type in common use in England from the end of the sixteenth century until the middle years of the seventeenth. It was attached with a screw to the exterior of the lockplate immediately behind the cock. To put the lock on "safe," the safety was manually pivoted to the rear, using the small projecting knob. In this position, it immobilized the sear by blocking the movement with a small extension which passed through a hole in the lockplate for this purpose (James D. Lavin, pers. comm. January 1999).

The only information we have from the historical documents is that the colonists were equipped with matchlock muskets. The most specific reference is clear on this point:

> The saluadges perceiuing so much subtilly devised how they might put out the fire in the Shallop, by which meanes they sawe they should be free from the daunger of our mens pieces, and to performe the same, one of the Saluadges came into the Shallop and taking the fire brand which one of our company held in his hand, thereby to light the Matches, as if he would light a pipe of Tobacco, as soone as he had gottenn yt into his hand, he presently threw it into the water & lept out of the Shallop (Quinn and Quinn 1983, p. 411).

Surely, one would expect, if they had more advanced firearms they would have been employed in the most dangerous exploring expeditions. Thus we only expected to find matchlocks and it came as a considerable surprise that the only identifiable part is from a snaphaunce. It could be that this was the only snaphaunce gun in the colony, the personal possession of a leader, say George Popham, who did not go exploring. All we can know at this point is that they were equipped with at least some state-of-the-art weaponry.

Gunflint

Fifteen pieces of flint are a distinctive blond color which is typical of some continental flints, especially from France (Smith 1960). Thirteen are just small flakes, but two are spall gunflints that exhibit wear along one edge consistent with use in a gunlock (Figure 169). Gunspalls are the earliest type of gunflint and would have been used in the first flintlocks (Hamilton 1980, p. 142). Thus these flints may be further evidence for the presence of a snaphaunce gun at Fort St. George. One was found in the storehouse not far from the

Figure 169. Spall gunflint (both sides), perhaps for a snaphaunce pistol (P455B).

snaphaunce safety lever, but unfortunately it had been removed from its original context to a mixed layer above the floor level. The other flint was found in the vicinity of the vice admiral's house. The size of these flints would be appropriate for a pistol, as are some of the lead balls described below.

Lead Munitions

Lead balls, shot, and scrap attest to the military component of the fort. There are 56 musket balls that were found across the site (Figure 170). These manifest a considerable range in size, denoting guns of different calibers (Table 10). The largest balls are consistent with the standard bore (.75 cal.) of an English matchlock musket for the early seventeenth century (Peterson, 1956, p. 14), but the other balls fit much smaller weapons (Figure 171a-f). It is possible that some of these are later intrusions into the site that were intended for trade guns or fowling pieces, but the relative uniformity suggests that they were conforming to a military, or at least expeditionary, standard. They indicate that many of the soldiers belonged to a military unit called the "shot." These soldiers carried a caliver, a weapon smaller and lighter in weight than the heavy military musket (ibid., p. 13) and thus more appropriate for exploring and skirmishing in the New World (ibid., fig. 9). Certainly, the caliver was found to be more effective in the Irish wars of this period and increasingly replaced the heavy musket (Falls 1997, pp. 39-40). Many of the soldiers at Fort St. George may have seen service in Ireland where they became accustomed to this preference.

A set of even smaller balls are .39 caliber (Figure 171g-h). These could have been used in a musket charged with buck-and-ball, but the fact that 14 of the twenty examples were concentrated in Raleigh Gilbert's house (Figure 172) and four of the remaining six were found in the vicinity of the vice admiral's house suggests that they were intended for a smaller weapon. Allowing for windage, these would fit the English pistol bore (Hamilton 1980, p. 130). Pistols were a mark of high rank which fits well with the proveniences of these balls at Fort St. George.

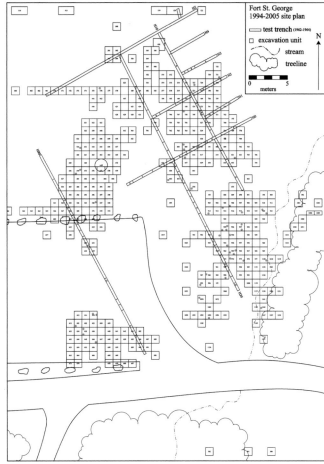

Figure 170. Distribution of lead musket balls. Although broadly distributed within the fort compound, the highest concentration is in the vicinity of the vice admiral's (and munition master's?) house.

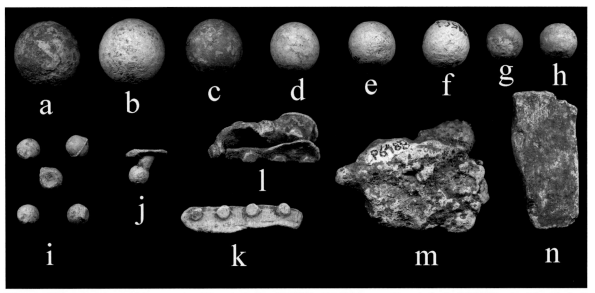

Figure 171. Lead munitions: a-b, .73 cal. balls (P176D, P648B); c, .63 cal. ball (P727D); d, .55 cal. ball (P920ED1); e-f, .51 cal. balls; g-h, .39 cal. balls (P623D); i, shot (P668FE1); j, shot with sprue still attached (P906A); k-l, sprue (P917B, H1-2); m-n, spills (P648B, P730C). (1:1)

Table 10. Measurements of lead balls from Fort St. George

Cat.No.	Weight(g)	Dia.(mm)	Dia.(in)	Gauge	Cat.No.	Weight(g)	Dia.(mm)	Dia.(in)	Gauge
H10B	12.1	13.0	.51	35	P783F	12.3	14.0	.53	28
H30K	12.0	13.0	.51	35	P785E	30.0	18.0	.69	12
H30L	11.7	13.3	.55	28	P805C*	15.8	15.0	.59	28
H80E	15.9	14.5	.59	22	P805C*	13.5	14.0	.55	28
P176D	30.7	18.0	.73	12	P807C	12.4	13.0	.51	35
P418A	4.6	9.9	.39	--	P815B	11.9	13.5	.54	28
P439D	7.2	11.5	.46	35	P821C**	9.8	18.0	.73	12
P449D	5.4	11.0	.44	35	P852A	31.0	18.0	.73	12
P474E	30.0	17.0	.67	12	P870A	12.1	13.0	.51	35
P474E	17.3	15.0	.55	28	P906B	28.5	18.0	.73	12
P534C	30.0	17.5	.69	12	P907D	4.5	9.5	.38	--
P546G	16.0	14.0	.56	28	P913B	11.2	12.5	.49	35
P614E	2.9	10.0	.39	--	P915B	13.7	14.0	.55	28
P618A	13.9	14.0	.55	28	P917B	13.1	14.0	.55	28
P618B*	15.5	15.0	.59	20	P920E1	13.5	14.0	.55	28
P621B	8.5	12.0	.50	35	P920ED1	14.9	14.0	.55	28
P623D	4.2	10.0	.39	--	P935C	30.1	18.0	.73	12
P623D	3.9	9.8	.39	--	P935C	4.2	9.0	.39	--
P623D	3.9	9.9	.39	--	P935E**	9.9	14.0	.55	28
P623D	3.7	9.5	.39	--	P937B	12.3	12.8	.51	35
P623D	3.9	9.8	.39	--	P937C	32.0	18.0	.71	12
P623D	3.9	9.3	.39	--	P944B	8.1	11.0	.45	--
P635B	15.7	15.0	.59	28	P946B	31.3	18.0	.73	12
P635B**	4.3	13.0	.51	35	P955B	10.6	13.0	.51	35
P635B	2.9	10.0	.39	--	P964B	31.4	18.0	.73	12
P636C	2.7	10.0	.39	--	P965B	31.3	18.0	.73	12
P636C	3.7	10.0	.39	--	P965C	9.7	12.5	.50	35
P636C	4.2	10.0	.39	--	P965C	19.6	15.6	.62	16
P636C	4.3	9.0	.39	--	P974C	11.2	12.4	.50	35
P636D	3.7	10.0	.39	--	P975B	11.3	12.7	.50	35
P646B	30.3	18.0	.73	12	P988A	30.1	18.0	.73	12
P658C**	1.2	9.0	.39	--	P990D1*	11.2	13.3	.52	35
P727D	22.3	16.0	.63	16	P995C1	11.9	13.1	.51	35
P730D	3.2	8.5	.35	--	P1070C	31.4	17.5	.69	12
P731D	13.5	13.0	.53	28	P1093ED1	28.8	17.0	.69	12
P748B	16.9	15.0	.59	28	P1150B	11.3	14.0	.55	28
P778C	11.0	13.5	.54	28	P1157B*	2.7	9.0	.35	--
P780A	17.2	14.5	.56	28	P1164B	11.4	13.0	.51	35

*Flattened
**Partial

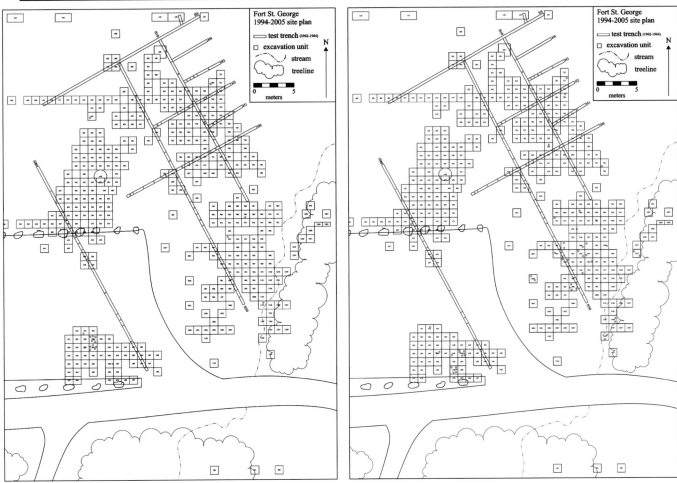

Figure 172. Distribution of lead pistol balls. The concentration of small caliber balls around the hearth of the admiral's house is sure evidence that Raleigh Gilbert cast his own munitions. That they were pistol size is further indication of his status.

Figure 173. Distribution of lead shot. Almost all of the lead shot was found in the admiral's house and the vicinity of the vice admiral's house and therefore may have been primarily ammunition that was used by the leaders.

There are only 51 pieces of shot, ranging between 4-7 mm in diameter (Figures 173 and 171i-j). They were cast in a gang mold, and the evidence of manufacture on site is represented by 83 segments of sprue (Figures 174 and 171k-l). Further proof of local casting of balls and shot is found in the large amount of lead stock, scrap and spillage: 188 pieces, totaling 1907.4 g in weight.[1] More than 63% of the pieces (120) and 60% of the weight (1142.9 g) were found in the vicinity of the vice admiral's house, indicating that this was the center of munition manufacture (Figure 175). Thus it may be no coincidence that, although we found no evidence of such a structure, this was also near where Hunt drew a little building that he identified as the munition master's house.

---

[1] One piece of spillage found in front of the hearth of Raleigh Gilbert's house shows on one side a rough surface indicating that it puddled on a sandy floor (Figure 171m), further evidence that this house did not have floorboards. Another spill from the location of the buttery/corporal's house, however, showed that it had fallen on a wooden board (Figure 171n).

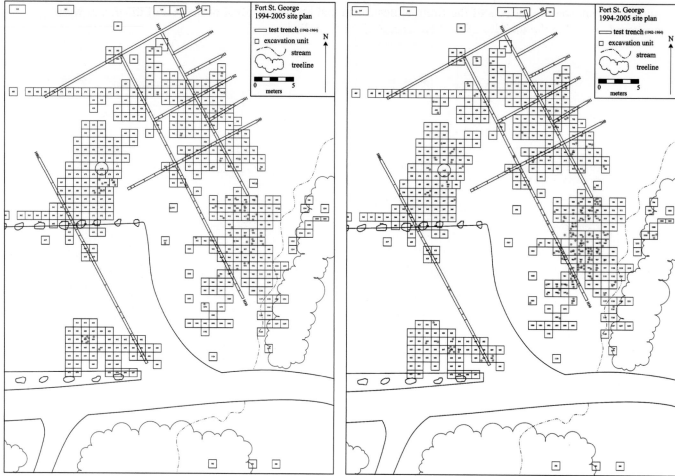

Figure 174. Distribution of lead sprue. The three concentrations of sprue define the three principle centers for the casting of lead balls and shot: the vicinity of the vice admiral's (munition master's?) house, around the hearth of the admiral's house, and in the southeastern corner of the storehouse.

Figure 175. Distribution of lead drips, spills and scrap. Significant evidence of lead casting is again seen in the admiral's house and storehouse, but the highest concentration is in the vicinity of the vice admiral's (and munition master's?) house which identifies it as the primary center of munition manufacture.

OTHER MATERIALS

Graphite

A piece of graphite from the admiral's house weighs 2.4 g. There is a depression in one side as though material had been removed by rubbing or grinding. It is speculated that it may have been used for lubricating gunlocks.

Flint

Sixty-eight pieces of European flint were found in the 1962-1964 and 1994-2005 excavations. All but two of these are the light to dark gray color characteristic of English, or Dover, flint. Most of these are small flakes or pieces that have been removed from larger nodules that may originally have been ship ballast, thus confirming the English origin of the lading. Only one flake exhibits wear along the edges, perhaps from use with a strike-a-light. The great majority of these English flint pieces (54) were found in the admiral's house, and eleven showed the effects of the fire that destroyed that residence. Most of the rest of the pieces were scattered around in the vicinity of the buttery and vice admiral's house.

Jet

There are two beads made of jet from the admiral's house. They are square in outline with flat backs. One also has a flat front, but the other is faceted into a four-sided pyramid (see Figure 63i). Both are 6 mm square, but vary in thickness from 4 mm to 6 mm. Similar examples are known from seventeenth- or eighteenth-century contexts where they have been described as rosary beads (e.g., Brain 1979, p. 221; Deagan 1987, pl. 8). These examples are cross drilled, however, and perhaps were sewn on clothing instead.

Bone and Shell

Two fragments of decorated bone are of uncertain functional identification and cultural affiliation. One is carved, the other engraved. The carved piece could be part of a large rosary bead or perhaps the handle of an implement of some refinement (Figure 176a). The engraved bone bears a design similar to some found on early prehistoric engraved bone from the southeastern United States (e.g., Jennings 1952, fig. 139u, no. 7), but presumably this is simply a matter of coincidence: the more obvious interpretation in this context is that it is a piece of a European knife handle (Figure 176b). Both objects were found in the vicinity of the vice admiral's house with typical assemblages of Fort St. George artifacts.

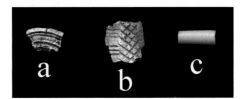

Figure 176. Bone and shell artifacts: a, carved bone (P945C1); b, engraved bone (P949C); c, shell bead (P454E). (1:1)

A shell bead is the only piece of wampum that has been found at the Popham site. It is tubular and highly polished, 10 mm in length and 3.5 mm in diameter (Figure 176c). It was found on the floor of the storehouse among a scatter of white glass trade beads, the European imitation of wampum.

DISCUSSION

The artifacts described above are consistent with the early seventeenth century, and since they are sandwiched between prehistoric levels and a late eighteenth- early nineteenth-century occupation, they may be considered diagnostic of the 1607-1608 dateline. (There are only a few stray artifacts from the site that date to the later seventeenth or early eighteenth centuries) As might be expected, the inventory of artifacts for this initial colonizing horizon is limited in variety and quantity, reflecting the austerity of an early seventeenth-century English military and trading outpost. The artifact categories are basic and virtually identical to those proposed by John Cotter fifty years ago for the initial settlement at Jamestown, and not substantially revised in subsequent excavations. The specific artifact types, however, may differ.

It is apparent that the colony was supplied on the cheap, for it will be observed that the artifact categories are not only limited but also generally composed of the least expensive manufactures: e.g., the coarsest earthenwares and simplest monochrome glass beads. Of particular note is the redundancy of items in the assemblage: the same types of artifacts occur over and over again. Only proportions differ between localities, which presumably indicate differences in activities and personages. The lack of variety might be expected considering the limited supply, and only one resupply, and provides a good idea of the survival kit considered necessary for these initial colonies. The relative poverty of material goods gives a real sense of how minimally supported the colonists were by their technology.

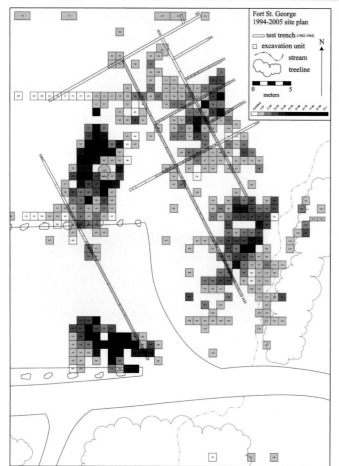

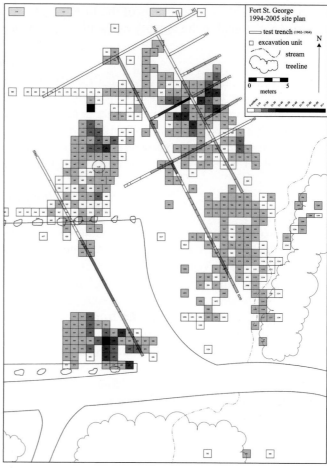

Figure 177. Distribution of all Fort St. George artifacts within the fort compound.

Figure 178. Distribution of ceramic storage containers: North Devon, varieties 1, 2, 3; West of England, Types A, C, D; olive jars. Although these wares are broadly distributed, they cluster most strongly in the storehouse and buttery.

Identifiable ceramics are mostly poor quality plainwares from the West of England, especially Devonshire, which makes good sense inasmuch as the colony was outfitted in Plymouth. The forms that can be recognized distinguish storage and cooking or serving functions. Other containers are Iberian olive jars, German stoneware jugs, and Dutch delftware apothecary pots. Hardware consists mostly of handwrought nails that presumably were used to construct the buildings within the fort and the pinnace *Virginia*. The military component of the venture is represented by armor, gun parts and lead munitions. Tobacco pipes and glass bottles catered to the vices of this rough crew. The concessions to a gentler life-style for a privileged few are indicated by a few objects of copper, brass, pewter, gold and jet, and items of glass such as window glass, ale and wine glasses, a mirror, buttons and ornaments – token reminders of the comforts of home in the wilderness. The glass beads and lead bale seal recall one of the principal objectives of the colony which was the development of the Indian trade. Another economic activity – shipbuilding – is specifically represented by the iron roves and caulking iron. All together, this assemblage comprises what might be expected to be the bare necessities (and a few personal luxuries) for an initial military, colonizing, and trading outpost in the New World.

This modest assemblage does not compare with the far more numerous and varied artifacts found at Jamestown, but Jamestown was occupied by thousands of colonists for many decades. As a result, the first

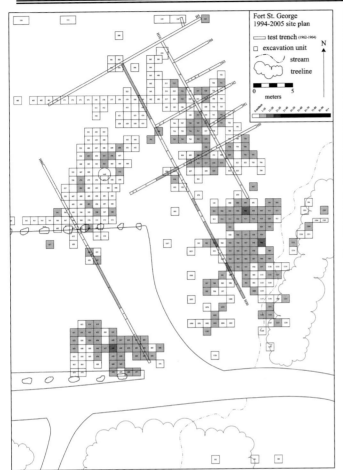

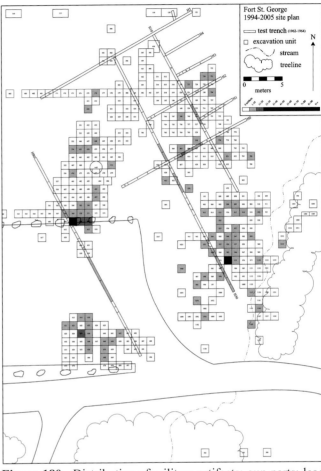

Figure 179. Distribution of ceramic cooking, serving and special purpose containers: Totnes; West of England, Type B; delftware; Bellarmine. As might be expected, these ceramics are concentrated in the residential locations.

Figure 180. Distribution of military artifacts: gun parts; lead munitions; armor and small roves. Military items are strongly represented in the southern end of the storehouse, around the hearth of the admiral's house, and in the vicinity of the vice admiral's house. The latter location, which may have been shared by the munition master, seems to have been the primary center for the casting of lead muntions.

year of occupation is obscured. Only at Popham can we see clearly that beginning. We may expect, if ever they are archaeologically isolated, to find similar beginnings at 1585 Roanoke and 1620 Plimoth Plantation.

The distributions of these artifacts on site also are informative. It appears that agriculture did not significantly displace artifacts horizontally from the original point of deposition and the distributions thus provide a template for the overall configuration of the fort (Figure 177). As might be expected, the greatest concentrations of artifacts are in the vicinities of the principal storage facilities, the storehouse and buttery, and the residential structures identified by Hunt as the admiral's house and the vice admiral's house. Significant assemblages were also found at other locales across the site, such as the kitchen, and the residential areas east of the lake and near the postern gate. Within these distributions are correlations of different artifact categories with specific structures within the fort that expose the social, economic and military parameters of public and private activities (Figures 178-182).

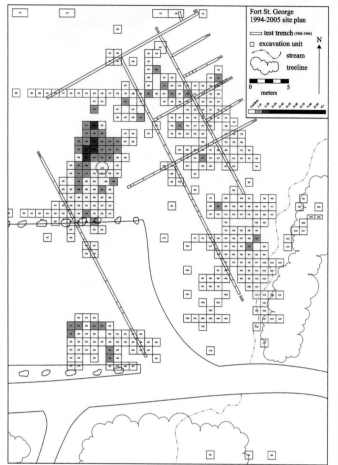

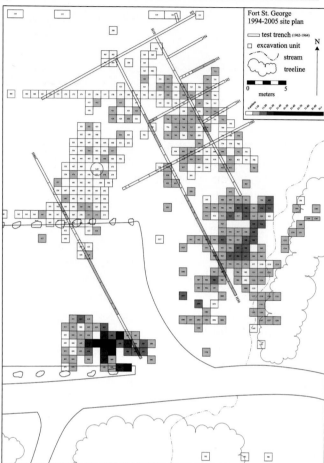

Figure 181.   Distribution of artifacts related to economic ventures (trading and ship building): white and blue glass beads and bale seal; caulking iron and large roves. Note that the distributions of these items reflect where they were stored on site, not the areas where they were put to use which is presumed to have been primarily off site.

Figure 182.   Distribution of prestige items: glass (bottles, wine and ale glassses, mirror, buttons, decorated beads, window); copper; pewter; gold; jet. These artifacts are almost entirely confined to the locations associated with the admiral and vice admiral, but the greater number and variety of items in the admiral's house reflect the higher status that may be inferred from the titles.

CONCLUDING THOUGHTS

We have at Popham an exciting opportunity to bring together a truly revealing integration of historical and archaeological information that will greatly expand our knowledge of the foundation of English America. This is not just an exercise in archaeology during the historic period, but a study of historical archaeology in which information from both history and archaeology are combined in such a manner that they intimately inform each other. It must be acknowledged that the key to this intimacy is that incredible document, the John Hunt map ("A pearl of no little price," as presciently observed by Ivor Noël Hume in 1994, p. 99). While we no longer expect perfection from Mr. Hunt, we are still amazed by his overall reliability. His rendering is a remarkably accurate guide to both excavation and interpretation: it is, to reverse the old cliché, a case of history as a handmaiden to archaeology. But the real point is that at Popham history and archaeology are equal partners as they inform us about the past. The fruit of this union prompts the following observations.

Fort St. George was a well-conceived settlement that was built to establish a permanent English presence. After fortifying the site, the colonists followed their Instructions for the Government of the Colonies (November 20, 1606) which ordered "first build your storehouse and those other rooms of publik and necessary use before any house be set up for private persons" (Brown 1890, p. 84). Both Hunt's drawing and the archaeology confirm that the storehouse was a large, timber-framed, wattle-and-daub, thatched-roof structure. The archaeology further reveals that it was earthfast, post-and-beam construction with interrupted sills, and that the major elements had been joined with mortises and tenons. The storehouse was obviously built to last by trained carpenters. It was early October by the time such a solidly built structure was sufficiently completed for the ships to begin off-loading the supplies, and by then the colonists would already have begun to feel the northerly winds roaring down the Kennebec and buffeting their exposed location. Houses were then quickly put up for the "private persons." These shelters were little more than rude huts built by untrained hands using a variety of techniques and materials. Even the second in command, Raleigh Gilbert, was lodged in inferior housing. Hunt again appears to depict a timber-framed, wattle-and-daub, thatched-roof structure which was the largest private residence within the fort. The archaeology confirmed many of these details, but revealed a more primitive form of construction than was employed in the storehouse which presumably could be erected more quickly. The archaeology also disclosed that the house burned during occupation and that much of the contents was consumed. This event corrects the historical record which states that it was the storehouse that burned. While this certainly would have been a disaster for Raleigh Gilbert, greatly altering his lifestyle, it would not have been as great a catastrophe as the loss of the storehouse would have been for the colony as a whole. Nevertheless, it may have soured Gilbert and contributed to his ultimate decision to turn his back on the adventure which in turn sealed its fate.

But for us the burning of Raleigh Gilbert's house was a stroke of good luck. The rubble in the destruction layer contained an assemblage of artifacts that contrasted significantly with the items found within the storehouse. The latter consisted mostly of inexpensive ceramics, hardware, trade goods, and munitions. These were cheap goods, but basic and necessary, and together they describe the public activities of the colony: defense, trade, shipbuilding. At Raleigh Gilbert's house, however, we have a glimpse of the private life of one of the leaders and we find that he came well-equipped with the finest ceramics and glassware from the site – and by inference the best foods and liquors – as well as the sartorial and military trappings that attest to his position within the colony, a faithful reflection of his status within English society.

That we should find at Popham a microcosm of English society is perfectly in line with the conceptions of the principal colonial advocates, as mentioned above, and differed not a wit from contemporary events in

Ireland. (The Pilgrim model of social equality, which we prefer to espouse today, was in fact the aberration among colonial establishments.) While the social distinctions were predictable, they rendered the ventures vulnerable to the loss of a few key men, especially if these men happened to be competent. President George Popham was described by Sir Ferdinando Gorges as "an honest man, but ould, and of an unwildy body, and timerously fearfull to offende, or conteste with others that will or do oppose him, but otherwayes a discreete, carefull man" (Thayer 1892, p. 135). Although in poor health George clearly was chosen because of his experience and maturity of judgment. Sir Ferdinando is not as kind in his assessment of Raleigh Gilbert: "desirous of supremasy, and rule, a loose life, prompte to sensuality, litle zeale in Religion, humerouse, head stronge, and of small judgment and experiense, other wayes valiant inough" (ibid.). Such a characterization, however, would seem to epitomize the qualities of a young aristocratic gentleman of the Elizabethan-Jacobean era, qualities that would particularly suit him for the role of adventurer and active right hand of the elderly and infirm George Popham. In fact, it is probable that had fate not intervened Gilbert would have grown into the role of president (Bradford 2000). He was, after all, the son of Sir Humphrey Gilbert and clearly inherited the adventurous spirit and force of will that might have served the colony well (see also Thayer 1892, p. 212).

The selection of other key personnel would seem to have been similarly thoughtful. Although family connections were certainly given prominent consideration, this would have provided a pool within which competence would have been recognized. Even the unnamed and unrelated lower orders were trained soldiers or skilled craftsmen. It is true that Sir John Popham saw colonization as a vehicle for the transportation of rogues and vagrants, and as lord chief justice was behind legislation to this effect, which caused his detractor John Aubrey to slander that the colony was "stockt and planted out of all the gaoles of England" (Stephen and Lee 1968, p.148). There is no evidence for this aspersion, though it remained as a stain on the record. It was repeated even by Henry Thayer, who conceded that the colonists were a very degenerate lot that included a preponderance of "worthless, unintelligent, inefficient...untrusty, unprincipled men" (Thayer 1892, pp. 210-211). Of course there may have been a few villains present, possibly including a Spanish spy, and the soldiers who probably composed half the company would have been a rough lot although presumably under discipline. But the general calumny is no more justified than the case lodged against the idle gentlemen of Jamestown. For it must be acknowledged that the Popham colonists industriously worked together to construct a defensible fort in about a month, while trained carpenters prefabricated and put up a large storehouse, skilled shipwrights assembled from scratch a pinnace that was so seaworthy it made at least two trans-Atlantic voyages, and a military cartographer made a map of Fort St. George that was state of the art in its precision of scaling and detail.

This last document is the nexus that ties this whole story together: personally, as well as historically and archaeologically. It reveals that John Hunt was an exceptionally experienced and accomplished draftsman, and it is certain that he belonged to the brotherhood of military cartographers who carefully recorded contemporary English campaigns, battles, and fortifications (Hayes-McCoy 1964). One of the most famous of these cartographers was Richard Bartlett who in a series of early seventeenth-century maps of the Irish wars exhibits many of the same stylistic conventions and oblique or "bird's-eye" picture-plan perspective as seen in the Hunt drawing. This may be no coincidence: Edward Popham, George's nephew who may have accompanied him to the Sagadahoc, was married to the daughter of a Richard Bartlett, and his sister Katherine was married to a John Hunt (Popham 1752). That they are the vary same Richard Bartlett and John Hunt would seem a likely proposition, as well as further evidence that important positions were kept in the family. But nepotism did not sacrifice expertise, and the important inference here is that competent individuals were chosen for the venture.

Thus, although the general historical consensus yet holds that the Popham Colony was stillborn because it was established "by the wrong people, in the wrong place, at the wrong time" (Morey 2005, p. 120), the new archaeological evidence encourages the conclusion that the planning, organization and selection of at least the principal people of the colony were far more thoughtful than generally has been credited historically. Similar conclusions are becoming increasingly apparent in the new research at Jamestown (Kelso 1997, pp.

22-28, 2006, pp. 189-190; Kelso, Luccketti, and Straube 1997; Kelso and Straube 2003, p.73). The foundation of English America was probably as sophisticated as contemporary means, personalities, ambitions and abilities could provide, but ultimately was subject to the vagaries of fortune that allowed one venture to survive while another failed.

POSTSCRIPT

At the start of this project, a rather more expansive program and set of objectives had been envisioned. During my long career in aboriginal archaeology I had developed a strong interest in contacts between different peoples and the acculturation processes that occurred as a result of these contacts (Brain 1969, 1989; Brain et al. n.d.). I came to focus on the most dramatic contact situation of all, that between the Native Americans and the various European explorers and colonists who recorded their experiences beginning in the sixteenth century (Brain 1979, 1985, 1988). When I changed venue from the southeast to the northeast, these thoughts still prevailed. The main reason I decided to search for Fort St. George was to establish a datum for a study of contact and acculturation between the local Abenaki and the first English colonists. I had not planned to advance much beyond proving the location of the fort because little if any of that ephemeral settlement was expected to have survived. Once I realized the potential of the site, however, I was far too captivated by that brave but doomed effort to move on. I subsequently tried to entice various graduate students into conducting a survey of nearby aboriginal sites, many shell mounds of which are visible from Fort St. George on Cox's Head and Long Island, but none has yet accepted the challenge. I hope someone will, for the lower Kennebec would provide an unparalleled case study comparing the Fort St. George period with Cushnoc and then Clarke and Lake.

APPENDIX A
HISTORICAL DOCUMENTS

Three documents from the hands of men who were at Fort St. George exist. These are the Robert Davies journal, the John Hunt map, and the George Popham letter. At least four other journals were written – by Raleigh Gilbert, John Eliot, James Davies, and Christopher Fortescue – but they apparently have not survived. They are referred to by Samuel Purchas (1625) who had intended to publish them, "but our voluminousnesse makes me afraid of offending nicer and queasier stomackes: for which cause I have omitted them." Quinn and Quinn (1983, pp. 444-445) conclude that Purchas then discarded them and so we are most unfortunately deprived of the "offending" details.

1. THE ROBERT DAVIES JOURNAL

The Robert Davies journal is known from a copy in the Lambeth Palace Library, London (Figure A1, next page). It is incomplete, missing at least one page at the back. It describes the voyage to the Sagadahoc and the first month and a half at Fort St. George. Robert Davies was pilot of the *Mary and John,* and so the journal stops when the ship returned to England in early October. Information about the founding of the colony is spare indeed and the journal is mostly of interest to the maritime historian. William Strachey published the complete journal in 1612 and added a brief synopsis of the progress of the colony after the *Mary and John* left that he had gathered from other sources. The additional detail enhances the document, but because of some editorial changes Strachey's text should always be compared with the Lambeth Palace copy. Reprinting of both versions is not justified here because of the length, but they have been published many times (e.g., Thayer 1892, Quinn and Quinn 1983) and the most relevant passages are cited in the text herein.

2. THE JOHN HUNT MAP

Physical Characteristics of the Map[1]

The Simancas copy of Hunt's map of "St. Georges fort" is stunning (Figure A2). Although excellent reproductions were made for Brown's *Genesis of the United States* and Thayer's *Sagadahoc Colony* (Figure A3), neither duplicates the fine draftsmanship nor attention to details that are displayed in this copy.

The map is in excellent condition and drawn with a sure hand on high quality handmade laid paper. The general lack of staining and surface dirt, and the absence of corrections or evidence of notations relating to surveying and scaling, as well as the sure-handed rendering of the delicate detail, indicates that the Simancas plan is a contemporary copy that was redrawn from another perhaps less elaborate but more realistic working map made in the field. The Simancas copy, then, is fit for a king's eye; lending credence to the theory that it was a copy provided to the Spanish as propaganda to intimidate and keep them at bay.

---

[1] Notes by John W. Bradford and Jeffrey P. Brain during a visit to the Simancas Archives on December 9, 2003. The castle now containing the archives is the former summer palace of Spanish Kings, including Philip III. In some respects little has changed since that time, although in December 2003 the castle was undergoing extensive renovations.

Figure A1. Sample pages from the Davies journal showing the entries for August 15 to 21, 1607 which describe the arrival at the Sagadahoc and the first explorations up the river "to See whear they myght fynd the most Convenyent place for thear plantation." Having chosen their place, on "Thursdaye beinge the 20th of Auguste all our Companyes Landed & thear began to fortefye our presedent Captain Popham Sett the fryst spytt of ground unto ytt and after hem all the rest followed & Labored hard in the trenches about ytt. Frydaye the 21st of Auguste all handes Labored hard about the fort Som in the trentch Som for fagettes and our ship Carpenters about the buildinge of a small penis [pinnace] or shallop." That this is a transcribed copy of the original journal is indicated by the relatively clean and unweathered appearance of the pages, and by the consistently well-formed and unaltered script, as well as the absence of the author's name on the title page. Dimensions of original page 15 x 20cm. (Lambeth Palace Library, MS 806 item 14)

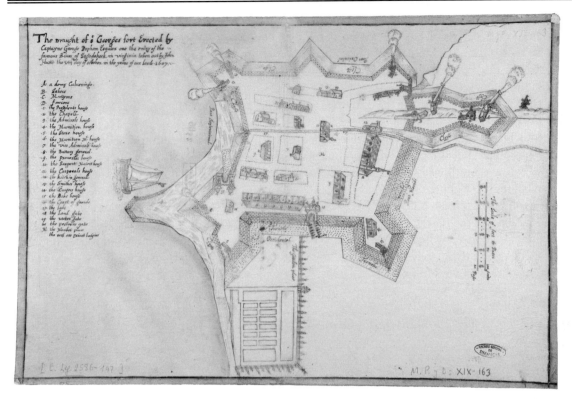

Figure A2. John Hunt map: Simancas copy. Dimensions of original 43 x 29cm. (Ministerio de Cultura de España, Archivo General de Simancas, MPD, 19, 163)

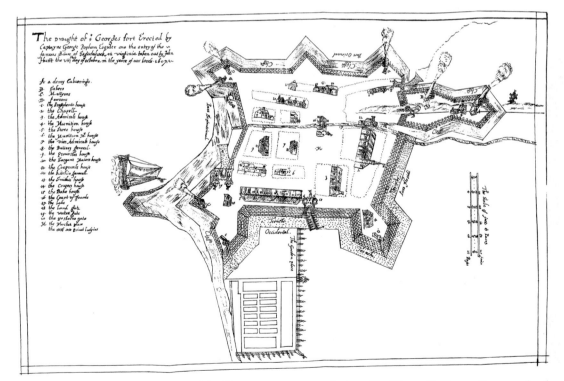

Figure A3. John Hunt map: copy of the Simancas map commissioned by Henry O. Thayer for reproduction in his book, *The Sagadahoc Colony* (1892). Some details are enhanced, but others are obfuscated or omitted, so the map must be used with care. (Collections of Maine Historical Society, FF52)

The overall dimensions of the plan, including the 3/16th inch border, are 11½ x 17¼ inches. Sometime long after it was drawn, perhaps when the Brown and Thayer copies were made, it was reinforced with a linen backing. There is an old crease down the center from top to bottom, indicating that the map was folded in half at some time before the linen backing was added. There is very little foxing which indicates that the map was left untouched for centuries in a stable and sealed atmosphere. The 3/16 inch border, which clearly is original, is colored with a sepia wash. The ink in the drawing is also sepia, but it is unclear whether the color is original or the result of fading. That it is original is suggested by the fact that some of the lines have been touched up with a darker ink (e.g., silhouette and doorway of Court of Guarde, parts of buildings #7 and #13, angles of rampart near storehouse, postern gate, and shoreline past postern gate). The salt water area defining the high tide line to the east and north was colored with a light gray-blue wash to distinguish it from the land area.

The map belongs to a genre of chorography that was popular in the early seventeenth century referred to as a "bird's eye" picture-plan (Hayes-McCoy 1964, p. xi). It was clearly drawn by a very accomplished surveyor-cartographer of the Bartlett school of military draftsmen. The skill, detail, and stylistic conventions are of the highest contemporary quality (see Harvey 1993, fig. 44; Brain 1998a). John Hunt is assumed to be the cartographer because the map was "taken out" by him. Whether John Hunt was also the designer of the fort is not known but whoever it might have been was likewise a military engineer of the first order.

Analysis of the Features Depicted on the Map

Fortifications

It is obvious that the type of fortifications selected – the ditch and reinforced earthen rampart – was specifically chosen to protect against the perceived greater danger of attack by European (French) ships. Had they been located farther from the coast and were only concerned with native assault they might have opted for a simpler wooden palisade à la Jamestown (Kelso et al. 1999, pp. 32-33). The primary physical defense was the location which was strengthened by ditch and rampart on the two land sides, rampart only on shore. The ramparts were simply dirt reinforced with faggots (fascines), the latter perhaps being represented by the masonry-like pattern drawn by Hunt. More likely, however, that pattern was simply a stylistic convention that was meant to indicate "wall" and to differentiate it from the trench which was stippled. (That the stippling is also used for the paths down from the water and postern gates suggests that they may have been covered ways). According to Hunt's scale, the landward ditch and rampart are each about 15' wide; therefore, the depth of the ditch and height of the wall were designed to have been approximately equal. Actually, the 2000 excavations revealed that the ditch was about 20' wide but quite shallow. The only indication Hunt gives us for the height of the rampart is that the doorways in the land gates and water gate are ca. 10' high, which seems excessive although possible. Since there was no ditch to provide dirt for the shoreside rampart perhaps it was constructed from the rocks and trees scattered about the site. The ditch was a dry moat, as shown by the fact that the stream is not diverted into it, but instead bisects it.

Armaments

According to William Strachey, Fort St. George was armed with "12 pieces of ordinaunce," but John Hunt shows only nine cannons on his map which he identifies as one demi-culverin, two sakers, two minions, and four falcons. The heaviest artillery, the demi-culverin and sakers, were placed in the citadel which was situated on the ledge forming the first terrace of Sabino Head (Figure A4). This location was the highest point within the fort and it afforded a clear field of fire for the artillery which had sufficient range to hit any ships attempting to enter the Kennebec. The lighter guns controlled Atkins Bay and the land approaches.

Citadel

The outline plan of the walls conforms perfectly to the topography of the ledge (Figure A4). This highest point was chosen as the placement for the biggest guns which had a clear field of fire to the navigable channel at the mouth of the river. Hunt shows this also as the location of the president's house, just as the lord would have resided in the strongest point in a medieval castle. The house has at least two sections (and the luxury of 2 chimneys) and appears to be a split-level indicating the uneven topography. The larger section has a peaked roof, atop which flies a swallowtail pennant. No evidence of a structure is apparent on this bare rock ledge.

Figure A4. Citadel.

Windmill

Hunt places a windmill on the next terrace above the citadel where the Cogan battery of Fort Baldwin was later placed (Figure A4). This terrace was on the highest point closest to the fort. This mill would have been used for grinding grain, and so may never have been built if the colonists never got around to growing the grain. Again, bare rock prohibits investigation.

Chapel

Quite fittingly, the chapel is located on the highest ground within the fort – except for the citadel, that is, which was needed for the big guns and president's house. This is the second largest building within the compound and architecturally is the most complex with a steeple on one end and decorative elements over the door (Figure A5, see also Figure A19). The construction may not have been as sophisticated as the storehouse, however, as Hunt clearly shows that the principal rafters are not tied to the posts, but are irregularly joined to the wall plate as in crotchet construction. No evidence of a structure was encountered during brief tests in 1994, and the permission for further investigation was subsequently withdrawn.

Figure A5. Chapel.

Storehouse

The largest and most important structure, excavations have confirmed the accuracy of Hunt's drawing regarding placement of posts, scale, wattle-and-daub walls, thatched roof, position of door; but it is only seven bays long, not eight as he drew it (Figure A6). Dimensions are approximately 19' x 69'. Hunt must have left before it was finished. The archaeology suggests that it was probably shortened one bay because of change in topography as the ground suddenly sloped upward and had to be cut away even to accommodate the seventh bay. Questions that remain unresolved: whether the tops of the posts which are clearly drawn as separate elements are meant to indicate capitals or beam ends; the significance of the three circles or balls over the door (see Figure 19); and the reason for the apparent holes in the roof. It seems unlikely that the latter are dormers because we found no evidence of a loft where colonists could have been quartered; neither does Hunt show a chimney, nor did we find a hearth (they certainly would not have wanted fire in the storehouse) so colonists could not have resided there. Perhaps the openings are a clerestory for lighting the dark interior of the large building.

Figure A6. Storehouse.

Buttery and Corporal's House

The buttery was close to the main storehouse, but separate and closely guarded because of its contents (Figure A7). It was also closest to the water gate so that the heavy butts had to be transported the least distance. Like the storehouse it was not heated, but the attached corporal's house does have a chimney. We found evidence of at least one structure at this location in the 1994/2001-2005 excavations.

Figure A7. Buttery and corporal's house.

Munition House

Following typical European practice, the magazine was placed within one of the bastions (the southwestern one which was the farthest from the shore). Hunt seems to draw it with a flat, hipped roof or perhaps he is indicating two attached structures in a T or L arrangement, most likely the latter (Figure A8). There are no chimneys, of course!

Figure A8. Munition house.

Bake House and Smith's House

These buildings with the most dangerous – largest, hottest, most permanent – fires were placed together (Figure A9) and apart from other structures, especially the magazine which was on the opposite side of the compound about as far away as

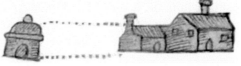

Figure A9. Bake house and smith's house.

possible. The bakery presumably was a North Devon portable oven as indicated by the domed structure, but may never actually have been in use if they had no flour because they had no grain (see windmill comment). The smithy is attached to the smith's house, and both have chimneys of course. This corner of the site could not be investigated by us.

Kitchen

The kitchen (Figure A10) was located where the stream enters the compound and therefore where the water would have been cleanest. Test excavations in 1994 were inconclusive at the predicted location.

Figure A10. Kitchen.

Court of Guard (Corps de Garde)

This headquarters of the watch is in the exact center of the fort, equally accessible to all quarters and thus able to respond to any alarm most efficiently. Why it straddles the stream (Figure A11) has always been a mystery, perhaps explained only by its precisely central location. The paved town road covers all, or most, of the predicted location.

Figure A11 (right). Corps de garde.

Admiral's House

This appears to be the most substantial individual dwelling, even bigger than the president's house according to Hunt, which would seem to suggest the occupant's standing in the colony. The 1999-2000 excavations confirmed that the structure was built and the artifacts found reveal the presence of an individual of considerable status. Construction was found to be less sophisticated than the storehouse and seemingly as drawn by Hunt (Figure A12). There are holes in this roof, too, but the theory of a clerestory proposed for the storehouse makes little sense for this relatively small structure. Maybe it did have a loft, although we found no evidence of one.

Figure A12. Admiral's house.

Vice Admiral's House

This is shown as a relatively modest structure (Figure A13), and since none of the colonists is definitely identified with this title it may be assumed that the office was minor or honorary. The 2001-2004 excavations, however, produced a fine assortment of artifacts similar to the admiral's house in quality, as well as evidence of construction and burning at the general location indicated by Hunt. But no building could be identified.

Figure A13. Vice admiral's house.

Provost's House

This is one of the larger structures drawn by Hunt and one of the most complicated (Figure A14). It has one, possibly two additions, and appears to have two chimneys. Considering the provost's function, the added room may have been intended as a gaol. Excavations in 2001-2005 found no evidence of this structure.

Figure A14. Provost's house.

Munition Master's House

The munition master's house is a small building between the storehouse and vice admiral's house (Figure A15). The location near other officers' abodes indicates the importance of this gentleman. Although he is not near the magazine, it is noteworthy that strongest archaeological evidence of lead munitions manufacture was found in the vicinity. The 2001-2004 excavations, however, found no trace of a structure at this location.

Figure A15. Munition master's house.

Cooper's House

The only cooper mentioned is Lancelot Booker who returned to England on the Gift of God in December 1607, so this house may not have been built (Figure A16). Hunt's rendering suggests it would have been one of the minimal kinds of structures erected for, and by, the lesser colonists (see Private Lodgings).

Figure A16. Cooper's house.

Sergeant Major's House

Robert Davies was designated the sergeant major of the colony, but since he apparently returned to England on the Mary and John in October 1607 it is unlikely that his house was ever built. The structure indicated by Hunt is a very small house attached to a huddle of private lodgings (Figure A17). We were not able to investigate this part of the site.

Figure A17. Sergeant major's house (number 10 at left) and the humble houses of ordinary colonists.

Private Lodgings

Housing for the common colonists must have been extremely rudimentary. Hunt draws a variety of forms, some of which may have been reasonably substantial, but most were probably small jerry-built hovels (Figure A17).

Gateways

It is doubtful that these were ever as elaborate as drawn by Hunt (Figure A18), but were probably quite imposing affairs. Access paths to the water gate and postern are stippled which is the same convention Hunt uses for the fortification trench (i.e., excavated area) which suggests that these may have been covered ways as discussed under fortifications above. The flags Hunt shows on the gates are too small to make out, but would be an appropriate place to fly the Cross of St. George.

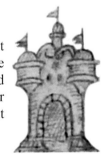

Figure A18. Land gate.

Doors

Rounded doorways are common in vernacular architecture. They make sense with masonry or cob construction, but they might not have been as suitable with timber-framed wattle-and-daub walls. Maybe it is just Hunt's stylization or perhaps it does reflect prevailing custom: the medieval style of door was the gothic pointed doorway which gradually gave way to round heads which then were replaced in the later seventeenth century by flat lintels as the Georgian and then neoclassical styles began to gain popularity. The decorative elements above the doors of the church and storehouse are of special interest. The decorated door frame is typical of Devonshire (Figure A19), although in this case it might just be that Hunt was indulging in one of his elaborations.

Figure A19. Doorways of storehouse (left) and chapel (right) from the Thayer copy. In center is an early eighteenth-century doorway from Poundsgate in Devon (Beacham 2001, fig. 3.13).

Jetty or Dry Dock

Hunt clearly shows this feature to be artificially modified using the same stylization as for the ramparts (Figure A20). He also crosshatches it, presumably to indicate that it is a feature distinct from the beach. But is it a jetty as has been assumed? Atkins Bay was too shallow even then for ships to approach any closer than Champlain's channel. Furthermore, the water gate clearly accesses directly down to a beach landing between this feature and the northeast bastion: ships must have been off loaded into boats which brought the goods ashore there. The best orientation of the Hunt map to landforms and topography clearly places the "jetty" not at the present trestle ledge, but between it and another ledge to the west (Figure A21, see also Figure 32). The colonists could have connected the two ledges far enough out to create a dry dock. This would have been a very logical place to build the *Virginia*, which not coincidentally is depicted by Hunt right next to it. Dry dock construction was a known method in contemporary England (Bradford 1999; see also Friel 1995, fig. 3.10) and is specifically mentioned by Strachey in the construction of the pinnace *Deliverance* in Bermuda (1609-1610): "we towed her out in the morning spring tide from the wharf where she was built," wharf here denoting a mole or dam (creating a dockyard and dry dock) as further described by Strachey: "our governor had caused a solid causeway of an hundred load of stone to be brought from the hills and neighbor rocks and round about her ribs from stem to stern, where it made a pointed balk and thereby brake the violence of the flow and billow" (Wright 1964, p. 56). That certainly would seem to describe what Hunt draws. All they had to do was close the bulwark when the tide was out creating a cofferdam, and then open it for launching when the tide was in. It might be observed that the northern exposure would not have provided the most felicitous location for shipbuilding, but the same holds true for the siting of the fort as a whole and yet there it is – clearly they made do with what nature provided.

Figure A20. Jetty – more likely a dry dock – and the *Virginia*.

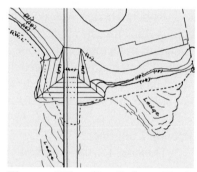

Figure A21. Detail from U. S. Army Corps of Engineers 1905 map showing rock ledges that could have been converted into a dry dock (see cover illustration). (National Archives RG77, CS1, SH22)

Boat

What presumably is the pinnace *Virginia* is shown afloat just off the tip of the jetty or dry dock (Figure A20). Obviously, the *Virginia* had not been launched by early October, but like the fort Hunt wished to show it fully finished and not still under construction. In fact, she is not only afloat but under full sail and riding the waves. Hunt's peculiar perspective gives us full view of both the bow and the stern. Among the details that are clearer in the Simancas copy than the published versions of Brown and Thayer is that the flag atop the mainmast is clearly the cross of St. George.

Garden

The rectangles probably indicate raised beds. The fence presumably would have been simple pickets to keep out animals, especially deer. We may doubt that the garden ever was a going affair, at least not until the spring of 1608, and even then would have been quite limited in what could have been grown. Later visitors mention only herbs and fruit trees growing on site.

Lake

Earlier researchers suggested this word is a misprint for "lade" or "labe," but "lake" is a perfectly good contemporary old English word for "a small stream of running water" (*Oxford English Dictionary*, p. 1561); "a small stream or channel: brook, rivulet" (*Webster's Third*, p. 1265). The archaeology not only confirmed the presence of this feature, but also that it had been engineered by the colonists. That is, a natural stream had been captured and channeled in order to provide a controlled supply of fresh water.

Scale

Archaeology has found the scale of feet and paces to be extremely accurate, and most interestingly has proven that the foot used then had already been established as approximately the same unit of measure now in use.

3. THE GEORGE POPHAM LETTER

This letter (Figure A22) was written at Fort St. George and sent to King James I aboard the *Gift of God* when it sailed for England on December 16, 1607. As an official report to the king, the letter was written in Latin, but as revealed in the English translation it is also an incredible piece of propaganda.

At the feet of his Most Serene King humbly prostrates himself George Popham, President of the Second Colony of Virginia If it may please the patience of your divine Majesty – to receive a few things from your most observant and devoted, though unworthy servant, I trust it will derogate nothing from the lustre of your Highness, since they seem to redound to the glory of God, the greatness of your Majesty, and the utility of Great Britrain, I have thought it therefore very just that it should be made known to your Majesty, that among the Virginians and Moassons there is none in the world more admired than King James, Sovereign Lord of Great Brittain, on account of his admirable justice and incredible constancy, which gives no small pleasure to the natives of these regions, who say moreover that there is no God to be truly worshipped but the God of King James, under whose rule and reign they would gladly fight. Tahanida, one of the natives who was in Great Brittain has here proclaimed to them your praises and virtues. What and how much I may avail in transacting these affairs and in confirming their minds, let those judge who are well versed in these matters at home, while I, wittingly avow, that all my endeavors are as nothing when considered in comparison with my duty towards my Prince. My well considered opinion is, that in these regions the glory of God may be easily evidenced, the empire of your Majesty enlarged, and the welfare of Great Brittain speedily augmented So far as relates to Commerce, there are in these parts, shagbarks, nutmegs and cinnamon, besides pine wood, and Brazilian cochineal and ambergris, with many other products of great value, and these in the greatest abundance. Besides, they positively assure me, that there is a sea in the opposite or Western part of this Province, distant not more than seven days journey from our fort of St. George in Sagadahoc – a sea large, wide and deep, the boundaries of which they are wholly ignorant of. This cannot be any other than the Southern ocean, reaching to the regions of China, which unquestionably cannot be far from these regions. If, therefore, it may please you to keep open your divine eyes on this matter of my report, I doubt not but your Majesty will perform a work most pleasing to God, most honorable to your greatness, and most conducive to the weal of your kingdom, which with ardent prayers I most vehemently desire. And may God Almighty grant that the majesty of my Sovereign Lord King James may remain glorious for ages to come. At the Fort of St. George, in Sagadahoc of Virginia, 13 December, 1607.

         In all things your Majesty's Devoted Servant

        George Popham

        (Translation from Thayer 1892, pp. 118-119)

Figure A22. George Popham letter to James I dated 13 December 1607. Dimensions of original 21 x 30 cm. (PRO CO.1.1)

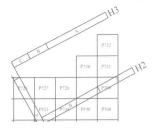

APPENDIX B
ARCHAEOLOGICAL CATALOGING SYSTEMS
OF THE 1962 AND 1994-2005 EXCAVATIONS

1. LOCATION AND CATALOG OF THE 1962 HADLOCK EXCAVATIONS.

Trenches that were dug across the site during the 1962 investigations by Wendell Hadlock and his crew were encountered during the course of our excavations. Enough sections were identified to enable us to reconstruct the principal excavation grid (see Figure 18) on the ground and relate it to our plan of excavations (Figure B1). This correlation allowed us to avoid or reinvestigate Hadlock's trenches according to the objectives of our subsequent investigations.

The Hadlock grid was oriented approximately 60° east of north (although there was some deviation from this standard), and those trenches running NE-SW were numbered between 0 and 5 while those at right angles were given designations 10, 30, and 80 (as determined by the number of feet they were southwest of the "zero point"). The trenches comprising the grid were 15 to 18 inches wide, and approximately the same in depth. They were dug in arbitrary sections of various lengths without regard for distinctions in the vertical stratification.

The artifacts collected during these excavations were identified as lots from the linear sections of the trenches, for example, "Trench 2, 10' - 25' SW." Occasionally, the depth and stratigraphic association of individual artifacts were given, but generally provenience was only identified by trench section. In cataloging this collection, we followed Hadlock's numbering system for the trenches, but added the prefix "H" so that there would be no confusion with our designations. To each section of a trench we assigned a letter according to the order in which it was dug. Thus, the catalog number for the above example is H2C.

There are also collections that came from locations other than the principal grid. These include the contents of the nineteenth-century well which we cataloged as H100, and the materials from a 110 foot-long trench that was dug from east to west along the bank line of the private property on the west side of the Popham site (see Figure 17). The latter was designated H110, following Hadlock's numbering system. Apparently, no collections survive (or at least cannot be identified) for the other locations excavated in 1962, nor for the mining of the bank line in 1964.

The entire catalog of collections and their proveniences that we have been able to reconstruct is presented in Table B1.

2. FIELD CATALOG OF THE 1994-2005 EXCAVATIONS.

All evidence of Hadlock's excavation plan and "zero point" had disappeared by 1994. Therefore, a new plan was imposed on the site before we began excavations. An arbitrary datum was established near the northwest corner of the parking lot at Latitude 43° 45' 11.3660" N, Longitude 69°47' 19.9801" W (see Figure 34). This datum was permanently marked with a capped galvanized iron pipe (2.5" x 18") that was set flush to the modern ground surface.[1] A dimple was punched into the center of the cap and all horizontal and vertical measurements made during the subsequent excavations are in reference to this point.

Excavation units were laid out along a metric grid oriented to 1994 magnetic north from datum. The standard unit was a 1 x 1 m square, although deviations from this norm were sometimes required in order to fulfill objectives or conform to topographic conditions. An alphanumeric identification system was used to

---

[1] Two additional permanent markers were also installed: a backsight was established 35.05 m north of datum on the 1994 magnetic north line; a secondary datum was set at S5 E30. Both markers are capped galvanized iron pipes (2" x 12").

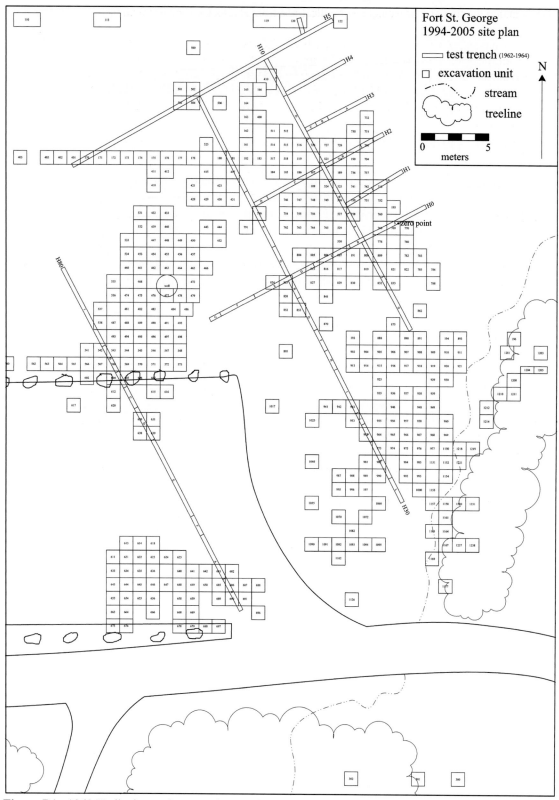

Figure B1. 1962 Hadlock trenches superimposed on 1994-2005 excavation plan. Hadlock's datum was the "zero point" located in Trench 0.

Table B1. Catalog number and provenience of collections from Hadlock's 1962 excavations.

H	No provenience. Assigned to collections that had no identification; some of these may be from excavations outside the grid in 1962 or from the 1964 mining of the bank for which there are no collections. The H is sometimes followed by a serial number that was assigned during subsequent analysis by Hadlock and others.	**H10A**	Trench 10, 2' - ca. 9' NW
		H10B	Trench 10, 9' - 18' NW
		H10C	Trench 10, ca. 41' - 50' NW
		H10D	Trench 10, 28'6" - ca. 41' NW
		H10E	Trench 10, 18' - 28'6" NW
		H10F	Trench 10, 0' - 8' SE
		H10G	Trench 10, 8' - 23' SE
H0	Trench 0, no further provenience known	**H30A**	Trench 30, 37' - 40' SE
H0A	Trench 0, 10' SW - 6+' NE	**H30B**	Trench 30, 0' - 3'6" SE
H0B	Trench 0, 10' - 16' SW	**H30C**	Trench 30, 26' - 50' NW
H0C	Trench 0, 18' - 24' SW	**H30D**	Trench 30, 3'6" - 11'6" SE
H0D	Trench 0, 24' - ca. 31' SW	**H30E**	Trench 30, 10' - 26' NW
H0E	Trench 0, ca. 31' - 40' SW	**H30F**	Trench 30, 11'6" - 19' SE
H0F	Trench 0, 40' - 50' SW	**H30G**	Trench 30, ca. 2' - 10' NW
H0G	Trench 0, 50' - 53' SW	**H30H**	Trench 30, 19' - 22' SE
H1	Trench 1, no further provenience known	**H30I**	Trench 30, 22' - 34' SE
H1A	Trench 1, 3' SW - 6'6" NE	**H30J**	Trench 30, 34' - 37' SE
H1B	Trench 1, 0'[3'] - 10' SW	**H30K**	Trench 30, 40' - 51' SE
H1-2	Between Trenches 1-2, NE of zero point	**H30L**	Trench 30, 51' - 60' SE
H2A	Trench 2, 0' - 6'6" NE	**H80A**	Trench 80, ca. 40' - ca. 49' SE
H2B	Trench 2, 0' - 10' SW	**H80B**	Trench 80, ca. 49' - ca. 62' SE
H2C	Trench 2, 10' - 25' SW	**H80C**	Trench 80, 0' - ca. 5'6" SE
H2D	Trench 2, 25' - 30' SW	**H80D**	Trench 80, ca. 5'6" - ca. 14' SE
H2-3	Between Trenches 2-3, 3.5' NE	**H80E**	Trench 80, ca. 14' - ca. 35' SE
H3A	Trench 3, 4' SW - ca. 8' NE (?)	**H80F**	Trench 80, ca. 35' - ca. 40' SE
H3B	Trench 3, 4' - 6' SW	**H80G**	Trench 80, 0' - ca. 4' NW
H3C	Trench 3, 6' - 10' SW	**H80H**	Trench 80, ca. 4' - ca. 12' NW
H5	There are no collections identified as being from Trenches 4 or 5, but one of the first trenches dug before the numbering system was in place is almost certainly what was later designated 4 or 5. Since Trench 5 is the more plausible candidate, the collection is assigned this catalog number.	**H80I**	Trench 80, ca. 12' - ca. 33' NW
		H100	Bottom of well
		H110A	Trench 110, 0' - 7' W
		H110B	Trench 110, 7'- 23' W
		H110C	Trench 110, 23' - 41'6" W
		H110D	Trench 110, 41'6" - 46' W
		H110E	Trench 110, 46' - 58' W
		H110F	Trench 110, 58' - 62' W
		H110G	Trench 110, 62' - 80' W

identify each of these units: a prefix "P" (for Popham) to avoid confusion with the Hadlock numbers, a unit number, and a letter indicating an arbitrary or natural level of excavation. Often a number was added after the letter to distinguish a feature that was found within a level. If more than one feature was found each was assigned a separate number (B1, B2, B3, etc.). If a feature continued down through more than one level it retained its original designation, but with the new level added (CB1, DB1, EB1, etc.). Artifacts found *in situ* in each level were piece-plotted and were given a sequential number identified with a number sign. Thus the thirteenth artifact found in feature 2 of level C of unit 645 would be P645C2#13.

Unfortunately, when the excavations began we had no idea that we were about to undertake a ten-year project. Had we been so prescient, we would have established a master grid that had a logical layout of excavation unit numbers. There is some coincidence of blocks of numbers with specific years or locations (e.g., all P100-P300 numbers were excavated in 1994; all excavations at the admiral's house were given P600 numbers). But exceptions abound (e.g., not all P600 numbers were confined to the admiral's location and they were excavated in more than one year). The reason for this is that different segments were excavated at different times for different reasons. Therefore, in the same location there might be sequential numbers in contiguous units or they might be quite mixed and even centuries apart (e.g., in the buttery location there are numbers in the P100s, P500s and P700s). In an attempt to clarify the situation, Table B2 provides a concordance of excavation numbers with the year of excavation and, where they coincide, with the locations of the principal structures that we investigated.

Table B2. Catalogue of excavation unit numbers, year(s) of excavation, and provenience (if at one of these four principal locations: storehouse, buttery, admiral's house, vicinity of vice admiral's house) of the 1994-2005 excavations.

Unit #	Year	Location	Unit #	Year	Location	Unit #	Year	Location
P100	1994		P195	1994		P456	2005	*Store.*
P102	1994		P196	1994		P457	2005	*Store.*
P103	1994		P197	1994		P460	1998/9	*Store.*
P104	1994		P200	1994		P461	1999	*Store.*
P105	1994		P201	1994		P462	2005	*Store.*
P106	1994		P202	1994		P463	2005	*Store.*
P108	1994		P300	1994		P464	2005	*Store.*
P110	1994		P301	1994		P465	1997	*Store.*
P113	1994		P302	1994		P466	1997	*Store.*
P119	1994		P400	1997	*Store.*	P467	1999	*Store.*
P120	1994		P401	1997		P468	1999	*Store.*
P122	1994		P402	1997		P472	1997	*Store.*
P150	1994		P403	1997		P474	1999	*Store.*
P161	1994	*Store.*	P405	1997		P475	1999	*Store.*
P162	1994	*Store.*	P407	1997		P476	1998	*Store.*
P163	1994	*Store.*	P410	1997		P477	1998	*Store.*
P164	1994		P411	1997/8	*Store.*	P478	1997	*Store.*
P165	1994		P412	1997	*Store.*	P479	1997	*Store.*
P166	1994		P415	1997	*Store.*	P481	2005	*Store.*
P170	1994		P417	1997	*Store.*	P482	2005	*Store.*
P171	1994		P418	1998	*Store.*	P483	1998	*Store.*
P172	1994		P421	1998	*Store.*	P484	1998	*Store.*
P173	1994		P423	1997	*Store.*	P486	1997	*Store.*
P174	1994		P424	1997	*Store.*	P487	2005	*Store.*
P175	1994	*Store.*	P428	1998	*Store.*	P488	2005	*Store.*
P176	1994	*Store.*	P429	1997	*Store.*	P489	2005	*Store.*
P177	1994	*Store.*	P430	1997	*Store.*	P490	2005	*Store.*
P178	1994	*Store.*	P431	1997	*Store.*	P491	2005	*Store.*
P179	1994	*Store.*	P432	2005	*Store.*	P492	2005	*Store.*
P180	1994	*Store.*	P433	1997	*Store.*	P493	2005	*Store.*
P181	1994	*Store.*	P439	2005	*Store.*	P494	2005	*Store.*
P182	1994	*Store.*	P440	2005	*Store.*	P495	2004/5	*Store.*
P183	1994		P443	1997	*Store.*	P496	2004/5	*Store.*
P184	1994		P444	1997	*Store.*	P497	2004	*Store.*
P185	1994		P446	1998/9	*Store.*	P498	2004	*Store.*
P186	1994	*Buttery*	P447	2005	*Store.*	P500	2003	
P187	1994	*Buttery*	P448	2005	*Store.*	P501	1998	*Store.*
P188	1994	*Buttery*	P449	2005	*Store.*	P502	1998	*Store.*
P189	1994	*Buttery*	P450	2005	*Store.*	P503	1998	*Store.*
P190	1994	*Buttery*	P452	1997	*Store.*	P504	1998	*Store.*
P191	1994	*Buttery*	P453	1998/9	*Store.*	P506	1998	*Store.*
P193	1994	*V.Adm.*	P454	2005	*Store.*	P511	2003	
P194	1994	*V.Adm.*	P455	2005	*Store.*	P512	2003	

Unit #	Year	Location	Unit #	Year	Location	Unit #	Year	Location
P514	2003		**P565**	1998		**P647**	1999/0	*Admiral*
P515	2003		**P566**	1998	*Store.*	**P648**	1999	*Admiral*
P516	2003		**P567**	1999	*Store.*	**P649**	2000	*Admiral*
P517	2003		**P568**	1999	*Store.*	**P650**	2000	*Admiral*
P518	2003		**P569**	1999	*Store.*	**P653**	1999/0	*Admiral*
P519	2003		**P570**	1999	*Store.*	**P654**	1999/0	*Admiral*
P520	2003		**P571**	1999	*Store.*	**P655**	1999/0	*Admiral*
P521	2003		**P572**	1998	*Store.*	**P656**	1999	*Admiral*
P523	1998	*Store.*	**P573**	1998	*Store.*	**P658**	2000	*Admiral*
P524	2003	*Buttery*	**P602**	1999	*Store.*	**P659**	2000	*Admiral*
P525	2003	*Buttery*	**P604**	1999	*Store.*	**P663**	1999	*Admiral*
P526	2003	*Buttery*	**P605**	1999	*Store.*	**P664**	1999	*Admiral*
P527	2003	*Buttery*	**P606**	1999	*Store.*	**P666**	1999	*Admiral*
P529	2003	*Buttery*	**P607**	1999	*Store.*	**P668**	2000	*Admiral*
P530	2003	*Buttery*	**P611**	2000	*Admiral*	**P669**	2000	*Admiral*
P531	1998	*Store.*	**P612**	1999	*Store.*	**P673**	1999	*Admiral*
P532	1998	*Store.*	**P613**	2000	*Admiral*	**P674**	1999	*Admiral*
P533	1998/9	*Store.*	**P614**	2000	*Admiral*	**P678**	1999	*Admiral*
P534	1998/9	*Store.*	**P615**	1999	*Store.*	**P679**	1999	*Admiral*
P535	1998	*Store.*	**P616**	1999	*Store.*	**P680**	2000	*Admiral*
P536	1998	*Store.*	**P617**	1999		**P681**	2000	*Admiral*
P537	2005	*Store.*	**P618**	2000	*Admiral*	**P682**	2000	*Admiral*
P538	2005	*Store.*	**P620**	1999		**P685**	2000	*Admiral*
P541	2004	*Store.*	**P621**	2000	*Admiral*	**P686**	2000	*Admiral*
P542	2004	*Store.*	**P622**	2000	*Admiral*	**P687**	2000	*Admiral*
P543	2004	*Store.*	**P623**	2000	*Admiral*	**P688**	2000	*Admiral*
P544	2005	*Store.*	**P624**	2000	*Admiral*	**P689**	2000	*Admiral*
P545	2004/5	*Store.*	**P625**	2000	*Admiral*	**P690**	2000	*Admiral*
P546	2004/5	*Store.*	**P630**	1999		**P691**	2000	*Admiral*
P547	1998	*Store.*	**P631**	1999		**P696**	2000	*Admiral*
P548	1998	*Store.*	**P633**	2000	*Admiral*	**P697**	2000	*Admiral*
P552	2000		**P634**	2000	*Admiral*	**P700**	2005	
P553	2000		**P635**	1999/0	*Admiral*	**P704**	2005	
P554	2000		**P636**	2000	*Admiral*	**P712**	2005	
P555	2000		**P638**	1999		**P726**	2001	
P556	2000		**P639**	1999		**P727**	2001	
P557	2000		**P640**	2000	*Admiral*	**P728**	2004	
P558	1998		**P641**	2000	*Admiral*	**P729**	2004	*Buttery*
P559	1998		**P642**	2000	*Admiral*	**P730**	2004	
P560	1998		**P643**	1999/0	*Admiral*	**P731**	2005	
P562	1998		**P644**	1999/0	*Admiral*	**P732**	2005	
P563	1998		**P645**	1999/0	*Admiral*	**P734**	2001	*Buttery*
P564	1998		**P646**	2000	*Admiral*	**P736**	2004	*Buttery*

Unit #	Year	Location	Unit #	Year	Location	Unit #	Year	Location
P737	2004		**P819**	2004	*Buttery*	**P930**	2003	*V.Adm*
P741	2004	*Buttery*	**P821**	2001		**P935**	2001	*V.Adm*
P742	2004	*Buttery*	**P822**	2001		**P936**	2002	*V.Adm*
P746	2001		**P824**	2001		**P937**	2002	*V.Adm*
P747	2001		**P825**	2001		**P938**	2003	*V.Adm*
P748	2001	*Buttery*	**P827**	2001		**P939**	2003	*V.Adm*
P749	2001	*Buttery*	**P829**	2005	*Buttery*	**P941**	2001	*V.Adm*
P750	2004	*Buttery*	**P830**	2005		**P942**	2001	*V.Adm*
P751	2004	*Buttery*	**P832**	2005		**P943**	2002	*V.Adm*
P752	2005		**P833**	2003		**P944**	2001	*V.Adm*
P754	2001		**P838**	2001		**P945**	2001	*V.Adm*
P755	2001		**P841**	2005	*Buttery*	**P946**	2003	*V.Adm*
P756	2001	*Buttery*	**P852**	2001		**P947**	2003	*V.Adm*
P757	2001	*Buttery*	**P853**	2001		**P948**	2003	*V.Adm*
P758	2004	*Buttery*	**P862**	2002		**P949**	2002	*V.Adm*
P760	2004	*Buttery*	**P870**	2001		**P953**	2002	*V.Adm*
P762	2001		**P875**	2003		**P955**	2001	*V.Adm*
P763	2001		**P888**	2004	*V.Adm.*	**P956**	2001	*V.Adm*
P764	2001		**P889**	2003	*V.Adm*	**P957**	2001	*V.Adm*
P765	2001	*Buttery*	**P890**	2004	*V.Adm*	**P958**	2001	*V.Adm*
P768	2004	*Buttery*	**P891**	2002	*V.Adm*	**P960**	2002	*V.Adm*
P769	2005	*Buttery*	**P893**	2004	*V.Adm*	**P963**	2001	*V.Adm*
P770	2005	*Buttery*	**P895**	2001		**P964**	2001	*V.Adm*
P778	2001	*Buttery*	**P903**	2002	*V.Adm*	**P965**	2001	*V.Adm*
P779	2005	*Buttery*	**P904**	2002	*V.Adm*	**P966**	2001	*V.Adm*
P780	2005	*Buttery*	**P905**	2001	*V.Adm*	**P967**	2001	*V.Adm*
P782	2005		**P906**	2003	*V.Adm*	**P968**	2002	*V.Adm*
P783	2005		**P907**	2004	*V.Adm*	**P969**	2002	*V.Adm*
P785	2005		**P908**	2004	*V.Adm*	**P973**	2001	*V.Adm*
P786	2005		**P909**	2004	*V.Adm*	**P974**	2002	*V.Adm*
P788	2005		**P910**	2004	*V.Adm*	**P975**	2002	*V.Adm*
P790	2005		**P911**	2004	*V.Adm*	**P976**	2002	*V.Adm*
P791	2005		**P913**	2002	*V.Adm*	**P977**	2002	*V.Adm*
P804	2001		**P914**	2002	*V.Adm*	**P981**	2003	*V.Adm*
P805	2001		**P915**	2001	*V.Adm*	**P982**	2001	*V.Adm*
P806	2001		**P916**	2003	*V.Adm*	**P984**	2002	*V.Adm*
P807	2001		**P917**	2003	*V.Adm*	**P985**	2002	*V.Adm*
P808	2004	*Buttery*	**P918**	2002	*V.Adm*	**P987**	2003	*V.Adm*
P809	2001	*Buttery*	**P919**	2003	*V.Adm*	**P988**	2003	*V.Adm*
P815	2001		**P920**	2003	*V.Adm*	**P989**	2002	*V.Adm*
P816	2001		**P921**	2004	*V.Adm*	**P990**	2001	*V.Adm*
P817	2001		**P925**	2001	*V.Adm*	**P992**	2002	*V.Adm*
P818	2005	*Buttery*	**P929**	2003	*V.Adm*	**P993**	2002	*V.Adm*

Unit #	Year	Location	Unit #	Year	Location	Unit #	Year	Location
P995	2002	*V.Adm*	P1102	2004		P1201	2004	
P996	2003	*V.Adm*	P1126	2002		P1203	2004	
P1000	2002	*V.Adm.*	P1150	2002		P1204	2004	
P1017	2004		P1151	2002		P1205	2004	
P1025	2004		P1152	2002		P1208	2003	
P1040	2002		P1153	2002		P1210	2003	
P1055	2002		P1154	2002		P1211	2003	
P1060	2002		P1155	2002		P1212	2003	
P1070	2002		P1157	2002		P1214	2003	
P1072	2004		P1158	2002		P1218	2003	
P1082	2004		P1161	2002		P1219	2003	
P1090	2002		P1163	2002		P1221	2003	
P1091	2004		P1164	2002		P1230	2003	
P1092	2004		P1167	2002		P1231	2003	
P1093	2004		P1169	2002		P1237	2003	
P1094	2004		P1177	2002		P1238	2003	
P1095	2002							

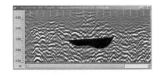

APPENDIX C
A GEOPHYSICAL SURVEY AT FORT ST. GEORGE:
SITE OF THE 1607-1608 POPHAM COLONY, PHIPPSBURG, MAINE

Peter Sablock
Department of Geological Sciences, Salem State College, Salem, MA

A geophysical survey of selected portions of Fort St. George, site of the 1607 Popham Colony, Phippsburg, Maine, USA, was conducted in order to verify the location of the trace of the defensive ditch, and other structures as recorded on the 1607 John Hunt map. The geology consists of the metasedimentary Cape Elizabeth Formation (Ordovician), discontinuously overlain by the clays and sands of the regressive marine Presumpscott Formation (Holocene). Seismic refraction and electrical resistivity surveys were conducted. In the seismic refraction survey the ditch was not apparent, presumably because the density contrast between the trench infill and surrounding undisturbed sediment did not generate a unique velocity for the infill. A pole-dipole resistivity survey did not produce usable results. We believe that the irregular bedrock surface allowed moisture to pool in bedrock lows producing a series of low resistivity zones which obscured the location of the ditch. A magnetometer survey was not completed due to the extreme twentieth-century magnetic clutter at the site. A ground penetrating radar survey was conducted with variable results. On most of the radar profiles the ditch is as shown on the Hunt map. The overburden thins to the north and in these locations the trace of the ditch is much less distinct although still identifiable. The radar profiles show a ditch with a low angle counterscarp and a much steeper scarp. We assume that the original profile was somewhat preserved on the radar sections due to the looser packing and higher moisture content of the sediments washed into the ditch after the site was abandoned.

LOCATION

The site is located at Sabino Head, Phippsburg, Maine. Sabino Head is a north-facing headland extending into Atkins Bay on the western side of the mouth of the Kennebec River. The site datum adjacent to the public parking lot is located at approximately Latitude 43° 45' 11" N and Longitude 69° 47' 20" W, North American Datum 1983 (NAD83).

SITE GEOLOGY

The bedrock of Sabino Head consists of the Ordovician Cape Elizabeth Formation – a muscovite schist of metamorphosed back arc sediments. The Cape Elizabeth Formation is, in turn, intruded by pegmatites of the Phippsburg Granite. The rocks have a fairly constant orientation of N15°E, 75°NW. The bedrock surface is highly irregular with up to 2 m of very local relief.

The Cape Elizabeth Formation is overlain by the Upper Pleistocene-Lower Holocene Presumpscott Formation, a regressive marine unit from 0-3 m thick consisting of fine to medium grained sand with silty interbeds. The Presumpscott is discontinuous and drapes the topography, in some places 2 m thick and in other places not covering the underlying Cape Elizabeth.

Due to cultivation, civilian construction, and the military construction of Fort Baldwin much of the top 1 m of overburden has been extensively reworked and backfilled. Given the large amount of cultural activity on the site (post 1607) the actual target of this survey, the trench, is really only the deepest remnant of the original feature. This remnant, partially excavated in 2000, was transected at a depth of 130 – 160 cm (Brain 2001, p. 22). The trench infill consists of water-laid organic fine silts and sands (ibid.). The site is relatively level with a 1:47 topographic gradient from west to east and 1:42 south to north along the grid lines. This shallow gradient means that a topographic correction would not have to be applied to either seismic, resistivity or radar data.

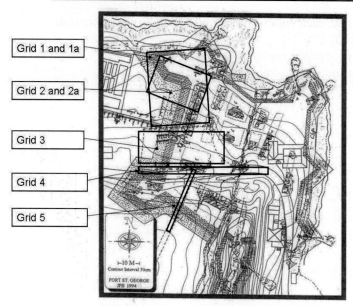

Figure C1. Locations of the five geophysical grids at Fort St. George.

PURPOSE OF THE GEOPHYSICAL SURVEY

The purpose of this survey was to attempt to delineate the trace of the defensive trench on the western and southern faces of the curtain wall and northwest bastion of the fort. The existence of the ditch had been confirmed by previous excavations but remote sensing would provide the most efficient method of delineating the full extent of the trace of the ditch as well as confirming the location of structures located under the paved town road as indicated on the Fort St. George map (see Figure 32).

METHODS

The data were collected over the course of four days during the fall and summer of 2004-2005. It was assumed that the primary target, the defensive ditch, would be a broad, linear feature, perhaps as wide as 5 m. Thus the geophysical survey grids could be relatively coarse. Five grids were established using a total station (Figure C1). The first geophysical grid began at archeological grid N0E0 and ended at N35E0. This grid was coincident with the archeological grid and consisted of transects from the base line running from west to east, beginning at N0E0 and ending at N35E0, at 1 m intervals. On all transects the data were collected from west to east. The second grid was oriented to identify the trace of the trench along the southern face of the northwest bastion of the fort. Thus, the transects ran from southwest to northeast along a baseline beginning at N11E15 and ending at N19E0. Transects were spaced at 2 m intervals along this grid from southeast to northwest, beginning on the east end of the baseline. The third, fourth and fifth grids were established to transect the parking lot, the paved town road and the public path to Fort Baldwin. These grids were also on a 2 m interval. The grid lengths totaled 1800 m. Some of the area under Grid 1 had been extensively excavated and a 1 m spacing was selected to detect these excavations. This would allow calibration of the various pieces of equipment.

Seismic refraction was carried out using a Geometrics Smartseis 12 channel seismograph. Seismic data were processed using Rimrock Geophysics SIPT2 software. A Geometrics 856 magnetometer with gradiometer and a Fisher M97 valve box locator were employed for the magnetic survey. A 24 electrode array Iris Syscal Kid was used for the resistivity/conductivity surveys and data post processed with RES2DINV and RES3DINV. Finally, a GSSI SIR 20 ground-penetrating radar with 200 MHz and 400 MHz antennae and attached survey wheel was used for the radar surveys. The data were processed using RADAN 5.0. The survey grid was georeferenced with a CMT GPS-HP-L4 with a real time DGPS receiver and differentially corrected.

DATA ACQUISITION

In order to quickly characterize and interpret the results a series of quick measurements were made. First, an 18 mm tube core was taken to refusal (approximately 80 cm). This gave an indication of general site stratigraphy and lithology. Second, on a daily basis, a Portable Soil Moisture Meter with a 36" probe was used to determine moisture content in the top meter of unconsolidated sediment. Moisture content is important in interpreting radar, resistivity and seismic results. The moisture content of the subsurface will affect the speed of transmission of acoustical energy (seismics) and electromagnetic energy (radar) in unconsolidated material, and subsequent estimation of target depth. Moisture content is the key physical parameter measured in resistivity surveys.

Two seismic refraction lines were run across the site, each with forward, reverse and center shotpoints. The lines were 48 m long with 12 geophones on 4 m takeouts, with a 5 m offset shotpoint and stacking of 5 records. After viewing the high level of low frequency background noise (presumed to be a result of the nearshore ocean/river floor interactions) a high pass acquisition filter of 20 Hz was installed. The energy source was a 4 kg sledgehammer on a steel plate. Seismic refraction provided a depth to bedrock, estimation of moisture content (via predicted velocities of equivalent dry material) at deeper levels and rough stratigraphy.

A quick survey of the site was conducted using the Fisher M97 in order to determine the suitability of a magnetic gradiometer survey. The site was found to have an excess of late nineteenth- through twentieth-century metallic clutter so a magnetometer survey was not conducted.

Ease of use and ideal site conditions (level with cropped grass) dictated that the majority of the geophysical survey work would be conducted using ground penetrating radar (GPR). The GPR survey was primarily conducted with the 400 MHz antenna. The acquisition parameters for the 400 MHz antenna were set to 100 scans per second, 512 samples per scan, 50 scans per meter, stacking of 5, high and low pass filters of 100 and 800 respectively, and a range (listening window) of 60 nS. Acquisition signal gains values were set to default antenna values. The parameters for the 200 MHz antenna were identical with the exception of high and low pass filters of 25 and 600 respectively and a range of 80 nS. Antenna position along the transects was calibrated over a 10 m test run using a GSSI survey wheel attached to the antenna and set to mark the radar record at 1 m intervals.

The dielectric constant varied on the three days that GPR was employed, from 7 to 18, depending upon sediment moisture content. This number represents a vertical average of the site conditions with the estimate reflecting a heavier qualitative weighing of conditions at the 1-2 m depth level.

A total of 36 transects, using the 400 MHz antenna, were made on the archeological-geophysical coincident grid, N0E0 to N35E0 (Figure C1). These transects were 22 m long. In addition, four 22 m transects were made with the 200 MHz antenna at N6E0, N9E0, N12E0 and N15E0. For discussion purposes this grid will be called 'Grid 1' for the 400 MHz antenna and 'Grid 1a' for the 200 MHz antenna transects.

The second geophysical grid oriented SE-NW, contained 14 variable length 400 MHz transects. The transect length decreased from 24 m in the SE to 14 m in the NW, terminating against the shoreline. Five 200 MHz transects were also run on this grid coincident with 400 MHz lines 7, 8, 9, 10 and 11. For discussion purposes this grid will be called 'Grid 2' for the 400 MHz antenna and 'Grid 2a' for the 200 MHz antenna transects.

The third, fourth and fifth geophysical grids – the parking lot, paved town road and public path to Fort Baldwin respectively – contained 29 transects. These grids were purely GPR grids at 1 m spacing. The parking lot grid consisted of 9 transects at 1 m intervals running from west to east, progressing from north to south and 8 transects running from north to south progressing from west to east. These parking lot transects were difficult to run due to the number of parked cars that blocked access. Eight transects were run along the town road from west to east progressing from north to south. Four transects were run from the south edge of the parking lot south towards Fort Baldwin along the public path.

A total of seven resistivity lines were run. All were laid normal to the presumed trend of the defensive ditch on Grids 1 and 2a. Each line consisted of 24 electrodes at 1.5 m intervals. The data were acquired with the array in both Wenner and pole-dipole configurations with a stacking of 5 records per electrode. The Wenner array is commonly used for profiling and a large body of interpretational data is available. The pole-dipole array is a more complex setup and interpretation can be difficult but the advantages of reduced telluric noise and stronger signal strength as well as improved depth penetration outweigh the disadvantages. The asymmetrical results obtained using the pole-dipole spread were negated by reversing the lines. Resistivity lines were run on Grid 1 locations N6E0, N9E0, N12E0, N15E0 and Grid 2 locations N7E0, N9E0, and N11E0. The resistivity data were processed by comparing the actual resistivity field curves against a model cross section generated by estimating layer thickness and resistivity values (model pseudosection). A least squares optimization was run to converge the pseudosection and measured values. The results provide a fairly reliable resistivity cross section.

All post processing of the radar records was done with RADAN® 5.0. It was decided to analyze the records with a minimum of processing – the raw data were preserved as much as possible. However, each radar record was reviewed and two processing corrections were applied to each record in the following order:

a) remove antenna cross-talk and ground coupling – an average adjustment of -1.76 nS was applied to each record;

b) the radargrams were viewed with a logarithmic color scale transform to enhance lower amplitude signals;

c) a high pass horizontal boxcar filter at 100 MHz to remove multiples.

A Kirchoff migration function was applied to the data sets to remove any diffraction caused by a steep sided feature such as a scarp or counterscarp. However, migration tended to obscure the data and it was decided not to apply the functions to the data sets. Time slice/depth slice analyses, with various widths for the window, were performed but were inconclusive due to the coarse nature of the grid.

RESULTS

N0E0 is located at Latitude 43° 45' 11.3660" N and Longitude 69° 47' 19.9801" W, +/-20 cm, North American Datum 1983 (NAD83).

Seismic Refraction

Refraction was unable to detect the primary target, the ditch, due to the extremely irregular rock-overburden interface. This irregular surface scattered the refracted energy. In addition, velocity inversions generated by backfilling were probably present in some areas across the site. However, seismic refraction provided usable site stratigraphy on a gross level as well as average depth to bedrock. A three layer model was generated with a near surface backfill velocity range of 350 m/s, an intermediate layer of the original Presumpscott Formation with a velocity of 460–510 m/s, and a third, bedrock, layer with velocities of 3800–4580 m/s.

Electrical Resistivity

The results from the electrical resistivity survey were very satisfactory. This is due to the fact that the ditch contains less compacted, finer grained, infill material with a higher porosity and lower permeability than the surrounding material. The lower permeability allows the infill to retain slightly more moisture thus showing as a lower resistivity area on the profiles. Figure C2 shows the resistivity results for the Grid 1 line N9W6 to N9E18. The ditch is the low resistivity zone in the center of the bottom profile. The upper two profiles are the apparent measured resistivity and the model resistivity respectively. Figure C3 shows the results for the line run from N12W6 to N32E12. The trench infill shows as low resistivity values surrounded by the higher resistivity, more permeable, undisturbed sediments. The trench infill begins and ends at approximately 7.5 m and 15 m respectively. The excessive width of the trench can be explained by the fact that the electric line intersects the trench at an angle and the original, higher angle, scarp and counterscarps degraded and eroded. The high resistivity layer over the trench infill is interpreted as sandy backfill and cultural reworking over the succeeding nearly 400 years.

Ground Penetrating Radar

In general, GPR was the remote sensing method of choice at Fort St. George. Although the disturbed nature of the site prevented the building of accurate plan views, significant information could be extracted from simple cross sections along individual radar lines. Perhaps the most valuable data obtained from the radar profiles were the location and approximate size of the ditch along the southern curtain wall under the public path to Fort Baldwin. The most intriguing data are from the large, deep feature under the eastern end of the paved town road. Finally, a parking lot transect yielded a very distinct cross section of the ditch along the northern face of the southwestern bastion.

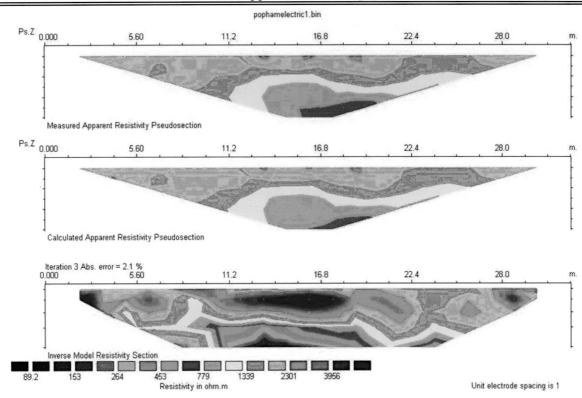

Figure C2. Resistivity line across the western fortification ditch. The uppermost diagram is the measured resistivity, the middle diagram is the pseudosection, and the bottom diagram is the calculated resistivity which shows the ditch as a low resistivity zone from 8.4 m to 17.2 m.

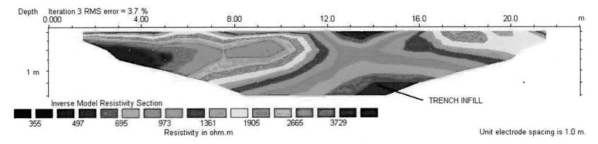

Figure C3. Resistivity line across the southern face of the northwest bastion.

Geophysical Grids 1 and 1a

Grid 1 and Grid 1a from N0 to N13 show a very good correlation with the predicted trace of the trench both in width and trend as drawn on the Hunt map and georectified by Jeffrey Brain (see Figure 32). North of N13 the location of the counterscarp becomes less distinct. Grid 2 and Grid 2a have a very general correlation with the predicted location of the scarp but little or no correlation with the counterscarp. In general, when an anomalous reflector indicated the presence of the trench this reflector occurred between 28 and 40 nS representing a depth of 140 to 200 cm. The trench appeared as an area of relatively low amplitude reflectors surrounded by higher reflectors. This is to be expected since the original glacio-marine stratigraphy of the site would have been disturbed when the trench was excavated and replaced by relatively well sorted fluvial sediments as the trench filled in. Along many of the transects the reflectors rest upon a high amplitude, nearly horizontal, reflector which may represent a gravel-cobble layer. The wall has no associated radar signature. Where Grid 1 transects exceeded 16 m in length, the excavations at the storehouse were detected.

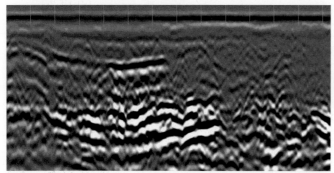

Figure C4. Section of GPR profile across the western fortification ditch along the N6 radar transect. The whiter area represents the ditch infill.

Several additional, non-natural, straight-sided features were identified. These were presumed not to be associated with the fort because they were too shallow and to the west of the trench. One anomalous feature was found, extending into the depth range of the trench, within the boundary of the fort (Grid 2 below).

A total of 22 transects, each of 22 m length were run to locate the trench bordering the west curtain wall. These began at the N0 datum and continued at 1 m intervals to N21. The trench was detected on all transects with the exception of transects N0, N1, N10, N11 and N14. The trench was detected at depths of from 120 cm to 180 cm. In cross section the trench is not symmetric – a steep scarp is faced by a shallow dipping counterscarp. The floor of the trench averages 3 m in width.

Radar signature correspondence with the predicted trench location is excellent from N3 to N13 (Figure C4). The absence of a trench signature on transects N0 and N1 are attributed to parking lot construction and archeological excavations. Transects N10 and N11 clearly show the presence of a linear feature all along the transect, similar to a utilities trench of some type. The same may be true for transect 14 which shows a deep fill structure along the entire transect. Transects 15–18 locate the scarp but indicate that the counterscarp shallows to the west in a very gradual manner. In point of fact, the trench appears to widen with a very shallow counterscarp and shallower scarp dip along these transects. It almost appears that the trench walls were purposely flattened. Transects 19–22 continue the trend of a wide trench but the scarp retains the steeper dip characteristic of the more southerly transects. Grid 1a, with transects at N6, N9, N12 and N15, shows the same trend in much coarser fashion. In addition, a sharp reflector, bedrock/gravel or cobble, appears at 2-3 m.

Geophysical Grids 2 and 2a

A total of 14 variable length transects were run on Grid 2 at 2 m intervals. Five variable length transects corresponding to Grid 2 transects 7, 8, 9, 10, and 11 were run on Grid 2a. The results are not as clear as those for Grids 1 and 1a. Transects 1, 2 and 3 run within the projected trend of the wall. These transects have some disturbed zones and anomalous reflectors which I attribute to later construction activity. The trench appears less distinctly than on Grid 1 on transects 6, 7, 8, 9, 10 11, 12 and 13 but it appears to have the same characteristic steep scarp and less steep counterscarp (Figure C5). More importantly, it trends more to the west and south (southerly by as much as 4 m) than expected. However, this does not eliminate a space problem – even locating the bastion trench several m south may not provide enough room for bastion walls and a gun platform. Coastal erosion must be considered. In addition, the bedrock interface as determined by Grid 2a increases in depth to 3–3.5 m as it approaches the shoreline. Several large rocks crop out, or are just below the surface along transects 10, 11 12, and 14. In all cases anomalous features terminate against these rocks. Grid 2a data indicate that these are boulders and not bedrock. It may be that the position of the trench was adjusted to fit these boulders into the scarp and counterscarp. A seismic survey should be conducted to determine if these rocks are indeed outcrop. In general, the farther north the transects run the more disturbed the ground becomes, with much more evident post-Popham activity obscuring the trench signature.

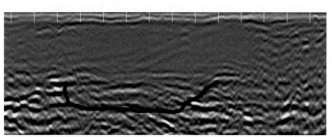

Figure C5. Section of GPR profile across the southern face of the northwest bastion. The outlined area indicates the ditch.

Finally, an interesting feature occurs at N25- N28 trending to the NE from E23 to E 24 along transect 15. It is sharp sided and extends down to 1.8 m.

Geophysical Grid 3

The radar grid over the parking lot was productive. It located the trace of the ditch, the location of previous archaeological site work and several unaccounted for anomalies. The various lines produced ditch profiles from quite indistinct to well defined. The grid was not fine enough, however, to locate the western gate.

Interesting results were obtained along line 9, adjacent to the island separating the parking lot from the town road. Along this profile, from west to east, the ditch is not apparent. It may be that the ditch extends outside of the reservation area and thus the radar line actually begins in the ditch. A large steep-sided feature extending 2 m to the bottom of the record occurs from 8 to 14 m, and another distinct anomaly occurs from 17 to 21 m. The latter of these two anomalies may be excavations at the admiral's house. Finally another anomaly, to the depth of the profile at 2 m, exists from 31 to the end of the profile at 36 m and probably represents more of the excavations at the admiral's house.

Profile line 7, 2 m to the north of line 9 is equally rewarding. The ditch is apparent from 6 to 14.2 m as a deep, broad anomaly with a sloping western counterscarp. The floor of the ditch is approximately 1.2 m broad. The remainder of the line is featureless. Profile line 5, 2 m north of line 7, contains three anomalies, only one of which can possibly be related to the Fort St. George map. These anomalies occur from 3 to 7 m, 7.8 to 11.3 m (probably the ditch) and 12.8 to 16.6 m. All of these anomalies are indistinct. The last anomaly is quite interesting with shallow, sloping sides.

On line 1 of the eight north-south transects across the parking lot the best cross section of the ditch appears (Figure C6). On this transect the ditch appears at a depth of 1.6 m, symmetric, 5 m broad at 1.6 m and narrows to 1.5 m at the bottom. The ditch occurs approximately 2 m south of the georectified location on the Fort St. George map (see Figure 32).

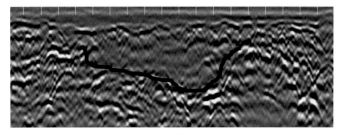

Figure C6. Section of GPR profile across the fortification ditch of the southwest bastion. The outlined area indictaes the ditch.

Geophysical Grid 4

The radar lines along the paved town road, eight in total, were only somewhat productive. The ditch is apparent at the western edge of the lines. The ditch anomaly occurs at a depth of 1.4 m and extends from the western edge of the lines east a distance of 8.5 m (Figure C7). The shape is asymmetric with a shallow western face and a steeper eastern face, as would be expected. The location of the ditch under the road indicates that either the western curtain wall extended this far south or that the radar line runs down the long axis of the ditch along the north facing wall of the southwest bastion.

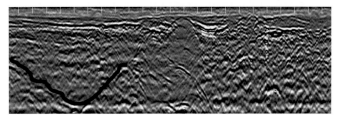

Figure C7. Section of GPR profile from west end of transect along the paved town road. The outlined area indicates the ditch.

An anomaly from 18 to 28 m is apparent, although indistinct, on the two northernmost lines. This may be the southeast corner of the admiral's house as it appears under the road. At the very end of the radar lines (just as the paved town road turns south) – at approximately 51 m, there is evidence of a very large deep disturbance. This anomaly extends from 0.8 m to the bottom of the profile at 2.2 m (Figure C8). The anomaly extends to the end of the radar line at 60 m. This feature may represent the course of the stream that was diverted eastwards across this location in the nineteenth century (see Figure 12).

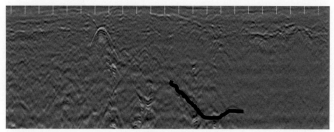

Figure C8. Section of GPR profile from east end of transect along the paved town road. The outlined area is the anomalous drop that probably indicates the former course of the stream

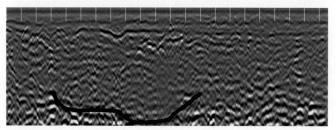

Figure C9. Section of GPR profile from transect along the public path to Fort Baldwin. The outlined area indicates the ditch of the southern wall.

Geophysical Grid 5

The three radar lines running from north to south, up the hill along the public path posed acquisition problems. The water bars along the path and occasional large exposed boulders prevented good coupling between the different antennae and the ground. The depth of the overburden was not known in this area, therefore two different antennae were used: 200 MHz and 400 MHz. The results were variable. In both cases, however, the supposed trace of the ditch was visible. There are also numerous additional anomalies along these lines. The ditch was identified based upon two lines of evidence. The first was a correspondence with known ditch profiles and the second was the anticipated location of the ditch. The profiles show a feature deeper (2.5 m) than other ditch sections but also broader at 5 m (Figure C9). The ditch occurs at approximately 22 m and ends at 27 m. As was expected, the ditch is 2 to 3 m south of the proposed location.

CONCLUSIONS

The geophysical data showed a good correspondence with the historical and archaeological map correlation (see Figure 32). In general, radar was the best method used for several reasons. First, the soil conditions were appropriate. Second, the topography was relatively flat allowing quick data acquisition without the need for a terrain correction. The third reason was the ease of data collection. However, the radar could not be used until the results were verified by another geophysical method. In this case electrical resistivity provided the corroboration with a good match to the radar data.

The data shows that the ditch exists at depth levels ranging from 1.3 to 2.5 m below the present ground surface. It is generally asymmetric with a shallow counterscarp and steeper scarp. It must be assumed that the profile has been degraded by erosion when the ditch was still exposed on the surface, producing the broad profile.

Many additional anomalies were detected along the various lines but no definitive statement can be made regarding them. They are, however, cultural and not the result of natural processes. The vast majority of these features bear no relation to any feature on the Hunt map and are assumed to postdate Fort St. George.

APPENDIX D
ARCHITECTURAL REMAINS

Architectural remains from Fort St. George include both organic and inorganic materials.

ORGANIC

The major categories of organic remains are wood, wattle and thatch that were preserved by being charred and/or buried. The wood includes posts, sills and other timbers from the frames of the buildings, as well as wattling that was used to fill in the walls.

Posts

The biggest pieces of preserved wood were the bottoms of the posts that were the principal supporting members of the earthfast structures (Figure D1, see also Figure 40). The tops of these stubs were often charred by the fire that destroyed the building, and the anaerobic environment of the posthole further conserved the wood. Thus enough remained of some posts, especially in the south end of the storehouse, to determine that they had been hewn to a roughly square or rectangular cross section and that the bottoms were sawn flat. Where they were identified, the posts from the side walls of the storehouse were cut from pitch pine (*Pinus rigida*), an easily worked but durable wood that is common in the region. The ridgepole post in the north gable end, however, has been identified as spruce which is not considered as strong or as durable as the pitch pine (Bruce Hoadley, pers. comm., 1998). A characteristic of the pitch pine is that the knots "are so filled with resin that they resist decay long after the stump has rotted away" (Peattie 1950, p. 23). In the storehouse, for example, a timber lying on the floor had deteriorated to a mere stain except for the knots which were still well preserved along its length (see Figure 57); and numerous knots were found associated with the lake indicating construction nearby although no timbers were preserved.

Sills

The sills of the storehouse were interrupted, that is, they were individual sections between the posts that appeared to be attached at each end by a mortise-and-tenon joint. They were the same width as the posts (app. 25 cm) but were only about 5 cm thick, and also appeared to be cut from pitch pine. Insofar as could be determined, the wall studs were toenailed into the sills.

Figure D1. Bottom of storehouse post from excavation unit P538. This was the penultimate post (going from north to south) in the west wall of the storehouse. The post was roughly squared, although one face is still rounded, and measures 30 cm to a side. The height of this remnant is 68 cm.

Timbers

Timbers include studs, beams, rafters, and other superstructural elements. We did not find any evidence of flooring, either at ground level or in a loft. Otherwise, the fragmentary condition of these poorly preserved pieces and the chaotic jumble into which they had collapsed precluded differentiation of the various elements. Most of the wood was too far deteriorated to be identified, but some of it appeared to be a softwood such as pine. Most of these secondary timbers appear to have been unshaped and in many cases the bark was not even removed. Measurable studs in the west wall of the storehouse had diameters of at least 4 cm. A large number of handwrought nails among the debris indicate that much of the joinery among these elements was nailed.

Wattles

Fragments of charred wattling were common in the storehouse. These fragments and impressions in daub indicate that a variety of materials of different sizes was used in the walls of this structure. The size ranged from 1-2.5 cm in diameter. A similar range was found in the admiral's house where the better preservation indicates the use of softwoods. Although the branches that were used were mostly stripped before they were installed, impressions of fragments of bark in the daub appear to be some species of pine an identification reinforced by what seem to be impressions of pine needles in some of the daub.

Thatch

Both the storehouse and the admiral's house had thatched roofs. The material used was probably a species of *Phragmites* although no definite samples have survived: The thatch is represented by globules of silica that formed during the combustion of the roof. Another material that may have been used is horsetail (*Equisetum fluviatile* or *hyemale*), a tough native plant that was abundant in the Popham area. In fact, it is still common and grows on site so that modern remains must be distinguished from archaeological.

INORGANIC

The inorganic materials used in construction by the Popham Colonists were stone, clay, and daub.

Stone

No stone foundations have been found at Fort St. George, but a chimney base and hearth area made of stone was present in the admiral's house. The stone used was the gneiss that is found naturally in the Popham area. Cobbles and small boulders were selected for the chimney base and although rounded forms were incorporated there was an obvious preference for flattish rocks that could be stacked. Large flat rocks were used for the hearth.

The bed of the lake (the stream that ran through the site) was lined with small cobbles that channeled and contained the water.

Clay

Gray marine clay was brought in and mixed with tempering materials, such as grasses and twigs, and then plastered on wattles to make walls. Sometimes the clay was also tempered with sand, which may have been more fireproof and therefore was used in chimneys.

Daub

When subjected to heat, clay plaster becomes fired daub. Daub that was produced in a hot, oxidizing fire tends to be hard and orange-red in color. On the other hand, a slow, smoldering fire may bake the clay in a reducing atmosphere which produces a soft, crumbly and thoroughly blackened daub. Thus the kind of daub can tell us much about the intensity of the fire that destroyed a building, and even that different parts of a building may have burned in different ways. For example, it is probable that the northern end of the storehouse was subjected to a hotter and more intense fire, while the southern end suffered a slower fire that continued to smolder for a long time after the walls had collapsed. The daub here was thoroughly cooked, rather than fired, and in some cases was reduced to cinders which often exhibit a silica glaze that probably derived from the organic tempering or thatch. Daub was relatively rare in the storehouse, however. Often, even when we had clear evidence of a fallen wall with the remains of charred studs and wattles, the soil matrix, also clearly subjected to the heat and fire that charred the wood, was composed of the local sandy subsoil with little apparent clay content.

The admiral's house, on the other hand, appears to have been destroyed by an intense interior blaze that fired the inside surface of the wall brick hard, but left the exterior surface essentially untouched. Daub from the chimney is easily identified not only by the sand tempering, but by the surface coating of soot. This daub was hard fired by being continuously subjected to relatively long periods of heating rather than brief intervals of high temperature.

Analysis of the daub from the admiral's house reveals that it was composed of clay with variable sand content that was tempered with grass and perhaps twigs (these could have been accidentally mixed in), as well as "chaff" which is our term for short straw-like pieces that leave round vesicles. The daub was plastered on the wattling in a coat averaging only about 1 cm thick. The surfaces of the walls were smoothed, but not otherwise finished. Since the parging appears to have been applied to both the interior and exterior of the wall, and the wattles range 1-2.5 cm in diameter, the overall thickness of the walls must have been at least 4.5 cm. The wattle impressions in the daub are roughly parallel at intervals that vary from touching to widely spaced (several centimeters or more) and none appear to cross indicating they were laid in one direction only, presumably woven horizontally between studs or other framing members. The same pattern was observed in the storehouse.

APPENDIX E
AN ALTERNATE DISCUSSION OF THE ARCHITECTURAL EVIDENCE FOUND AT THE STOREHOUSE AND THE ADMIRAL'S HOUSE

Peter Morrison

The following was originally a chapter of a master's thesis presented to the Graduate School of the University of Maine entitled: *Architecture of the Popham Colony, 1607-1608: An Archaeological Portrait of English Building Practice at the Moment of Settlement* (Morrison 2002). The text and figures have been updated to reflect two further seasons of excavation in the storehouse area and four further years of discussion and thought.

STOREHOUSE

After the colonists began their fortifications in August 1607, they turned to the construction of the storehouse. As depicted by John Hunt in October 1607, the storehouse was eight bays in length and two bays wide (see Figure A6). An arched door was located in the third bay from the north, and each of the remaining bays had a window.

Hunt further showed that the storehouse roof employed a vertical "king-post" between the center of its end tie-beams and the roof peak. Quite possibly, such posts were used at every rafter pair along the building's length. Hunt also depicts a series of six apparent roof openings. The builders might have intended these as smoke vents. The storehouse only would require smoke vents if it served a function additional to storage, perhaps as barracks. If this was the case, then the garret probably would not have had a floor, which would have prevented smoke from rising to the vents. On the other hand, these openings might have served to admit daylight into the otherwise pitch-dark garret or loft or to the main floor below. Because there are so many openings, it seems likely that illumination was their primary purpose. In addition, it seems probable that the colonists would have desired to keep fires well away from their vital stores. This is particularly the case since, prior to completion of the separate munition house, the storehouse may have housed gunpowder.

Unfortunately, it is impossible to discern how the storehouse roof was clad based on Hunt's vague representation. Presumably the roof was thatched, and the lines that Hunt drew up the slope of the roof might have been a stylized representation of that material. Perhaps instead, the lines represent battens or weights that helped hold the thatch in place, or perhaps they represent shingling. However the colonists roofed the storehouse, the Hunt drawing suggests they used the same material to cover the majority of the buildings in the fort. Only the chapel, whose roof exhibits longitudinal lines overlain by more substantial vertical structures, was illustrated differently (see Figure A5).

Three hundred and eighty-seven years after it was erected, discovery of a posthole and post mold from the storehouse provided the first proof that structural remains of the colony still survived. Based on that alone, we knew that the colonists were using an earthfast framing technology. Over the course of five more field seasons, from 1997 to 1999 and 2004 to 2005, seventeen additional postholes/post molds were recorded. Based on the location of these, it was a simple matter to determine the size and shape of the storehouse. Such characteristics as the depths of the posts and postholes, the positioning of post molds within their postholes, and the contents of the holes and molds, revealed information about more ephemeral aspects of the building, such as how the building was framed. Excavators were pleasantly surprised to find that the ground also contained other evidence of the building, including sills, wattle and daub, and perhaps thatch.

Eight posthole/post mold sets were found marking the entire east wall of the structure. Seven postholes and post molds have been uncovered along the west wall; one additional posthole and post mold set is presumed to survive, but was not excavated. Three posthole/post molds have been uncovered on the center line of the building including one at each gable end.

All of the postholes and post molds from the storehouse are similar to each other in most respects. The fill within the postholes was a mixture of soil material naturally occurring on the site, and as a group the holes that were excavated contained very few artifacts. This is consistent with the notion that the storehouse was built early in the settlement, as there were not yet many lost articles to be accidently incorporated into the backfill of the holes. This also indicates that the storehouse was built in a single episode.

The postholes are consistently circular to oval in plan, and range from 65 cm (2' 2") to 110 cm (3' 8") in diameter. In a few cases, the firm subsoil, below the level of most root and animal activity, preserved the shape of individual shovel cuts. These revealed that the colonists excavated their holes using flat-bladed spades rather than rounded shovels. The post molds varied from 20 cm (8") to 30 cm (12") in diameter. Several of the post molds were sufficiently clear to show that the posts originally had been at least partially hewn or sawn to a rectangular cross section. Actual wood was found at the bottom of all of the post molds that were fully excavated along the walls. R. Bruce Hoadley of the Wood Technology Department, University of Massachusetts, Amherst identified the wood as that of a native, hard-grained, resinous pine which was probably pitch pine. This firmly establishes that the colonists were framing their buildings from trees cut on site, rather than assembling frames prefabricated in England. Charcoal has been found in the upper reaches of a number of the post molds indicating the building was destroyed by fire.

The dimensions given above apply specifically to the wall posts and their holes. The center-line posts were somewhat lighter and their holes correspondingly shallower and smaller. The north gable center posthole, for instance, was 50 cm (1' 8") in diameter.

The post molds along each wall are in near perfect alignment, and nowhere does a post stray from a straight line by more than about 12 cm (5"). Further, the building's east and west walls are very nearly parallel, resulting in a building about 5.75 m (18' 10") wide. The variation in width averaged just 7 cm (3"), though the widest part of the building was 19 cm (8") more than the narrowest part. Along each wall, post spacing is more variable. The east wall posts averaged 2.99 m (9' 10") apart, measured center to center, and this distance typically varied by just 7 cm (3").[1] On the west wall, the posts averaged a slightly longer 3.07 m (10' 1") apart, but the variability was much greater. Here, the distance typically varied by 32 cm (13"), and the longest distance of 3.54 m (11' 7") was 80 cm (2' 7") more than the shortest distance of 2.74 m (9' 0"). The additive result is that the east and west walls differ in their overall lengths: the west wall is 21.5 m (70' 6") long, while the east wall is 20.91 m (68' 7") in length.

As these represent measurements with reference to the posts' centers, the overall dimensions of the finished building would have been slightly greater reflecting the measurements from the outside of the posts. The full dimensions of the building would have been about 21.2 m (69' 7") along the east wall; 21.75 m (71' 4") along the west wall; 6.1 m (20' 0") along the north wall; and 6 m (19' 8") along the south wall. The difference in post spacing also led to differences in the angles formed by the sidewalls and the individual bents. Because the building is nearly rectangular overall, the angles average 90°, ±3°. In one case, however, the angle formed between the wall and the bent is nearly 8° from perpendicular.

Many of the wall post molds appear to be located towards the exterior sides of the postholes (Figure E1). That is, posts that formed the east wall of the structure stood near or against the east side of their holes, while posts that formed the west wall of the structure stood near or against the west side of their holes. In the five

---

[1] These distances are from post centers to post centers. As the posts averaged about 30 cm in diameter, the space between posts would be 30 cm less than the distances given.

places where both the seventeenth-century ground surface and the bottom of the postholes could be identified, the holes were found to have been excavated between 69 cm and 88 cm (27" and 35") deep. Notably, the hole for the center post at the north end of the building was 50 cm (20") shallower than either of the neighboring corner posts.

In some instances, the post molds extended to the bottoms of their holes. In other cases, one or more rocks had been placed under the post to raise it above the bottom of the hole. The correction in elevation created by the stones was usually about 10 cm (4") or less, but one post near the middle of the west wall was raised over 30 cm (12") from the bottom of its hole.

The near perfect alignment of post molds marking each wall line may indicate that the storehouse was raised in preassembled sidewall sections. In other words, the builders used "normal" assembly. If the storehouse was built in sidewall sections, we can further conclude that the wall plates were placed on top of the posts, and the tie-beams on top of the plates. The apparently consistent placement of the wall posts near the outside of the holes indicates the manner in which the posts were raised. When a builder raises a post, he first lays the post on the ground, its base overhanging the prepared hole. As the post is raised, the near edge of the hole forms the fulcrum on which the post pivots. Typically, the butt of the post slides into place against the far side of the hole from where the post lay on the ground (Carson et al. 1988; Tom Gerhardt, pers. comm., 2002). The observation

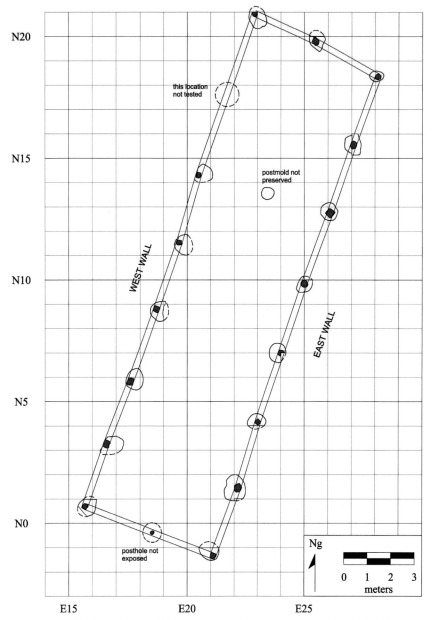

Figure E1. Spatial relationship between post molds and postholes in the storehouse. The west wall post molds are located predominantly on the exterior or "outboard" side of their respective postholes. Some of the east wall post molds show a similar tendency. Since a post base typically settles on the opposite side of a hole from where it was raised, this positioning indicates that the storehouse posts were raised from the interior of the building's footprint. The pattern further suggests that the posts were raised in assembled longitudinal wall sections, though the pattern could also be created by setting the posts individually from the building interior. The same relative positioning of molds within the holes would be unlikely in a building raised in transverse bent sections.

that many of the storehouse post molds tend to be situated near or against the exterior side of their holes means that the carpenters framed the wall sections inside the footprint of the building and raised them

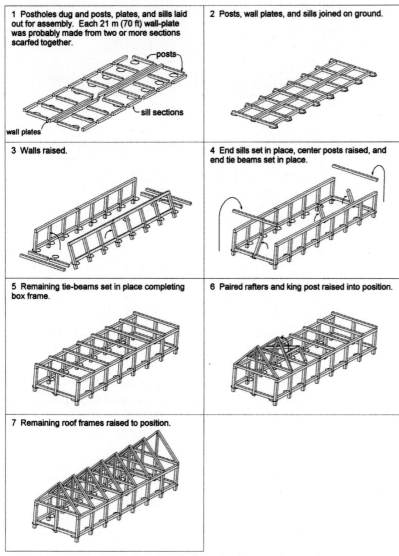

1 Postholes dug and posts, plates, and sills laid out for assembly. Each 21 m (70 ft) wall-plate was probably made from two or more sections scarfed together.

posts

sill sections

wall plates

2 Posts, wall plates, and sills joined on ground.

3 Walls raised.

4 End sills set in place, center posts raised, and end tie beams set in place.

5 Remaining tie-beams set in place completing box frame.

6 Paired rafters and king post raised into position.

7 Remaining roof frames raised to position.

Figure E2. Assembly of major timbers in the storehouse frame. Steps 1 through 5 are conjectured from archaeological data; the use of king posts with each pair of rafters in the roof, steps 6 and 7, is conjecture based on John Hunt's depiction.

outward (Figure E2). It is not known if this has any real cultural significance; building inside the footprint may have been done simply to conserve limited workspace within the fort. This may have been particularly useful since the storehouse was adjacent to the western defensive wall.

The posts were not the only timbers to leave their mark in the ground. Clear evidence of ground sills survived along the sidewalls in the south half of the storehouse. Most of the sills burned. In some instances, they survived as linear arrangements of small charcoal fragments, whereas in other cases the charcoal retained substantial structure. A few small pieces of actual wood survived from a sill at the south gable end. In several instances the relationship between sill and post mold was sufficiently clear to confirm that the sills were pieced together between posts and were not continuous timbers. In one case in particular (P538), the preservation was even sufficient to show that the end of the sill section partially intruded into the outline of the post mold. This probably indicates that the sill was tenoned into the side of the post.

Evidence of other timbers also survived in the southern end of the storehouse. In these cases, the timbers appeared to be elements that had fallen during the demolition of the structure, and were therefore displaced. While some could be seen to overlie others, it was generally not possible to determine what parts of the building's superstructure were represented. A possible exception was found in P545 and P546 where the clear trace of a timber was aligned transversely across the building (see Figure 57). Very likely, this was a tie beam.

Wattle and daub was a common kind of infilling used in seventeenth-century English buildings, and the colonists used it in the storehouse. Pieces of the daub survived because it was burned, turning it into stable brick-like chunks. Imprints left in the daub indicate that it was pressed into wattle that was generally about 1 cm in diameter. In a few instances, both the wattle imprint and the smoothed interior or exterior face of the wall were preserved on a single piece of daub. These indicate that the total thickness of the infilled wall was about 5 cm. Imprints of grass leaves have also been found in the daub. While the grass might have been used as a binder to strengthen the daub, it may also have been incorporated into the mixture by chance. If the grass is eventually identified, it may be possible to determine whether it is a variety native to Sabino Head or whether it grew in some other nearby location.

In a situation highly unusual on archaeological sites, the wattle itself survived in parts of the storehouse's southern end (see Figures 45 and 50). Here, the sections of wattle panel on both the east and west walls within about a meter of the sill were charred but not entirely consumed by fire. Low to the storehouse floor, the fire appears not to have been as intense, resulting in the wattle's survival. Surprisingly, little or no fired daub was found directly associated with the wattle. The wattle might not have been coated in this area, but it seems more likely that the low intensity of the fire that permitted the survival of the wattle failed to heat the daub sufficiently to fire and preserve it.

To summarize, John Hunt shows us that the storehouse was one story tall. Though he showed the building to be eight bays in length and two bays wide, it was in fact only seven bays in length. The building was framed using hole-set posts and interrupted ground sills. As no discernable trenches were discovered, it is likely that the sills sat at grade.

The arrangement of post molds within their postholes suggests that the carpenters raised the building using normal assembly. That is, the east and west walls were each preassembled flat on the ground. These assembled units would have included the posts and wall plate, at least, but apparently sill sections as well, mortised between the posts. Due to the length of the building, over 21 m (70'), each plate was probably pieced together from two or more shorter and more manageable sections. Once the walls were raised, the east and west walls were connected together by tie beams. Thus, the tie beams sat atop the plates. Just what combination of joints were used to effect the junction between the post, plate, and tie beam, is not clear. With nothing else to influence our conclusion, the simplest and most likely joint would seem to have utilized a common jowled post, commonly referred to as a "gunstock" post. In this complex arrangement, the top of the expanded wall post is shaped with one tenon that fits a mortise in the longitudinal wall plate and a second tenon to fit a mortise in the

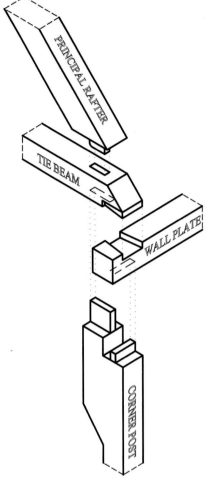

Figure E3. Typical joinery used to connect post, wall plate, tie beam and rafter in normally assembled buildings.

transverse tie beam. In addition, the tie beam is firmly secured to the wall plate using a half dovetail joint (Figure E3). It is the half dovetail joint that counters any tendency of the walls to spread apart under the pressure of the roof.

This combination of joints was commonly used in England and it is consistent with the current analysis that the structure was erected in wall sections. However, we have no direct evidence for its use, and, in fact, have another line of evidence indicating that it is not the whole story, or is altogether incorrect. In particular, John Hunt's map indicates some kind of device at the top of each post, an architectural detail he also recorded for the Court of Guard (see Figure A11). Perhaps Hunt was merely illustrating a decorative but structurally insignificant finial combined with an otherwise typical jowled post. More likely, he wished to indicate a small brace, bracket, or other reinforcement. A further possibility is that the post was jowled, but that the expansion was oriented longitudinally along the sidewalls and transversely along the end walls. Arranged this way, the plate may have been interrupted at each post or tie beam analogous to the interrupted sills, rather than having been made from just one or two long timbers. Another suggestion is that Hunt meant to indicate something not usually recognized in English colonial construction, such as an anchor-bent type joint, as found in Germany and the Netherlands (Richard Harris, pers. comm., 2006) and in the Hudson River Valley in the United States.

The problem with these two suggestions is that they are difficult to reconcile with the analysis of the archaeological evidence presented here, since both interrupted plates or anchor-bent construction would indicate bent-section construction. Their consideration is useful, however, in that they are examples of a wider spectrum of joinery options that were potentially available. In the end, the correct answer as to what kind of joinery was used in the storehouse will have to fit both the archaeological evidence and documentary evidence. When we finally hit on this answer, it will likely provide an "ah-ha!" experience to all concerned.

Once the walls were raised, several subsidiary posts were installed to provide additional support. The center line post molds and postholes indicate that the builders utilized additional posts at the gable ends and at the third bent, counting from the north. Possibly, the interior post suggests the site of a transverse partition, in which case the building had at least two cells, or perhaps the additional support indicates that a portion of the garret was indeed given a floor, requiring extra support. Each gable end also possessed a king post located directly above the center post and extending from the tie-beams to the peak of the roof. Presumably, king posts were used at every bent to help support the weight of the roof, but they may have been installed only at those bents that had a center post, or only at the ends.

The ground sills were apparently assembled as part of the preassembled wall sections. The clearest evidence for this was found in P538, where the end of the ground sill was seen to intrude into the outline of the post mold. This suggests that a tenon on the sill fit into a mortise on the post; such a joint would most easily have been assembled while the wall frame rested on the ground. If not, the sills would have simply been laid on the ground between the posts after the walls were raised into place.

Though the excavators found clear evidence of sills, no evidence was found to indicate that the structure had a wooden floor. Probably, the building had earthen floors, but the possibility that it had a wooden floor or a partial wooden floor cannot be ruled out. The sills were heavy timbers, and as a result they partially survived the fire that destroyed the storehouse and the weathering processes of another 400 years in the ground. In contrast, floor planks would have been fairly thin and might not have survived in any recognizable form. Any sleepers used to support the floors would have been heavier beams, though probably smaller than the sills. If the sleepers themselves did not rest directly on the ground, then girts would also have been needed to bridge the width of the bays. These would have been very heavy timbers and the fact that no sign of such timbers was found is a strong indication that they never existed, at least at the south end of the building where preservation was best.

The early completion of the storehouse was vital to the colony so that the ships could be off-loaded and returned to England for further supplies. The storehouse may also have been needed for temporary housing while other shelters were completed, particularly after the ships left. From the Davies journal, we know that intense effort was put into raising the structure in the first month of the settlement. The archaeological evidence shows that this work was directed by a master carpenter with the assistance of skilled laborers. The trees needed for the structure were not brought from England, but were cut on location. Once the timbers were hewn or sawn square, the builders laid out and partially assembled the frame on the ground. If the building was assembled in wall sections it shows that the builders had the skills to work with the relatively complicated joinery needed in normal assembly and demonstrates that the presumed benefits that could accrue from using the simpler joinery related to reverse construction were outweighed in the builders' minds by the benefits of normal construction. Although we cannot know for sure what building method they chose, factors that they considered might have included perceived advantages in the use of limited ground space while the timbers were laid out and assembled, the simplified personnel requirements that came from reducing the time during which the carpenters needed additional crew to actually raise the building, and perhaps a simple preference based on greater familiarity with one building method over another.

ADMIRAL'S HOUSE

The evidence for the storehouse construction was relatively straightforward. As we excavated most of its footprint over the course of five seasons, the details were laid out for us to see. Not so with the admiral's house. Interpretation of that structure was made difficult because of rebuilding on the same location and because a large part of that location was inaccessible due to the paved town road that crosses over it. Still, a good case can be made for the story of the admiral's house and how it was built.

John Hunt's drawing indicates that this structure was the third largest building at Fort St. George; only the storehouse and chapel were larger (see Figure 5). According to the Hunt map, the

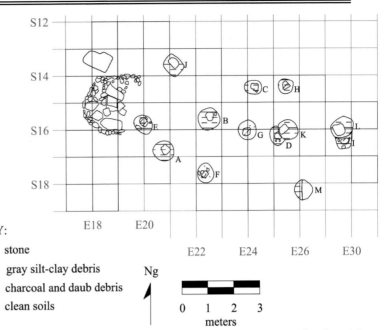

KEY:
◯ stone
⬭ gray silt-clay debris
◌ charcoal and daub debris
◒ clean soils

Ng

0 1 2 3
meters

Figure E4. Hearth, postholes, post molds, and large stones on the site of the admiral's house.

structure was four bays long and one bay wide. It was oriented east-west, approximately perpendicular to the storehouse, and had a chimney at its west end. The drawing also shows that the door provided entrance into the second bay from the west end. As in the storehouse, the roof appears to have been built with covered openings, somewhat like dormers. Since this building had a chimney, smoke holes were not necessary, lending further support to the suggestion that such openings provided light to a second floor, or garret.

By comparing the Hunt map to the known location of the storehouse, Jeff Brain was able to determine the approximate location of the admiral's house. He decided that the house site probably lay partially under the paved town road where it would remain inaccessible to us for the present, though hopefully preserved for future study. It also appeared that the site partially lay under the unpaved Fort Baldwin parking lot. The 1999 and 2000 excavations confirmed both of these expectations.

In the predicted location of the admiral's house, Brain's team discovered nine postholes with post molds, a half-excavated posthole in which a mold was not found, a hearth, and two separate debris fields. In addition to these, they found three posthole-like features. Each of these features lacked a post mold but contained one large stone. These, too, may have been related to the construction of the admiral's house. The stone base of the hearth consisted of large flat-lying and closely fitted slabs of schist at its center (Figure E4). These were surrounded by a semicircular arrangement of smaller stones. Around the whole feature was a narrow trench, again semicircular in plan.

Brain interprets this constellation of features as indications that the admiral's house was partially destroyed by fire and subsequently repaired. In his view, the apparently random distribution of postholes represent a contingency building thrown up in a hurry, possibly by unskilled laborers trying to complete work before the onset of winter.

The current analysis offers a different interpretation. I believe that the burned wood and fired daub indicate that the original admiral's house was completely destroyed by fire. Furthermore, I feel that the pattern of postholes and the distribution of demolition debris provides evidence that the colonists built a new structure slightly offset to the north of, and at a different orientation to, the original building. Both buildings were built in regular bays. Thus, while they might have been built quickly, they were not nearly as crude as they first appeared.

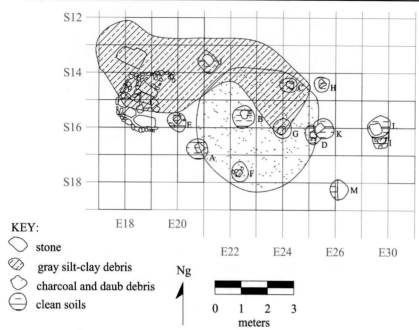

KEY:

- ⬡ stone
- ⬡ gray silt-clay debris
- ⬡ charcoal and daub debris
- ⬡ clean soils

Ng

0　1　2　3

meters

Figure E5. Extent of debris fields containing gray silty clay, and fired daub and charcoal.

As Brain points out, "[the post-holes] do not at first glance seem to form a coherent pattern." He goes on to say that the key to making sense of the profusion of postholes and their confusing arrangement is in the differing contents of the post-holes and post molds. Most of the postholes contained only mixed, nearly artifact- and debris-free soils, very much like those found in the storehouse. Two postholes were very different in that they contained dense concentrations of charcoal and fired daub within their fill. Consequently, the holes must have been excavated after the burning episode.

The nine post molds can be grouped according to their contents, as well. Four of the molds contained dense concentrations of char-coal and fired daub, similar to what was found in two of the postholes. The presence of this debris indicates that hollows were left in the place of the posts at a time when a great deal of burned wood and fired daub was available to fill them, probably immediately after the building burned. The remaining five post molds, on the other hand, did not contain this concentration of burned demolition debris. These molds were characterized by gray clay that had filtered into the pocket left near the ground surface as the upper portion of the posts decayed. Deeper in the same molds, darkened humic soils indicated the presence of decayed wood *in situ*. These molds were the remains of posts that decayed slowly over time. The gray clay derived from unfired daub that washed into the resulting pockets when little or no burned debris was available to fill the mold.

The two kinds of holes and two kinds of molds combined to form three different groupings of hole-mold complexes. The first group contained natural soil in their holes and demolition debris, burned daub and charcoal, in their molds. In these cases, the holes were dug prior to the fire, and the molds were filled with demolition from that fire. The second group contained demolition debris in their holes, but contained decayed wood and gray clay in their molds. In these instances, the holes were dug after the fire. The posts, however, did not burn, indicating that they were part of a building that decayed slowly over time after abandonment. The third set contained natural soil in their holes and decayed wood and gray clay in their molds. These features were apparently contemporary with the second set that contained debris in their holes. To understand why the contents of the holes differ, it is necessary to understand the extent of two other important features of the site: a field of charcoal and burned daub, and a second debris field that contained unfired daub. It is also necessary to look at the soil stratigraphy in this part of the site.

At the base of excavation was the natural undisturbed glacial till. This horizon was dark reddish brown in color and sandy loam in texture. It contained many cobbles. Above this subsoil was what was, in 1607, the ground surface. This was a horizon of very dark gray to black humic loam with fine to medium sized bits of charcoal and fired daub.

Spread across part of the admiral's house area was a debris field containing a relative abundance of early seventeenth-century artifacts, charcoal, and fired daub. This debris field was centered at S16 E23, and extended more than two meters horizontally in each direction (Figure E5). The fired daub, charcoal, and relative abundance of domestic artifacts, including burned and fire-damaged items, indicate that this was demolition from a dwelling, and in particular a dwelling that was occupied at the time of the fire.

Partially overlying this artifact- and debris-rich layer was a stratum consisting largely of gray silty clay. The gray silty clay was distinctly thickest on and around the hearth. The material became thinner towards the east, but excavators noted that it ultimately terminated with an abrupt edge in that direction. Furthermore, they noted that this east boundary coincided with the location of a post mold. This layer had relatively few artifacts, though those that it did contain were attributable to the 1607-1608 occupation. The majority of artifacts in the western part of the gray silty clay were architectural in nature, particularly nails. The silty clay contained very few domestic artifacts.

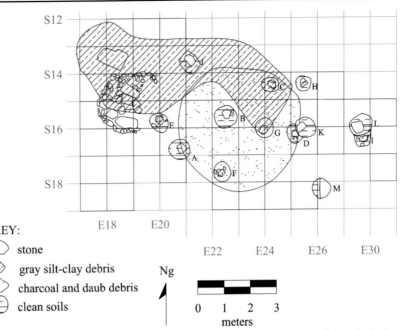

KEY:
◇ stone
◈ gray silt-clay debris
◇ charcoal and daub debris
◒ clean soils

Figure E6. Features representing the hypothetical first house of the admiral. Each posthole was free of artifacts and debris; each post mold contained artifacts, charcoal and fired daub.

As Brain notes, this very fine-grained gray material is geologically out of place at Fort St. George and had to have been brought onto the site. This gray silty clay is believed to have been used as daub. The fact that this material was not fired suggests that it came from a building that did not burn but rather disintegrated over time in the weather. Thus, there were two distinct demolition levels, not just one. The first, stratigraphically deeper and slightly older level is from a house that burned. The second and more recent level represents a house that slowly collapsed, possibly over a period of years.

Scattered on top of the gray silty clay were many more flat stones. These were most densely concentrated around the hearth, and they probably were originally part of that structure. As they did not exhibit the coherent arrangement seen in the hearth base, these overlying stones were clearly displaced, possibly through the action of plowing. Their stratigraphic position on top of the gray silty clay shows that they only collapsed once most of the daub had washed out of the surrounding walls or chimney. Possibly, they originally formed part of the fireback.

Above the stones and silty clay were 10-20 cm of sediments that had accumulated on site between 1608 and the 1982. These were sandy loam in texture and very dark gray in color, mottled with dark brown. This layer of sediments contained a mixture of artifacts including historic-period Native American artifacts, seventeenth-century English colonial artifacts, and nineteenth- and twentieth-century American artifacts. This horizon was a plowzone, and its contents were fairly well mixed throughout. Fifty centimeters of sand and gravel sat above this, extending to the parking lot surface. This thick layer of fill dates from 1982 when the Bureau of Parks and Lands imported it to the site to build the current parking lot.

At first glance, the postholes and post molds do not form any clear rectangular patterns of the kind made by the storehouse posts. Several lines of posts do stand out, however, and these provide a clue as to what may have occurred. In particular, post molds A, B, and C form a perfect line (Figure E6). Furthermore, they are at equal distances apart: 2.09 m between A and B, and 2.02 m between B and C. Also, post D is the same distance from post C (2.03 m) and is located at a nearly 90° (actually 83°) angle from the ABC line. These

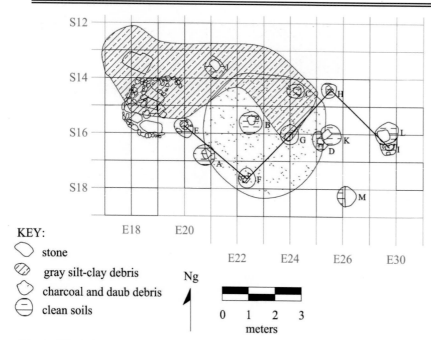

KEY:

⬭ stone

▨ gray silt-clay debris

⬡ charcoal and daub debris

⊖ clean soils

Ng

0 1 2 3
meters

Figure E7. Features representing the hypothetical second house of the admiral. Post molds contained humic soils and gray silty clay (unfired daub) and few artifacts; postholes F and G contained burned debris from the first house, while postholes E, H and I contained little burned debris and few artifacts.

four post mold/postholes are of the same type. That is, they each contain artifact-free natural soils in their holes, and demolition debris in their molds. These observations suggest a unity between the four features.

Posts F, G, and H form a similar line (Figure E7). Here, the distances are not quite equal: from F to G is 2.14 m while the distance from G to H 2.44 m. Two other posts are situated at nearly 90° to the FGH line. Post E lies 3.01 m to the northwest of F (95° off the line), while post I lies 3.08 m to the southeast of H (90° off the line). This pattern is made up of two different kinds of postholes and post molds. Holes E, H, and I contain nearly artifact- and demolition-free sediments. The holes for posts F and G, on the other hand, contain large quantities of demolition debris

and artifacts. All five of these features have similar molds, containing darkened soils, in some cases small amounts of decayed wood and, in each case, gray silty clay.

From these alignments, I believe that posts A, B, C, and D can be connected to show a partial outline of one structure. This is interpreted as the admiral's first house. Possibly, it was begun prior to October 1607 in time for John Hunt to have seen and drawn it. This building burned sometime during the course of the next year. The debris from its demolition fell primarily within the building's footprint forming the charcoal and fired daub debris field and filling the voids left by the building's burned-out posts. Thus, the distribution of debris consisting of the fired daub and charcoal correlates with the footprint of the admiral's first house, though as Brain points out this debris field is not fully as extensive as the building footprint to which I say it is related.

Almost immediately after the destruction of the first building, a new building was raised. The partial footprint of the admiral's second house is marked by posts E, F, G, H, and I (Figure E7). All of these post holes may be contemporary with each other, but they contain different kinds of fill. The explanation for this may be found in the position of each posthole in relation to the footprint of the original building. Those postholes dug outside of the first building's footprint contain little or no demolition debris, while the two postholes dug inside of the first building's footprint contain large quantities of debris.

A few strategically placed excavation units could confirm whether this scenario is correct. If it is correct, we can predict the likely location of additional postholes and post molds (Figure E8) and it should be possible to predict what kind of material will be found in each, even before they are found. A predicted posthole at S12.5 E 23 (no. 1) should contain nearly sterile natural soils, perhaps with a little bit of daub and charcoal, and a post mold without debris. Predicted posthole 2 should have natural soils, but with a mold full of debris. As a possible posthole with clean fill was already found at that location, the unexcavated portion of that hole might contain a debris-filled mold. However, this same location falls on the possible site of a posthole and post mold from the replacement structure. That being the case, there could be two sets of postholes and post molds, one set intrusive into the other. If that is so, the earlier mold will contain debris, as will the later intrusive hole, but the mold associated with the intrusive hole will contain humus capped by gray silty clay. Similar predictions can be made for the remaining conjectural posts. Posthole/post molds 3, 4, and 5 should be similar to those at A, B, C, and D, while posthole/post mold 6 should be most like those at H and I.

Judging from the relationship between the hearth, the gray clay layer, and the clay-filled post molds, it may be hypothesized that the known hearth was part of the second building rather than the first, but none of the building's bays appear to encompass the hearth. Possibly, evidence of additional posts exist and we simply failed to

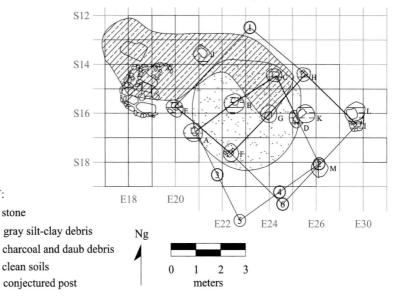

KEY:
⬭ stone
⬯ gray silt-clay debris
⬠ charcoal and daub debris
⊖ clean soils
③ conjectured post

Ng

0 1 2 3
meters

Figure E8. Possible locations of additional postholes and post molds relating to the admiral's hypothetical first and second houses.

identify them. However, an alternative explanation is better supported by the evidence at hand. If post E is at the northwest end of Gilbert's second house, then the hearth and its chimney were located outside of that wall. This scenario makes use of the semicircular trench that surrounded the hearth, which excavators referred to as a "builders' trench." Post molds were not observed in the trench, but if small poles were used, they could have been missed. These hypothetical small posts or poles could then have formed the framework for a wattle-and-daub fireplace and chimney. Alternatively, the poles might have been closely set in the form of a palisado, and daubed. As the gray silty clay is thickest on and around the hearth, it very likely represents daub primarily from the chimney rather than a wall. The Hunt map does not show any exterior end chimneys. Brick examples of exterior gable chimneys are legion in Tidewater Maryland and Virginia, as well as in England, but those date from later years.

By the current reconstruction, Raleigh Gilbert's first house and the storehouse were skewed out of alignment by nearly 45°. The rebuilt house was skewed about 22° from the axis of the storehouse. These conclusions fit poorly with the orderly arrangement portrayed by Hunt, with the storehouse and admiral's house set at nearly right angles. This suggests that Hunt was indeed "tidying up" the fort, at least on paper.

Robert Davies did not mention any major fires in his description of the early months at Fort St. George. Assuming that such an event would have attracted his notice, it follows that the destruction of the admiral's first house occurred after October 8, 1607 when Davies left the colony. Since the Hunt map was apparently sent back to Europe on that same voyage, it is likely that the house depicted would have been the admiral's first house.

The carpenters raised both the admiral's first and second houses utilizing hole-set posts. Beyond that, we do not even know such basics as the orientation of either building's main axis or the number of bays they had. Further conclusions, such as whether the posts were raised individually or in already framed wall or bent sections, are beyond the available information. There are hints, however, that this information is preserved in the ground and someday might be recovered. Notably, posts A, B, and C are positioned in the same position relative to their postholes. This regularity shows that they were all raised from the ground in the same direction. Without knowing the orientation of the building, and where these posts were located on that building, we cannot yet decide whether normal or reverse assembly was used, or perhaps even, if the posts were raised individually.

The analysis of the admiral's houses leaves us with equivocal conclusions and many unanswered questions. To Brain, the evidence suggests a single building that suffered a fire and was repaired. In his view, its posts were raised individually, resulting in a building sufficient for the exigency, but not one intended for the long term. To me, the evidence indicates that there were two successive buildings on the same site, and that both the first and second were erected in regular bays. Furthermore, it appears to me that Raleigh Gilbert's houses were built with as great, or nearly as great, a level of skill as was the storehouse. In the limited data we have, it is notable that the widths of the bays in the admiral's two successive houses and the precision with which the various walls were squared to each other, is in keeping with those found in the storehouse. The colony might have had a limited number of carpenters whose first priorities were to raise the public structures, and particularly the storehouse. Once those were completed, however, it is reasonable that they would have turned their attention to construction of the president's and the admiral's houses. If any members of the colony were able to preserve some standards in the building of their New World homes, it would be these gentlemen.

BIBLIOGRAPHY

Alcock, N. W., M. W. Barley, P. W. Dixon, and R. A. Meeson
   1996 *Recording Timber-Framed Buildings: An Illustrated Glossary*. Council for British Archaeology, Practical Handbooks in Archaeology, no. 5. Walmgate, York.

Alcock, N.W., and Nancy Cox
   2000 *Living and Working in Seventeenth Century England: An Encyclopedia of Drawings and Descriptions from Randle Holme's original manuscripts for The Academy of Armory* (1688). The British Library. London. (CD-ROM)

Allan, J. P.
   1984 *Medieval and Post-Medieval Finds from Exeter, 1971-1980*. Exeter Archaeological Reports, vol. 3, Exeter City Council and the University of Exeter. Alan Sutton Publishing, Ltd. Gloucester, Gloucestershire.

Allan, J. P., and Peter Pope
   1990 "A New Class of south-west English Pottery in North America," *Post-Medieval Archaeology*, vol. 24, pp. 51-60.

Allen, John Logan
   1997 *North American Exploration*, vol. 1, *A New World Disclosed*. University of Nebraska Press. Lincoln, Nebraska.

Andrews, Kenneth A.
   1964 *Elizabethan Privateering 1585-1603*. Cambridge University Press. Cambridge.

Andrews, Wayne, ed.
   1967 *Concise Dictionary of American History*. Charles Scribner's Sons. New York.

Ardesoif, J. P.
   1772 *An Introduction to Marine Fortification and Gunnery*. W. Dawkins. Gosport, Hampshire.

Atkin, Malcolm
   1985 "Excavations on Alms Lane (Site 302N)," in M. Atkin, A. Carter, and D. Evans, eds., *Excavations in Norwich, 1971-1978*, part II. East Anglian Archaeology Report, no. 26, Norwich Survey, University of East Anglia. Norwich, Norfolk.

Babits, L. E.
   1976 "The Evolution and Adoption of Firearm Ignition Systems in Eastern North America: An Ethnohistorical Approach," *The Chesopiean*, vol. 14, nos. 3-4, pp. 40-82.

Baker, Emerson W.
   1985 *The Clarke & Lake Company: The Historical Archaeology of a Seventeenth-Century Maine Settlement*. Occasional Publications in Maine Archaeology, no. 4. Maine Historic Preservation Commission. Augusta, Maine.

Baker, Emerson W., Edwin A. Churchill, Richard D'Abate, Kristine L. Jones, Victor A. Konrad, and Harald E. L. Prins
   1994 *American Beginnings: Exploration, Culture, and Cartography in the Land of Norumbega*. University of Nebraska Press. Lincoln, Nebraska.

Baker, James W.
   1997 *Plimoth Plantation: Fifty Years of Living History*. Plimoth Plantation, Inc. Plymouth, Massachusetts.

Baker, Norman B.
   1967 *Early Houses of New England*. Charles E. Tuttle Co. Rutland, Vermont.

Ballard, Edward
   1863 *Memorial Volume of the Popham Celebration, August 29, 1862*. Bailey and Noyes. Portland, Maine.

Banks, Charles Edward
   1929 "New Documents Relating to the Popham Expedition, 1607," *American Antiquarian Society Proceedings*, vol. 39, pt. 2, pp. 307-334.

Barbour, Philip L., ed.
   1969 *The Jamestown Voyages Under the First Charter, 1606-1609*. Hakluyt Society. London.

Barley, M. W.

1971   *The House and Home: A Review of 900 Years of House Planning and Furnishing in Britain*. New York Graphic Society Ltd. Greenwich, Connecticut.

1987   *The English Farmhouse and Cottage*. Alan Sutton. Gloucester, Gloucestershire.

Beacham, Peter

2001   *Devon Building: An Introduction to Local Traditions*. Devon Books. Tiverton, Devonshire.

Beaudry, Mary C., Karin J. Goldstein, and Craig Chartier

2003   Archaeology of the Plymouth Colony in Massachusetts," in J. Tuck, ed., *The English in America, 1497-1696*. The Colony of Avalon Foundation. Ferryland, Newfoundland.

Beckenstein, Myron

2004   "Maine's Lost Colony," *Smithsonian*, vol. 34, no. 11, pp. 18-19.

Beresford, Guy

1982   "The Reconstruction of Some Saxon Buildings at Goltho, Lincolnshire," in P. Drury, ed., *Structural Reconstruction: Approaches to the Interpretation of the Excavated Remains of Buildings*. British Archaeological Reports, British Series, no. 110. Oxford.

Bettesworth, A., and C. Hitch

1981   *The Builder's Dictionary: or, Gentleman and Architect's Companion*. Association for Preservation Technology. Washington.

Bettey, J. H.

1982   "Seventeenth Century Squatters' Dwellings: Some Documentary Evidence," *Vernacular Architecture*, vol. 13, pp. 28-30.

Bickerton, L. M.

1984   *English Drinking Glasses, 1675-1825*. Shire Publications Ltd. Aylesbury, Buckinghamshire.

Biggar, H. P.

1922   *The Works of Samuel de Champlain*, vol. 1, *1599-1607*. The Champlain Society. Toronto, Ontario.

Billings, Warren M.

1975   *The Old Dominion in the Seventeenth Century: A Documentary History of Virginia, 1606-1689*. Institute of Early American History and Culture. Williamsburg, Virginia.

1993   *Jamestown and the Founding of the Nation*. Thomas Publications. Gettysburg, Pennsylvania.

Blades, B.S.

1986   "English Villages in the Londonderry Plantation," *Post-Medieval Archaeology*, vol. 20, pp. 257-269.

Bolton, Charles Knowles

1929   *The Real Founders of New England*. F. W. Faxon Co. Boston.

Bourque, Bruce J.

2001   *Twelve Thousand Years: American Indians in Maine*. University of Nebraska Press. Lincoln, Nebraska.

Bradford, John W.

1999   "Where was the Virginia Built?" Manuscript. West Point, Maine.

2000   "Raleigh Gilbert, Esquire." Manuscript. West Point, Maine

Bradley, Robert L.

1978   *Maine's First Buildings: The Architecture of Settlement, 1604-1700*. Maine Historic Preservation Commission. Augusta, Maine.

1979   "Historical Archaeology in Maine: Problems and Future Direction," in D. Sanger, ed., *Discovering Maine's Archaeological Heritage*. Maine Historic Preservation Commission. Augusta, Maine.

1981   "Parking Lot Construction at Popham." Inter-Departmental Memorandum, Maine Historic Preservation Commission. Augusta, Maine.

Brain, Jeffrey P.

1969   "Winterville: A Case Study of Prehistoric Culture Contact in the Lower Mississippi Valley." Ph.D. Dissertation, Yale University. New Haven, Connecticut.

1979   *Tunica Treasure*. Papers of the Peabody Museum, Harvard University, vol. 71. Published jointly by the Peabody Museum, Harvard University, and the Peabody Museum of Salem. Cambridge and Salem, Massachusetts.

1985   "Introduction: Update of De Soto Studies Since the United States De Soto Expedition Commission Report." *Final Report of the United States De Soto Expedition Commission*. Classics in Anthropology Series,

Smithsonian Institution Press. Washington.

1988   *Tunica Archaeology.* Papers of the Peabody Museum, Harvard University, vol. 78.   Cambridge, Massachusetts.

1989   *Winterville: Late Prehistoric Culture Contact in the Lower Mississippi Valley.* Mississippi Department of Archives and History, Archaeological Report, no. 23. Jackson, Mississippi.

1994   "Archaeological Investigation of Fort St. George." Report to the National Geographic Society (Grant Number 5234-94). Peabody Essex Museum. Salem, Massachusetts.

1995   "Fort St. George: Archaeological Investigation of the 1607-1608 Popham Colony on the Kennebec River in Maine." Peabody Essex Museum. Salem, Massachusetts.

1997   "Fort St. George II: Continuing Investigation of the 1607-1608 Popham Colony on the Kennebec River in Maine." Peabody Essex Museum. Salem,, Massachusetts.

1997a   "Introductory Remarks," in J. P. Brain, ed., *Contributions to the Historical Archaeology of European Exploration and Colonization in North America.* The Review of Archaeology, vol. 17, no. 2, pp. 1-5.

1998   "Fort St. George III: 1998 Excavations at the Site of the 1607-1608 Popham Colony on the Kennebec River in Maine." Peabody Essex Museum. Salem, Massachusetts.

1998a   "Fort St. George on the Kennebec," *Bermuda Journal of Archaeology and Maritime History,* vol. 10, pp. 41-52.

1999   "Fort St. George IV: 1999 Excavations at the Site of the 1607-1608 Popham Colony on the Kennebec River in Maine." Peabody Essex Museum. Salem, Massachusetts.

2000   "Fort St. George V: 2000 Excavations at the Site of the 1607-1608 Popham Colony on the Kennebec River in Maine." Peabody Essex Museum. Salem, Massachusetts.

2001   "Fort St. George VI: 2001 Excavations at the Site of the 1607-1608 Popham Colony on the Kennebec River in Maine." Peabody Essex Museum. Salem, Massachusetts.

2002   "Fort St. George VII: 2002 Excavations at the Site of the 1607-1608 Popham Colony on the Kennebec River in Maine." Peabody Essex Museum. Salem, Massachusetts.

2003   "Fort St. George VIII: 2003 Excavations at the Site of the 1607-1608 Popham Colony on the Kennebec River in Maine." Peabody Essex Museum. Salem, Massachusetts.

2003a   "The Popham Colony: An Historical and Archaeological Brief," *The Maine Archaeological Society Bulletin,* vol. 43, no. 1, pp. 1-28.

2003b   "Popham: The First English Colony in New England," in J. Tuck, ed., *The English in America, 1497-1696.* The Colony of Avalon Foundation. Ferryland, Newfoundland.

2003c   "In Search of Bartholomew Gosnold, 1602." Peabody Essex Museum. Salem, Massachusetts.

2004   "Fort St. George IX: 2004 Excavations at the Site of the 1607-1608 Popham Colony on the Kennebec River in Maine." Peabody Essex Museum. Salem, Massachusetts.

2005   "Fort St. George X: 2005 Excavations at the Site of the 1607-1608 Popham Colony on the Kennebec River in Maine." Peabody Essex Museum. Salem, Massachusetts.

n.d.   *Popham: The Archaeology of a Place.* Manuscript. Peabody Essex Museum. Salem, Massachusetts.

Brain, Jeffrey P. and John R. Grimes

1992   "We Claim These Shores: Native Americans and the European Settlement of Massachusetts Bay," *Register.* Peabody Museum. Salem, Massachusetts.

Briars, Peter C. D.

1971   *The English Country Pottery: Its History and Techniques.* Charles E. Tuttle Co. Rutland, Vermont.

Brereton, John

1602   *A Briefe and True Relation of the Discouerie of the North Part of Virginia* (facsimile reproduction 1903). Dodd, Mead and Company. New York.

Bridenbaugh, Carl

1980   *Jamestown: 1544-1699.* Oxford University Press. New York.

Briggs, Martin S.

1932   *The Homes of the Pilgrim Fathers in England and America (1620-1685).* Oxford University Press. Oxford.

Brittingham, Joseph B., and Alvin W. Brittingham, Sr.

1947   *The First Trading Post at Kicotan (Kecoughtan), Hampton, Virginia.* The Franklin Printing Co. Newport News, Virginia.

Brown, Alexander, ed.
   1890   *The Genesis of the United States* (2 vols.). Houghton Mifflin and Company. Boston.
Brown, R. J.
   1979   *The English Country Cottage*. Robert Hale Ltd. London
Bruce, Curt, and Jill Grossman
   1975   *Revelations of New England Architecture: People and Their Buildings*. Grossman Publishers. New York.
Brunskill, R. W.
   1970   *Illustrated Handbook of Vernacular Architecture*. Universe Books. New York.
Burrage, Henry S.
   1906   *Early English and French Voyages, 1534-1608*. Charles Scribner's Sons. New York.
   1914   *The Beginnings of Colonial Maine, 1602-1658*. Marks Printing House. Portland, Maine.
Cabart, Hubert
   1983   "Céramiques et verreries des XVIIe et XVIIIe siècles provenant de la fouille de la rue Saint-Dominique à Châlons-sur-Marne. *Société d'Agriculture, Commerce, Sciences et Arts de la Marne*, vol. 97, pp. 231-263.
Calloway, Colin G., ed.
   1991   *Dawnland Encounters: Indians and Europeans in Northern New England*. University Press of New England. Hanover, New Hampshire.
Camp, Helen B.
   1975   *Archaeological Excavations at Pemaquid, Maine, 1965-1974*. Maine State Museum. Augusta, Maine.
Candee, Richard M.
   1976   "The Architecture of Maine's Settlement: Vernacular Architecture to about 1720," in D. Thompson, ed., *Maine Forms of American Architecture*. Downeast Magazine. Camden, Maine.
   1992   *Building Portsmouth: The Neighborhoods & Architecture of New Hampshire's Oldest City*. Portsmouth Advocates, Inc. Portsmouth, New Hampshire.
Canny, Nicholas, ed.
   1998   *The Oxford History of the British Empire*, vol. 1, *The Origins of Empire: British Overseas Enterprise to the Close of the Seventeenth Century*. Oxford University Press. Oxford.
Carey, George
   1966   "Fort St. George Historical Research." Ms. Maine Bureau of Parks and Recreation. Augusta, Maine.
Carson, Cary, Norman F. Barka, William M. Kelso, Garry Wheeler Stone, and Dell Upton
   1988   "Impermanent Architecture in the Southern American Colonies," in R. St. George, ed., *Material Life in America, 1600-1860*. Northeastern University Press. Boston.
Cave, Alfred A.
   1995   "Why Was the Sagadahoc Colony Abandoned? An Evaluation of the Evidence," *The New England Quarterly*, vol. LXVIII, no. 4, pp. 625-640.
Chandler, Eliot. J.
   1997   *Ancient Sagadahoc*. Conservatory of American Letters. Thomaston, Maine.
   2000   "John Parker: Georgetown's First Resident," *Discover Maine: Maine's History and Nostalgia Magazine*, Greater Bath-Brunswick Region edition, pp. 54-58.
Charles, F. W. B.
   1981   "Post-construction and the Rafter Roof," *Vernacular Architecture*, vol. 12, pp. 3-19.
   1982   "The Construction of Buildings with Irregularly-spaced posts," in P. Drury, ed., *Structural Reconstruction: Approaches to the Interpretation of the Excavated Remains of Buildings*. British Archaeological Reports, British Series, no. 110. Oxford.
Clark, Charles E.
   1983   *The Eastern Frontier: The Settlement of Northern New England, 1610-1763*. University Press of New England. Hanover, New Hampshire.
Coffin, Robert P. Tristram
   1965   *Kennebec: Cradle of Americans*. Down East Enterprise, Inc. Camden, Maine.
Coleman-Smith, R., and T. Pearson
   1988   *Excavations in the Donyatt Potteries*. Phillimore and Co. Chichester, Sussex.
Cook, Olive
   1982   *English Cottages and Farmhouses*. Thames and Hudson Ltd. London.

Cornwall, I. W.
   1958   *Soils for the Archaeologist*. Phoenix House. London.
Cotter, John L.
   1958   *Archeological Excavations at Jamestown, Virginia*. United States Department of the Interior, National Park Service, Archeological Research Series, no. 4. Washington.
   1994   *Archeological Excavations at Jamestown, Virginia* (2nd ed.). Archeological Society of Virginia, Special Publication, no. 32. Courtland, Virginia.
   1997   "Historical Archaeology: A Retrospective," in J. P. Brain, ed., *Contributions to the Historical Archaeology of European Exploration and Colonization in North America*. The Review of Archaeology, vol. 17, no. 2, pp. 5-9.
Courtney, Paul
   1988   "Small Arms Accessories of the Mid-Seventeenth Century," *Finds Research Group 700-1700, Datasheet 11*. Reprographic Unit, University of Oxford. Oxford.
Cousins, Rodney
   2000   *Lincolnshire Buildings in the Mud and Stud Tradition*. The Heritage Trust of Lincolnshire. Sleaford, Lincolnshire.
Cranmer, Leon E.
   1990   *Cushnoc: The History and Archaeology of Plymouth Colony Traders on the Kennebec*. Maine Archaeological Society, Inc. and Maine Historic Preservation Commission, Occasional Publications in Maine Archaeology, no. 7. Augusta, Maine.
Craven, Wesley Frank
   1957   *The Virginia Company of London, 1606-1624*. Virginia 350th Anniversary Celebration Corporation. Williamsburg, Virginia.
Crompton, Amanda
   2000   "A Planter's House at Ferryland, Newfoundland," *Avalon Chronicles*, vol. 5, pp. 1-48.
Cronon, William
   1983   *Changes in the Land: Indians, Colonists, and the Ecology of New England*. Hill and Wang. New York.
Crossley, David
   1990   *Post-medieval Archaeology in Britain*. Leicester University Press. London.
Cuff, Robert H.
   1997   *New-Founde-Land at the Very Centre of the European Discovery & Exploration of North America*. Harry Cuff Publications Ltd. St. John's, Newfoundland.
Cumming, W. P., R. A. Skelton, and D. B. Quinn
   1971   *The Discovery of North America*. McClelland and Stewart Limited. Toronto, Ontario.
Cummings, Abbott Lowell
   1979a   *The Framed Houses of Massachusetts Bay, 1625-1725*. Harvard University Press. Cambridge, Massachusetts.
   1979b   "Massachusetts and Its First Period Houses: A Statistical Survey," in A. L. Cummings, ed. *Architecture in Colonial Massachusetts*. The Colonial Society of Massachusetts. Boston.
Daniels, J. Stuart
   1950   *The Woodchester Glass House*. John Bellows Ltd. Gloucester, Gloucestershire.
Deagan, Kathleen
   1987   *Artifacts of the Spanish Colonies of Florida and the Caribbean, 1500-1800*, vol. 1, *Ceramics, Glassware, and Beads*. Smithsonian Institution Press. Washington.
Deetz, J. Eric
   2001   "...set upon cratchets...," in W.M. Kelso, J.E. Deetz, S.W. Mallios and B.A. Straube, eds., *Jamestown Rediscovery VII*. The Association for the Preservation of Virginia Antiquities. Richmond, Virginia.
   2002   "Architecture of Early Virginia: An Analysis of the Origins of the Earth Fast Tradition." MA thesis, School of Archaeological Studies, University of Leicester. Leicester, Leicestershire.
Deetz, James
   1973   "Ceramics from Plymouth, 1635-1835: The Archaeological Evidence," in I. Quimby, ed., *Ceramics in America*. University Press of Virginia. Charlottesville, Virginia.

1979   "Plymouth Colony Architecture: Archaeological Evidence from the Seventeenth Century," in A. L. Cummings, ed., *Architecture in Colonial Massachusetts*. The Colonial Society of Massachusetts. Boston.

1993   *Flowerdew Hundred: The Archaeology of a Virginia Plantation, 1619-1864*. University Press of Virginia. Charlottesville, Virginia.

Diderot, Denis

1959   *A Diderot Pictorial Encyclopedia of Trades and Industry* (2 vols.). Dover Publications, Inc. New York.

Dixon, Philip

1982   "How Saxon is the Saxon House?," in P. Dreary, ed., *Structural Reconstruction: Approaches to the Interpretation of the Excavated Remains of Buildings*. British Archaeological Reports, British Series, no. 110. Oxford.

Dow, George Francis

1972   *Domestic Life in New England in the Seventeenth Century*. Benjamin Bloom, Inc. New York.

Dozes, Eli B.

1999   *Phippsburg*. Arcade Publishing. Charleston, South Carolina.

Drake, Samuel Adams

1888   *The Making of New England, 1580-1643*. Charles Scriber's Sons. New York.

Draper, J. O.

1984   *Post-Medieval Pottery, 1650-1800*. Shire Publications Ltd. Aylesbury, Buckinghamshire.

Drury, P. J., ed.

1982   *Structural Reconstruction: Approaches to the Interpretation of the Excavated Remains of Buildings*. British Archaeological Report, British Series, no. 110. Oxford.

Dunnack, Henry E.

1924   *Maine Forts*. Charles E. Nash and Son. Augusta, Maine.

Dwelley, Marilyn J.

1980   *Trees and Shrubs of New England*. Down East Books. Camden, Maine.

Dyson, Stephen L., ed.

1985   *Comparative Studies in the Archaeology of Colonialism*. British Archaeological Reports, International Series, no. 233. Oxford.

Egan, Geoff

1985   "Leaden Cloth Seals," *Finds Research Group 700-1700, Datasheet 3*. Reprographic Unit, University of Oxford. Oxford.

Egan, Geoff, and Hazel Forsyth

1997   "Wound Wire and Silver Gilt: changing fashions in dress accessories c.1400- c.1600," in D. Gaimster and P. Stamper, eds., *The Age of Transition: The Archaeology of English Culture 1400-1600*. The Society for Medieval Archaeology Monograph, no. 15, and Oxbow Monograph, no. 98. Oxford.

Egan, Geoff, and R. L. Michael

1999   *Old and New Worlds*. Oxbow Books. Oxford.

Evans, Coriander, W.

1957   *Some Notes on Shipbuilding and Shipping in Colonial Virginia*. Virginia 350th Anniversary Celebration Corporation. Williamsburg, Virginia.

Evans, E. Ester

1974   "Folk Housing in the British Isles in Materials Other than Timber," in H. J. Walker and W. G. Hag, eds., *Man and Cultural Heritage*. Geoscience and Man, vol. 5, School of Geoscience, Louisiana State University. Baton Rouge, Louisiana.

Falls, Cyril

1997   *Elizabeth's Irish Wars*. Syracuse University Press. Syracuse, New York.

Faulkner, Alaric, and Gretchen Fearon Faulkner

1985   "Acadian Maine in Archaeological Perspective," *Northeast Historical Archaeology*, vol. 14, pp. 1-20.

1987   *The French at Pentagoet, 1635-1674: An Archaeological Portrait of the American Frontier*. Occasional Publication in Maine Archaeology, no. 5, Maine Historic Preservation Commission and New Brunswick Museum. Augusta, Maine.

Fearn, Jacqueline

1995   *Thatch and Thatching*. Shire Album, no. 16. Shire Publications Ltd. Princes Risborough, Buckinghamshire.

Fiske, John
 1893 *The Beginnings of New England, or the Puritan Theocracy in its Relations to Civil and Religious Liberty.* Houghton Mifflin Co. Boston.

Fitzhugh, William W.
 1985 *Cultures in Contact: The Impact of European Contacts on Native American Cultural Institutions, A.D. 1000-1800.* Smithsonian Institution Press. Washington.

Fitzhugh, William W., and Jacqueline S. Olin, eds.
 1993 *Archeology of the Frobisher Voyages.* Smithsonian Institution Press. Washington.

Fordney, Chris
 2002 "The Forgotten Colony," *National Parks Magazine,* vol. 76, nos. 3-4, pp. 46-50.

Forman, Henry Chandlee
 1957 *Virginia Architecture in the Seventeenth Century.* Virginia 350th Anniversary Celebration Corporation. Williamsburg, Virginia.

Fournier, Paul J.
 1965 "Popham Colony Established by Objects," *Down East Shopper,* October 7.

Friel, Ian
 1995 *The Good Ship: Ships, Shipbuilding and Technology in England, 1200-1520.* British Museum Press. London.

Furnivall, Frederick J.
 1877-1908 *Harrison's Description of England in Shakspere's Youth* (4 parts). New Shakspere Society. London.

Gailey, A.
 1984 *Rural Houses of the North of Ireland.* John Donald Publishers Ltd. Edinburgh.

Gaimster, David
 1997 *German Stoneware 1200-1900: Archaeology and Cultural History.* British Museum Press. London.
 1999 *Maiolica in the North: The Archaeology of Tin-glazed Earthenware in North-West Europe, c. 1500-1600.* British Museum Occasional Paper, no. 122. London.

Gaimster, David, and Paul Stamper, eds.
 1997 *The Age of Transition: The Archaeology of English Culture 1400-1600.* The Society for Medieval Archaeology Monograph, no. 15, and Oxbow Monograph, no. 98. Oxford.

Gaulton, Barry, and James A. Tuck
 2003 "The Archaeology of Ferryland, Newfoundland, until 1696," in J. Tuck, ed., *The English in America, 1497-1696.* The Colony of Avalon Foundation. Ferryland, Newfoundland.

Gibson, Susan G., ed.
 1980 *Burr's Hill: A 17th Century Wampanoag Burial Ground in Warren, Rhode Island.* Studies in Anthropology and Material Culture, vol. 2, The Haffenreffer Museum of Anthropology, Brown university. Providence, Rhode Island.

Gidwitz, Tom
 2006 "The Little Colony That Couldn't," *Archaeology,* vol. 59, no. 2, pp. 30-35.

Gilbert, William
 2000 "Finding Cupers Cove: Archaeological Excavations at Cupids, 1995-1999." Baccalieu Trail Heritage Corporation. Carbonear, Newfoundland.
 2003 "Finding Cupers Cove: Archaeology at Cupids, Newfoundland, 1995-2002," in J. Tuck, ed., *The English in America, 1497-1696.* The Colony of Avalon Foundation. Ferryland, Newfoundland.

Godfrey, Eleanor S.
 1975 *The Development of English Glassmaking, 1560-1640.* The University of North Carolina Press. Chapel Hill, North Carolina.

Gordon, Andrew, and Bernhard Klein, eds.
 2001 *Literature, Mapping, and the Politics of Space in Early Modern Britain.* Cambridge University Press. Cambridge.

Gorges, Sir Ferdinando
 1658 *A briefe narration of the original undertakings of the advancement of plantations into the parts of America, Especially showing the beginning, progress and continueance of that of New-England.* Nathaniel Brook. London.

Gould, Mary Earle
    1949   *The Early American House*. Charles E. Tuttle Co., Inc. Rutland, Vermont.
Grant, Alison
    1983   *North Devon Pottery: The Seventeenth Century*. University of Exeter. Exeter, Devonshire.
Green, H. J. M.
    1982   "The Origins and Development of Cruck Construction in Eastern England," in P. Drury, ed., *Structural Reconstruction: Approaches to the Interpretation of the Excavated Remains of Buildings*. British Archaeological Reports, British Series, no. 110. Oxford.
Guidoni, Enrico
    1987   *Primitive Architecture*. Rizzoli International Publications, Inc. New York.
Hadlock, Jean
    1962   "Fort Saint George." Manuscript. Maine State Museum. Augusta, Maine.
Hadlock, Wendell S.
    1962   "Hadlock Still Hopeful 1607 Colony Will be Found Soon," *Bath Times,* August 28.
Haile, Edward Wright, ed.
    1998   *Jamestown Narratives: Eyewitness Accounts of the Virginia Colony. The First decade: 1607-1617*. Round House. Champlain, Virginia.
Hamilton, T. M.
    1980   *Colonial Frontier Guns*. The Fur Press. Chaldron, Nebraska.
Harrington, Jean Carl
    1962   *Search for the Cite of Ralegh: Archeological Excavations at Fort Raleigh National Historic Site, North Carolina*. Archeological Research Series, no. 6, National Park Service. Washington.
Harrington, Peter
    1992   *Archaeology of the English Civil War*. Shire Archaeology Series, no. 68. Shire Publications Ltd. Princes Risborough, Buckinghamshire.
Harris, Richard
    1980   *Timber Framed Buildings*. Arts Council of Great Britain. London.
Harrison, William
    1994   *The Description of England: The Classic Contemporary Account of Tudor Social Life*. Republication of 1968 edition copyrighted by The Folger Shakespeare Library. Dover Publications, Inc. Mineola, New York.
Hartley, Dorothy
    1987   *Made in England*. Century Hutchinson Ltd. London.
Harvey, P. D. A.
    1993   *Maps in Tudor England*. University of Chicago Press. Chicago.
Hary, Debby
    1962   "Journal of excavations directed by Wendall Hadlock, David Oxton field crew chief, at Popham, Fort Pownell, Islesford and Fort George." Manuscript. Maine Historic Preservation Commission. Augusta, Maine.
Haslam, Jeremy
    1984   *Medieval Pottery*. Shire Publications Ltd. Aylesbury, Buckinghamshire.
Hatch, Charles E., Jr.
    1957   *The First Seventeen Years: Virginia, 1607-1624*. Virginia 350th Anniversary Celebration Corporation. Williamsburg, Virginia.
Hayes-McCoy, G. A.
    1964   "Introduction," in G. A. Hayes-McCoy, ed., *Ulster and Other Irish Maps, c. 1600*. Stationary Office for the Irish Manuscripts Commission. Dublin.
Heath, Ian, and David Sque
    1993   *The Irish Wars, 1485-1603*. Osprey Publishing Ltd. Botley, Oxfordshire.
Henkes, H. E.
    1994   *Glas zonder glans, vijf eeuwen gebruiksglas uit de bodem van de Lage Landen, 1300-1800*. Coordinatie Commissie van Advies inzake Archeologisch Onderzoek binnen het Ressort Rotterdam. Rotterdam.
Higgins, Pat
    2000   "Popham Colony: Not Just a Footnote," *Imagine Maine* (www.imaginemaine.com).

Hill, W. Scott
   1891   "The Site of Fort Saint George, Erected by Captain George Popham, in 1607," *The Kennebec Journal*, pp. 1-5.

Hoadley, R. Bruce
   1998   "Comments on Wood Samples." Wood Technology Department, University of Massachusetts. Amherst, Massachusetts.

Hodges, Charles T.
   1993   "Private Fortifications in 17th-Century Virginia: A Study of Six Representative Works," in T. R. Reinhart and D. J. Pogue, eds., *The Archaeology of 17th-Century Virginia*. Archeological Society of Virginia Special Publication, no. 30. Courtland, Virginia.

Hoffman, Paul E.
   1987   *Spain and the Roanoke Voyages*. Published for America's Four Hundredth Anniversary Committee by the North Carolina Department of Cultural Resources. Raleigh, North Carolina.

Horning, Audrey
   2001   "Dwelling Houses in the Old Irish Barbarous Manner: Archaeological Evidence for Gaelic Architecture in an Ulster Plantation Village," in P. J. Duffy, D. Edwards and E. Fitzpatrick, eds., *Gaelic Ireland c. 1250 - c. 1650: Land, Lordship and Settlement*. Four Courts Press. Dublin and Portland.

Howe, Henry F.
   1943   *Prologue to New England*. Farrar and Rinehart. New York.

Howell, Roger, Jr., and Emerson W. Baker
   1988   *Maine in the Age of Discovery: Christopher Levett's Voyage, 1623-1624, and a Guide to Sources*. Maine Historical Society. Augusta, Maine.

Hudson, J. Paul
   1957   *A Pictorial Booklet on Early Jamestown Commodities and Industries*. Virginia 350th Anniversary Celebration Corporation. Williamsburg, Virginia.
   1980   *Treasures from Jamestown*. Archeological Society of Virginia, Special Publication, no. 7. Richmond, Virginia.

Huggins, Peter, Kirsty Rodwell, and Warwick Rodwell
   1982   "Anglo-Saxon and Scandinavian Building Measurements," in P. Drury, ed., *Structural Reconstruction: Approaches to the Interpretation of the Excavated Remains of Buildings*. British Archaeological Reports, British Series, no. 110. Oxford.

Hughes, Thomas P.
   1957   *Medicine in Virginia, 1607-1699*. Virginia 350th Anniversary Celebration Corporation. Williamsburg, Virginia.

Humber, John L.
   1986   *Backgrounds and Preparations for the Roanoke Voyages, 1584-1590*. Published for America's Four Hundredth Anniversary Committee by the North Carolina Department of Cultural Resources. Raleigh, North Carolina.

Hurst, John G., David S. Neal, and H. J. E. van Beuningen
   1986   *Pottery Produced and Traded in North-west Europe, 1350-1650*. Rotterdam   Papers VI. Museum Boymans-van Beuningen. Rotterdam.

Hutchinson, Peter A.
   1998   "Once Upon a Fort...:The Continuing Puzzlements of John Hunt's 1608 Plan for the Popham Colony's Fort St. George." Manuscript. University of Maine. Orono, Maine.

Innocent, C. F.
   1916   *The Development of English Building Construction*. Cambridge University Press. Cambridge. (Reprinted 1971 by David and Charles Ltd. Newton Abbot, Devon.)

Isaacson, Mrs. Peter A.
   1964   "Feel Site of Popham Colony is Definitely Established," *Down East Shopper*, April 2.

Isaacson, Mrs. Peter A., et al.
   1965   *Phippsburg – Fair to the Wind*. Phippsburg Historical Society, Inc. Lewiston, Maine.

Jacobson, Timothy
   1991   *Discovering America: Journeys in Search of the New World*. Key Porter Books Ltd. Toronto, Ontario.

Jacobus, Donald Lines
    1938   "Richard Seymer of the Popham Colony: The First English Preacher in New England," *The New England Quarterly*, vol. 11, no. 2, pp. 367-372.

James, Stephen R., Jr.
    1988   "A Reassessment of the Chronological and Typological Framework of the Spanish Olive Jar," *Historical Archaeology*, vol. 22, no. 1, pp. 43-66.

Jennings, Jesse D.
    1952   "Prehistory of the Lower Mississippi Valley," in J. B. Griffin, ed., *Archeology of Eastern United States*. The University of Chicago Press. Chicago.

Jester, Annie Lash
    1957   *Domestic Life in Virginia in the Seventeenth Century*. Virginia 350th Anniversary Celebration Corporation. Williamsburg, Virginia.

Johnson, Matthew
    1993   *Housing Culture: Traditional Architecture in an English Landscape*. Smithsonian Institution Press. Washington.

Johnston, J. D.
    1980   "Settlement and Architecture in County Fermanagh, 1610-41," *Ulster Journal of Archaeology*, vol. 43, pp. 79-89.

Jones, Olive, and Catherine Sullivan
    1985   *The Parks Canada Glass Glossary for the Description of Containers, Tableware, Flat Glass, and Closures*. Studies in Archaeology, Architecture and History. National Historic Parks and Sites Branch, Parks Canada. Ottawa.

Jope, E. M.
    1960   "Moyry, Charlemont, Castleraw and Richhill: Fortification to Architecture in the North of Ireland 1570-1700," *Ulster Journal of Archaeology*, vol. 23, pp. 97-123.

Kelso, William M.
    1995   *Jamestown Rediscovery I: Search for 1607 James Fort*. The Association for the Preservation of Virginia Antiquities. Richmond, Virginia.
    1996   *Jamestown Rediscovery II: Search for 1607 James Fort*. The Association for the Preservation of Virginia Antiquities. Richmond, Virginia.
    1997   "Historical Archaeology and Archaeological History: A View from Jamestown," in J. P. Brain, ed., *Contributions to the Historical Archaeology of European Exploration and Colonization in North America*. The Review of Archaeology, vol. 17, no. 2, pp. 22-28.
    2006   *Jamestown: The Buried Truth*. University of Virginia Press. Charlottesville, Virginia.

Kelso, William, J. Eric Deetz, Seth W. Mallios, and Beverly A. Straube
    2001   *Jamestown Rediscovery VII*. The Association for the Preservation of Virginia Antiquities. Richmond, Virginia.

Kelso, William M., Nicholas M. Luccketti, and Beverly A. Straube
    1997   *Jamestown Rediscovery III*. The Association for the Preservation of Virginia Antiquities. Richmond, Virginia.
    1998   *Jamestown Rediscovery IV*. The Association for the Preservation of Virginia Antiquities. Richmond, Virginia.
    1999   *Jamestown Rediscovery V*. The Association for the Preservation of Virginia Antiquities. Richmond, Virginia.

Kelso, William, and Beverly Straube
    1997   "1996 Interim Report on the APVA Excavations at Jamestown, Virginia." The Association for the Preservation of Virginia Antiquities. Richmond, Virginia.
    2000   *Jamestown Rediscovery VI*. The Association for the Preservation of Virginia Antiquities. Richmond, Virginia.
    2003   "Jamestown Phoenix," in J. Tuck, ed., *The English in America, 1497-1696*. The Colony of Avalon Foundation. Ferryland, Newfoundland.

Kenyon, John P.
    1985   *Stuart England* (2nd ed.). Pelican Books. Harmondsworth, England.

Kimball, Fiske
1922 *Domestic Architecture of the American Colonies and of the Early Republic.* Charles Scribner's Sons. New York.

King, Julia A., and Edward E. Chaney
2003 "Lord Baltimore's Neighborhood: Standards of Living on the Seventeenth-Century Patuxent Frontier," in J. Tuck, ed., *The English in America, 1497-1696.* The Colony of Avalon Foundation. Ferryland, Newfoundland.

Kizer, Taft
1998 "Donyatt," in *Jamestown Ceramic Research Group.* The Association for the Preservation of Virginia Antiquities. Richmond, Virginia. (www.apva.org)

Kupperman, Karen Ordahl
1984a *Roanoke: The Abandoned Colony.* Rowman and Allanheld. Totowa, New Jersey.
1984b "Climate and Mastery of the Wilderness in Seventeenth-Century New England," in D. Hall and D. Allen, eds., *Seventeenth-Century New England.* The Colonial Society of Massachusetts. Boston.

Lacey, Brian
1994 "The Archaeology of the Ulster Plantation," in M. Ryan, ed., *Irish Archaeology Illustrated.* Country House. Dublin.

Lane, Gardner
1962 "Fort St. George Supposed Site - Popham Beach, Maine." Field Notes, May 27 - June 27, 1962. Historical Archaeology Laboratory, University of Maine. Orono, Maine.
1966 "An Archaeological Report on Excavations Carried Out at Sabino Head in Popham Beach, Maine – The Site of Fort St. George – 1607-1608 A.D." Manuscript, Maine Bureau of Parks and Recreation. Augusta, Maine.

Lapham, W. B., comp.
1888 *Popham Beach as a Summer Resort, with a Sketch of the Popham Colony and the Ancient Province of Sabino.* Maine Farmer Job Print. Augusta, Maine.

Leach, Douglas Edward
1966 *The Northern Colonial Frontier, 1607-1763.* Holt, Rinehart and Winston. New York.

Lee, Christopher
2003 *1603: The Death of Queen Elizabeth I, the Return of the Black Plague, the Rise of Shakespeare, Piracy, Witchcraft, and the Birth of the Stuart Era.* St. Martin's Press. New York.

Leger, M. C.
1919 *The Catholic Indian Missions in Maine 1611-1820.* Catholic University of America, Studies in American Church History, vol. 8. Washington.

Lenz, Peter A., ed.
n.d. "Voyages to Norumbega: Vineland; Meta Incognito; New Founde Lande; Saguenay; Breton's Illand; Sagadahock; Semeamis; Mastachusit & Patuxet c. 997-1620." Manuscript distributed by editor.

Lescarbot, Marc
1612 *Histoire de la Nouvelle France.* Jean Millot. Paris.

Letts, John B.
1999 *Smoke Blackened Thatch: A Unique Source of Late Medieval Plant Remains from Southern England.* English Heritage and University of Reading. London.

Levermore, Charles Herbert
1912 *Forerunners and Competitors of the Pilgrims and Puritans.* The New England Society. Brooklyn, New York.

Lewis, J. F.
1893 *Text Book of Fortification and Military Engineering, Part II.* Harrison and Son. London.

Lindsay, J. Seymour
1970 *Iron and Brass Implements of the English House.* Alec Tiranti. London.

Lloyd, E. W., and A. G. Hadcock
1893 *Artillery: Its Progress and Present Position.* J. Griffin and Company. Portsmouth, Hampshire.

Luccketti, Nicholas M., William M. Kelso, and Beverly A. Straube
1995 "Field Report 1994." Jamestown Rediscovery, The Association for the Preservation of Virginia Antiquities. Jamestown, Virginia.

Luccketti, Nicholas, and Beverly Straube

1998 "1997 Interim Report on the APVA Excavations at Jamestown, Virginia." The Association for the Preservation of Virginia Antiquities. Richmond, Virginia.

1999 "1998 Interim Report on the APVA Excavations at Jamestown, Virginia." The Association for the Preservation of Virginia Antiquities. Richmond, Virginia.

Luckenbach, Al

1995 *Providence 1649: The History and Archaeology of Anne Arundel County, Maryland's First European Settlement*. The Maryland State Archives and The Maryland Historical Trust. Annapolis, Maryland.

McCann, John

1995 *Clay and Cob Buildings*. Shire Album, no. 105. Shire Publications Ltd. Princes Risborough, Buckinghamshire.

McCarthy, Michael R., and Catherine M. Brooks

1988 *Medieval Pottery in Britain, AD 900-1600*. Leicester University Press. Leicester, Leicestershire.

McCartney, Martha W.

2001 *Jamestown: An American Legacy*. Eastern National. Williamsburg, Virginia.

McGhee, Robert

2003 "The First English house in the New World," in J. Tuck, ed., *The English in America, 1497-1696*. The Colony of Avalon Foundation. Ferryland, Newfoundland.

McManis, Douglas R.

1975 *Colonial New England: A Historical Geography*. Oxford University Press. New York.

Mahoney, Sarah

2003 "Popham Beach's Forgotten Colony," *Know*, May/June, pp. 46-47.

Maine Historical Society

1856 *Collections of the Maine Historical Society*, vol. 4. Portland, Maine.

Mallios, Seth, and Beverly Straube

2000 "1999 Interim Report on the APVA Excavations at Jamestown, Virginia." The Association for the Preservation of Virginia Antiquities. Richmond, Virginia.

Mancall, Peter C., ed.

1995 *Envisioning America: English Plans for the Colonization of North America, 1580-1640*. Bedford Books. Boston.

Marken, Mitchell W.

1994 *Pottery from Spanish Shipwrecks, 1500-1800*. University Press of Florida. Gainesville, Florida

Maverick, Samuel

1885 "A Briefe Discription of New England and the Severall Townes Therein, Together with the Present Government Thereof," *New England Historical and Genealogical Register*, vol. 39, pp. 34-35.

Meinig, D. W.

1986 *The Shaping of America: A Geographical Perspective on 500 Years of History*, vol. 1, *Atlantic America, 1492-1800*. Yale University Press. New Haven, Connecticut.

Meirion-Jones, Gwyn I.

1973 "Settlement and Vernacular Architecture in Brittany," *Vernacular Architecture*, vol. 4, pp. 3-6.

Mercator's Log

2001 "America's Forgotten Colony," *Mercator's World*, vol. 6, no. 2, p. 10.

Mercer, Eric

1975 *English Vernacular Houses: A Study of Traditional Farmhouses and Cottages*. Her Majesty's Stationery Office. London

Miller, Helen Hill

1983 *Passage to America: Ralegh's Colonists Take Ship for Roanoke*. Published for America's Four Hundredth Anniversary Committee by the North Carolina Department of Cultural Resources. Raleigh, North Carolina.

Miller, Henry M.

2003 "Lord Baltimore's Colony of Maryland and its Capital of St. Mary's City, 1634-1695," in J. Tuck, ed., *The English in America, 1497-1696*. The Colony of Avalon Foundation. Ferryland, Newfoundland.

Miller, Henry M., D. L. Hamilton, Nicholas Honerkamp, Steven R. Pendery, Peter E. Pope, and James A. Tuck, eds.

1996 *The Archaeology of Sixteenth- and Seventeenth-Century British Colonization in the Caribbean, United*

States, and Canada. Society for Historical Archaeology, Guides to Historical Archaeological Literature, no. 4. Tucson, Arizona.

Miller, J. Jefferson, II, and Lyle M. Stone
  1970 *Eighteenth-Century Ceramics from Fort Michilimackinac: A Study in Historical Archaeology*. Smithsonian Studies in History and Technology, no. 4, Smithsonian Institution Press. Washington.

Miller, Orloff G.
  1991 *Archaeological Investigations at Salterstown, County Londonderry, Northern Ireland*. University Microfilms International. Ann Arbor, Michigan.

Milton, Giles
  2000 *Big Chief Elizabeth: The Adventures and Fate of the First English Colonists in America*. Farrar, Straus and Giroux. New York.

Montgomery, Susan J., et al.
  1984 "Unearthing New England's Past: The Ceramic Evidence." Scottish Rite Masonic Museum of Our National Heritage. Lexington, Massachusetts.

Morey, David C., annotator
  2005 *The Voyage of* Archangell, *James Rosier's Account of the Waymouth Voyage of 1605, A True Relation*. Tilbury House Publishers. Gardiner, Maine.

Morison, Samuel Eliot
  1930 *Builders of the Bay Colony*. Houghton Mifflin Co. Boston.
  1971 *The European Discovery of America: The Northern Voyages, A.D. 500-1600*. Oxford University Press. New York.
  1972 *Samuel de Champlain: Father of New France*. Little, Brown and Company. Boston.

Morrison, Peter H.
  2002 "Architecture of the Popham Colony, 1607-1608: An Archaeological Portrait of English Building Practice at the Moment of Settlement." MA thesis, Department of History, University of Maine. Orono, Maine.

Morriss, Richard K.
  2002 *The Archaeology of Buildings*. Tempus Publishing Ltd. Stroud, Gloucestershire.

Murphy, Cullen
  1998 "Jamestown Revisited," *Preservation*, July/August, pp. 40-51.

National Trust
  2000 *Compton Castle*. National Trust (Enterprises) Ltd. London.

Nichols, Ray
  1997 "Sagadahoc Colony in the Land of Norumbega." Manuscript. University of Missouri. St. Louis, Missouri.

Nixon, Douglas A.
  1999 "A Seventeenth-Century House at Ferryland, Newfoundland (CgAf-2, Area B)." MA thesis, Department of Anthropology, Memorial University of Newfoundland. St. John's, Newfoundland.

Noël Hume, Ivor
  1956 "A Century of London Glass Bottles, 1580-1680," *The Connoisseur Year Book*, pp. 98-103.
  1962 "Tudor and early Stuart glasses found in London," *The Connoisseur*, August, p. 269.
  1969a *A Guide to Artifacts of Colonial America*. Alfred A. Knopf. New York.
  1969b *Glass in Colonial Williamsburg's Archaeological Collections*. Colonial Williamsburg Archaeological Series, no. 1. The Colonial Williamsburg Foundation. Williamsburg, Virginia.
  1982 *Martin's Hundred*. Alfred A. Knopf. New York.
  1994 *The Virginia Adventure, Roanoke to James Towne: An Archaeological and Historical Odyssey*. Alfred A. Knopf. New York.
  2000 "Message from Maine: Two Virginias and One Mystery Map," *Colonial Williamsburg*, vol. 22, no. 4, pp. 67-72.
  2003 "Hunting for a Little Ladle," *Colonial Williamsburg*, vol. 25, no. 4, pp. 24-29.

Noël Hume, Ivor, and Audrey Noël Hume
  2001 *The Archaeology of Martin's Hundred, Part I: Interpretive Studies*. University of Pennsylvania Museum of Archaeology and Anthropology, and The Colonial Williamsburg Foundation. Philadelphia, Pennsylvania, and Williamsburg, Virginia.

Oliver, Paul
    1975   *English Cottages and Small Farmhouses: A Study of Vernacular Shelter.* Arts Council of Great Britain. London.
Oswald, Adrian
    1951   "English Clay Tobacco Pipes," *The Archaeological News Letter*, vol. 3, no. 10, pp. 153-159.
    1955   "The Evolution and Chronology of English Clay Tobacco Pipes," *The Archaeological News Letter*, vol. 5, no. 12, pp. 243-250.
    1960   "The Archaeology and Economic History of English Clay Tobacco Pipes," *The Journal of the British Archaeological Association*, vol. 23, pp. 40-102.
    1975   *Clay Pipes for the Archaeologist.* British Archaeological Reports, British Series, no. 14. Oxford.
Outlaw, Alain Charles
    1990   *Governor's Land: Archaeology of Early Seventeenth-Century Virginia Settlements.* University Press of Virginia. Charlottesville, Virginia.
Pearce, Jacqueline
    1992   *Post-Medieval Pottery in London, 1500-1700: Border Wares.* Museum of London, HMSO. London.
Peattie, Donald C.
    1950   *A Natural History of Trees of Eastern and Central North America.* Houghton, Mifflin Co. Boston.
Peavey, Elizabeth
    2002   "Dig It!," *Down East*, vol. 49, no. 2, pp. 60-63.
Perkins, James E., and Jane Stevens
    1974   *One Man's World: Popham Beach, Maine.* The Bond Wheelwright Company Publishers. Freeport, Maine.
Peters, J. E. C.
    1977   "The Solid Thatch Roof," *Vernacular Architecture*, vol. 8, p. 825.
Petersen, James B., and David Sanger
    1991   "An Aboriginal Ceramic Sequence for Maine and the Maritime Provinces," in M. Deal and S. Blair, eds., *Prehistoric Archaeology in the Maritime Provinces: Past and Present Research.* Reports in Archaeology, no. 8, Council of Maritime Premiers, Maritime Committee on Archaeological Cooperation. Fredericton, New Brunswick.
Peterson, Harold L.
    1956   *Arms and Armor in Colonial America.* Bramhall House. New York.
    1969   *Round Shot and Rammers.* Bonanza Books. New York.
Pflederer, Richard L.
    2005   "Before New England: The Popham Colony," *History Today*, vol. 55, no. 1, pp. 10-17.
Pittman William E.
    1993   "A Survey of 17th-Century Chesapeake Ceramic Typologies," in T. R. Reinhart and D. J. Pogue, eds., *The Archaeology of 17th-Century Virginia.* Archeological Society of Virginia Special Publication, no. 30. Courtland, Virginia.
Platt, Colin
    1978   *Medieval England: A Social History and Archaeology from the Conquest to 1600 AD.* Routledge. London.
Poole, William Frederick, Edward Ballard, and Frederic Kidder
    1866   *The Popham Colony: A Discussion of its Historical Claims with a Bibliography of the Subject.* Wiggin and Lunt. Boston.
Pope, Peter E.
    2003   "The English at Newfoundland in the Century after Cabot," in J. Tuck, ed., *The English in America, 1497-1696.* The Colony of Avalon Foundation. Ferryland, Newfoundland.
Popham, C. F. J.
    1987   "Sir John Popham: Portrait of a Sixteenth Century Judge." Manuscript for Popham Reunion. London.
Popham, Frederick W.
    1976   *A West Country Family: The Pophams from 1150.* Paradigm Print. Gateshead, Durham.
Popham, John
    1752   "The Genealogy or Descent of the Honourable Family of the Pophams of Somersetshire exactly drawn down to the worship Edward Popham of Huntworth in the County of Somerset Esq. 1640, and continued from that Time to the Year 1752 by John Popham Gent. of New Inn." Illuminated genealogical scroll in the possession

of Captain Philip Brooke-Popham of Bagborough House, North Taunton, Somerset.

Preston, Richard Arthur
    1953   *Gorges of Plymouth Fort: A Life of Sir Ferdinando Gorges, Captain of Plymouth Fort, Governor of New England, and Lord of the Province of Maine.* University of Toronto Press. Toronto.

Purchas, Samuel
    1625   *Hakluytus Posthumus, or Purchas his pilgrimes.* W. Stansby for H. Fetherstone. Glasgow.

Quinn, David Beers
    1940   *The Voyages and Colonizing Enterprises of Sir Humphrey Gilbert.* Hakluyt Society. London.
    1965   *The New Found Land: The English Contribution to the Discovery of North America.* The Associates of the John Carter Brown Library. Providence, Rhode Island.
    1971   *North American Discovery, ca. 1000-1612.* Harper and Row. New York.
    1974a *England and the Discovery of America, 1481-1620.* Alfred A. Knopf. New York.
    1974b *The Hakluyt Handbook* (2 vols.). The Hakluyt Society. London.
    1977   *North America from Earliest Discovery to First Settlements: The Norse Voyages to 1612.* Harper and Row. New York.
    1985   *Set Fair for Roanoke: Voyages and Colonies, 1584-1606.* Published for America's Four Hundredth Anniversary Committee by the University of North Carolina Press. Chapel Hill, North Carolina.
    1988   "Colonies in the Beginning: Examples from North America," in S. Palmer and D. Reinhartz, eds., *Essays on the History of North American Discovery and Exploration.* Texas A & M University Press. College Station, Texas.

Quinn, David B., and Alison M. Quinn, eds.
    1982   *The First Colonists: Documents on the Planting of the First English Settlements in North America, 1584-1590.* Published for America's Four Hundredth Anniversary Committee by the North Carolina Department of Cultural Resources. Raleigh, North Carolina.
    1983   *The English New England Voyages, 1602-1608.* The Hakluyt Society. London.

Quinn, David B., Alison M. Quinn, and Susan Hillier
    1979   *New American World: A Documentary History of North America to 1612,* Volume 3, *English Plans for North America. The Roanoke Voyages. New England Ventures.* Arno Press. New York.

Ray, Anthony
    2000   *English Delftware in the Ashmolean Museum.* Ashmolean Museum. Oxford.

Reineking-von Bock, Gisela
    1971   *Steinzeug.* Kunstgewerbemuseum Catalog, vol. 4. Cologne.

Reinhart, Theodore R., and Dennis J. Pogue, eds.
    1993   *The Archaeology of 17th-Century Virginia.* Archeological Society of Virginia. Special Publication, no. 30. Courtland, Virginia.

Reps, John W.
    1980   *Town Planning in Frontier America.* University of Missouri Press. Columbia, Missouri.

Reynolds, Peter J.
    1982   "Substructure to Superstructure," in P. Drury, ed., *Structural Reconstruction: Approaches to the Interpretation of the Excavated Remains of Buildings.* British Archaeological Reports, British Series, no. 110. Oxford.

Rice, Douglas Walthew
    2005   *The Life and Achievements of Sir John Popham, 1531-1607: Leading to the Establishment of the First English Colony in New England.* Fairleigh Dickinson University Press. Cranbury, New Jersey.

Robbins, Roland Wells
    1969   *Pilgrim John Alden's Progress: Archaeological Excavations in Duxbury.* The Pilgrim Society. Plymouth, Massachusetts.

Roberts, Keith
    2002   *Matchlock Musketeer, 1588-1688.* Osprey Publishing Ltd. Botley, Oxfordshire.

Roberts, Robert B.
    1988   *Encyclopedia of American Forts.* MacMillan Publishing Co. New York.

Robinson, P.
    1979   "Vernacular Housing in Ulster in the Seventeenth Century," *Ulster Folklife,* vol. 25, pp. 1-28.

Rowse, A. L.
   1955   *The Expansion of Elizabethan England.* Macmillan and Co., Ltd. London.
   1959   "New England in the Earliest Days," *American Heritage,* vol. 10, no. 5, pp. 23-29, 105-111.
Ruempol, A. P. E., and A. G. A. van Dongen
   1990   *Pre-industrial Utensils.* Museum Boymans-van Beuningen. Rotterdam.
Salisbury, Neal
   1982   *Manitou and Providence: Indians, Europeans, and the Making of New England, 1500-1643.* Oxford University Press. New York.
Sanger, David, ed.
   1979   *Discovering Maine's Archaeological Heritage.* Maine Historic Preservation Commission. Augusta, Maine.
Scease, Matt
   2001   "Rebuilding Maine's First Ship," *Down East,* June, pp. 81, 97-98.
Sewall, Rufus King
   1859   *Ancient Dominions of Maine.* Elisha Clark and Company. Bath, Maine.
Shepard, Anna O.
   1965   *Ceramics for the Archaeologist.* Carnegie Institution of Washington Publication, no. 609. Washington.
Shirley, John W.
   1985   *Sir Walter Ralegh and the New World.* Published for America's Four Hundredth Anniversary Committee by the North Carolina Department of Cultural Resources. Raleigh, North Carolina.
Simmons, William S.
   1970   *Cautantowwit's House: An Indian Burial Ground on the Island of Conanicut in Narragansett Bay.* Brown University Press. Providence, Rhode Island.
Simpson, Mildred
   1963   "Diggers Invade Popham Beach Area in Quest of Original Colony Site," *Kennebec Journal,* July 13.
Skowronek, Russell K.
   1987   "Ceramics and Commerce: The 1554 *flota* Revisited," *Historical Archaeology,* vol. 21, no. 2, pp. 101-111.
Smith, Alan, ed.
   1957   *Virginia 1584-1607: The First English Settlement in North America.* Theodore Brun Fine Editions Limited. London.
Smith, Carlyle S., translator
   1960   "Two 18th Century Reports on the Manufacture of Gunflints in France," *The Missouri Archaeologist,* vol. 22, pp. 40-69.
Smith, John
   1624   *The Generall Historie of Virginia, New-England, and the Summer Isles with the names of the Adventurers, Planters, and Governours from their first beginning An: 1584 to this present 1624.* Michael Sparkes. London.
   1631   *Advertisements for the unexperienced Planters of New England, or anywhere.* London.
Smith, J. T.
   1982   "The Validity of Inference from Archaeological Evidence," in P. Drury, ed., *Structural Reconstruction: Approaches to the Interpretation of the Excavated Remains of Buildings.* British Archaeological Reports, British Series, no. 110. Oxford.
   1985   "Short-lived and Mobile Houses in Late Seventeenth-century England," *Vernacular Architecture,* vol. 16, pp. 33-34.
Snow, Dean R.
   1976   "The Ethnohistoric Baseline of the Eastern Abenaki," *Ethnohistory,* vol. 23, no. 3, pp. 291-306.
South, Stanley, Russell K. Skowronek, and Richard E. Johnson
   1988   *Spanish Artifacts from Santa Elena.* South Carolina Institute of Archaeology and Anthropology, Anthropological Study, no. 7, University of South Carolina. Columbia, South Carolina.
Spectre, Peter H., and David Larkin
   1992   *A Goodly Ship: The Building of the Susan Constant.* Houghton Mifflin Company. Boston.
Stephen, Leslie, and Sidney Lee, eds.
   1968   *The Dictionary of National Biography.* Oxford University Press. London.

Stephenson, Roy
     1999   "Tin Glazed Ware in London: A Review," in G. Egan and R. L. Michael, eds., *Old and New Worlds*. Oxbow
             Books. Oxford.
Strachey, William
     1612   *The Historie of Travell into Virginia Britania.* Reprinted 1849 and 1953 by Hakluyt Society. London.
Straube, Beverly
     1998   "Totnes-type," in *Jamestown Ceramic Research Group*. The Association for the Preservation of Virginia
             Antiquities. Richmond, Virginia (www.apva.org).
Straube, Beverly, and Nicholas Luccketti
     1996   "1995 Interim Report." The Association for the Preservation of Virginia Antiquities. Richmond, Virginia.
Strickland, Charles R.
     1950   "The First Permanent Dwellings at Plimoth Plantation," *Old-Time New England* (Bulletin of the Society for
             the Preservation of New England Antiquities), vol. 40, no. 3, pp. 163-169.
Styles, John
     2001   "Innovation and Design in Tudor and Stuart Britain," *History Today*, vol. 51, no. 12, p.49.
Sullivan, James
     1795   *The History of the District of Maine*. I. Thomas and E. T. Andrews. Boston.
Summerson, John
     1963   *Architecture in Britain, 1530 to 1830*. Penguin Books Ltd. Harmondsworth, Middlesex.
Tabor, William H.
     2002   "Maine's Popham Colony," *Athena Review*, vol. 3, no. 2, pp. 62-68.
Tapley, Lance
     2000   "Discovering an Archaeological Time Capsule," *American Archaeology*, vol. 4, no. 4, pp. 12-19.
Thayer, Henry O.
     1892   *The Sagadahoc Colony*. Gorges Society. Portland, Maine.
Thomas, Davis
     1988   "In Search of Norumbega," *Down East*, November, pp. 74-79.
Thwaites, Reuben Gold.
     1896   *The Jesuit Relations and Allied Documents*, vol. 2, *Travels and Explorations of the Jesuit Missionaries in
             New France, 1610-1791*. The Burrows Brothers Company. Cleveland, Ohio.
Tisdale, D. A.
     2000   *Soldiers of the Virginia Colony, 1607-1699*. Dietz. Williamsburg, Virginia.
Tozer, Eliot
     2001   "Maine's Lost Colony," *Yankee*, May, p. 19.
     2003   "Finding the Lost Colony," *Early American Life*, vol. 34, no. 2, pp. 42-45.
Tuck, James A.
     1997   "The Forgotten Colonies: Seventeenth-Century English Settlement in Newfoundland, Canada," in J. P. Brain,
             ed., *Contributions to the Historical Archaeology of European Exploration and Colonization in North
             America*. The Review of Archaeology, vol. 17, no. 2, pp. 28-32.
Turner, E. Randolph, III, and Antony F. Opperman
     1993   "Archaeological Manifestations of the Virginia Company Period: A Summary of Surviving Powhatan and
             English Settlements in Tidewater Virginia, circa A.D. 1607-1624," in T. R. Reinhart and D. J. Pogue, eds.,
             The Archaeology of 17th-Century Virginia. Archeological Society of Virginia Special Publication, no. 30.
             Courtland, Virginia.
Vanes, Jean
     1977   "The Port of Bristol in the Sixteenth Century." Issued by the Bristol Branch of the Historical Association.
             The University, Bristol.
Viereck, Philip, ed.
     1967   *The New Land: Discovery, Exploration, and Early Settlement of Northeastern United States, from Earliest
             Voyages to 1621, Told in the Words of the Explorers Themselves*. The John Day Co. New York.
Wahll, Andrew J.
     1980   "Fort Saint George Reconsidered." Manuscript. Derwood, Maryland.

Wahll, Andrew J., ed.
  2000 *Sabino: Popham Colony Reader 1602-2000*. Heritage Books, Inc. Bowie, Maryland.
Wall, Suzanne, E.
  2003 "Final Report for the Analysis of the Red Soil Samples from Fort St. George in Popham, Maine." Report on file, Peabody Essex Museum. Salem, Massachusetts.
Warren, Bud
  2000 "Toughing It Out At Popham: English Settlers Give Up After Two Years," *Discover Maine: Maine's History and Nostalgia Magazine*, Greater Bath-Brunswick Region edition, pp. 51-53.
Waterman, Thomas Tileston
  1950 *The Dwellings of Colonial America*. The University of North Carolina Press. Chapel Hill, North Carolina.
Watkins, C. Malcolm
  1960 "North Devon Pottery and its Export to America in the 17th Century," *Contributions from the Museum of History and Technology*, paper 13, pp. 17-59. Smithsonian Institution. Washington.
Wilcoxen, Charlotte
  1987 *Dutch Trade and Ceramics in America in the Seventeenth Century*. Albany Institute of History and Art. Albany, New York.
Wiliam, Eurwyn
  1982 "Straw-rope Underthatch in South-West Wales," *Vernacular Architecture*, vol. 13, pp. 36-38.
Williamson, William D.
  1832 *The History of the State of Maine from its First Discovery, A.D. 1602, to the Separation, A.D. 1820, Inclusive* (2 vols.). Glazier, Masters and Co. Hallowell, Maine.
Willis, Raymond F.
  1984 "Empire and Architecture at 16th-Century Puerto Real, Hispaniola: An Archeological Perspective." Ph.D. dissertation, University of Florida. Gainesville, Florida.
Willmott, Hugh
  2002 *Early Post-Medieval Vessel Glass in England, ca. 1500-1670*. Council for British Archaeology, Research Report, no. 132. Walmgate, York.
  2005 *A History of English Glassmaking*. Tempus Publishing Ltd. Stroud, Gloucestershire.
Wilson, Joseph Kennard
  1902 "The Door-Step of New England," *New England Magazine*, vol. 27, no. 1, pp. 3-14.
Wilson, Margaret
  2005 "New England in the Earliest Days: The *Virginia* of Sagadahoc and the Establishment of an English Colony on the Kennebec River in 1607," *Maritime South West*, no. 18, pp. 169-183.
Wingood, Allan J., Peggy Wingood, and Jonathan Adams, compilers
  1986 *"Sea Venture": The Tempest Wreck*. Sea Venture Trust. Bermuda.
Winship, George Parker
  1905 *Sailors Narratives of Voyages along the New England Coast, 1524-1624*. Houghton Mifflin. Boston.
Wright, Adela
  1991 *Craft Techniques for Traditional Buildings*. B. T. Batsford. London.
Wright, J. Leitch, Jr.
  1971 *Anglo-Spanish Rivalry in North America*. University of Georgia Press. Athens, Georgia.
Wright, Louis B., ed.
  1964 *A Voyage to Virginia in 1609*. Charlottesville, Virginia.
Wright, Louis B., and Elaine W. Fowler, eds.
  1971 *West and By North: North America Seen through the Eyes of its Seafaring Discoverers*. Delacorte Press. New York.
Yarwood, Doreen
  1963 *The Architecture of England from Prehistoric Times to the Present Day*. B. T. Batsford Ltd. London.
Youings, Joyce
  1986 *Ralegh's Country: The South West of England in the Reign of Queen Elizabeth I*. Published for America's Four Hundredth Anniversary Committee by the North Carolina Department of Cultural Resources. Raleigh, North Carolina.

INDEX

Primary references for documents, excavations and artifacts are indicated in boldface.

copper – pg 140

p. 137 Iron – see Nail

(handwritten annotation: Metal — p. 137)